THOR   RPAY, (

JOHN HUME
and the SDLP
Impact and Survival in Northern Ireland

JOHN HUME
and the SDLP

Impact and Survival in Northern Ireland

GERARD MURRAY

IRISH ACADEMIC PRESS

DUBLIN: PORTLAND, OR

First published in 1998 by
IRISH ACADEMIC PRESS
44, Northumberland Road, Dublin 4, Ireland
and in North America by
IRISH ACADEMIC PRESS
c/o ISBS, 5804 NE Hassalo Street, Portland, OR 97213
website: http://www.iap.ie

© Gerard Murray 1998

British Library Cataloguing in Publication Data

Murray, Gerard
    John Hume and the SDLP: Impact and Survival in Northern Ireland.
    (New directions in Irish history)
    1. SDLP 2. Political parties—Northern Ireland—History—
    20th century 3. Northern Ireland—Politics and government—
    1969–1994
    I. Title
    324.2'4109'72'09047

ISBN 0 7165 6441
ISSN 1393-5356 New Directions in Irish History

A cataloguing record is available from the Library of Congress

Typeset in 11 pt on 13 pt Sabon
by Artwerk, Dublin.
Printed by Colour Books Ltd., Dublin

Contents

List of Abbreviations

Árd Fheis – Annual Conference
CIA – Central Intelligence Agency
Dáil Eireann – Irish Parliament
DNC – Democratic National Committee
DUP – Democratic Unionist Party
EAGGE – European Agricultural Guidance and Guarantee Fund
EEC – European Economic Community; EC – European Community; EU – European
    Union; ERDF – European Regional Development Fund
Garda Siochana – Irish Police Force
IIP – Irish Independence Party
INC – Irish National Caucus
INLA – Irish National Liberation Army
IRA – Irish Republican Army
LHL – Linen Hall Library, Belfast
MBW – Making Belfast Work
MEP – Member of the European Parliament
MORI – Market and Opinion Research International
NDI – National Democratic Institute for International Affairs
NDP – Nationalist Democratic Party
NED – National Endowment for Democracy
NIO – Northern Ireland Office
NIPC – Northern Ireland Political Collection
NORAID – Irish Northern Aid Committee
Oireachtas – Senate (of the Irish Republic)
OUP – Official Unionist Party
PR – Proportional Representation
PRONI – Public Records Office of Northern Ireland
PUP – Progressive Unionist Party
RTE – Radio Telefis Eireann
RUC – Royal Ulster Constabulary
SDG – Social Democratic Group
SDLP – Social Democratic and Labour Party
Sinn Féin (Ard Chomhairle) – (National Executive)
Tanaiste – Deputy Prime Minister (of the Irish Republic)
Taoiseach – Prime Minister (of the Irish Republic)
TD – Teachta Dala – Elected Member (of the Irish Parliament Government)
UDA – Ulster Defence Association
UDP – Ulster Democratic Party
UDR – Ulster Defence Regiment
UPNI – Unionist Party of Northern Ireland
UUP – Ulster Unionist Party
UUUC – United Ulster Unionist Council
UWC – Ulster Workers' Council

Acknowledgements

My grateful thanks go to the SDLP for their invaluable assistance and in particular to Gerry Cosgrove, general secretary. I wish to express my appreciation to the following: the staff of the Public Records Office of Northern Ireland (PRONI), the library staff at the University of Ulster at Jordanstown and Queen's University, Belfast; BBC Northern Ireland, in particular to June Gamble and Gráinne Loughran, Broadcast Archivist at the Ulster Folk and Transport Museum, the Linen Hall Library in particular Yvonne Murphy, Head of the Northern Ireland Political Collection; to Belfast Central Library; and Edinburgh University.

I should like to thank the following at the University of Ulster: my main supervisor Professor Paul Arthur for supervising my doctoral thesis on the SDLP and his constructive criticism; Professor Henry Patterson for identifying the subject as an area absent in research; Professor Keith Jeffery for making publication of this book possible.

A special note of thanks go to the International Social Sciences Institute at Edinburgh University for inviting me as a Visiting Associate for their 1997/98 annual theme of 'Trust'. In particular I should like to acknowledge the assistance of Professor Malcolm Anderson, Director of the Institute; Dr Halla Beloff Acting Director; Dr Eberhard Bort, Assistant Director and Research Fellow; and Dilys Rennie. The institute's academic facilities have been an enormous bonus in getting this book completed. A special note of thanks to Professor Adrian Guelke for his support and for writing the preface to this book. Also a note of appreciation to all those individuals who allowed me to interview them and to Martin Gilroy, James Hillis and Damian Smyth.

I would like to thank Rosy Addison for her invaluable editing skills and patience with my changing deadlines. The final thank-you has to go to my family and friends who are too numerous to mention individually for their loyal support and encouragement over the last few years.

Gerard Murray,
April 1998.

Preface

The contribution of the SDLP to the achievement of the Good Friday Agreement was probably greater than that of any other party in Northern Ireland. As Gerard Murray demonstrates in this important addition to the literature on the Northern Ireland problem, this can only be judged in the context of the party's strategy over many years. In fact, the party had a relatively low profile in the intensive week of negotiations that led up to the Good Friday Agreement. But while some of the most innovative elements in the Agreement reflect evolution in the thinking of moderate Unionists, it nevertheless remains true that the Agreement bears the imprint of the SDLP's ideas more than those of any other political organisation in the province. The display of emotion shown by the party's negotiators at Stormont when the news came through that the Agreement had secured the acceptance of all the parties was an appropriate reflection of the years of effort that the party had put in to achieving such an outcome.

Yet the party remains curiously neglected in the literature on Northern Ireland. As might be expected, journalists have found violence and the extremes of the political spectrum more appealing as subjects than the party of constitutional nationalism. The party's long-serving leader, John Hume, has been the subject of two popular biographies and is one of a small number of Northern Ireland's politicians widely recognised internationally. However, the academic literature on both Hume and the SDLP remains extremely thin. Ian McAllister's book on the party is now over twenty years old and lacked the sources available to Gerard Murray for his path-breaking study.

Murray's thorough research into the party's own records and extensive interviews with major figures in the party gives his account an authority without rival in the field of the study of party politics in Northern Ireland. In the process, he lays to rest many myths that have grown up round the SDLP, in particular that the party has simply been a vehicle for the ideas of John Hume and that it has been inconsistent in its approach to the quest for a negotiated settlement. What emerges from Murray's account is that the pursuit of an Irish dimension has always been a key element in SDLP policy, with wide support throughout the party. He provides a corrective to the common impression that the party became much more nationalist in its orientation after the departure of Gerry Fitt and Paddy Devlin and Hume's assumption of the leadership. Murray traces Hume's internationalisation of the Northern Ireland problem through the European Community, showing how Hume's post-nationalist political philosophy chimed in with the ethos underlying European integration. He also shows how Hume used his links with politicians in the United States to influence attitudes there.

However, Murray's study is also very far from being a hagiography of Hume. He is sharply critical of a number of aspects of Hume's leadership of the party, particularly the failure to rectify the abysmal organisational base of the party. He also explores the divisions that arose in the party over strategy, particularly the criticism Hume encountered over the priority he gave to his personal quest for a cease-fire by the Provisional IRA, in part because of its negative impact on Unionist opinion, but also because of a failure to involve senior members of the party in the dialogue with Sinn Féin. He argues that Hume's failure to involve the party more directly in these ultimately successful efforts was a major weakness, which damaged the party in the context of its electoral battles with Sinn Féin in 1996 and 1997. As Murray notes at the end of the book, a key issue is whether in the pursuit of the peace process, the future of the party as an electoral force has been sacrificed. One consequence of the course that Hume pursued is that the SDLP's stake in the success of the Good Friday Agreement is also greater than that of any other party in Northern Ireland. Murray's pioneering work is a significant step to filling a large hole in the study of the politics of Northern Ireland.

Adrian Guelke,
(Professor of Comparative Politics, Queen's University of Belfast.)

Belfast, 12 May 1998.

Introduction

There is a gap in academic literature dealing specifically with the evolution of Nationalist politics within Northern Ireland in recent years. In particular, there is a shortage of research work on the Social Democratic and Labour Party (SDLP) formed in August, 1970. Ian McAllister has written *The Northern Ireland Social Democratic and Labour Party*, which covers the period up to 1976. He has produced a thorough chronology and a detailed account of the SDLP from its inception in August 1970 until the cessation of the Constitutional Convention in March 1976. But his work does not examine fully the political thinking within the SDLP that eventually led to the publication of *Towards a New Ireland* in September 1972. Nor did his investigations include unpublished SDLP policy discussion papers prior to the production of the 1972 policy document. These early papers add new insights into the SDLP's formative years. Significantly they detail the SDLP position in relation to the constitutional issue of Northern Ireland and the Party's subsequent understanding and strategy for attaining its political objective of Irish unity.

Consequently, the first objective of this book has been to examine, in Chapter One, this new material which sheds important light on SDLP attempts to articulate its identity and to shape its strategy for the way forward. It is important to establish the political thinking which lay behind the 1972 policy document which has affected everything subsequently in relation to resolving the Northern Ireland conflict. *Towards a New Ireland* has remained the core of SDLP political philosophy. The launch of the SDLP exemplified revisionist thinking within Nationalist politics in Northern Ireland, continuing the momentum for change started by the National Democratic Party in 1965 and the rise of the Civil Rights Movement during the late 1960s. The Party's initial enthusiasm to form a government within Northern Ireland became an unrealistic objective due to the tactics of Unionist politicians and a change in British Government policy towards Northern Ireland. After the failure of Sunningdale and the Constitutional Convention, it became clear to the SDLP that a purely internal solution to the Northern Ireland problem would never work. Chapters Two and Three demonstrate the efforts by the SDLP to keep the Irish dimension to the Northern Ireland conflict alive despite the political vacuum in Northern Ireland politics from 1976 onwards.

This work outlines the ways in which the SDLP has been proactive in moving towards its ultimate objective of Irish unity or, to use SDLP phraseology, an 'agreed Ireland'. It examines the willingness within the SDLP to agree to a consociational solution to the Northern Ireland conflict, given its long-term objective of a united Ireland. The development of the SDLP political strategy over the course of its existence was affected by factors such as the rise of Sinn Féin as a political entity and the inflexibility of the Unionist parties. So this book attempts to establish the degree to which Government policy towards Northern Ireland contributed to the SDLP conclusion that a purely internal solution would never work. In reacting to these factors, it is necessary to explain how the SDLP survived the political turbulence of the Northern Ireland troubles by successfully incorporating external assistance.

Chapters Three and Four examine the SDLP search for a political strategy and continuing momentum in the midst of a political void in Northern Ireland politics. By the end of the 1970s, the SDLP priority under the new leadership of John Hume was to develop an Anglo-Irish process as the stable framework towards creating change in Northern Ireland. Chapter Five details the obstacles to the SDLP campaign to get the British and Irish Governments to develop and promote an Anglo-Irish framework to the Northern Ireland conflict. Chapter Six details the SDLP's private input into the *New Ireland Forum Report*. This report provided the principles which led to the signing of the *Anglo-Irish Agreement* in November 1985. Chapter Seven evaluates the *Anglo-Irish Agreement* from the SDLP viewpoint and its impact on the Catholic community. Chapters Eight and Nine explore the aim of the Hume/Adams process which commenced in 1988, and its political impact on the SDLP. The process raises the serious question can the SDLP survive politically against the rising spiral of electoral support for Sinn Féin demonstrated in the 1996 and 1997 election results in Northern Ireland.

Chapter Ten demonstrates how exogenous factors, such as the American and European dimensions, have played an important role in SDLP strategy to pressurise the British Government into adopting the Party framework for resolving the Northern Ireland conflict. The chapter examines the impact of Hume's leadership with reference to his role in the international scene of the United States and Europe. The strength of Hume's role within the Party and the extent to which his political philosophy based on post-Nationalism dominates SDLP thinking, is analysed. Chapter Eleven examines the role of the Social Democratic Group (SDG) established under the auspices of the National Democratic Institute for International Affairs in the United States in an attempt to strengthen the organisational base of the SDLP. But, as early as 1989, the SDG was no longer operational and the organisational base of the SDLP a shambles. This chapter raises serious questions why the SDLP failed to use the SDG as a flagship to rectify the abysmal organisational base of the party; and therefore, to what extent the SDLP is democratically managed, if at all, under John Hume's leadership.

The book is restricted to a political analysis of the SDLP and does not undertake to demonstrate an in-depth study of the Party's social and economic policies. The study has involved analysis of SDLP data from three main sources: (1) The SDLP's private records deposited at the Public Record Office of Northern Ireland (PRONI). These records document the Party's earliest internal discussion papers in relation to all matters from the SDLP's inception in 1970 through to the mid-1980s;

(2) Interviews with current and former senior SDLP members along with other political representatives in Northern Ireland and the Republic;

(3) The main Irish and British newspapers from 1976 until 1997, along with SDLP radio interviews on BBC Radio Ulster, deposited at the Ulster Folk and Radio Museum.

If constitutional issues and reform are to be fully addressed in Northern Ireland and if new material on SDLP political thinking can be added to constructive discussion and debate, then the following Chapters may shed some light on the political sensitivities of the Province.

I

Origins and Formation

1965–1974

CHAPTER ONE

The National Democratic Party and the Civil Rights Movement

By the end of the 1960s, the Catholic population of Northern Ireland was frustrated with the sterile politics of the Nationalist Party. Attempts by the 'National Unity Movement', established in 1959, to induce the Nationalist Party to build a more active party structure were unsuccessful. A meeting organised by National Unity at Maghery, Armagh, in April 1964 failed to bring the Nationalist Party into contact with the changed times, new needs and developing attitudes among the minority community. The constitutional issue was no longer the primary concern of the Catholic population. Advances in the British Welfare State and access to higher education substantially increased the quality of living for many Catholics who saw new possibilities for active participation within the Northern Ireland State. The Nationalist Party failure to identify this new mood in the Catholic community led to the formation of the National Democratic Party (NDP) in 1965.

As early as 1964, the future leader of the Social Democratic and Labour Party (SDLP) John Hume suggested a movement from a traditional Nationalist viewpoint among Catholics in Northern Ireland to a more moderate position. Calling for Catholics to recognise the legitimacy of the Protestant tradition he felt that a United Ireland could only come about by evolution and consensus with the support of the northern majority.[1] There was a growing awareness among the Catholic intelligentsia that they had social, economic, and political interests in the affairs of Northern Ireland. These issues needed to be addressed by strong political organisation from within the minority community. From the outset, the NDP had rejected and replaced the negativism of the old Nationalist Party. Prior to the establishment of the NDP, the only politics within Northern Ireland was fundamentally Unionist politics. There were no structured or cohesive Nationalist politics. The only formal political organisation was the Nationalist Party which, as a political force, failed to look after the interests of the minority community. By contrast, the NDP confronted the realities of partition and gave *de facto* recognition to the Northern Ireland state: it wanted to see the end of partition, but only by democratic means. In the meantime, it wanted to participate in the social, economic and political life of Northern Ireland.[2]

According to former general secretary John Duffy, the NDP was the, 'bedrock of SDLP membership'. Out of almost four-hundred people who first joined the SDLP, nearly eighty per cent had been NDP members.[3] The NDP was instrumental in the SDLP getting off the ground, structurally and politically. Former NDP members had experience of the structures and organisational requirements of a modern political party, so the NDP provided the SDLP with a polity on which to model itself.[4]

The NDP wanted to end partition, but by mutual agreement between the two traditions within Northern Ireland.[5] The Party was willing to accept that Northern Ireland remained within the United Kingdom until a majority of the people within Northern Ireland wanted otherwise. The concept that the majority within Northern Ireland decide any new political settlement, as outlined in NDP policy documents,[6] and later adapted by the SDLP signified a major shift in Catholic political representation in Northern Ireland. The foundation of the SDLP demonstrated a major move from the traditional Nationalist position. Traditional nationalism held to the principle that it was the majority in the whole island which mattered and that a minority such as the Unionists had no right to opt out.[7] The new thinking of the NDP became the cornerstone of the earliest political philosophy and subsequent policy documents of the SDLP.

There had been a fresh perspective introduced by the NDP: it brought a degree of revisionism within Nationalist political thinking in Northern Ireland: it abandoned abstentionist politics which had been the predominant policy of the Nationalist Party. For the first time in Northern Ireland's history, the rise of the NDP had demonstrated a significant shift in Nationalist thinking towards the acceptance of the Northern Ireland State. The NDP had also participated in the Civil Rights Movement. Initially, economic and social matters were considered more important than the constitutional issue by the minority community. There had been no question that the unity of Ireland was the primary aim of the party when it was formed. It did not consider itself a Nationalist party in the traditional or previously-understood meaning of the term. It was a party which wished to see the eventual unity of Ireland, but its primary aim had been the achievement of Civil Rights. Debating and questioning social and economic matters within Northern Ireland had been their primary objective.

Even from its origins in 1965, the NDP had failed to make significant progress as a political organisation because it had been allied to the old Nationalist Party. The NDP did not organise in areas where the Nationalist Party had a Stormont MP. It only fought seats in areas where the Nationalist Party did not function,[8] in essence, that meant they were no threat to the Nationalist Party.

The principles behind the formation of the National Democratic Party in 1965 became the foundation of SDLP philosophy in 1970. The NDP had tried to combine all the progressive and liberal strands of political thinking which were activated during the 1960s. It had wanted to create an alternative political force to Unionist politics on the basis of social democracy. It had initiated the first demonstration of a political organisation representing the minority population within Northern Ireland while simultaneously giving *de facto* recognition to the Northern Ireland State. The Party definition of Nationalism was outlined in the Manifesto for the General Election in June 1970: 'Real Nationalism, such as has never been tried in Northern Ireland, expressed in a concern for the people who are the nation, is a necessary ingredient of internationalism.' Negotiated unity of the island should take place within a European context claimed the NDP and this principle has remained a fundamental element of John Hume's political philosophy.

In their Manifesto for the election, the NDP outlined a number of demands which were to become the basis of the SDLP's formative discussion papers. They wanted:

- A Council of Ireland, with representatives from both Dublin and Belfast, to promote harmonious cross-border relations and economic development between North and South.
- A *Bill of Rights* guaranteeing basic Civil Rights for all in Northern Ireland.
- Repeal of the *Special Powers Act* and other repressive legislation.
- Proportional Representation in all, including Local Government, elections.

The NDP went on to outline 'that the only long-term solution to Ireland's troubles is the creation by consent of a thirty-two county Republic'.[9]

The SDLP emerges out of the Civil Rights Movement
The SDLP superseded both the Nationalist Party and the NDP as the main political representative of the minority tradition. McAllister has pointed out that, at its inauguration, the SDLP seemed more a coalition of diverse political interests linked only by a common opposition

to Unionism than a political party. 'This apparent disunity was the result of the total absence of an indigenous tradition of Catholic parliamentary politics in Northern Ireland.[10]

As an organisation the SDLP emerged from the Civil Rights Movement. The Party was founded by people who were already Stormont MPs. Gerry Fitt left Republican Labour to become the Party's first leader. John Hume, Paddy O'Hanlon and Ivan Cooper were active in Civil Rights campaigns. Paddy Devlin was a former Northern Ireland Labour MP; Austin Currie held the constituency of East Tyrone for the Nationalist Party and Paddy Wilson–murdered on 26 June 1973–was a Republican Labour Senator. They could see the need in the 1969 Stormont elections for a strong political opposition to the Unionist majority and anticipated that this could be best attained through co-ordinated opposition and a proper party structure.

Hume and Currie drew up the original statement of principles for the SDLP which was signed by Hume, O'Hanlon, Cooper, Devlin, Fitt and Currie. One of the main aims outlined in the document was a call for the Civil Rights of all the citizens of Northern Ireland to be observed. The document also had a strong Irish dimension. It stated that one of its major goals was, 'To promote co-operation, friendship and understanding between North and South with the view to the eventual reunification of Ireland through the support of the majority of the people in the North and in the South'.[11] This was a view which Paddy Devlin believed showed the SDLP's acceptance of the, 'majority's right to opt out'.[12] However, Currie reflected, 'It was obvious by the phraseology in relation to consent that we still had our doubts in relation to a decision being taken entirely purely within a Northern Ireland context. That was something that developed and was quite new thinking at that time'.[13]

Far from being a projection of the old Nationalist Party, the SDLP promoted a new perception of Irish unity which faced up to the realities of partition and thus addressed the core of the Northern Ireland problem. Its immediate priority was to achieve the objectives of the Civil Rights movement in relation to social and economic issues. The SDLP initially set out to harness support for Civil Rights that existed on the streets and present an effective parliamentary opposition at Stormont until such times as it might be possible to form a coalition government with liberal-minded Unionists. The Party was created on the basis that reform was attainable in Northern Ireland and that there was a place for the minority. One of the Party's first policymakers, Ben Caraher, said, 'I think if people had then been asked what is your dream, your dream would have been to participate in a coalition government with the Northern Ireland Labour Party and some liberal Unionists. Agreement within Northern Ireland, if it worked, might destroy many Unionists' fears, and agreement in Northern Ireland might be a preliminary to agreement in Ireland.'[14]

Ben Caraher's early thinking about minority participation in the administration of Northern Ireland demonstrated the initial optimism of the leaders of the newly-formed SDLP. This could be interpreted as an extension of the euphoria carried over from the Civil Rights movement. Caraher has recalled, 'The big difference between the SDLP and the old Nationalist Party was over the question of unity. Unity was practically the only policy of the old Nationalist Party. We thought it would be a mistake to make unity of the country the primary and over-riding aim that determined all other policies. Unity was only one of the aims of the SDLP and it wasn't its first aim. However, the SDLP never diluted that aim.'[15]

In relation to the Civil Rights Movement, Austin Currie recalled, 'On the one hand the Unionists were asserting that they were British. At the same time they were refusing to allow British standards in Northern Ireland. The Civil Rights Movement aimed at the Achilles' heel of Unionism. It put emphasis on non-violence. It put the empha-sis on British rights because those had been the weaknesses in the past.'[16] To that extent, Currie argued that the SDLP was not initially a Nationalist movement. It was a movement determined to attain British standards of equality within Northern Ireland. Currie acknowledged that, when the SDLP was formed in 1970, the issue of 'Nationalism was being put on a back burner'. He felt the minority community recognised that they had to live within Northern Ireland for a consid-erable period of time and had to make the best of that situation. Twenty-five years on Currie argued that, 'A modern, democratically-organised political party was essential to put the maximum pressure on the Unionist and British governments and to solidify and build upon by political action what had been achieved on the streets.'[17]

Again almost twenty-five years later, Gerry Fitt reflected on the Civil Rights Movement, 'As far as I am concerned the Civil Rights Movement was about an end to discrimination, it had nothing whatso-ever to do with a United Ireland, though Unionists believed it to be a Republican conspiracy.'[18] Gerry Fitt, as a Westminster MP, was in a key position prior to the formation of the SDLP in August 1970. As the only SDLP public representative at Westminster, the Party needed Fitt in its early years to inform British political opinion of the com-plexity of the Northern Ireland conflict. Fitt has recalled, 'When the

SDLP was formed I was hoping against hope desperately that we were bringing into being a social democratic and labour party that would engage the sympathies across the sectarian divide in Northern Ireland.'[19]

Paddy Devlin also initially held out hope that the newly formed SDLP could 'integrate anti-Unionist groups into one coherent political force by seriously stretching across the forbidden Catholic-Protestant divide in an effort to fuse traditions and loyalties into one harmonious society'.[20] Like Devlin, Fitt intended the SDLP to be 'a broad-based cross-community labour party with a portfolio of reforming policies based on the civil rights demands'.[21]

The Irish dimension was always a key element in the SDLP overall political policy on constitutional issue. Ivan Cooper, one of a sprinkling of Protestant representatives in the SDLP argued that the Irish dimension was fully accepted by all the leading members of the new Party, 'All our discussions made it clear that the Irish dimension was important. Devlin and Fitt gave their allegiance to that principle. For those of us in rural areas we felt there had to be some type of all-Ireland institution. It wasn't defined, but it was felt that there had to be some type of executive function in relation to the Irish dimension. There had to be some formal link with the South. The SDLP leadership knew it could not go into partnership government without an Irish dimension.'[22]

Political instability and violence within Northern Ireland in the early 1970s made it difficult for the SDLP to consolidate into an effective opposition. The bastion of Unionist control was breaking down around the Stormont Government and this heightened the suspicion and mistrust of the Unionist administration towards the newly-formed SDLP. The SDLP saw the Irish dimension in very similar terms to the NDP: Irish unity could only come about with the consent of the majority within Northern Ireland.

As early as 1964, Hume noted that Unionists 'must accept that Nationalism in Ireland is an acceptable political belief'.[23] He also outlined in a column he wrote regularly for the *Sunday Press* in the period 1969-70,[24] the elements of his overall strategy. They were 'contained in the "three Rs", Reform, Reconciliation and Reunification.'[25] In the early years of Hume's political career, he wished to see the cause of the Northern Ireland conflict properly defined.

The Civil Rights Movement in the late 1960s provided the basis for the SDLP to develop and evolve. It was the experience of those who took part in the Civil Rights Movement which shaped the need for social democracy in the Party. Throughout Northern Ireland, a number of liberal activists were concerned about social, economic and political equality for all the citizens of the State,[26] but were not drawn to the SDLP because of the polarisation of the two communities within Northern Ireland. As a consequence, the majority of the Party rank-and-file and leadership were drawn from the minority community.

From the Party's formation in 1970, it sought to attract moderate Unionists into its ranks and penetrate the 'sectarian barriers' of Northern Ireland politics. The party leader, Gerry Fitt, declared the Party's support for reform within the Stormont administration. In line with the rest of the founding members of the SDLP he declared, '...we intend to work for the reunification of this country with the consent of the vast majority of its people'.[27]

Paddy O'Hanlon has acknowledged that, when the SDLP was formed, the founding members of the Party realised the Irish dimension had to be part of an evolutionary process.[28] Ivan Cooper, like Fitt and Devlin has strongly claimed that never at any time during their formative years did the SDLP consent to devolved government within Northern Ireland without some expression of an Irish dimension. He has said, 'Our expectations of power-sharing were not very high in the early days. We saw ourselves as a very strong cohesive opposition at Stormont. However, we were all dedicated to bringing Stormont down once the Unionists deflected from implementing the various reforms. They had to be kicked and dragged along the way....It was not until mid- 1973 that we seriously thought about becoming part of a government. We were coming around to the joint sovereignty concept. The Irish dimension was always on our minds because we had to sell it to our constituencies. However, our top priority was to get an accommodation within Northern Ireland. We thought more in a European context.' [29]

O'Hanlon has argued that the SDLP was founded on the philosophy of social democracy, 'We were a social democratic unit. We knew exactly what we were. We were in the mainstream of European thought and that is exactly were we wanted to stay – not Irish thought but European thought as a European party.'[30] Currie has explained the basis of the SDLP's Socialist principles in moderate terms, 'The backbone of the SDLP tended to be teachers. Whether they were in Belfast, Derry or Dungannon, teachers tended to be quite radical, most of them would have to have been left-of-centre, although not too left-of-centre. They would not have to have been ideological. To that extent they were probably ahead of their time and more European in their thinking than any other political party. To that extent, also, I suppose ahead of their time in so far as "European Socialism" was more social democracy than anything else. The social democratic philosophy within the SDLP was therefore forward-looking.'[31]

John Hume fought his first election against Eddie McAteer 'on the basis of seeking a mandate to establish a political party based on social democratic principles.'[32] Crystallising the tenets of the new party, Hume wanted it to be called the Social Democratic Party. But O'Hanlon remembered that the 'Belfast brethren' wanted 'Labour' added on to the end of it, bluntly adding, 'The knock-about-farce boys had to have Labour in it for Belfast'.[33] If labour was not in the title, Fitt was not having anything to do with the Party.[34] Hume has said, 'The mandate we sought was a broad-based party based on social democratic principles and the less splits there were the better. Therefore, it was better to have taken Fitt on board.'[35] 'We made it very clear from the beginning that the SDLP would be based on social democratic principles on the European model.'[36] Hume was greatly influenced by European politics and the manner in which the European institutions were evolving. He believed the Northern Ireland problem was insoluble purely within the boundaries of Northern Ireland. Therefore, it was necessary to change the context of the problem. Placed within a European context the conflict according to Hume's thesis all sides appeared increasingly reconcilable.[37]

Hopes of Reform and Compromise Diminish
Tensions at the end of 1969 saw the emergence of the Provisional IRA on the streets of Northern Ireland. Government measures such as the Falls Curfew in July 1970 'had a profoundly alienating impact upon the wider Catholic community'.[38] Such actions contributed to the Provisionals taking the role of defenders of the Catholic community, particularly in the working-class areas within Northern Ireland. Sabine Wichert has pointed out that 'the SDLP arrived too late to be able to halt the drift towards extremism and violence and thus take reforming Catholic interests to Stormont'.[39]

William Faulkner's 'Committee Proposals' for members of the opposition at Stormont in June 1971 were welcomed by Fitt, Devlin and Currie although they were viewed by the SDLP as being too little too late. The SDLP would have operated the committee system as a method of reforming the political system, but the majority of the Party outside Belfast wanted some type of formal link with the Republic of Ireland.

Ian McAllister has written that Hume, 'doubted whether the will existed in the Unionist Party to implement the proposals'.[40] The committee system put forward by Faulkner marked a sign of moderation by Unionists. On the other hand this was off-set by the strong Unionist security policy of internment. Faulkner was mistaken to believe that the SDLP would participate in a committee system that would allow the Unionist government to implement stringent security policies.

Unionists blamed Hume for being the manipulator who eventually led the SDLP to leave Stormont formally. The shooting of Seamus Cusack and Desmond Beattie by the British Army in Derry on 8 July 1971 led Hume to demand a Public Enquiry. When an enquiry did not take place, Hume declared that the SDLP would formally withdraw from Stormont. Devlin recalled that both he and Fitt did not support Hume's stance which, however, had the backing of the majority within the SDLP.[41] Hume was afraid that the Provisionals would take advantage of Nationalist sentiment in Derry at this time and would take over from the moderation of the SDLP. Ken Bloomfield has said: 'Hume's decision, though, may well have been strategic rather than tactical, since of all Northern Ireland politicians he has been the most inclined to think in grand conceptual terms and in long timescales.'[42] Stormont was rapidly losing credibility within SDLP circles and its impartiality was seriously questioned by mid-1971. Any new system of government within Northern Ireland had to deprive the Unionist Party of its monopoly of power. The SDLP sought the abolition of Stormont, the transfer of security to Westminster and 'as a precondition to talks – the ending of internment'. The Party believed that if such measures emerged, 'it would deliver such a blow to the Unionist power structure that it would turn inwards and begin to devour itself'.[43]

When the SDLP officially withdrew from Stormont on 16 July 1971, it was really an official recognition by the party that Unionist domination at Stormont was an irreversible. From July 1971, Westminster rather than Stormont 'had emerged as the centre of lobbying and attention' for the SDLP.[44] Withdrawal from Stormont opened the SDLP to accusations from Unionists that the Party was reverting to the abstentionist politics of traditional Nationalism; a view incidentally shared by both Fitt and Devlin.[45] Gerry Fitt told the BBC that, 'People thought that we were half Unionists and that we had forgotten the people who voted for us.'[46] The SDLP was left in an awkward dilemma. Their abstention from Stormont left the Party 'politically impotent'.[47]

Internment was introduced on 9 August 1971 and thirteen civilians were killed in Derry on 30 January 1972. The implementation of internment resulted in an increase in the IRA bombing campaign. Support for the IRA within Republican strongholds of Northern Ireland increased significantly. The effect of internment and stringent security measures led the SDLP to refuse to become involved in political talks with the Government while internment continued, 'The mood in the Catholic community since internment had been such that a more co-operative attitude from the SDLP might well have done it severe political damage.'[48]

Continuation of internment throughout 1974 caused Paddy Devlin's resignation during the era of the power-sharing Executive.[49] In contrast, Fitt never displayed the public sympathy to internment which some members of the SDLP demonstrated for pragmatic reasons. Fitt has said, 'Was I supposed to shout and scream in opposition to internment? There is no way I was going to do that'.[50] This was a politically dangerous strategy for Fitt to begin, as Republicans henceforth directed their hostility towards him. It started the impetus that eventually led to him to leave the political stage in Northern Ireland and brought about his defeat in the 1983 General Elections.

Former SDLP veteran Paddy Duffy has argued that even if the Unionists had been more forthcoming in implementing reforms within the Northern Ireland State, this would not have led the SDLP to cancel the Irish dimension which was an integral aspect of its policies, 'The Unionists offered too little too late. We would not have seen an internal arrangement as a permanent settlement, but rather as only an interim settlement. There would have to be some involvement with the South in some way or other. We were convinced that there had to be an Irish dimension because there couldn't be a permanent settlement unless you had one. The Party was flexible over what form the Irish dimension would take. We looked at federation, confederation and condominium. A federal system of government was probably the most realistic option which consisted of some type of arrangement between the South and the North. There was no way we were going to be British.'[51] It was becoming clearer to the SDLP that the Northern conflict could not be resolved within an exclusively Northern Ireland context.

Basically, the SDLP believed that all identities in Northern Ireland had to be accommodated in a new political settlement. The structure of the administration and its external relationships with the rest of Ireland and Britain had to command the allegiance of both communities. For this to happen the SDLP understood the need which existed to articulate an entirely new and much more comprehensive definition of Irish unity, which could have a validity for both traditions.[52]

Each of the two communities in Northern Ireland have shaped their identities in terms which transcend the borders of Northern Ireland. Unionists perceive themselves to be British, in the sense that they are part of a nation which exists throughout the United Kingdom. Northern Nationalists understand their identity as belonging to the thirty-two counties of Ireland which constitute the territory of the Irish nation. Therefore, the SDLP argued that a compromise which accommodated both traditions had to be found, rather than a new balance which would suppress the British identity and give victory to the Nationalist one.[53] In contrast to traditional Nationalism, the SDLP rejected the notion that the answer to the conflict was simply the ending of partition.

Denis Haughey has pointed out that the SDLP's earliest thinking focused on the necessity of accommodating both identities of the two traditions within Northern Ireland. Any acceptable administration and its external relationship with the United Kingdom and the Republic of Ireland had to command the allegiance of all sections of the community, 'That has always been our view. It took various forms at various times. The essential elements were always there whether it was our original proposals of joint sovereignty or later acceptance of a power-sharing executive with a council of Ireland.'[54]

John Duffy was one of the main authors of the SDLP's earliest policy discussion papers until January 1972. He produced a series of recommendations for resolving the Northern Ireland conflict in six early draft papers which were completed by the end of 1971. Duffy's proposals were based on the Council of Ireland idea which were set out in the *1920 Government of Ireland Act*. While the SDLP stated its long-term objective for a thirty-two-county Socialist Republic this was not a viable option in the short-term.[55] Documents focused on an interim strategy for drawing up a new political framework within Northern Ireland involving the two Governments and the Unionist community.

Based on the premise that the Stormont administration had to be replaced forthwith, the SDLP proposed that powers from Unionist control, 'should pass to a one-hundred-member Commission broadly representative of the Northern Ireland community' with the exception of security matters. It was anticipated that the Commission would provide a provisional system of administration in Northern Ireland for eighteen months until elections to a new system of government could be created by the middle of 1973 at the latest. The inaugural Commission would have the same powers as the Northern Ireland House of Commons and Senate, with the exception of judicial, police and security matters. The commission would be formed in consultation with the two governments, the Unionists and the SDLP.[56] Security was to be transferred initially to a non-political, expert body which was to be Chaired by a non-British or Irish legal figure symbol. It would have the power to recommend a United Nations force, if necessary.[57]

The proposals suggested that 'The Commission should elect, from among its own number, a Chairman, Vice-Chairman and Executive Committee of fifteen....Twelve of the fifteen members of the Executive should be elected by the Commission specifically to be the heads and depute heads of the existing Ministries of the Northern Ireland Government'. After consultation with the Commission and the Irish Government, the British Government should legislate a *Bill of Rights* and an *Anti-Discrimination Act* for Northern Ireland which would guarantee equality for all its citizens.[58]

In the policy documents the SDLP called on the British and Irish Governments to create a Supreme Council of Ireland to be composed of an equal number of representatives from Northern Ireland and the Republic. The Council would have effective powers in: security legislation in Northern Ireland and the Republic; economic development; the creation of an eventual integrated economy, including parity of living standards and welfare payments; the initiation of research into harmonisation of all legislation North and South; education, social and cultural matters; a final Court of Appeal in disputes arising under the *Bill of Rights* and *Anti-Discrimination* legislation.[59] The Supreme Council was to review Anglo-Irish relations every ten years; for instance in terms of legislative harmonisation between both parts of Ireland. After eighteen months, the SDLP proposed that the provisional administration, namely the Commission, should be replaced by a eighty-seat council. Elections to the new council were to be by proportional representation. It was to have a similar role to the Commission mentioned in the earlier part of the proposals.

The September 1971 document also called on the Government to declare that it had no interest in perpetuating the partition of Ireland. It stated that Britain should actively support reunification whenever this could be achieved. Reunification had to be based in terms acceptable to the majority of people in Northern Ireland and had to have their consent. British Government should actively seek out such terms in consultation with the Northern Ireland Council, the Government of the Republic and the Supreme Council of Ireland.[60] Also, in a small up-date of the document in December 1971, the SDLP outlined a proposition that the Republic of Ireland 'should declare her willingness to re-examine, in consultation with the Supreme Council of Ireland and the Northern Ireland Council, such parts of her constitution as may be held to be offensive to any section of the Irish people, and to contemplate amendments.' Further, 'The Republic of Ireland, in conjunction within the Northern Ireland Council, under the overall guidance of the Supreme Council of Ireland, should make arrangements for voters in Northern Ireland to participate in future elections of the President of Ireland.'[61]

Although the SDLP proposals in the discussion documents for a eighty-seat council in Northern Ireland, complemented with an elected executive and the continuation of the Supreme Council of Ireland, were viewed as a long-term measure, in effect they still only represented an interim solution. The purpose of the SDLP interim measures were 'aimed in the first instance at peace within Northern Ireland' but would 'also have the effect of creating the conditions which will facilitate in the long-term the unity of our country by consent', a process that was estimated to take fifteen years.

Duffy's analysis set out the three sets of relationships which were needed for resolving the conflict, namely, accommodation within Northern Ireland; between North and South; and between Britain and Ireland. This was a framework which was to be based on the totality of relationships and eventually taken up by the two Governments in the early 1980s. The underlying principle behind any new constitutional arrangements was to create the basis of equality for both traditions within Northern Ireland. These earliest internal SDLP policy discussion papers which preceded the key document *Towards a New Ireland* produced in September 1972 acknowledged that the interdependence between North and South of the island was the core ingredient for a long-term settlement. The SDLP defined the obstacle to unity in late 1971 documentation not as 'British imperialism', a traditional Nationalist sentiment, 'but rather the strength of the fears of the Protestant/Majority community'.

In the second of two discussion papers set out in September 1971 by the SDLP Interim Executive and Research Group, recommendations were made for a Conference with the aim of creating a new political environment in Northern Ireland protecting Catholics from discrimination and 'relieving the Protestant community of their apprehension of being coerced into an all-Ireland Republic'. The political philosophy contained in this paper founded the principles behind the power-sharing Executive in 1974 and the discussions emanating from the Sunningdale Conference. The document proposed internal reform within Northern Ireland by establishing a *Bill of Rights, Fair Practices Act*, Proportional Representation in all elections and an alternative system of government to the Westminster model. A Council of Ireland was to act as the official mechanism for developing cross-border economic and social co-operation. Development of a joint security authority represented by all three Governments to take responsibility for border policing was recommended.[62]

John Duffy attempted to base future SDLP policies in a realistic context despite the long-term aim of Irish unity. After January 1972, Duffy's line of thinking was abandoned by the SDLP who felt that his policy direction was not radical enough. It was argued that Duffy's proposals were simply a repackaging of the Council of Ireland proposals as set out in the *1920 Government of Ireland Act* and that something more original was required.[63] There was also criticism from the Republic. Duffy commented in an internal party memorandum that a prominent southern politician told him his proposals were impractical since they made 'for unreasonable and unworkable change in the South'.[64] It would appear however that the SDLP abandoned the direction of Duffy's discussion papers due to a leak by a senior party figure of a crucial internal policy document.[65] According to John Duffy, Party leader Gerry Fitt leaked this information to British Labour Party sources either directly or indirectly through the media.[66] To retain its distinct and separate stance from Government policy in Northern Ireland the SDLP started to focus its attention from January 1972 on the idea of condominium which became the basis of its *Towards a New Ireland*.

For the SDLP, Northern Ireland's institutions were the property of the Unionist community, and the minority community was alienated from them. To end this alienation, new institutions would have to be created which incorporated the specifically Irish identity of the Catholic population. Caraher has argued that it was impossible to advocate an all-Ireland State because a large section of the Protestant community viewed its identity as British. They did not want to be part of a United Ireland. In these circumstances, a condominium proposal whereby Northern Ireland would be governed jointly by Britain and the Republic was the only realistic solution.[67]

The SDLP now felt the formation of a condominium was a method of dealing with the existence of the two communities within Northern Ireland and their conflicting loyalties. Cooper suggested that the SDLP must examine ways of 'making Northern Ireland into a territory pertaining to the Sovereign Parliaments of Britain and the Irish Republic and having two recognised citizenships...for the inhabitants to choose between'[68] and continued that, '...as long as the settlement is on the basis of the Ulster Protestants having their identity, their desired citizenship guaranteed and the Catholics are merely guaranteed jobs and a fair look in, you will not have a settlement for peace'.[69]

Ben Caraher elaborated that a condominium would give guarantees against Unionists being absorbed into a United Ireland simultaneously maintaining their identity and link with Britain. Conversely, a condominium would give to the minority community's Irish identity official recognition. It offered an end to Protestant political domination, a share in power, the end of discrimination, the withdrawal of British troops and a Sovereign Power as a watchdog over the interests of the minority.[70] The Republic would have 'an agreed political role in the North and political recognition of Irish nationality for the first time in every part of the island'.[71]

Caraher envisaged Northern Ireland becoming a condominium of the Republic of Ireland and the United Kingdom, whose citizens would have the option to choose either British or Irish citizenship to reconcile 'the existence of two different communities with differing and conflicting loyalties'. The condominium proposals gave the Party a 'distinctive position' in relation to the constitutional issue. He felt that to agree to a Council of Ireland with 'vaguely defined consultative functions'[72] could leave the electorate unable to distinguish between the SDLP and the Alliance Party or the Northern Ireland Labour Party.[73]

The SDLP refused an invitation from the Secretary of State, William Whitelaw and the British Government to attend the Darlington Conference arranged for 25-27 September 1972. It was virtually impossible for the SDLP to enter normal dialogue while internment continued since it would have provided militant Republicans with propaganda that the SDLP was giving tacit support to British internment policy. Instead, a weekend conference in Donegal in August 1972 consisting of SDLP Executive and MPs was held to work out a formal response to the Darlington Conference. John Duffy recalled that John Hume, Paddy Fox and Ben Caraher would have steered the SDLP in the direction of supporting the condominium concept.[74] The Party used the early policy discussion papers on condominium put forward by John Duffy, Ben Caraher and Ivan Cooper as the basis on which to put forward proposals for the Darlington Conference.[75]

John Hume played a major role in the formulation of the final draft of *Towards a New Ireland*, which called on Britain to make a formal declaration of intent for a United Ireland and also proposed an interim system of government in the form of joint sovereignty by Dublin and Westminster. *Towards a New Ireland* was probably the document around which there was most internal SDLP party discussion.[76] According to Ivan Cooper, everybody in the SDLP was in agreement with its philosophy, '...at all times there had been an acceptance within the SDLP that there had to be an Irish dimension'.[77] Caraher has indicated that Hume provided the political momentum in the SDLP at this time and supported his condominium paper; he recalled that the Party subscribed in principle to the condominium concept of Northern Ireland governed jointly by Britain and the Republic.[78] Caraher remembered feeling uneasy about the final draft of the document published as *Towards a New Ireland* on 20 September 1972. He felt the final draft was written both in reaction to the strong anti-British feeling which was surfacing within the minority community and as a reaction against the fear that hard-line Republicanism threatened to take over from constitutional Nationalism. Caraher believed that Nationalist sentiment was potent throughout the entire minority community at the time and has said, 'There was a very strong United Ireland movement among the minority community, far stronger than since the War [of Independence 1918-1921]. When we talked about the condominium concept, a lot of us felt that there had to be something about a United Ireland in our policy.' He has added, 'The final condominium document produced proposals for an eventual United Ireland. I felt that distorted the real meaning of condominium. It produced an imbalance. The purpose of the institutions I was proposing to set up was not to gradually work towards a United Ireland. My condominium was intended to be stronger than joint sovereignty. It was not a preparation for anything, but was intended to be an actual solution there and then. It left the door open for a United Ireland if there was an agreement.'[79]

Many Catholics were happy to see the collapse of Stormont when it became apparent that Unionists were reluctant to implement reform and the creation of confidence-building measures necessary to start integrating this section of the community into Northern Ireland society. The implementation of internment in August 1971 still left bitter anti-British feelings within the Catholic community. Direct Rule did not ensure the immediate end of internment. When thirteen civilians were killed in Derry on 30 January 1972 by the Parachute Regiment and when British military operations such as 'Operation Motorman' took place on 31 July 1972 – a British military operation to restore 'no-go areas' to normal administration – the sense of continuing British oppression of the minority community was reinforced.

The IRA increased its violence at this time. Twenty-six bombs went off in Belfast on 21 July 1972 killing eleven people and injuring one hundred and thirty others in what became known as 'Bloody Friday'. The collapse of the IRA cease-fire which had lasted from 26 June 1972 to the 9 July 1972 led to an all-out security clamp-down on the Provisionals by the Government. Devlin has said, 'The breakdown of talks with the Provos was a salutary lesson for us in the SDLP, for it showed that the IRA was incapable of engaging in the political process.'[80]

William Whitelaw believed the collapse of the IRA cease-fire strengthened Catholic support for a strong security offensive against the Provisionals. He anticipated that the SDLP would become more co-operative with the Government in negotiations about new political arrangements and on issues of security.[81] In his memoirs he noted, 'I needed to encourage the SDLP to build up their strength and their co-operation with the Government and the security forces'.[82] The Government viewed the SDLP, 'as the main Catholic party' who 'were engaged in a struggle for support within the Catholic community with the Provisional IRA'.[83]

Paul Bew and Henry Patterson have pointed out that, in the post-internment period, the SDLP held a stronger anti-partitionist stance than Lynch's Fianna Fáil Government in the Republic.[84] It was the Irish Government which placed pressure on the SDLP to enter into dialogue with the British Government. The Irish Government was opposed to direct involvement in the affairs of Northern Ireland. Its strategy was to coerce the SDLP to become more co-operative with the British in order to reach some form of internal compromise in Northern Ireland.[85] A General Election in the Republic in March 1973 brought to power a new coalition Government consisting of Fine Gael and the Labour Party. Like the Lynch administration, the coalition priority was to put aside traditional arguments for Irish unity and to pressurise the British for radical reform within the Northern state which would be acceptable to the minority community.

On 20 March 1973, the British Government published a *White Paper* outlining plans for a Northern Ireland Assembly. The SDLP welcomed the proposed size of the assembly and its method of election which was in keeping with their recommendations. Westminster control of law and order, prisons and the police, instead of being within the remit of the Northern Ireland Assembly, was the preferred option outlined in early SDLP policy discussion documents. The SDLP believed that the Irish dimension could best be expressed through a Council of Ireland as outlined in the – *White Paper* and acknowledged,

'... that the future for this island particularly in the context of the EEC lies in developing ultimate integration by agreement between North and South and we believe that an all-Ireland institution with clearly defined powers and with that aim in view should be the clearly expressed view of the British Government in this *White Paper*.'[86] The SDLP welcomed the *Charter of Rights* contained in the *White Paper*, as they had sought a *Bill of Rights* in earlier discussion documents. Yet the *White Paper* failed to address the future of policing within Northern Ireland adequately. The SDLP wanted to see 'a newly constituted Police Service'.[87]

Both the Government *Green Paper* based on the Darlington talks published on 30 October 1972, and its subsequent *White Paper* published on 20 March 1973 contained a significant Irish dimension. The SDLP felt there was enough of its philosophy contained in the *White Paper* to allow it to support a Northern Ireland Assembly. Bew and Patterson have noted that the SDLP justified its strategy for taking part in the 1973 Local Government Elections and the subsequent Assembly Elections on the basis 'that their victory as the main representatives of the North's Catholics would have dramatic effects on British policy and would lead to a quick ending of internment'.[88]

The Council of Ireland proposals contained in the *White Paper* were an acknowledgement by the British Government that cross-border institutions could address the Irish identity of the minority community in Northern Ireland but the SDLP expressed disappointment that the Irish dimension had not been defined in clearer terms. Ben Caraher commented,

> 'The Council of Ireland proposed by the British Government in 1973 was a dilution of the SDLP's condominium proposals. The British and Irish Governments were not prepared to go the whole condominium way. The Council of Ireland concept was influenced by the SDLP condominium proposals – namely the need for an all-Ireland institution and a formal relationship with Northern Ireland and the Republic. It was something which would give the Nationalist community within Northern Ireland a sense that the political institutions within Northern Ireland somehow reflected a sense of their own identity. It did not go as far as a condominium, but it was a step in that direction. We were not political absolutes.'[89]

Ironically, the Government proposals did contain the main principles of the SDLP unpublished policy discussion papers which put emphasis on a revival of the 1920 Council of Ireland proposals.

For the SDLP, any political arrangement between the two communities within Northern Ireland would only be acceptable if both sections of the Northern Ireland community had access to all levels of the decision-making process. Two national identities had to be recognised in Northern Ireland's relations with Britain and the Republic of Ireland. These were the principles behind the original *Towards a New Ireland*. They were also outlined in the Party Manifestos for the 1973 Assembly Election and the General Election in February 1974.

For the SDLP, the Irish dimension was significant not only from an Irish Nationalist perspective, but also in the context of the EEC. The Party believed that when the Republic joined the EEC in January 1973 there was a strong case for justifying a Council of Ireland. The SDLP remained 'convinced that the future for this island particularly in the context of the EEC lies in developing ultimate integration between North and South'[90] and felt that the Council of Ireland proposals contained in the – *White Paper* provided the basis for a formula in which quadripartite talks involving representatives from both sides in the North, the Republic and Britain could take place.[91]

Sunningdale and the Power-sharing Experiment

The power-sharing Executive projected in the Government *White Paper* of March 1973 was made up of Brian Faulkner's Unionist Party of Northern Ireland (UPNI), the Alliance Party and the SDLP. The most controversial dimension of the overall package discussed at the Sunningdale Conference which took place from 6 to the 9 December 1973 in Berkshire was that the Council of Ireland would promote co-operation between Northern Ireland and the Republic of Ireland, particularly in the economic and security spheres. It identified 'tourism, regional development, electricity and transport' as areas of inter-dependence from which the two states could benefit.[92] The process of harmonisation of these functions was set against the recent EEC membership by the United Kingdom and Ireland.[93] The British Government acknowledged that it was 'prepared to facilitate the establishment of institutional arrangements for consultation and co-operation between Northern Ireland and the Republic of Ireland'.[94]

It was anticipated that the Council of Ireland would operate 'at both inter-Governmental and inter-Parliamentary levels'.[95] The communiqué issued after the Sunningdale Conference accepted in principle the creation of a Council of Ireland. A study was to be conducted on the actual functions of the Council. The Council of Ireland was to include a 'council of ministers with executive and harmonising functions and a consultative role and a consultative assembly with advisory and review functions.'[96] What had been agreed between the two Governments at Sunningdale was to be later signed formally and registered at the United Nations.

The SDLP was generally happy with the *Sunningdale Agreement*, because the main proposals agreed in principle at the conference were already contained within the SDLP's early discussion papers. In particular, the Council of Ireland functions on cross-border social and economic issues and the promotion of a joint security authority by all three Governments on border policing were SDLP proposals outlined in the communiqué after the Sunningdale Conference. Also, the SDLP welcomed Article 11 of the *Sunningdale Communiqué* which dealt with human rights. This reiterated the SDLP desire to see the *European Convention on Human Rights and Fundamental Freedoms* as part of Northern Ireland internal legislation, a position outlined by the SDLP in *Towards a New Ireland*.[97]

On 28 May 1974 the power-sharing Executive collapsed as a result of the Ulster Workers' Council (UWC) Strike. Direct Rule was reimposed. The downfall of Sunningdale cannot be attributed just to the issue of power-sharing and the Council of Ireland. Two other factors contributed to its failure: one was the British General Election which brought a change of Government in February 1974; the second was the fact that nothing definite had been agreed at Sunningdale in relation to the Council of Ireland which increased Unionist fears as to their future role.

It was the first time that Catholic Nationalist politicians had actively participated in the government of Northern Ireland since the foundation of the state. It gave the SDLP a sense of significance and permanence as the major political party representing the minority population in Northern Ireland. The SDLP viewed the power-sharing administration as only part of an overall political settlement. Within any political agreement there had to be some form of Irish dimension, with at least some form of cross-border institution. The Party always felt that the Irish Nationalist community in Ireland could not give its full allegiance to a State which existed in a purely British context. For this reason alone, the SDLP would never have agreed solely to a power-sharing arrangement for Northern Ireland. The Council of Ireland was part of the overall political package. Perhaps the SDLP might have entertained the possibility of phasing in the Irish dimension over a particular timescale.[98]

Eddie McGrady recalled that the SDLP agreed to participate in a Stormont institution in return for Unionist agreement to participate in an all-Ireland institution: 'That was the *quid pro quo*. It was a very important principle, one would not have happened without the other. The first *pro* happened – that is the formation of the Executive, but the second *quid* didn't – which was then termed the Council of Ireland. People have forgotten that the *quid pro quo* still exists. Because we believe that whatever solution there is, there cannot be a solution unless it has those components....Sunningdale would not have worked without the all-Ireland dimension which was catered for through the Council of Ireland. The SDLP's strategy was based on addressing solutions to the Northern Ireland problem. Therefore, it could not put the Irish dimension to the one side and work within a purely Northern Ireland context. This would have meant the party would have only concentrated on social and economic problems and ignored the constitutional problems. We could not have done this because the conflict is not just about social and economic issues but is about the constitutional problem.'[99]

Dissension existed within the SDLP, as Fitt was later to admit that he supported an internal settlement at Sunningdale and opposed Irish Government involvement in the negotiations leading up to Sunningdale. Fitt blamed Hume for pressurising the Irish Government into developing a bigger role for the Council of Ireland concept than was originally envisaged. He has argued that the SDLP should have left the Irish dimension at Sunningdale to one side and focused on having the power-sharing Executive running for four or five years. This would have provided a time-span to build up confidence amongst the Catholics and the Protestants within Northern Ireland. He believed that an effective power-sharing Executive would have ended discrimination and provided everyone in Northern Ireland with equal opportunities. Fitt has contended that, perhaps, after confidence had been built up between the two communities, the Council of Ireland concept could have been explored.[100]

Fitt has said that power-sharing was a tremendous advance on anything the minority community had ever obtained within Northern Ireland and has claimed that it was the Council of Ireland which killed any hopes of keeping the power-sharing Executive in office. The Sunningdale experiment, according to Fitt, emphasised the power-sharing element first, then the Council of Ireland.[101] However, Fitt's interpretation was a minority view within the SDLP. The consensus within the party was that Unionists were opposed to the principle of power-sharing with the minority community. Unionists used the emotional vehicle of the Council of Ireland as a decoy for their real target – namely the power-sharing Executive.[102]

The fall of the power-sharing Executive in May 1974 led the Government to seek new policies for Northern Ireland. In the immediate aftermath of Sunningdale the SDLP maintained its position of seeking a 'partnership' resolution of the conflict.[103] The SDLP believed such a strategy was the only way forward for resolving the conflict. The principles of partnership from the SDLP perspective were basically about allowing the expression of both traditions within Northern Ireland to exist legitimately. Partnership required the agreement of the people of the North and the South to support any new institutions which were established. Although the SDLP gave *de facto* recognition to the Northern Ireland State, they did not recognise it as a social, cultural or geographical unit.[104] This attitude towards Northern Ireland became even more pronounced during the late 1970s.

Republicans viewed the SDLP as a 'partitionist Nationalist' body.[105] The IRA violence continued at a high level during the period leading up to and during the era of Sunningdale. Sinn Féin realised that if the Sunningdale experiment was successful it could lead to the demise of the Republican Movement and a permanent political solution within Northern Ireland. Therefore, the collapse of Sunningdale was welcome news not just in Loyalist circles but also in Republican strongholds. Gerry Adams has argued, 'From the point of view of British strategy the Sunningdale experience had succeeded for the first time in producing a fully-fledged Catholic partitionist party in the form of the SDLP, a party that was prepared to work the partitionist system.'[106] From the time the SDLP was formed in 1970, a tension developed between what Adams has described as 'partitionist Nationalism' represented by the SDLP and 'anti-partitionist Nationalism' by militant Republicanism. While the SDLP aspired towards a United Ireland, initially they were prepared to wait until Unionists gave their consent to such unity. From the Republican viewpoint, Anthony McIntyre has argued that British strategy at Sunningdale was aimed at bolstering 'the constitutional guarantee [for the Unionists] while at the same time incorporating constitutional Nationalism into the framework of the State, in a bid to marginalise Republicanism'.[107]

Bew and Patterson have argued that the Northern Ireland Office (NIO) speculated divisions between the urban and rural elements within the SDLP would lead to the party accepting a 'predominantly internal settlement' in order to compete with the Provisionals.[108] However, the NIO underestimated the weakness of Fitt, his leadership and his influence within the SDLP. The SDLP was still vehemently opposed to the Government position on policing and internment and so to keep support among the minority community away from the Provisional IRA or Sinn Féin, the SDLP took a strong position against the government on these matters. The NIO was not alone in underestimating the strength of support within the SDLP for a strong executive and harmonisation function for the Council of Ireland as outlined in the *White Paper* in March 1973. The Irish Government also failed to gauge this desire within the SDLP.

In the post-Sunningdale period some Government officials assumed that an institutionalised Irish dimension was no longer an integral part of SDLP policy. But the Party still sought a phased and orderly British Army withdrawal from Northern Ireland in conjunction with a political settlement.[109] After a joint meeting of the SDLP Executive and Assembly Party in June 1974, Party guidelines were issued on post-Sunningdale strategy. The Party called on the British Parliament to state clearly on what terms Northern Ireland would remain part of the United Kingdom. Any Northern Ireland settlement had to be based on the principle of partnership between both sections of the community in the North, namely power-sharing or participation in government at executive level. The Party decided to use the phrase 'Agreed Ireland' rather than 'United Ireland' in its political terminology.

The SDLP still supported the main thrust of the *1973 Northern Ireland Constitution Act* which provided a fair and practical framework for the establishment of power-sharing at government level. In new proposals drawn up in a draft policy discussion document in the aftermath of Sunningdale, the SDLP proposed a seventy-eight-member legislative assembly which should nominate a chief minister, whose task it would be to form a multi-party Government within Northern Ireland after talks with party leaders.[110]

The document proposed an Irish ministerial conference to promote North-South relations consisting of members from the Irish Government and the Northern Ireland Government.[111] It sought a *Bill of Rights* for both Northern Ireland and the Republic; it was to be drawn up for Northern Ireland by the newly created Assembly; and in the Republic, it was the responsibility of the Oireachtas to legislate a similar bill as part of an overall revised constitution.[112] In the draft document the SDLP called on the South to spell out exactly what it meant by unity,[113] and requested the Republic to draw up a new Constitution 'in which the aspiration to Irish Unity is proclaimed in such a way that it does not imply the annexation of the North by the Republic'.[114]

The Government produced a *White Paper* in July 1974 with the purpose of setting up a Constitutional Convention for Northern

Ireland.[115] The SDLP wanted power-sharing in Government and an Irish dimension to be a non-negotiable factor in the Convention discussions. There was a call from the SDLP for the Government to re-examine the basis of its policy towards Northern Ireland. British policy guaranteed the Unionist population that Northern Ireland could remain part of the United Kingdom so long as a majority so wished. However, the SDLP argued that the Government had a responsibility to make the Unionist population accept the sovereignty of the British Parliament over Northern Ireland of which the Unionists were a minority. They blamed successive Governments for not taking responsibility for the proper ruling of Northern Ireland and allowing Unionist politicians to veto any political initiatives.

In the immediate period after the collapse of Sunningdale, prior to the convention elections taking place, the SDLP was disappointed with Irish Government policy on Northern Ireland. They wanted both British and Irish Governments to declare that power-sharing in government and an Irish dimension expressed through agreed institutions in the North and South were non-negotiable ingredients of any forthcoming Constitutional Convention.

The SDLP accepted the principle that British policy provided Unionists with a guarantee that Northern Ireland would remain within the United Kingdom as long as a majority so wished. However, 'implicit in that guarantee was the understanding that the same Unionist population would accept and abide by the policies laid down by successive British Governments and Parliaments for the good government of Northern Ireland'. If Unionists rejected these principles, the SDLP believed that the 'fundamental basis of British policy towards Northern Ireland since 1920 would have to be re-examined'. The Government should 'declare that it will remain in Northern Ireland only until such time as agreed institutions of Government are established which allow the people of Ireland, North and South, to live together in harmony, peace and independence.'[116]

By moving away from the principles as outlined in the – *White Paper* of 1973 the SDLP argued that Constitutional Convention proposals gave the Unionists a guarantee, 'to dominate the minority in Northern Ireland and deprive them of basic Civil Rights'. The party argued that in such circumstances, the Unionist population, 'would have foregone any right to such guarantees, particularly those enshrined in the *Government of Ireland Act 1920*, the *Ireland Act 1949* and the *Northern Ireland Constitution Act 1973* [which] would have to be withdrawn'. Similarly to the condominium proposals contained in *Towards a New*

Ireland the Party now promoted the idea of eventual British withdrawal from Ireland, once agreed institutions between the North and the South were established. The SDLP wanted the British Government to pursue this strategy with the support of the Irish Government.[117]

The Northern Ireland Constitutional Convention failed to revive any prospect of a power-sharing administration for Northern Ireland. The SDLP was still adamant that there had to be power-sharing in government as well as an institutionalised Irish dimension. Denis Haughey spoke to a meeting of the SDLP North Antrim Constituency Council in February 1975 and summed up the SDLP attitude towards the constitutional issue at that time,

> 'Let no-one doubt the SDLP commitment to power-sharing and the Irish dimension. Let no-one fear for a moment that we will abandon these principles; our commitment to them is total. Those who ask us to abandon the Irish dimension are asking us to deny our identity; they are asking us not to be what we are. We do not demand that there must be an Irish dimension – we are saying that there is an Irish dimension. We are not saying that we have a right to be Irish if we choose to, we are saying that we are Irish. These facts and any solution which does not take account of them and give them expression will not be a solution that we will agree to.'[118]

During the Convention talks, Bill Craig who was leader of the Vanguard Unionist Progressive Party promoted the idea of a voluntary coalition with the SDLP. When it came to a vote on a voluntary coalition, only one Unionist, Craig himself, voted for it. Dissension among Unionists showed that few members within their rank-and-file were open to power-sharing. The hope of a temporary coalition advocated by Craig was rejected. With nothing else on offer, many in the SDLP believed that further progress in a solely Northern Ireland context was impossible. The only way out of this political *cul-de-sac* for the SDLP was to exercise influence on the major players in the Irish conflict, namely the British and Irish Governments.[119]

II

Searching for an Internal Compromise

1975–1979

CHAPTER TWO

Political Inertia

After the collapse of the Sunningdale experiment in 1974, the British Prime Minister, Harold Wilson, made a final attempt at a constitutional initiative within Northern Ireland before abandoning a policy designed to achieve a settlement. Over a period of three months in 1975, a Cabinet subcommittee chaired by Wilson discussed the possibility of withdrawal, repartition and the creation of a no-man's land 'along the border with the Republic'.[1] The subcommittee rejected all three possibilities, which it felt only tended to exacerbate the political situation in Northern Ireland.

As a consequence of talks between the IRA and senior Government officials during 1975 the SDLP and the Irish Government were concerned about the form a British withdrawal from Northern Ireland would take.[2] The Irish Government felt the British Government policy of open negotiation with the Provisional IRA seriously undermined the moderate position of the SDLP within Northern Ireland's minority population,[3] a view held by members of the SDLP itself.[4]

The Provisional IRA had maintained a truce for seven-and-a-half months during 1975 on the basis that the British Government was serious about negotiating a withdrawal from Northern Ireland. Brendan O'Brien has maintained that, following an interview with the most senior British official involved in the talks with the Provisionals, 'the talks were never about "disengagement" but if successful, they could have resulted in a complete withdrawal of the British Army from internal security'.[5] Rees has written that the SDLP leader at that time, Gerry Fitt and 'other SDLP leaders had consistently opposed the Provisional IRA and disliked any idea of their "political" role'.[6]

The Labour Government which returned to power in October 1974 used the IRA talks and truce 'as a key role in paving the way for the Ulsterisation strategy'.[7] Rees recalled that, in his first major speech to the House of Commons as Secretary of State he emphasised the cornerstone of his security policy was 'a progressive increase in the role of the civilian law-enforcement agencies in Northern Ireland'.[8] An IRA cease-fire was an ideal opportunity for the British Government to commence its strategy of Ulsterisation, namely, the progressive replacement of the Army by the RUC and UDR. Desmond Hamill has argued it would have enabled the Government to end internment 'and get the Province back to proper law and order. It was all part of a deliberate policy of politicising the Provisionals, thereby attaining long-term stability within the province'.[9] Rees hoped that prolonging the truce would weaken the structures of the IRA, leading the Provisionals to choose the political avenue and abandon the path of violence.[10]

The establishment of incident centres in Republican areas of Northern Ireland by the Government gave a new legitimacy to the Republican Movement[11] and undermined the position of the SDLP. Hamill has noted that the incident centres were 'part of a deliberate policy of politicising the Provisionals, and aimed at the long-term stability of the province'.[12] Although the incident centres were closed down in November 1975, ironically they strengthened the position of Sinn Féin in working-class districts and had a detrimental effect on the SDLP in these areas. The British Government supplied Sinn Féin with telex machines and direct phone lines to the Army commanders. This had the knock-on effect of developing a strong community structure for Sinn Féin which the SDLP has never been able to compete with. Brian Feeney has indicated that, 'Well into the 1980s, people in Ardoyne and the New Lodge talked about going to the incident centre which was by then a Sinn Féin Advice Centre'.[13] Although Sinn Féin did not enter the political arena until 1981, establishment of incident centres initiated the genesis of Sinn Féin organisational presence in working-class areas which, to date, has not diminished.

Changes in Government policy which attempted to foster normalisation in the late 1970s were rooted in the *1975 Gardiner Report* which recommended the end of special category status for prisoners; the end of internment; and the processing of paramilitary suspects through normal legal channels. All those convicted of 'terrorist' crimes in Northern Ireland after 1 March 1976 were to be treated as ordinary criminals and no longer awarded political status, reversing the decision to give Republican prisoners political status which had been made for those at Crumlin Jail in 1972. Policies of Ulsterisation and criminalisation were significant indications to the SDLP that the Government was no longer intent on devising a strategy for Northern Ireland on the basis of a consociational settlement.

The Constitutional Convention
The Constitutional Convention was established by the *White Paper*

published on 4 July 1974. It set out to provide a forum in which the local political parties could reach a consensus on how Northern Ireland could best be governed. The SDLP was alarmed that there was no compulsory provision in the legislation, 'requiring that a new system should contain power-sharing as of right or an Irish Dimension'.[14] The Convention came in two phases from May 1975 to November 1975 and from 12 January 1976 until March 1976. The SDLP criticised the *White Paper* for its ambiguity and lack of clarity. They sought government assurances that the prerequisite for any local initiatives must include power-sharing and an Irish dimension.

John Hume was of the opinion that the SDLP should take no active steps to prepare for the Convention Election. He wanted a legislative guarantee from the Government on its commitment to power-sharing and an Irish dimension. He stressed that the Loyalists should in some way be coerced into accepting this position before establishing a Constitutional Convention. Hume wanted the SDLP to boycott the election if the British Government did not agree to this ultimatum.[15]

Paddy Duffy, who reflected the general consensus within the SDLP at that time took an opposite view on Party strategy for the election. A boycott would only portray the SDLP as a hard-line Party unable to move forward. There was also the fear that Republicans would use the SDLP boycott as an ideal opportunity to assert their political leadership, seize the chance to have talks with Unionist politicians and use the elections as a means to elect their own leaders for such talks.[16]

In their manifesto *Speak with Strength* the SDLP defined the essence of the problem as having a wider implication than being confined to just Northern Ireland itself.[17] The manifesto outlined that there was also an Irish and British dimension to the conflict.[18] The SDLP fought the Convention Elections in May 1975 on the principles of power-sharing and an Irish dimension. The *White Paper* in March 1973 on a Northern Ireland Assembly remained the acceptable basis on which the SDLP would work internally within Northern Ireland.

Although the collapse of the power-sharing Executive left a large degree of despondency within the SDLP, there was some hope that a compromise between the Unionist Party of Northern Ireland (UPNI, former members of the Ulster Unionist Party who continued to support Brian Faulkner after Sunningdale), the Alliance Party and the SDLP could lead to an agreed strategy in the proposed Convention. The results of the May 1975 elections brought hopes of moderate politics within Northern Ireland to an abrupt end. The combined force of the SDLP (17), UPNI (5) and the Alliance Party (8) came to a meagre thirty out of a grand total of seventy-eight seats. The majority of forty-six seats gave Unionists the mandate they sought for a return to majority-rule government in Northern Ireland, based on the British Parliamentary system.

The success of the United Ulster Unionist Council (UUUC, established in January 1974 to oppose the Sunningdale Agreement) at the elections gave Unionists a mandate to reject the principle of power-sharing built into the 1973 Northern Ireland Constitution Act. Since the UUUC held the highest number of seats in the Convention, it felt justified in drawing up the final report for Westminster in November 1975 which only conveyed the Unionist viewpoint. The SDLP proposals were not included in the main text but, however, were mentioned in an appendix to the final report. In its submission, the SDLP sought maximum devolved power returned to a Northern Ireland assembly, but on a power-sharing basis. To get a mandate for acceptable new institutions within Northern Ireland by both communities, the SDLP suggested that two separate referendums take place in Northern Ireland and the Republic of Ireland simultaneously.[19]

The UUUC rejected 'any imposed institutionalised association [or] constitutional relationship with the Irish Republic'.[20] Nevertheless, the UUUC did acknowledge an Irish dimension in security and economic matters between Northern Ireland and the Irish Republic. Such arrangements might take place as part of normal diplomatic relations between Member States of the EEC. The report stressed that the Republic would have to give *de jure* recognition to the status of Northern Ireland. Also, it would have to relinquish its territorial claim over Northern Ireland before normal relations between both States could develop.[21]

Members of the SDLP, as well as the Irish Government, were concerned that the Constitutional Convention might be a mechanism for British withdrawal from Northern Ireland. Rees noted that the Irish Government 'wanted reassurance that the Convention was not a device for us to pull out leaving a Congo situation'.[22] The British Government was irresolute in developing an appropriate policy for Northern Ireland in the immediate post-Sunningdale period. Morgan has indicated that 'the Convention was only a substitute for a policy'.[23] It was felt within some quarters of the Northern Ireland Office that the Ulster Workers' Council strike had allowed Protestant populism to depart from constitutional politics. A similar trend of thinking could develop within the Catholic community in Northern Ireland.[24] In such circumstances, the Constitutional Convention provided a stopgap device to fill the political void which existed in Northern Ireland after the collapse of Sunningdale.

From the SDLP perspective Government talks with the Provisional IRA during 1975 led to suspicion as to Britain's real objective for holding the Constitutional Convention. In the aftermath of the failure of Sunningdale, the SDLP only felt demoralised further by Government suspension of constitutional politics in negotiating with the IRA. The Party held out scant optimism of the Convention finding a suitable framework for establishing a political settlement. Seamus Mallon felt that the Convention was an attempt by the British Government to write out the Irish dimension and move towards an internal settlement[25] and has argued, 'That is where it reached its crux – where in effect we had to devise a means of insisting on an Irish dimension'.[26]

Eddie McGrady has maintained that the 'Constitutional Convention was a public expression of all that was bad within Northern Ireland, rather than a sphere for healing and progress'.[27] He believed that initially, the SDLP hoped the Convention could evolve into some type of partnership arrangement. Denis Haughey believed that the Convention demonstrated how the Unionists have always thought in terms of having an election and the majority winning and has pointed out,

'Unionists have always wanted and still do talk about having an election for an Assembly. Let the Assembly work out its relationship with the South and relationship with Britain and so on. That is the traditional Unionist framework. Northern Ireland once established is forever. Have an election we win! That is the natural order.'[28]

However, Martin Smyth has said that Unionists went into the Constitutional Convention seeking a way that would somehow accommodate the minority community, yet maintain the basic principles of democracy, 'Sunningdale collapsed because it was undemocratic. It was not necessarily over power-sharing, but rather because the Executive did not have a mandate from the people on the way they wanted to be governed'.[29] In relation to the SDLP policy of partnership government at the time of the Constitutional Convention, Smyth has maintained:

'The SDLP could have gone to the electorate having formed their own distinctive policies along with Faulkner's UPNI, Craig's section of the Vanguard Unionists, Alliance and Northern Ireland Labour Party. If they had of [sic] won a majority of votes, we as a Unionist Party were prepared to become a constructive opposition....I still believe in democracy. You have got to have a proper opposition.

When you have partnership government – who is actually going to expose the weaknesses of that government? You cannot have a partnership government if within that government they are fighting cats and dogs.'[30]

To demonstrate SDLP willingness to recognise the concerns of the Unionist community, the Party put a full page advertisement in the *News Letter,* a predominantly Protestant morning newspaper, on 4 February 1976 which outlined the SDLP position on Irish unity and the constitutional issue, affirming that,

'... there can be no change in the status of Northern Ireland without the consent of the majority of its people. The SDLP has defined its aspirations very clearly, making clear that the only unity that has real value is that which comes about by free agreement.'[31]

There was much scepticism among Unionists about SDLP sincerity in taking such a moderate political stance. The advertisement was nevertheless generally interpreted by Unionists as a formal acknowledgement the SDLP would abide by the will of the majority of the people within Northern Ireland on the constitutional issue. In essence, it permitted Unionists to veto any North-South institutions.

A surprising development during the Convention talks were proposals put forward by William Craig in relation to the concept of a voluntary coalition. This idea was presented to the SDLP during a process of bilateral talks under the formal procedure of subcommittees. Craig had a concept of a coalition administration which was not dissimilar to the Churchill Coalition of 1940–1945. Craig suggested that the UUUC could 'join with the SDLP in a temporary or emergency coalition to run Northern Ireland for a four or five-year parliamentary term until the security situation improved and the political deadlock was resolved'.[32] Paddy Devlin has noted, 'I encouraged the view that the programme for a voluntary coalition could be widened out to include not only security, but an agreed social and economic policy'.[33]

Yet Maurice Hayes attributed this unexpected opportunity to compromise, to the external pressure of the Loyalist and Republican paramilitaries and commented in his autobiography, 'Both Hume and Craig looked over the parapet and saw anarchy, civil war and disaster. Craig wanted agreement on a strong government that would restore order and stability. The SDLP believed that a period of stability would induce economic growth which would help to remove Catholic disabilities'.[34] Hume felt that, although the SDLP was involved in negotiations with the Unionists in relation to a voluntary coalition, this was not a permanent solution to the Northern Ireland problem. He was not in favour of an agreement which would only last for a few months. Hume wanted negotiations which would provide a political framework which addressed the existence of the two distinct identities within Northern Ireland.[35]

Concerning voluntary coalition, Sean Farren claimed, 'The SDLP never accepted a purely internal settlement at any time. The closest we ever came to accepting something only within Northern Ireland was during the Constitutional Convention. This happened when Bill Craig conceded the Voluntary Coalition concept. Dissent in the Unionist camp during the Convention negotiations demonstrated that only a small minority of them were prepared for power-sharing. It became obvious that the number who were prepared to be involved in this concept was small and could not carry the day. Bill Craig got cut off by his own people and his idea was never tested.'[36]

The only other glimmer of hope coming out of the Constitutional Convention meetings were informal talks initiated between Paddy Devlin and John Hume of the SDLP and the Revd Martin Smyth and Capt Austin Ardill of the Ulster Unionist Party. These talks were an attempt to break the political deadlock after the collapse of the Constitutional Convention. There were five informal meetings between the representatives of the two parties. While considerable agreement was reached between the two parties, there was no consensus on the vital issue of power-sharing or the formation of an executive. Some of the areas of agreement had already been discussed during the former Convention talks. Throughout the talks, the SDLP insisted that there had to be a power-sharing dimension for any future arrangements for a Northern Ireland administration.

Talks between the two parties stopped on 6 September 1976. The collapse of the talks, according to the Unionists, was due to SDLP insistence on power-sharing as a basis for any future Northern Ireland Government. The Unionist delegation also wanted an election to enable the people of Northern Ireland to decide their view on power-sharing or majority rule.[37] For the SDLP, political consensus on arrangements for the future Government of Northern Ireland had to be based on separate referendums in Northern Ireland and the Republic.

The SDLP approach to the talks was to study Unionist objections to power-sharing and to propose amendments to the *1973 Northern Ireland Constitution Act* accordingly. The SDLP proposals were outlined in a joint statement by John Hume and Paddy Devlin who were both involved in the talks with the Unionist delegation. The SDLP believed that the *1973 Act* should be amended in the following ways:

1. Additional powers, particularly in relation to policing, should be devolved to any future administration. There should be a proviso of any other powers being available on request from the government upon an agreed vote of the Northern Ireland Assembly – such a vote to be clearly representative of both sections of the community.

2. The functions of the Secretary of State under the *1973 Act* should be discontinued and these functions exercised by a respected Northern Ireland figure to be known as a Lord President.

3. The cabinet should reflect the proportional strength of the parties in the Assembly or Parliament willing to form a Government.

4. These arrangements should be subject to a constitutional review at the end of the life of the second parliament. This would enable a thorough review to take place with the working of a new system and meet the objection that power-sharing is unworkable or that some ulterior objective lies behind it.

5. There should be, under the powers conferred by the Act, a positive and freely-negotiated agreement between North and South on matters of common concern.[38]

There was a degree of dilution in the Irish dimension by the SDLP. In section four, it was suggested that a review of the newly-created devolved administration should take place at the end of every second Parliament. It was an in-built democratic check to review power-sharing and allow the Unionists an opportunity to monitor the Irish dimension.

There was some recognition by the SDLP that power-sharing had to work over a period of time before an Irish dimension could evolve. Breakdown of these talks was a tragedy for Northern Ireland politics because it marked the beginning of a period of intransigence and a political vacuum: it indicated to the SDLP the end of any hope of compromise or progress with the Unionist community and marked a hardening of SDLP attitudes on constitutional issues.

Collapse of the inter-party talks between UUUC officials and representatives of the SDLP was a clear signal to the SDLP that the principles of power-sharing and an Irish dimension within the parameters of Northern Ireland were not going to work. The aftermath of the Constitutional Convention caused serious internal reflection within the SDLP. The Party felt that the responsibility for the hard-line position of the Unionists lay with the British Government who had not based its policy on the *1973 Northern Ireland Constitution Act*. From the SDLP perspective, Government inaction in relation to the constitutional issue only reinforced Unionist triumphalism after their success in bringing down the power-sharing Executive in 1974.

The SDLP believed that the only way to resolve the Northern Ireland conflict was for the British Government to create the circumstances in which both communities could address the causes rather than the symptoms of the conflict. It was necessary to remove the Unionist political veto on any forthcoming Government proposals for a political framework within Northern Ireland. Otherwise, the SDLP argued, it would be impossible to get Unionists to sit down on an equal footing with political representatives of the minority population to address the core issues of the conflict, namely, political identity and affiliation to the Northern Ireland state.

Consequently, the SDLP was opposed to further inter-party talks which were a futile exercise while the Unionists maintained a political veto on Government initiatives in relation to Northern Ireland. The Party felt Government policy encouraged Unionists to avoid facing up to the unacceptability of majority rule from the viewpoint of the minority community. A starting point for any political process within Northern Ireland, from the SDLP viewpoint, was to establish a political framework which first examined the causes of the conflict.

The SDLP viewed the Unionist veto as being totally unjust and undemocratic, and pointed to the contradictions within Unionist ideology. On the one hand, they were proclaiming to be loyal to the sovereignty of the British Parliament. On the other hand, the actions of the Ulster Workers' Council (UWC), which brought down the power-sharing executive in 1974, was an example of ambiguity within that ideology. The SDLP believed that if the Unionists claimed they were British, then the price of that allegiance must surely be to accept the decisions taken by Westminster. To act otherwise would only make a farce of the Unionist insistence that they were British citizens. The Unionist veto operated as a major impediment to real healing and reconciliation taking place between the two communities in Northern

Ireland. This proposition was aired by Seamus Mallon, a former convention member for Armagh, at a meeting of the National Labour Movement in Belfast on 20 September 1976. He considered that the British dimension of the Northern Ireland problem had been a negative, even a retarding, factor in the quest for political agreement. Attacking the British government, Mallon argued, 'On every occasion when faced with a challenge from extreme Unionism, this so-called Sovereign Government has taken the soft option, with increasingly disastrous results. One has only to look at the present political impasse to realise that Loyalist attitudes are based on the knowledge that their intransigence is underwritten by the lack of will of the British Government. Twice in the recent past – during the UWC strike and in defying the stated wish of the British Government and Parliament in the Northern Ireland Convention – extreme Unionism has seen the British Government capitulate to its demands. The confidence borne of this knowledge has been the most potent single factor in the failure to form an equitable administration here'.[39]

To the SDLP, removing the Unionist veto would make the Unionist community face up to their own insecurity of their identity and relationship with Britain and the rest of Ireland for the first time; the Party believed it was Unionist insecurity which had led them to develop a siege mentality when the Northern Ireland State was established in 1920. To continue the Unionist veto only exacerbated the symptoms of the Northern Ireland conflict.

SDLP Questions British Labour and Conservative Northern Ireland Policy

The SDLP soon realised that in the Constitutional Convention the Government had diluted its 1973 position in relation to the Irish dimension.[40] The Secretary of State, Merlyn Rees, brought the Convention back for a further four weeks starting from 4 February 1976. However, by 5 March 1976, Rees had to dissolve it because the local parties in Northern Ireland failed to reach political consensus. Rees said in the House of Commons, 'The Government do not consider it necessary or appropriate to create an institutional framework such as a Council of Ireland for relations with the Republic. Arrangements for co-operation should evolve positively and naturally as and when the need for them arises and is generally recognised and accepted'.[41] He also remarked,

'It is clearly not possible at this time to make progress towards a devolved system of Government for Northern Ireland. This still remains the Government's aim, but it does not contemplate any major new initiative for some time to come....the immediate need now is for a period of constitutional stability so that we can tackle the problems of criminality and unemployment. There is no need for any immediate change in the machinery of government for Northern Ireland.'[42]

This remained the British position in relation to policy within Northern Ireland, despite the fact that Merlyn Rees was replaced as Secretary of State by Roy Mason on 10 September 1976.

On 15 September 1976 the SDLP issued a press statement condemning the UUUC and the British Government inactivity in Northern Ireland affairs which marked the end of SDLP participation in inter-party talks, and served as a warning to the new Secretary of State that the British Government was obliged to become more actively involved in developing a strategy for resolving the conflict. In its statement, the SDLP said, 'We must face the reality now that agreement is not possible, given the present political stance of the majority parties and their adherence to the old "not an inch" mentality. In such circumstances inter-party talks are not a vehicle for agreement'.[43]

From the SDLP perspective, it was a Government responsibility to create the necessary political conditions for political progress. The SDLP used Mason's appointment as Secretary of State as an opportunity to demand the government clarify its immediate and long-term plans for Northern Ireland and asked for elucidation on fundamental questions relating to Northern Ireland:

1. The first thing that the British Government must now do is state bluntly what are their intentions, both short term and long term, for the future of Northern Ireland.

2. When the British Government say the Northern Ireland problem can only be solved by the people of Northern Ireland themselves, what do they mean? Are they stating that the British Government and Parliament have no role in the matter and are not capable of governing here? The implications of this question are fundamental and far reaching and the people of Northern Ireland deserve an answer.

3. When the British Government repeatedly underline their guarantees to the Unionist population of membership of the United Kingdom, are these guarantees unconditional? Are there any

terms to be fulfilled in order to retain membership of the United Kingdom? If so what are they? If not, is a section of the Unionist population, a tiny percentage of the UK population, to have a permanent veto on how Northern Ireland is to be governed within the UK?

4. Are the British Government willing and determined to implement their stated policy, democratically approved by virtually the entire British Parliament, as to the fairest method of governing Northern Ireland? To do so would be to accept what is their Sovereign responsibility. To refuse is to abandon those responsibilities, with fundamental consequences for everyone. What is the British position? [44]

The intention of the SDLP in asking these questions was to seek confirmation that the principles of power-sharing and an Irish dimension were still an essential component of Government Northern Ireland policy.

Roy Mason's appointment as Secretary of State for Northern Ireland heralded a coolness in relations between the Government and the SDLP. Kevin McNamara admitted that there was a frostiness between Gerry Fitt, then SDLP leader, and Roy Mason and attributed this detachment largely to the Government adoption of a new economic as well as a hard-line security policy towards Northern Ireland from Mason's tenure onwards.[45] The alleged maltreatment of suspects involved in paramilitary activities at Castlereagh Interrogation Centre placed immense pressure on the SDLP to condemn British Government security measures in Northern Ireland. The Party felt bound to represent the strong feeling of resentment towards the British Government within the Republican ghettos on this matter both to prevent a decrease in their own electoral support and also to modify increasing support for Republican violence.

Mason's term as Secretary of State marked a further move away from finding a political settlement to the Northern Ireland conflict. At his first press conference at Stormont on 27 September 1976, the Secretary of State was seen to be,'...worried at the poor state of the Ulster economy, and said his concern about that exceeded even his concern of the political and security problems. He had given instructions to all his Ministers to pay personal attention to the economic problem'.[46]

For the remainder of the 1970s the Government changed their focus on defeating terrorism from a purely military perspective by embracing a new economic strategy. The De Lorean Project in West Belfast marked a shift in policy. The Northern Ireland Development Authority accepted the De Lorean project in 1978 after it had been rejected by the Industrial Development Authority in Dublin and the Government of Puerto Rico and this indicates, perhaps, that the British Government were desperate to encourage massive overseas investment in West Belfast. The Government believed that by improving the economic and social environment of areas such as West Belfast the troubles could, possibly, be minimized.

On 28 October 1976, Cyril Townsend, MP for Bexleyheath, asked the Secretary of State if he intended to take an independent political initiative in an attempt to resolve the Northern Ireland conflict. In his reply, Mason referred Townsend back to a letter setting out the Constitutional Convention on 12 January 1976 and said:

'The Government want a devolved government, but, as we have consistently made clear, "no system of government within Northern Ireland would be stable or effective unless both parts of the community acquiesce in that system and are willing to work to support it. This means a system which will command widespread support throughout the community and in which both the majority and the minority will participate." '[47]

British policy in the short-term was not going to invest any resources in drawing up a formula for resolving the Northern Ireland constitutional issue. O'Leary and McGarry have suggested that under Roy Mason, 'wide-ranging political initiatives were shunned lest they heighten expectations and create instability'.[48]

Ivan Fallon and James Strodes have written that Roy Mason developed a specific scheme, '...[his] strategy was to combine a tough security policy designed to wipe out the Provos, with a massive programme of overseas investment designed to provide jobs and wean the young away from violence....Mason was hoping to show the Catholic community that, if they continued the path of peace and spurned the IRA, he would deliver jobs and prosperity for all, or at least for some'[49] While the SDLP found cold comfort in the policy of the Labour Government, they were to find little to achieve their stated aims and objectives in Conservative policy towards Northern Ireland. At the Conservative Party Annual Conference in 1976, representatives of the Ulster Unionist Party received a very warm welcome.[50] In one of the conference debates, it was argued that Northern Ireland was under-represented at Westminster. However, any increase in Westminster seats was viewed by the SDLP as leading Northern Ireland further down the road of integration within the rest of the United Kingdom.

Hard-line Unionist politicians in 1976 were still in a triumphant mood after the collapse of the power-sharing Executive. They still held very firmly to the policy of a return to a majority rule system of government which was largely the recommendation outlined in the *Constitutional Convention Report*. There was little chance of moving them beyond this position especially – when seen from the SDLP point of view – they were in a position of strength with political allies in the British Labour Party, in Government and in the Conservative Party.

The SDLP believed that Airey Neave, a Tory spokesman for Northern Ireland, was privately negotiating with Ulster Unionists on some form of devolved Government within Northern Ireland, in the event that the Tories would be elected to Government at the next General Election. The SDLP was apprehensive that these negotiations might signify a return to a Stormont-type of majority-rule administration. While no concrete deal between the Ulster Unionists and the Conservative Party was evident immediately after the 1976 Conservative Annual Conference, nevertheless the bond between the two parties was evidently renewed and tightened. The SDLP, by contrast, had no steadfast political support from the main political parties in Britain to advance its analysis. This uncertainty led to the SDLP Executive declining a meeting with Airey Neave who was visiting Northern Ireland on 14 October 1976. Neave wanted to meet the SDLP along with the other main political parties, to discuss possible political developments. The SDLP refusal to do so was founded on the suspicion that a back-hand deal had been struck between the Conservative Party and the Ulster Unionists during their recent meeting at the conference.

The SDLP chairman, Denis Haughey, was directed by his Executive on the 9 October 1976 to write to Neave outlining the Party position as to why they were unwilling to meet with him. In a letter addressed to Neave from Haughey, the following questions were asked:

1. Does the Conservative Party believe that the Westminster Parliament has the sovereign authority to determine the forms of government of Northern Ireland?

2. Does the Conservative Party accept that Northern Ireland is a deeply divided community and that a devolved government, based on sectarian majority rule is ungovernable?

3. Does the Conservative Party accept that any future devolved government in Northern Ireland must be a partnership government involving both sections of the community in executive government?

4. Does the Conservative Party accept that a large minority of people in Northern Ireland claim Irish nationality and have a right to the symbols and institutions which express that nationality?[51]

Neave immediately responded to Haughey by quoting a speech made in the House of Commons on 12 January 1976,

' I stated then the Conservative position, which has not changed. As you may remember, I said that what we wanted "a system of government which can command widespread support throughout the community, including the minority" and that "the greater the measure of support that can be achieved, the more likely it will be that this House can pass the necessary legislation"....During that debate we also referred to the fact that no Party in the Northern Ireland Convention had insisted that "power-sharing" be written into any new constitution, and supported the Government in saying that an institutionalised "Irish dimension" was not practicable.'[52]

Haughey replied to Neave complaining that the reply to his first two questions was totally unsatisfactory, pointing out that Neave had avoided answering the questions put to him. The reply that the Conservative Party wished to see the establishment of a Government which would have 'widest possible support' was interpreted by the SDLP as a dilution of the partnership-government principle which had previously been Conservative Party policy based on the *1973 Northern Ireland Constitution Act*. In reply to Neave's allegation that no party in the Northern Ireland Convention had insisted on power-sharing, Haughey said:

'I refer you to the SDLP manifesto of May 1975 on which we fought the Convention elections and the report which we made to the British Parliament in September 1975 when the Convention ended. In both cases we refer repeatedly to the setting up of "partnership institutions" and of "partnership system of government". These phrases are perfectly clear.'[53]

Haughey also affirmed that he interpreted Neave's answer to his final question as an admission by the Conservative Party that they no longer supported an institutionalised Irish dimension and the minority population's legitimate right to an Irish identity. Such a departure in Conservative policy lent credibility to Seamus Mallon's contention that SDLP political policy at the time was becoming obsolete and was no longer an effective strategy for bringing about political progress within Northern Ireland.

Despite frustration at Labour and Conservative Party policy on Northern Ireland, the SDLP Executive tried to pull their rank-and-file behind its stated policy of partnership-government in Northern Ireland. This was demonstrated by Party Chief Whip, Austin Currie, speaking in Letterkenny on 19 October 1976 when he insisted, 'SDLP policy is firmly based on the necessity of a partnership between North and South, and we believe that for this partnership to be effective it must be institutionalised.'[54]

Unionist insistence on a return to a majority-rule style of government at Stormont, and British Government refusals to accept the legitimacy of the Irish dimension led the SDLP choose a more hard-line approach in relation to the adoption of the Irish dimension and its future role.

Frustration within SDLP ranks: 'Independence' versus 'Partnership'

Different attitudes towards independence were held by leading members of the SDLP at that time. Ben Caraher wrote a paper on the subject giving a constructive review of how independence might work and could appeal to the Loyalist and Republican elements within Northern Ireland:

> '...advocates [of independence] claim that it satisfies the aspirations of the two political traditions; it should appeal to Republicans since it gets rid of the British and it should appeal to Loyalists since it safeguards them against absorption into a United Ireland. Furthermore, such a settlement makes each section of the community dependent on the other and forces them into finding an accommodation with each other... .'[55]

But Caraher also pointed out that independence was too simplistic a solution. To believe that a British withdrawal from Northern Ireland would lead the two communities to reconcile their different allegiances by peaceful methods would be unrealistic. Nevertheless, he noted that some elements contained within the concept of independence embraced the SDLP principles of an acceptable constitutional settlement. In particular, independence provided, in theory, a process whereby both traditions could sit down together and work out an acceptable system of government for themselves; it would include another SDLP premise whereby both communities would be in a position to define their relationship with the Republic and Britain.

Eddie McGrady, debating the independence issue, said, 'Negotiated independence is at variance with the basic concept and philosophy of the SDLP. The New Ireland would be a nightmare of paramilitarism feeding on the same old hatreds and divisions on each other. The only guarantee that can achieve lasting peace and provide for eventual solutions is peaceful co-existence within Northern Ireland, which is another way of saying genuine partnership in the community and government, partnership in our rights and duties, and partnership in our cultures and traditions'.[56] McGrady was opposed to independence and strongly favoured an internal settlement which embraced the SDLP principles of power-sharing and an Irish dimension.

On the other hand, Joe Hendron, SDLP Constituency Representative for West Belfast, was in favour of the idea of independence for Northern Ireland. He maintained, 'I believe that negotiated independence is an option that the people of Northern Ireland should consider over the next twelve months. Devolved government with the sharing of responsibilities at all levels, has been and remains the nucleus of SDLP policy and we will continue to pursue this'.[57]

Hendron was more in favour of working within the parameters of Northern Ireland and was less captivated by the Irish dimension. Like Gerry Fitt and Paddy Devlin, he appeared to be more concerned about working with the two communities in Northern Ireland and obtaining progress at that level.

Similarly, Paddy Devlin advocated a negotiated independence for Northern Ireland. He argued for independence on the basis that previous British strategy for Northern Ireland had failed to create the conditions for a broadly-based administration. He put forward the case that negotiated independence could enable the people of Northern Ireland to write their own constitution, independent of London. The European Community could act as a guarantor for both communities in the event that new political institutions were set up in Northern Ireland.[58]

In an article in the *Irish Times*, Devlin commented, 'The fundamental idea behind the proposed form of independence is to exclude the possibility of conquest of one side over the other; the possibility of one tradition dominating the other; the possibility of one religion subordinating the other to the extent of its complete suppression'.[59] In effect, Devlin was reflecting the core of SDLP philosophy by the end of 1976. The Party was looking for political structures which would enable both communities in Northern Ireland to negotiate some system of government on an equal footing. Furthermore, independence was one method of cancelling the Unionist veto, thus allowing progress to take place.

Another advocate of independence, Seamus Mallon, took the term to 'imply a Sovereign State, without a British presence, but perhaps retaining a tenuous British link'.[60] He went on further to remark that the independence concept was something which could 'suit a lot of books' and which merited serious consideration.[61]

The issue of independence stimulated heated debate at the 1976 SDLP Annual Conference. It reflected the disarray and disharmony in the SDLP to its policy of partnership. There was also disillusionment in the Party at Unionist intransigence and the lack of will in the British Government to exercise its authority. For the SDLP, the British Government was the stumbling-block in Northern Ireland: by never exercising its power over Unionist vetoes, then any political initiatives offering compromise and equality for both sections of the community seemed inoperable. The independence lobby in the SDLP was sceptical by the end of 1976 that the British Government and the Unionist political leaders were willing to support the SDLP policy of a partnership government within Northern Ireland. This section of the Party appeared to turn its back on the principles of moderation and compromise, turning its energies to demanding a British withdrawal from Northern Ireland. At the sixth SDLP Annual Conference, one-hundred and eleven delegates, including more than half the former convention members called upon the British Government to declare its intent to withdraw from Northern Ireland. The motion for British withdrawal was defeated at the conference by one-hundred and fifty-three votes to one-hundred and eleven, with twelve abstentions.

Seamus Mallon backed the motion for independence, defending his view on the basis that it did not contradict current SDLP policy. John Hume opposed the motion. He felt that the result of a quick British declaration of intent to leave Northern Ireland would lead to a scramble for power between the Nationalist and Unionist traditions in Northern Ireland. Hume spoke at the 1976 Annual Conference and summed up the aspirations of the anti-independence section within the SDLP. 'Let not frustration be the basis of Party policy...' he pleaded, '...The present policy is best, and people are turning away from it because they are disheartened at its lack of success to date. But as the Conference was told: it's not that partnership has been tried and failed. It has never been tried'.[62]

Gerry Fitt rejected independence as completely unrealistic. He felt that this lobby within the SDLP wanted Britain to withdraw from Northern Ireland but at the same time leaving their 'purse on the mantelpiece'.[63] Fitt attacked the independence lobby within the SDLP on the basis that one could not trust the Unionist majority in an independence situation.[64]

The 1976 conference placed considerable pressure on the Party to review its partnership policy. The narrow defeat of the Cookstown Branch Motion for independence was an indication of the tensions within the party over its long-term political strategy. The political vacuum in Northern Ireland by the end of 1976 allowed emotions to take hold of the SDLP. The independence issue was an outward manifestation of the difficulties the SDLP leadership faced in keeping their rank-and-file behind its policy of partnership. It reflected the internal frustrations which existed in the SDLP in the immediate aftermath of the Constitutional Convention; frustrations which a large section of the Party perceived as an inadmissible log-jam in finding an acceptable framework for resolving the constitutional issue of Northern Ireland.[65]

Denis Haughey has recalled that many in the SDLP were devoting their energies to breaking the political deadlock at this time,

'There were various times when a number of leading figures within the Party called for a declaration of British intent to withdraw and called for an examination of opportunities that might be presented by an independence situation. We settled on the view that really the log-jam could only be broken by joint action by the British and Irish governments. From the late [19]70s onwards, we were firmly committed to the Anglo-Irish strategy as the right approach.'[66]

Despite the intense debate within the SDLP which centred on independence, the Party maintained its strategy of partnership-government, although only marginally endorsed at the 1976 conference. The partnership policy document for the conference had been prepared by Ben Caraher largely influenced by John Hume. The policy document outlined,

'Partnership, as advocated by the SDLP, that is partnership between the two national traditions within Northern Ireland and partnership between North and South is the only policy that has the remotest chance of resolving the Northern Ireland problem because it is based on a correct analysis of the nature of the problem. It is also the only policy which can remedy the political instability of Northern Ireland because it is based on a recognition of the origin of that instability.'[67]

The concept of power-sharing as defined by the SDLP was synonymous with the term 'partnership' which involved:

- The sharing of power and responsibility at Government level between the two political traditions within Northern Ireland;

- The co-operation of both political traditions on the island of Ireland, through common political institutions to develop co-operation on problems common to both parts of the island as a focus of loyalty for that part of the Northern people that considered itself Irish;

- Maintenance of the position of Northern Ireland within the UK as long as a majority of the population of Northern Ireland wished it, which provided a focus of loyalty to that part of the Northern people which considered itself British.

Partnership from the SDLP viewpoint was about creating institutions of government within Northern Ireland that were acceptable to both traditions. Caraher's policy paper on 'partnership' asserted that the Northern Ireland conflict was essentially one of national aspirations and identities. 'The successful resolution of any political problem is dependent on a correct perception of the nature of the problem...' argued Caraher, and '...acceptance of the framework of the Northern Ireland State and formation of cooperation within that framework is an inadequate solution to the problem because it is based on a misunderstanding of the nature of the conflict.' He insisted,

'We reject the contention that all that is required is to find a formula to enable Catholics and Protestants to participate in a devolved Northern Ireland Government and to give the so-called Irish dimension a decent and discreet burial by a vague promise of co-operation and consultation with the government of the Republic. This version of co-operation is really a disguised form of domination. A solution which refuses to respect peoples own sense of their identity is not partnership; it is the maintainence [*sic*] of the domination of the British over the Irish tradition in Northern Ireland....partnership between the two national traditions within Northern Ireland and partnership between North and South, is the only policy that has the remotest chance of resolving the Northern Ireland problem because it is based on a correct analysis of the nature of the problem.'

Accordingly, the Caraher paper on partnership was the basis of the SDLP *Partnership in Ireland* document endorsed at the 1976 Annual Conference. One third of the delegates wanted SDLP policy on partnership referred back to the Executive. Seventy votes were cast in support of Party policy while thirty-two referred it back to the Party Executive.[68] The SDLP Executive was instructed at conference to undertake an immediate study of the feasibility of an independent Northern Ireland. The immediate task for the SDLP leadership at the beginning of 1977 was to pacify the independence lobbying group within the party. The independence issue and call for British withdrawal by a section of the SDLP was an external manifestation of the tensions within the Party caused by the complicated process of dealing with the British and Irish Governments as well as the Unionist leadership.

The independence factor could be interpreted in two ways. Firstly, it could be argued that Party members who wanted independence represented the more liberal and moderate strand of the SDLP. They were willing to abjure direct Dublin involvement in Northern Ireland affairs; an independent Ulster would facilitate the SDLP objective of placing both traditions in Northern Ireland on an equal footing.

Secondly, the greener – that is nationalist – faction in the SDLP was also included in the independence debate. The demise of Sunningdale and the Constitutional Convention reinforced their perception that the partnership policy was not feasible in Northern Ireland while the British remained. They envisaged independence as a first step towards Irish reunification. The degree and extent of the relationship between an independent Northern Ireland State and the Republic was to be negotiable.

In the final analysis, the independence issue demonstrated a public manifestation of the sense of frustration contained in the SDLP after the Constitutional Convention. During this period British withdrawal was not a policy proposal unique to the SDLP. Paddy Duffy did not feel the independence issue was a serious strategy within the SDLP. It was addressing the reality that neither Britain nor the Republic held any real interest in Northern Ireland after the failure of Sunningdale.[69] Despite considerable support for British withdrawal from Northern Ireland by the independence lobby within the SDLP, it is much more significant that the moderate elements within the SDLP marshalled the Party in line behind its partnership policy of co-operation with Unionists and a significant Irish dimension. A similar position was taken by Sinn Féin and Fianna Fáil in the Republic. Also, a corresponding stance was adopted by the Irish Independence Party established in 1977.

CHAPTER THREE

Strategic Options

Seamus Mallon: his Vision of Future SDLP Strategy

In the Autumn of 1976, Seamus Mallon asked probing questions relating to policy in a SDLP internal paper.[1] He wondered whether or not existing SDLP policy, adequate for the Sunningdale Agreement and as the basis of the *Constitutional Convention Report,* was practicable in the current political vacuum. For the SDLP partnership policy to be attainable, he proposed four conditions:

- There would have to be sufficient Unionist electoral support (which was not forthcoming).

- The British Government would have to be willing to re-activate a political framework guaranteeing the principle of power-sharing (a framework mechanism which was essential to the SDLP perception of attaining a settlement).

- The fundamentals of party policy would have to be 'sufficiently attractive to the minority community to ensure electoral support.'

- Any new administration within Northern Ireland 'must have the political and moral support of the government and people of the South.'

Mallon was emphasising the serious consequences for the SDLP in pursuing a weak political strategy in the aftermath of Sunningdale and the Constitutional Convention. He argued that the SDLP 'concept of an Irish dimension had been reduced to a "form of words" exercise rather than a tangible and dynamic expression of aspiration that was incorporated in the Sunningdale pact.' He expressed concern over whether or not the SDLP policy of partnership in attaining 'a positive and freely negotiated agreement between North and South on matters of common concern [would] counter-balance the ideological appeal of militant nationalism.'

Mallon believed the SDLP had to retain support from the Irish Government in relation to a meaningful Irish dimension and proposed three alternatives open to the Party:

- To retain its current policy of attempting to influence Unionist opinion; 'that a combined approach can be made to the British Government to implement agreement based on the 1973 Act' – as set out in the SDLP amended five-point submission.

- 'Fall in line with the British Government's attitude and accept direct rule and absence of initiatives and political movement until the devolution arrangements for Scotland and Wales are worked out.'

- Decide on a new strategy which would override the factors which were making the SDLP current policy of partnership inoperable, thereby, formally ending the present line of policy and carrying out a 'radical reappraisal of policy.'

In the internal paper, Mallon pointed out that there was no substantial support from within Unionism, 'to form a power-sharing administration or seek support for this from their electorate...That avenue has rightly been fully explored and found to be a cul-de-sac.

He also pointed out that the British Government did not intend to introduce a power-sharing administrative model of government within Northern Ireland, in the foreseeable future. As long as that was the Government stance, the Unionist position would not change. He stressed that SDLP policy had failed to provide an alternative to traditional violent Republicanism.

Mallon's paper provided important insights into SDLP political thinking during 1976, indicating the direction that the Party was going to take over the next couple of years. His paper was an attempt to get the SDLP to reappraise its strategy on the basis that power-sharing was no longer an attainable goal. In relation to SDLP strategy, Mallon suggested:

1. All negotiations and talks with Northern Ireland parties cease and we shift the emphasis away from the domestic political scene.

2. The British Government is publicly and privately pressurised to face up to the hypocrisy of their present stance by demanding that they (i) state their long-term intentions regarding Northern Ireland;

(ii) state clearly whether they intend to exercise their sovereignty to effect a solution.

3. Request the Irish Government to privately seek a British Government commitment to restore a political forum embracing the principles of power-sharing and a meaningful Irish dimension.

If the Irish Government did not get assurances from the British Government on these principles Mallon believed the SDLP and the Irish Government should state in public that the British dimension was standing in the way of political agreement in Northern Ireland, hence illuminating the requirement for a political process to be reached within an Irish context. He argued that this state of affairs would give new 'emphasis and dynamic to the Irish dimension...[changing]...the Irish involvement from the purely negative position it now adopts to a positive, indeed, dominating role.' This paper demonstrated an attempt by Mallon to redirect SDLP strategy beyond a purely British context to one which would also embrace the Irish Government.

The SDLP felt abandoned by the Fine Gael and Labour coalition Government in the Republic immediately after the Constitutional Convention. From the SDLP perspective, Dublin had relinquished prospective responsibility for Northern Ireland. Liam Cosgrave, Taoiseach and Head of Fine Gael and Labour coalition from March 1973–June 1977, no longer publicly supported the SDLP vision of an Irish dimension. Instead, he supported some form of devolution in Northern Ireland supported by the two communities.

Until the collapse of Sunningdale in 1974, Cosgrave preferred Northern policy had to be based ultimately on the principle of attaining a power-sharing administration within Northern Ireland. With the British Government, Dublin had believed the Sunningdale initiative would provide the basis of a permanent settlement within Northern Ireland. But following pressure from the SDLP, the Irish Government reluctantly accepted the expression of the Irish dimension as a necessary prerequisite to any permanent settlement within Northern Ireland.

The SDLP believed that, in the absence of a political initiative within Northern Ireland during the mid-1970s, Dublin once again had abrogated responsibility for Northern Ireland. When the principle of power-sharing became evidently less acceptable to the British Government and the Unionists, the SDLP felt that the Irish Government policy of a power-sharing arrangement within Northern Ireland was no longer viable. Sean Farren has recalled:

'The Labour Party in the South distrusted us. They saw the SDLP as a sectarian party. You had a certain amount of sniping at us within the Labour Party. The Labour Party was still under the influence of people like Noel Browne and Conor Cruise O'Brien. Particularly O'Brien, had adopted an attitude that it's better to do nothing in relation to Northern Ireland. That direct rule indefinitely was the best prescription for Northern Ireland. Our relations with Southern parties apart from leadership level was not cemented until the New Ireland Forum.'[2]

Further, the SDLP was infuriated by the Minister for Posts and Telegraphs, Conor Cruise O'Brien, when he made remarks about minority participation in the Constitutional Convention and bluntly dismissed the relevance of the Irish dimension. He argued that Dublin or London could not support an institutionalised Irish dimension as 'the Convention clearly excluded a power-sharing Executive'.[3] His remarks created tension between the SDLP and the Irish Government at this time. His comments also stirred fears within the SDLP that it no longer had the Irish Government on board as a political ally to promulgate their policy of partnership-government.

Nevertheless, the Irish Government was involved in behind-the-scenes negotiations with the British Government and Opposition during 1976 with the object of agreeing on a system of devolution in Northern Ireland which also embraced the principle of power-sharing. Roy Mason had prepared a speech for the House of Commons on 28 October 1976, in which he had been asked again by Cyril Townsend if he had developed an independent political initiative for Northern Ireland. The Irish Government had procured details of the text of Mason's speech. They felt it was an adumbrative speech which did not qualify his position on the issue of a devolved, power-sharing administration for Northern Ireland.

Garret FitzGerald, Irish Minister for Foreign Affairs, has recorded in his autobiography that the Irish Ambassador in London approached William Whitelaw to ensure Tory opposition support in the House of Commons for greater lucidity from Roy Mason on any initiative he intended for Northern Ireland. FitzGerald has noted that his Government was successful in getting Roy Mason to clarify what he meant by power-sharing by adding an additional sentence to his proposed statement in the House of Commons on 28 October 1976.[4] Mason outlined his understanding of a devolved government for Northern Ireland, 'This means a system which will command widespread support throughout the community and in which both the majority and the minority will participate'.[5]

The Irish Government had weakened its position in relation to the Irish dimension. A motion at the 1976 SDLP Annual Conference demonstrated Party dissatisfaction with the 'apparent unwillingness...[of the Irish Government]...to exert influence on Britain to implement her stated policy of power-sharing in Northern Ireland'. The motion was narrowly defeated by twenty-six to twenty-four votes.[6] If anything, the Irish Government lacklustre approach to the Irish dimension exacerbated the SDLP sense of isolation by the end of 1976.

There was very little prospect of a political initiative emerging during early 1977. Although the Secretary of State, Roy Mason, did admit in the House of Commons on 10 February 1977, 'I do not exclude interim arrangements for partial devolution, provided that they involve some real power and responsibility and are not merely advisory'[7] but he added, 'There has been no willingness to move by the [Official Unionist Party] OUP leadership. They told me frankly that at this stage they still stand by the majority *Convention Report*.'[8]

On 23 March 1977 the Callaghan Government was on the brink of collapse engineered by a Conservative motion of 'No-confidence' to be brought before the House of Commons. The Labour Party was in a vulnerable position after recent by-election defeats and the defection of two Labour MPs to the Scottish Labour Party.[9] Callaghan and Foot had urgent discussions with James Molyneaux seeking support from the Ulster Unionists and the Liberal Party to enable the British Labour Party to remain in office. David Butler has written that the Labour Party made limited commitments to the Unionists. He has observed,

'The Government could not give Mr Molyneaux what he demanded – a promise of devolution for Northern Ireland on the model proposed for Scotland – and without any mandatory provision for power-sharing with the Catholics. What Mr Callaghan did was to promise, unconditionally, a Speaker's Conference to examine Ulster representation at Westminster.'[10]

The SDLP initially opposed any increase to Northern Ireland's twelve seats at Westminster. They feared Unionists would be the main beneficiaries of such a move. They contended that in a deeply divided society such as Northern Ireland, the minority population was 'ill-served by the straight vote system.'[11] Mason talked about a Super Council for Northern Ireland, but this was looked upon by the SDLP as a further concession to the Unionists for their support at Westminster: such a strategy by the British Government did not appear neutral to the SDLP. It reinforced its fears that an era of Unionist domination might prevail. It did little to promote the SDLP policy based on partnership, which was totally disregarded by the Government.

Denis Haughey told the Draperstown branch of the SDLP 'that since the failure of the Convention...' he saw, 'the British Government's Northern Ireland policy as one of the major obstacles to the development of shared government'.[12] This view represented the general consensus in the Party towards the government in 1977; John Hume reinforced this view in an RTE Radio interview on 30 January and said,

'We believe that the British Government is sitting on the fence in a most irresponsible way, when they say that the solution to the problem of the North was a matter for the people of the North and the politicians of the North themselves. This was an incredible position for a sovereign government. They were saying that they have no role. Could one imagine them saying that if there was rioting and shooting on the streets of Leeds that such was a matter for the people of Leeds?'[13]

The SDLP found the Government position on sovereignty over Northern Ireland incomprehensible. Failure to get Government support for their partnership strategy led some members of the SDLP to believe that the Party could be taken over by the extreme 'green' wing. Party policy makers had a balancing–act to maintain between the moderate and the more extreme Nationalist sections of the SDLP during 1977.

Continuation of the SDLP partnership strategy was hard to maintain against a background of Government inaction on the constitutional issue. The SDLP went into the 1977 District Council Elections emphasising partnership philosophy. In the election Manifesto they stated,

'If we are to solve our problems then we must recognise the reality of life as it is and not as we would like it to be. The reality is that there is a deep division between the two traditions which has left us with the peculiar political situation that is here today. The past approach of each tradition, based on pursuit of victory for its point of view has always resulted in conflict, death and destruction and in

a deepening of bitterness and division. The only way forward therefore is to accept these differences and go forward on the basis of a
fully agreed partnership which accepts the traditions and attitudes
of people as they are without seeking to coerce them.'[14]

In the elections in May 1977, the SDLP received 20.6 per cent of the
votes cast, a total of one-hundred and fourteen seats, a rise from 13.4
per cent of the votes which the Party had received in the 1973 Local
Government Elections, but the percentage of votes was down from the
Convention Elections held in May 1975 when the Party received 23.7
per cent of votes cast.

Denis Haughey and Assembly Proposals

The SDLP was impressed by Mason's handling of a Loyalist strike by
the United Unionist Action Council in May 1977. Fears that another
strike would echo the 1974 Ulster Workers' strike were dissipated by
Government determination to stand up to the Loyalist extremists. The
strike also resulted in the UUUC Parliamentary Coalition being dissolved which led the SDLP to believe that there was hope of Unionist
moderation in Northern Ireland. In June 1977, the SDLP Chairman,
Denis Haughey, wrote an internal Party policy paper outlining the
shape a government initiative should take. The paper was based on the
principles espoused in the Government *White Paper* published in July
1974 which emphasised the need for a system of government in
Northern Ireland which could 'command the most widespread acceptance' among the community.[15] Haughey proposed a locally-elected
Assembly within Northern Ireland. He argued in his paper, 'On the
evidence of the Local Government Election results there is a healthy
chance that the power-sharing elements [of Unionists] would get up to
half the seats. In such a situation the pressure would be on the Official
Unionists, and there is evidence of changed thinking among some
members of that party'. Some of his proposals echoed those contained
in the Constitutional Convention. The main task of the Assembly was
'to consider what type of shared government is most likely to command
widespread support and respect in the North of Ireland'. The other
outstanding feature of the Assembly was that it was to have similar
powers of scrutiny and enquiry to the present Northern Ireland Select
Committee eventually introduced in December 1993. Haughey wanted
the Assembly to have the power to consider legislative matters and
make recommendations to the Westminster Parliament. He proposed
that a system of Proportional Representation (PR) should be undertaken

to appoint committees 'to oversee the work of the various Ministries and consult with the Ministers responsible'.[16] He argued in his paper that the Secretary of State should give preferential treatment to those parties open to partnership and not to those opposed to such a policy.

Putting theory into practice, however, was a difficult task for the SDLP. It proved too presumptuous to expect the Unionist mentality of domination to dissipate quickly. Its dilemma was further exacerbated by Government refusal to implement the partnership document and accept it as the basis for resolving the Northern Ireland conflict. The Party opposed the Government idea of interim devolution for Northern Ireland devolving a range of administrative powers back to the local councils.   Michael Canavan[17] summarised SDLP feeling at this time towards returning any local powers towards Northern Ireland. He felt that, 'To restore these powers would be to recycle the trouble. We are implacably opposed to such a move. We have moved a considerable distance from the Irish unity stance. The Loyalists have not moved – not an inch'.[18]

It was becoming increasingly clear to the SDLP that an internal solution to the Northern Ireland problem was no longer attainable. Paddy Duffy, Constituency Representative for Mid-Ulster, stated, 'Indeed, once power-sharing is rejected the British Government is left with no other logical option but to work towards a solution in an all-Ireland context with the Southern Government. Time for such a solution is fast approaching'.[19]

John Hume prepared a paper for an SDLP Executive and Constituency Representatives' meeting held on 13 August 1977.[20] This paper became the basis of the *Facing Reality* a document which was officially launched at the SDLP Conference in November 1977. Hume pointed out that British attempts to resolve the Northern Ireland problem in a purely British context had floundered. Earlier questions put to the Government by Denis Haughey, in 1976, on Government long-term and short-term intentions for Northern Ireland were unsatisfactorily answered according to Hume in this paper. Once more, Hume called for a re-examination of the British approach to the Northern Ireland conflict.

He called on the Government to channel all its energies towards developing a strategy for establishing a new political framework which could provide the administrative basis for implementing SDLP partnership strategy. Hume believed Government long-term strategy for an acceptable settlement in Northern Ireland should also encompass a role for the Irish Government as well as the local parties.

In the short-term Hume did not seek a British withdrawal from Northern Ireland. He acknowledged that British attempts to resolve the Northern Ireland conflict in a purely British context 'have failed and will continue to fail'. He wanted the Government to introduce administrative structures which would provide the basis for unity and agreement between the two parts of Ireland to take place. In an internal policy subcommittee paper he outlined, 'In the immediate future and as part of that long-term strategy the British Government should, in conjunction with the Irish Government initiate talks involving both Governments and the Northern Parties with a view to arriving at an agreed form of government for the North, within the long-term strategy'. Irrespective of the outcome of these talks, Hume wanted Westminster to enter into immediate talks with the Irish government 'to promote matters of common concern to both parts of Ireland'.

Simply reiterating the principles of *Towards a New Ireland* as the premise on which to advance the SDLP partnership strategy Hume echoed the 1972 policy document calling for the two Governments to sponsor joint socio-economic initiatives between both parts of Ireland. These appointed bodies were intended to initiate a 'programme for the harmonisation of the laws and services on both sides of the border'. Hume argued that such a strategy is a visible expression of the Irish dimension with the ultimate objective of 'long-term reconciliation'.[21]

For the remainder of the 1970s, Government inactivity in the political sphere and the stance taken by the Unionists in Northern Ireland contributed to the SDLP position on the Irish dimension. Hugh Logue, SDLP Constituency Representative for Derry, maintained, 'For any Party, which has pursued partnership with such vigour as the SDLP, the process which forces us to conclude that the Loyalists do not wish partnership, has been a painful one. Bluntly, the SDLP, which has taken more abuse from the Provisional IRA than anyone else, feels let down by the ordinary rank-and-file Unionists.'[22] The SDLP were not negating the principle of partnership-government, but rather reappraising its method of achieving this policy. The Party felt that, in return for Unionist support at Westminster, the British Government was prepared to bring Northern Ireland further down the road of integration. With this support behind them, the SDLP ranks believed the Unionists still held on to their mentality of majority rule within the Northern Ireland state.[23]

The SDLP frequently reiterated its analysis of the Northern Ireland conflict throughout the 1970s. Fundamentally, the island of Ireland had hitherto consisted of two separate political units, one a sovereign state and the other a non-sovereign one. From the SDLP viewpoint, the implementation of its partnership policy in Northern Ireland provided the strongest possibility for the necessary reconciliation between the two communities to take place. In addition, it provided the basis for the two communities to work out their relationship with the rest of Ireland and also Britain. This was the core of SDLP ideology and it was necessary, as a first step, to overcome the age-old fears and suspicions between the two traditions within Northern Ireland.

From the SDLP position, as the 1970s unfolded, the Unionists still refused to countenance the principles of power-sharing. Also, the Government continued to operate within a purely British context. In reality, the SDLP believed that to retain the current *status quo* simply enabled Unionism to avoid the fact that a large section of the minority community was dissatisfied with their status. The problem for the minority was its inability to express legitimate political aspirations and sense of identity within the existing political structures and institutions of Northern Ireland.

Extracts from Paddy Duffy's internal policy discussion paper at this time demonstrate SDLP resolve to develop its policies beyond internal parameters. Duffy has claimed,

> 'While the Party remains committed to the position that any Northern Irish administration must be on the basis of power-sharing it will henceforth operate in a wider field of activity and seek to achieve its objective on the many fronts upon which progress can be made other than in the strict Northern Irish context.'[24]

Facing Reality in essence retained the SDLP partnership philosophy as the core of long-term Party strategy. Significantly, it called for the Irish Government to have a role in bringing about a new system of government for Northern Ireland. Regardless of the success or pace any talks between the two Governments and local parties accomplished, both governments were to press ahead and identify a whole range of projects and schemes within the socio-economic sphere.[25]

Leaks about the SDLP forthcoming policy document and its strong Irish dimension placed the party in the extreme Nationalist camp from the Unionist perspective. Furthermore, when the Queen made a Silver Jubilee Visit to Northern Ireland in August 1977 added controversy was generated for the SDLP. Prominent members of the Party received invitations to official functions during the Royal visit. Their

absence from these functions was viewed by Unionists as further confirmation that the SDLP was a traditional Nationalist party. Despite
the SDLP absence at these functions, the Party Executive had taken no
definite decision to boycott Royal functions. Fitt described the visit by
the Queen and her agreement to attend a Speaker's Conference at
Westminster as a great psychological boost to the Unionists,[26] therefore, leaving little occasion for the SDLP to celebrate. At the 1977
SDLP Annual Conference, the Party endorsed the *Facing Reality* document as their official policy for attaining its objective of a partnership
government within Northern Ireland.

Paddy Devlin leaves the SDLP

Devlin argued that his main political interest was to attempt to
improve the social and economic conditions of both communities in
Northern Ireland. Like Fitt, he said he held no strong desire for an
Irish dimension to any new political arrangements for Northern
Ireland. He was an advocate of the SDLP partnership policy within
Northern Ireland, but privately never supported its commitment to the
Irish dimension. This would indicate that, unlike the majority of his
former colleagues in the SDLP, he was more interested in identifying
an internal solution to the Northern Ireland conflict.

After the disintegration of Sunningdale, Paddy Devlin was gradually
losing interest in the SDLP. When asked why he felt sour towards the
SDLP in an interview, he said:

> 'It was gradual. The Party was going in a different direction from
> me. They were going towards Dublin and the Catholic Church. I
> was already feeling awkward after the collapse of the Executive, by
> such things as people writing articles about us as the Catholic
> SDLP Party. Things like that imply closeness to the Catholic reli-
> gion. I wanted no religion near politics.'[27]

Undoubtedly, Devlin was vehemently angry at the SDLP label as a
Catholic Party. When he joined the Party, he believed it would develop
Socialist credentials. He attributed the lack of Socialism in the Party as
another key factor in his departure from the SDLP.[28] Devlin totally
opposed National Democratic Party infiltration to the SDLP. In addition, he was hostile to John Hume. This stemmed from the SDLP
nomination of Hume as the Party contestant for the European
Elections in 1979. This was a position many felt Devlin would like to
have occupied himself.[29] Also, he was critical of the SDLP for develop-

ing too strong a base in Derry and in the rural areas of Northern Ireland. He recalled:

> 'The SDLP's failure was that it did not change politics within the North of Ireland. It failed to do that and became an Irish Nationalist party. There were too many middle-class Nationalists in the party. They were not genuine Labour men or social democrats. They were just Nationalists except their faces were different from the old Nationalist Party which had existed before that.'[30]

The climax of Devlin's political career within the SDLP was his appointment as Minister of Health in the 1974 power-sharing Executive. At Sunningdale, Devlin would have gone a long distance towards a settlement within Northern Ireland.[31] Commenting on the Sunningdale era, Devlin claimed:

> 'It was the power-sharing dimension to Sunningdale which led to the UWC Strike in May 1974, and not the Council of Ireland. As early as October 1974, Craig had met Loyalist leaders in Larne before the Council of Ireland had ever been discussed, and he was arranging dummy strikes at the Ballylumford power station.'[32]

For Devlin, this was conclusive evidence that a partnership-system of government between the two communities in Northern Ireland was unlikely to materialise. He became increasingly disillusioned after the collapse of Sunningdale and membership of the SDLP became less accommodating to him and less feasible for him.

Devlin welcomed Brian Faulkner's Committee System in June 1972 which was to give the opposition at Stormont a more effective role. Devlin responded to the Faulkner proposals by remarking that they showed 'plenty of imagination, his finest hour since I came into the House.' However, the SDLP fell behind Hume's decision to withdraw from Stormont over the suspicious shooting of Seamus Cusack and Desmond Beattie in Derry on 8 July 1971. Devlin recalled, 'Gerry and I were livid with anger. Just at a time when there were signs that we might be getting somewhere, the old Nationalist knee-jerk of abstention was brought into play.'[33] Devlin was one of the more enthusiastic members of the SDLP interested in Craig's voluntary coalition concept. He believed it offered the potential to restore the principle of power-sharing which had been the political framework for devolved government during the era of the power-sharing Executive. It could have provided the basis for a measure of co-operation between the two communities in some form of devolved administration within Northern Ireland. Hence, an opportunity for the SDLP to develop a Socialist programme of government along with their Unionist counterparts. Devlin has asserted, 'Craig's idea was that we should join in defining a common ground within the constitutional framework. Paisley turned and wouldn't go with it. Hume was also on the run and wasn't going to settle for devolved arrangements.'[34] Significantly, the discussions surrounding the voluntary coalition neglected the constitutional issue. Instead, they were discussions about social, economic and security issues avoiding the controversial issues of the border or severing the link with Britain. Devlin would have been willing to relinquish the Irish dimension during these negotiations if constructive agreement had been reached between the SDLP and the UUUC. This was Devlin's last direct involvement in political negotiations for the SDLP at that time.

In his resignation speech from the Constituency Representatives group on 26 August 1977, Devlin stated that the SDLP was reneging on its earlier promises for a full-scale evaluation of the independence issue. More importantly, Devlin referred to the advertisement in the *News Letter,* which outlined SDLP commitment, 'on the status of Northern Ireland not being changed without the consent of the majority of its people and that the SDLP would work at all times for the best interest of the people of Northern Ireland'.[35] Devlin has insisted, 'When we set up the Party in August 1970, if we had been able to work towards the objectives set out that morning. We could have changed politics in the North of Ireland forever. We failed to do that'.[36] Devlin commented in his autobiography, 'It seemed to me that Party strategy was solely directed towards consolidating the Catholic vote. The direction we were travelling in was in line with the old Nationalist Party, most certainly not the way I wanted to go.'[37] The original idea for establishing the SDLP, Devlin has argued, was to establish a party which could bind both sections of the community together within Northern Ireland, 'on the basis of their working-class interests'. He has explained, 'We wanted the Party somewhere in the middle to attract people from both sections of the community but who had mainly a working-class interest. We envisaged the trade unions joining. I am basically a trade unionist and a Socialist. I am not a Catholic or an Irish Nationalist. I don't see politics going any place unless there is some effort to unite the Protestant and Catholic people.'[38] Throughout his political career Devlin undoubtedly, sincerely fought sectarianism. He believed the way forward for Northern Ireland politics was to promote non-sectarian Socialist policies in which the economic and social issues concerning Protestant and Catholic alike could be promoted. Devlin intended the SDLP to be 'a broad-based cross-community Labour Party with a portfolio of reforming policies based on the Civil Rights demands'. Devlin's dream was to combine workers 'in common cause on a non-sectarian basis and wiping out tribal divisions'.[39]

Devlin and Fitt supported an internal settlement of the Northern Ireland conflict. Devlin believed that power-sharing was a device which could enable Socialist politics to act as a basis for reconciliation between the two communities. Over a period of time, 'realigning political parties on the just distribution of wealth and incomes'[40] was his main aim. In relation to the SDLP, Devlin maintained, 'The Party was now populated with straightforward Nationalists who were Catholic by religion and conservative in economic and social policies.'[41] Hume's success during 1977 in the international arena accentuated the SDLP policy of partnership-government in Northern Ireland. Hume was able to use his influence with senior Irish-American politicians to get President Carter to publicly support SDLP partnership strategy. Devlin dismissed *Facing Reality* 'as a hastily drafted piece of froth' released to coincide with Carter's expected intervention on Northern Ireland. Devlin claimed that senior members of the Party had advance information of Carter's forthcoming statement and hoped to exploit its content and release for personal reasons as well as those connected with the Party.[42]

Paddy Devlin maintained he resigned his position as Chairman of the SDLP Constituency Representatives' Group in protest both against the Party reappraisal of its partnership policy and also against their movement towards more Nationalist tendencies. In relation to the constitutional issue, he argued against any joint British and Irish Government involvement in preliminary discussions with Northern Ireland parties.[43] He felt that this would lead ultimately to an administration being imposed on the people of Northern Ireland. The Devlin concept of partnership was different from the main body of the SDLP. He felt that 'negotiations for a future administration within Northern Ireland in the initial stages are a matter for Northern Ireland parties. The second stage brings the sovereign powers into the negotiations to underpin an inter-party agreement.'[44] Much of Devlin's disappointment with SDLP strategy was due to Hume's increasing dominance within the Party. 'I fundamentally disagree with his strategy' said Devlin, 'I would have wanted him to embrace the Unionist tradition as well. In the short-term he has been a winner, but in the long-term he has to gain the trust and respect of the Loyalist.'[45] John Duffy has pointed out that both Devlin and Fitt disagreed with the policies upheld by many others as well as Hume. Paddy Devlin and Seamus Mallon were often at loggerheads. Duffy believed that neither of them wanted a situation where there was a formal party structure.[46] Devlin, like Fitt, was not a team player, but rather was very much an individualist.[47]

Surprisingly, Michael Murphy argues that Devlin was not a natural ally of Gerry Fitt. Austin Currie confirmed this in an interview with Murphy. Currie has recalled, 'It was an up-and-down relationship and depended upon how one of them reacted to particular things and to particular personalities at particular times. It was never an easy relationship. Gerry, to a large extent, felt that he had to be careful about Devlin because after all, Devlin was in West Belfast and could have created difficulties there.' In another interview, Murphy asked Fitt about his relationship with Devlin. Fitt replied, 'Paddy was from the Falls Road. I was not. I was an import from the other side of the city, coming in. I was like Jesus Christ on the Falls Road and Paddy was bound to resent this. A quite natural feeling. He always had a bit of a chip on his shoulder. My natural ally in the SDLP was Austin Currie. It should have been Paddy. We were together on most things but there was always the personal thing.'[48]

Devlin felt angry that Fitt did not succumb to his viewpoint at the time of his dismissal from the SDLP. Devlin commented that, 'Gerry would have taken the same views as mine, but he didn't fight. He left me to do the fighting while he got off-side. Gerry was a terrible lightweight.'[49] Murphy argued that Devlin believed he 'provided most of the Socialist input into SDLP policy' and since Fitt, 'always professed that he was a Socialist above anything else, he should have logically backed Devlin'.[50] Fitt lacked the fortitude to stand by his Socialist credentials and was swayed by the general mood within the SDLP at the time to take a 'greener', traditional Nationalist position. Not only was the SDLP a Catholic party in Devlin's estimation but it, 'had reverted to sterile Nationalism'.[51]

Devlin and Fitt were distinct individualists within the SDLP in numerous ways. For example, although a former Republican, Devlin supported the police force within Northern Ireland, the RUC, which was a view that contributed to his feelings of isolation in the SDLP.[52] Regarding an internal settlement in Northern Ireland, Alex Maskey of Sinn Féin argued that Paddy Devlin's stance in relation to the constitutional issue of Northern Ireland demonstrated marked revision. Maskey has recalled:

'I know [*sic*] Paddy Devlin a long, long time. Paddy Devlin was an outright Republican for some considerable time. He would never have countenanced dealing with an exclusive Northern Ireland state scenario. To have gone on and criticised the SDLP for being too Nationalist completely revises his own position that I don't think it stands scrutiny.'[53]

Despite Devlin's sincerity, there are contradictions and inconsistencies in the accusations he levelled at the SDLP. As Mallon has argued, 'the weakness of the SDLP in Belfast was due to Devlin's and Fitts's failure to organise at a time when things were running with them'.[54] It is extraordinary to believe that Devlin did not assent to the Irish dimension in line with his former colleagues when the SDLP was established in 1970. Devlin was involved submitting policy for *Towards a New Ireland*. He also participated in numerous SDLP delegations with Hume both to the Irish Government and opposition in Dublin during the early 1970s.[55] Therefore, there is inconsistency in Devlin's onslaught on SDLP constitutional strategy of which he himself had formerly approved.

The Irish Independence Party (IIP) was established on 7 October 1977. Among its leaders were Frank McManus, a former Unity MP for Fermanagh-South Tyrone, and Fergus McAteer a Derry Nationalist. Initially, there was trepidation within the SDLP that the IIP might supplant the Party as the main voice of the Nationalist community. The main objective of the IIP was to secure an overall British withdrawal from Ireland so they sought the assistance of the Irish Government and exerted international pressure on the EEC and America to persuade Britain that it was in her best interests to leave.[56]

Sean Hollywood, a former SDLP councillor for Newry and Mourne, reflected,

'To a large extent...[the SDLP]... did move in a green direction and that came mostly with the foundation of the Irish Independence Party. The IIP was not strong in many places, but my analysis which is not generally the accepted one, is that it was strong in the places were the people who were funding the SDLP lived at that time.... It was a crucial moment for the SDLP. The SDLP moved in their direction to take them on in their own ground, rather than standing by its own position.'[57]

Significantly, the IIP did echo a call for British withdrawal from Northern Ireland which was also prevalent within a considerable section of the SDLP in the immediate aftermath of the Constitutional Convention. However, IIP emphasis on the British presence in Ireland as being the central obstacle to a political settlement became the essential differentiation point between it and the SDLP. Further, the IIP called for a British withdrawal to take place from Northern Ireland without Unionist consent, another sharp difference between the two parties.

Currie maintained the IIP tried to capitalise on the Provos, 'without having the guts or commitment to go the whole hog'.[58] Brian Feeney believed:

'The IIP were not a threat to the SDLP. They represented very conservative, right-wing Catholics who were exclusively rural. They were a rival with Sinn Féin rather than the SDLP. They went to Sinn Féin in 1982 to offer and stand in the assembly elections on behalf of Sinn Féin. The IRA told them to bugger off because they had an organisation.'[59]

The militant dimension of the IIP was more likely to lead to former abstentionist voters to the IIP in Republican areas, rather than cause any significant decrease in SDLP electoral support. The weakness of the IIP was demonstrated when Sinn Féin wiped them out in the October Assembly Elections in 1982. The IIP acquired 3.3 per cent of the vote in the 1979 General Election and 3.9 per cent in the 1981 Local Government Elections, 'but faded thereafter when its vote swung over to Sinn Féin'.[60] Regardless of the IIP, the SDLP would have pressed ahead to promote a stronger Irish dimension of partner-ship-government. This had more to do with Hume's recent success and confidence on the international scene than with the arrival of the IIP.

The IIP did have an impact on the SDLP in the Westminster Elections in 1979, particularly in Derry and Mid-Ulster. Mallon claimed, 'Paddy Duffy would have literally won a seat in Mid-Ulster, but for the spoiling tactics of the IIP'. Mallon also recalled, 'In the Republic, Fianna Fáil temporarily turned its loyalty away from the SDLP to that of the IIP. There were some people in the Republic of Ireland who flirted with them for a period, but I think they got the message fairly quickly'.[61] The only defections from the SDLP to the IIP were by members from North Antrim led by John Turnly. Although one of the few Protestant members of the SDLP, Turnly's departure did not give rise to a sense of panic. Gerry Fitt, then SDLP leader, described Turnly's behaviour as eccentric. He argued that Turnly, 'always expressed views very similar to those of Provisional Sinn Féin'.[62] Therefore, despite the arrival of the IIP on the political scene in 1977, they did not have any serious impact on the SDLP.

By the end of 1977, the SDLP believed the Irish Government had to be actively involved with London in resolving the Northern Ireland problem. The parameters of that resolution had to move beyond a purely British context. The SDLP was determined to maintain pressure on the British Government about the importance of the Irish dimension. Mallon argued that the continuation of an exclusively British context for the Northern Ireland problem only vindicated Unionist conditioning to downgrade the significance of the Irish dimension. It gave legitimacy to Unionist supremacy over the minority community in Northern Ireland. Mallon maintained:

'At all stages, the British Government by its failure to react positively has fostered this attitude, and indeed, by unconditionally guaranteeing the constitutional position of Northern Ireland, has reinforced Unionist adherence to it. In doing so, the legitimate aspirations of the non–Unionist population have been treated with utter condescension, and their claims for recognition of their Irish identity relegated to the role of an optional extra, to be granted if and when agreed to by Unionism.'[63]

He criticised the Irish Government belief that the SDLP 'expression of national aspirations was obscurant, and therefore ultimately politically unviable, was a singular disservice to the minority community'.[64]

The Secretary of State, Roy Mason, told the House of Commons on 24 November 1977, that it was his intention to reintroduce devolved power to Northern Ireland. He envisaged the inception of a unicameral assembly within Northern Ireland, playing a consultative role in legislative matters. Mason believed these measures could provide the basis for eventual legislative devolution to progress. The proposals were to incorporate the safeguarding of minority interests within Northern Ireland.[65] In relation to Mason's interim devolution proposals, the SDLP insisted they would only take part in talks using their *Facing Reality* document as the framework for political development.[66]

The SDLP was suspicious that Mason's interim devolution proposals were too similar the Molyneaux proposals for administrative devolution for genuine progress to be made. Eddie McGrady felt that any attempt 'to enter into pacts and undertakings with Unionists at Westminster, in reality, meant that the Government was, "putting the Northern Ireland problem on the long finger".'[67] Hume warned the SDLP, 'that a drift towards integration with Britain was happening while there was no political movement in the North'.[68]

By the start of 1978, SDLP strategy towards the Unionist community was changing. The Party had repeatedly identified the Unionist veto as a major impediment to reaching any final agreement to the Northern Ireland problem. A large section of the Catholic population felt totally isolated by their inability to express their sense of identity and allegiance within the Northern Ireland State. Any such framework drawn up by the Government in a purely British context would continue to ignore the legitimate aspirations of a large section of the Catholic population to their Irish identity. The veto destroyed any SDLP hope of addressing the key issues which were at the core of the conflict.

Consequently, the SDLP felt it was a futile exercise to operate internally within Northern Ireland to secure the implementation of their partnership policy by Westminster. Seamus Mallon has recalled that at the time:

'The Party was being left behind and if things proceeded as at present there would be no Party left in a couple of years. The Party could not accept anything less that full power-sharing and a substantial Irish dimension. The current British equation was that interim devolution equalled power-sharing and cross border cooperation and the Irish dimension. That was totally unacceptable.'[69]

Mallon suggested securing British disengagement in a joint or simultaneous call with the Irish Government. In addition, if the British were to establish suitable structures of government, it would give them the best excuse for leaving Northern Ireland.

Eddie McGrady made it clear that the SDLP had been patient, moderate and accommodating in its approach to the Northern Ireland situation during the 1970s. McGrady's argument seemed to be a new call for the SDLP to initiate an Anglo-Irish strategy in 1978. He asserted:

'Unionist leaders have failed to grasp the extent of our significant concession which was made for the Northern Ireland majority by the SDLP. That concession was the recognition by the political minority in Northern Ireland of the right of the Unionist majority to have a final veto on the ultimate solution. This substantial concession recognised for the first time the existence of Northern Ireland, in spite of the fact that the Unionist majority was carefully constructed to be that majority and morally has no claim to the normal democratic rights and privileges of natural majorities.'[70]

McGrady continued to point out that despite the shortcomings of the Northern Ireland State, the SDLP was willing to participate in it. He hinted that since Unionists had rejected the concession which acknowledged their majority status as separate, the SDLP should work within 'the more democratic and in the more realistic terms as part of the majority in Ireland'. Therefore, by definition, the Unionists become a minority in Ireland. McGrady said, 'Future SDLP policies on the constitutional position may require withdrawal of the guarantee that the constitutional position will not be changed except by the consent of the majority of Northern Ireland'.

Federalism

In the Republic, Fianna Fáil has always held a strongly traditional Irish unity stance towards the issue of Northern Ireland. During their periods in government, they have tended to be less sympathetic to the Unionist position than the Coalition Government parties comprising Fine Gael and the Labour Party. In an RTE interview, the Taoiseach, Jack Lynch, reflected SDLP strategy in relation to both parts of Ireland. He argued that the British Government should state its intention to withdraw from Ireland. His position corresponded to that of the SDLP in that he was not calling for an instant withdrawal from Ireland, but rather the initiation of a process towards that objective.[71]

Nonetheless, there was a difference in policy between the SDLP and Fianna Fáil on the constitutional question of Northern Ireland. *Facing Reality* emphasised the SDLP policy of a federal solution to the problem. Fianna Fáil was slower to become involved in a discussion on federalism. However, both parties recognised the need to be seen saying broadly similar things,[72] and it was evident to the SDLP during 1978 that there was a need develop a joint Nationalist strategy between all the main constitutional parties within Ireland about the Northern Ireland problem.

As a result in 1978 Denis Haughey pointed out that current SDLP policy was being examined with an impressive body of opinion moving towards a solution in an Irish context.[73] The SDLP sought to consolidate its contacts within the main parties in the Republic with the objective of putting pressure on the British Government to nudge the

dimension. From the SDLP perspective, this was a contentious political factor within the Catholic community.

By early 1979, the SDLP had ruled out two solutions for resolving the Northern Ireland conflict. They dismissed the proposal of an independent Ulster as being economically and politically unworkable. Such a solution would not reduce the sectarian tensions between the two communities. In addition, the SDLP recognised that the traditional Nationalist aspirations for a united Ireland based on a thirty-two-county unitary model were no longer a realistic idea, leading the party to accept the validity of Unionist opposition to such an initiative.

The federal system appeared the more realistic option to the SDLP. The immediate task, as a result of one of the motions passed at the 1978 Annual Conference was to establish the feasibility of such a system. The difficulty of persuading Unionists to distinguish a federal option from a traditional 'United Ireland' remained. An SDLP sub-committee examined different systems of government in a federal arrangement. In their analysis of federalism a range of difficulties had to be overcome. There were three alternative systems of government within a federal context:

1. **A Two-Part System**
   The Irish Government would govern the present twenty-six-counties and would be the ultimate federal authority over both parts of the island. Northern Ireland would be an autonomous administration with the exception of powers reserved for the federal government.

2. **A Three-Part System**
   The Irish Government would be the regional government of the twenty-six counties which now make up the Republic. Northern Ireland was also to have a Regional Government. A newly-created Federal Government would have ultimate authority over each.

3. **A Four-Province System**
   The creation of a regional administration would be grounded on a four-province basis and each subject to a Federal Authority.

A major difficulty the SDLP anticipated in a federal arrangement was whether the present six counties of Northern Ireland would be retained within a new federal arrangement. Another option was to consider whether areas lying beside the present border could opt for whichever regional jurisdiction they preferred. The SDLP had problems as to whether a Northern Ireland Regional Government would take the form of a power-sharing administration or a majority-rule system of Government. The extent of Northern Ireland representation in a federal system of government had to be measured and established. These matters, along with reconciling the question of the nationality of citizens in a federal state and the new state relationship with Britain, were delicate issues which had to be addressed.[81]

From the SDLP perspective, the positive aspect of federalism was its ability to break Unionist reliance on the British Government for the protection of their tradition and identity. According to SDLP thinking, the Unionists' true identity could be better facilitated within an all-Ireland framework. John Hume argued at an Oxford Union debate,

> 'One of the tragedies of Ireland has been that the Protestant tradition always relied for its security, not on its own strength of members, convictions or tradition, but on Acts of the British Parliament. I can think of no more insecure foundation for the protection of any tradition. Irish history is littered with such Acts of Parliament offering guarantees to the Protestant tradition in Ireland which were cast aside the moment political expediency demanded it.'[82]

Consequently, the SDLP priority during 1979 was to establish a political process which would break the political log-jam in Northern Ireland.

The SDLP thesis was simply that the creation of the Northern Ireland State only came about to buttress Unionist interests. The history of Northern Ireland has shown that the minority community has continually felt alienated within the structures of that state. The SDLP believed that to support the existing Northern Ireland State continually would only reinforce the alienation of the minority. New structures of government had to be created in Northern Ireland to which both communities could give their allegiance. The fall of Stormont in 1972 was a sign that a 'new political order' was essential for Northern Ireland.[83] Any new order had to embrace the Unionist tradition. Hume called for greater emphasis on the Irish dimension in response to the perceived 'integrationist' policy of the British Government in 1976 and 1977.

CHAPTER FOUR

Change in Leadership

Towards a New Ireland – A Policy Review Document
In a real sense, by 1979, the SDLP had acknowledged a total stalemate in Northern Ireland politics. It believed the only way forward was for the British and Irish Governments to create the necessary political structures within Northern Ireland over and above the heads of the local political parties. The experience of Sunningdale and the Constitutional Convention illustrated that the local parties in Northern Ireland were not politically mature enough to agree on new structures which reflected the legitimacy of the Irish dimension. Further, the SDLP felt that a joint approach by the British and Irish governments paved the way for a political framework which could eventually be presented to the local parties within Northern Ireland.

The primary objective of the SDLP during 1979 was to get the two Governments to negotiate an administration to which the two communities in Northern Ireland could give their allegiance. The SDLP wanted the British Government to realise that the Northern Irish problem could only be resolved by embracing the Irish dimension as part of an overall settlement. They believed, moreover, that treating the problem purely by security measures was not going to resolve the conflict. The imbalance in Northern Ireland policy was the unconditional guarantee of the British Government to the Unionists that they could remain part of the United Kingdom without giving reciprocal guarantees to the Nationalist community's aspirations.

The SDLP attacks on the politics of consecutive British Governments had to be balanced alongside Party criticism of the policy of the Republic towards Northern Ireland. In an internal Party discussion paper, the SDLP asserted:

'The actions and attitudes of Southern people and Southern Governments have a direct bearing upon Northern Ireland. It is inevitable that this should be so when over one-third of the people of the North look to Dublin as their real capital and the centre of their national identity. The Republic is involved in the problem. It must be involved in the solution.'[1]

Quadripartite talks involving the British and Irish Governments and the political representatives of the two traditions in Northern Ireland were sought by the SDLP as the best method of securing a political initiative.

In pursuing its policy of an 'Agreed Ireland' during 1979, the SDLP realised that it was impossible to develop a political initiative exclusively between the political parties in Northern Ireland. An SDLP policy review paper noted that:

> 'The increasing electoral strength of Paisleyism, the lack of leadership and commitment to devolution of the Official Unionist Party, the alienation of large sections of the population, resulting from paramilitary influence on the one hand and security strictures on the other, convince us that it is now impossible to reach the agreement necessary to create an administration which would command the active support of sufficient numbers of people within both communities.'[2]

Either the Government could impose a settlement, or outside bodies such as the EEC and the United States could use the necessary power and resources to help create change in Northern Ireland. The SDLP believed that a settlement imposed by the Government 'would inevitably involve the British Government in direct military conflict with extreme loyalist paramilitaries and with the Provisional IRA'. Consequently, the Party was convinced that the British would not adopt such a strategy which, in essence, implied instant British withdrawal. For the SDLP, 'such an approach might well result on conditions being imposed that could be unacceptable to the SDLP and the minority community'.

For the SDLP, 'a solution must shift from the Northern Irish political parties to outside factors which have the power and the resources to create change'. The main attraction of this approach was that it did not require an electoral mandate within Northern Ireland and it enabled political progress to continue 'without the constant threat of veto by any political grouping in Northern Ireland'.

A joint Anglo-Irish approach by the two Governments could be a mechanism of overcoming Unionist resistance to any new political initiative. It could mark the weakening of Unionist guarantees which blocked political progress in Northern Ireland. Sean Farren, SDLP Vice Chairman, speaking to North Antrim Constituency Council, maintained, 'To make meaningful discussion possible the SDLP has called for the withdrawal of these guarantees in their present form. Such a move would clearly break the political stalemate and oblige all parties to realistically face the problem of finding a solution to our present crisis.'[3] Consequently, throughout 1979, the SDLP supported a joint Anglo-Irish initiative by both Governments as the best formula for creating a political framework for resolving the Northern Ireland conflict. In addition, the Party endeavoured to have the issue of the Northern Ireland Constitution placed within the wider framework of the whole island of Ireland, the United Kingdom and the EEC. Within this wider framework, both Governments could develop cross-border co-operation in socio-economic matters between the Republic and Northern Ireland.[4] To attain this objective, the SDLP sought the support of political allies in the international arena of Europe and the United States, and in the domestic spheres of Ireland and the United Kingdom.[5]

According to SDLP thinking, the advantage of having a joint Anglo-Irish strategy meant in essence, that a political framework could proceed without depending on the initial agreement of the local parties within Northern Ireland. More importantly, it marked the official demise of an internal framework in relation to a constitutional settlement by the SDLP. This strategy became the best option of integrating the Irish dimension as part of an overall political settlement. The key factor in a joint Anglo-Irish approach was the in-built mechanism to proceed with a political initiative regardless of Unionist protest. Ideally, from an SDLP stance, 'the removal of a popular mandate diminishes the spectre of Paisleyism in electoral terms'.[6]

So, the first SDLP draft outline for *Towards a New Ireland* indicated the Party felt that Unionists could participate in an Anglo-Irish framework as the British Government would look after their interests. In addition, it also believed that perhaps the Sinn Féin leadership might view a joint Anglo-Irish strategy along with cross border co-operation 'as a tacit declaration of eventual British disengagement'. The clever part of such a scheme was that 'the absence of an electoral mandate would prevent the strength of Paisleyism intimidating other Unionist parties'. It was a strategy which the SDLP felt enabled political movement to continue in Northern Ireland regardless of the extremism of Republican violence and Unionist intransigence.

By implication, the SDLP held Unionists responsible for the failure of an internal settlement through their refusal to accept a political initiative within Northern Ireland which embraced the political aspirations of the minority community. It was evident to the SDLP that agreement on an acceptable form of government through the normal democratic channels of negotiation between the locally elected political parties within Northern Ireland was not forthcoming. Therefore the SDLP proposed, in an internal policy review document, the establishment of a special Constitutional Commission which would study in depth any proposals put forward by the local parties on matters relating to Northern Ireland and which could be implemented regardless of local party support for it.[7]

It was anticipated that the Constitutional Commission would be created by the British and Irish Governments. Its role would be to assist the two Governments in reaching a satisfactory constitutional settlement. It would be made up of 'constitutional experts, headed possibly by a person of international standing from outside Northern Ireland and representatives of political parties from Northern Ireland, Britain and the Republic of Ireland'.[8] Separate commissions were recommended concerning social and economic issues. Significantly, the European dimension influenced SDLP deliberation regarding these commissions whose role would be to identify areas in the social and economic spheres in Northern Ireland and the Republic which would benefit from streamlining and greater efficiency. The SDLP policy review document specified areas such as agriculture and fisheries, tourism, industry and commerce, health and social services, policing, education, arts and sport as areas which would benefit from joint cross-border co-operation. Accordingly, the SDLP paper suggested that EEC funds should be administered on an all-Ireland basis for such projects.

This internal draft policy document also challenged the responsibilities and role which the Republic had to play in resolving the Northern Ireland conflict. The conduct of the commissions, in effect, meant an erosion of Irish Government powers pertaining to certain economic and social issues in the South. The paper indirectly called for the demise of the dominant Catholic ethos in the South and a move towards a more pluralist State. These themes were later elaborated more fully by the SDLP in the negotiations leading to the publication of the *New Ireland Forum Report* in May 1984. However, the essential thesis of the SDLP draft policy document concentrated on the gradual diminution of British rule within Northern Ireland. In addition, it focused on persuading the main constitutional parties in the Republic along with the SDLP 'to formulate a set of proposals which would form the basis of discussion on Irish unity'.[9]

Principles contained in several draft SDLP policy documents throughout 1979 became the basis of *Towards a New Ireland*. This policy document was overwhelmingly endorsed by the SDLP 1979 Annual

Conference. The motion backing the policy document called, '...the British and Irish Governments to agree to and promote a joint Anglo-Irish process of political, social and economic development'.[10] The key figures behind this policy document were Seamus Mallon, Sean Farren and Paddy Duffy. Other senior personalities in the Party, including John Hume and Denis Haughey, also contributed to the policy review.

In the document the SDLP insisted that it was now the responsibility of the two Governments to draw up a suitable political framework implementing their principles of 'partnership'. Thus, the SDLP was challenging the two Governments to adopt the Northern Ireland conflict as their 'common problem'.[11] The policy document fell short of endorsing an outright federal solution to resolving the Northern Ireland conflict. Instead, by the end of 1979, the SDLP had reinterpreted this concept somewhat, moving more to open-ended terms of reference for the two Governments to create a political framework for a final constitutional settlement.

The policy document called on the British Government to acknowledge the inefficacy of its current Northern Ireland policy and re-examine its strategy: British policy had only contributed to Unionist refusal, 'to enter into any meaningful dialogue about the problem'. The Irish Government was asked to state its terms for Irish unity and to demonstrate what this implied socially, economically and politically to alleviate Unionist fears. However, the SDLP was unable to press ahead with this strategy with the Republic's main political parties until the start of the New Ireland Forum talks in 1983.

As well as a viable administration in Northern Ireland, the SDLP proposed that the two Governments establish a Standing Commission. The role of this commission would be to develop government structures within Northern Ireland in the context of Northern Ireland's position within the island of Ireland, the United Kingdom and the EEC. Further, on the economic and social fronts, both Governments were to create cross-border bodies to identify projects beneficial to both parts of Ireland. This would take place in the context of an expanding European economic community.

Atkins' Constitutional Conference

The SDLP on the whole welcomed the new Conservative administration elected to office in May 1979. For the SDLP, it marked an end of Government reliance on Unionist support in the House of Commons and secret deals taking place. Brid Rodgers, SDLP Chairperson, reflected the optimistic mood in the SDLP to the newly-elected British administration, saying, 'The new British Government had moved away from Roy Mason's hand-washing attitude of sort-it-out-amongst-your-selves and was showing signs of facing up to its responsibilities. That was certainly a move in the right direction'.[12] The British Government published a *Green Paper* on 20 November 1979, raising proposals for a Conference for the political parties in Northern Ireland. Paragraph 4 of the Government document stated,

> 'It is at present the clear wish of a substantial majority of the people in Northern Ireland to remain part of the United Kingdom. The Conference will therefore not be concerned with the constitutional status of the Province and will not be asked to discuss issues such as Irish unity, or confederation, or independence. Nor, since there is no prospect of agreement on them, will the Conference be invited to consider either a return to the arrangements which prevailed before 1972, or a revival of the system which obtained in the first five months of 1974. New patterns must be sought which take full account of the needs and anxieties of both sides of the community.'[13]

Opposing the Conference because it lacked any emphasis on the Irish dimension, the SDLP initially refused to take part in it as they felt it would only represent a Unionist viewpoint.[14] Also, the principle of power-sharing or, to use SDLP terminology, 'partnership-government' enshrined in the *1973 Northern Ireland Constitution Act* was abandoned. The stated aims of the Constitutional Conference failed to acknowledge the legitimate Irish aspirations of Northern Ireland's minority community. Fitt differed from Hume over his interpretation of what partnership meant; he viewed partnership at a political level between the two communities in Northern Ireland as a realistic goal for the foreseeable future whereas Hume and the majority of the SDLP rank-and-file wanted some type of formal link with the Republic.

The SDLP was only willing to take part in the Conference if the agenda was expanded to allow the Party to discuss their own proposals.[15] Consequently, the SDLP wrote to Atkins stating that if the Conference agenda were broadened, the SDLP would be willing to participate in it. After an Executive Meeting on 15 December 1979, the SDLP decided it would take part in the Constitutional Conference. This decision was taken on the basis of a six-point agreement reached between Hume and Atkins. This basically enabled the Party to discuss the Irish dimension outside the terms of reference for the Constitutional Conference at a parallel conference.

Accordingly, the Constitutional Conference commenced at Stormont on 7 January 1980. The SDLP proposals to the Conference on 8 January 1980 were presented by John Hume. Predictably, they called on the British Government to reappraise its responsibility towards Northern Ireland. Hume said, 'The British Government's approach to the Northern Ireland problem has been totally consistent since 1920 in that the whole of its policy was to underline and guarantee one identity in a situation where the problem resulted from a clash of identities'.[16] The SDLP believed the first step for the government to resolve the Northern Ireland problem was to adopt a joint British and Irish government approach to resolving the conflict.

Hume initially only gave a lukewarm and guarded welcome to Akins' Conference. He considered its operation as a first step in the SDLP desire to have a wider Anglo-Irish framework. The new SDLP leader, believed it 'was the first step in a developing process which presupposes that there will be other steps'. According to Hume, the British Prime Minister, Margaret Thatcher, told him that the Government had no definitive policy on Northern Ireland. The purpose of the Atkins' Conference was to report to the cabinet on attitudes on Northern Ireland before the British Government would embark upon any new political initiative.[17]

Austin Currie clarified the SDLP position towards the Constitutional Conference:

'The SDLP has made it clear from the beginning that it sees the current Akins's [sic] Conference as only the first step towards a solution, and so also in different words has Mr Atkins. Such a scenario, if it does not involve an imposed solution, and the British have denied such an intention, must necessarily involve a further conference or conferences. It is the sincere wish of the SDLP that at the earliest possible stage a quadripartite conference will be held involving the two Sovereign governments and representatives of the two communities in the North.'[18]

In addition, Seamus Mallon who was considered to be one of the so-called 'greener' Nationalist members of the Party, threw support behind Atkins' Conference. He maintained:

'Most people recognise that this Conference is neither the ideal forum to deal with the many complex problems which face us, nor is it anything which would lead to a lasting solution. However, it is a very important – indeed crucial – first step and should be given every opportunity to develop so that at the very least the political parties can clearly understand, if not agree with, each other's positions, fears and aspirations.'[19]

As the sessions of the Conference proceeded during 1980, it became apparent to the SDLP that the British Government was not going to infuse the Irish dimension into its overall policy towards Northern Ireland. Atkins told the Commons on 7 February 1980 that, 'The object of the Conference is to identify the highest level of agreement on the transfer to locally elected representatives in Northern Ireland of some of the powers of government'.[20] The Conference was distinctly reiterating former British internal policy in relation towards Northern Ireland. The Secretary of State made this abundantly clear in the House of Commons on 8 May 1980 when he said:

'I am not convinced that the introduction of a formalised all-Ireland relationship between the North and South on political matters would do anything to advance the cause which we are following, namely, to seek to re-establish democratic control of affairs in Northern Ireland by Northern Ireland people. We are not seeking to solve the future of Northern Ireland. That is not for us. As I have said, we are seeking to re-establish some democratic way of controlling affairs in Northern Ireland. That is what we are about.'[21]

Consequently, the SDLP submitted proposals on devolution to the Constitutional Conference strictly within the limits of the economic and social spheres. In brief, the SDLP put forward six main proposals:

* A unicameral legislature which would be elected, by proportional representation, for a fixed term which might be of four or five years.

* From the legislature a Cabinet would be formed, the members of which would be the political heads of the Northern Ireland Departments.

* The Chairman of the Cabinet would be the Chief Executive. The Chief Executive would be appointed by the Secretary of State, but he would have no departmental portfolio.

* The Cabinet would conform to the principle of collective responsibility within an agreed socio-economic programme.

* The arrangement would be temporary only. There would be statutory provision that they should be subject to review after two terms (eight to ten years).

* The SDLP proposed the status of a devolved administration as subordinate to that of a sovereign Assembly. Therefore, any budgets for Northern Ireland social and economic programmes had to be controlled by Westminster.[22]

On 2 July 1980, the British Government published another *White Paper* which outlined the results of the Constitutional Conference and suggested possible ways forward.[23] Paragraph 6 of the *White Paper* stated,

'The Conference had the merit of bringing together, for the first time for some years, leading members of all but one of the main Northern Ireland political parties for detailed and sustained discussion of the problems involved in establishing a new administration in Northern Ireland. These exchanges were of value to the Government and, it is hoped, to the parties. They did not lead to a negotiated agreement for a future pattern of government. That was never expected: the Conference was aimed at establishing the highest level of agreement between the parties rather than identifying a single detailed scheme of government to which all would subscribe.'[24]

Atkins' Constitutional Conference failed to provide a political framework for resolving the Northern Ireland problem. The SDLP blamed this failure on the Government still working strictly within the parameters of an internal settlement. Atkins proposed an assembly and executive body having a range of responsibilities not dissimilar to the powers held under the 1974 Assembly. While the proposals contained safeguards for minority interests, there were no guarantees that the minority were to have seats in the executive.[25] Nonetheless, the SDLP welcomed the acknowledgement in the government proposals which stated that, 'New institutions of government which the minority community cannot accept as its institutions will not bring stability and so will not be worth having.'[26] In particular, the SDLP was pleased with the sentiments expressed in Paragraph 22 of the *White Paper* which 'encouraged the growth of a new and deeper relationship between the United Kingdom of Great Britain and Northern Ireland and the Republic of Ireland.'[27]

On 27 November 1980, the Secretary of State, announced in the House of Commons:

> '... we have to conclude that there is not sufficient agreement between the political parties to justify the government bringing the proposals to the House for setting up a devolved administration at this stage. In the words of Paragraph 64 of Cmnd. 7950, we shall now explore other ways of making the government of Northern Ireland more responsive to the wishes of the people, and such alternatives could involve a progressive approach to a transfer of powers. The principles enunciated in successive command papers will, of course, continue to apply and I shall be consulting the local political parties.'[28]

The SDLP was totally opposed to substantial powers being invested in local government authorities within Northern Ireland without the implementation of power-sharing at executive level. In February 1980 Eddie McGrady had written a paper on local government in Northern Ireland. While it was not part of the SDLP's formal submission to the Constitutional Convention, it nevertheless set the tone of the SDLP position in relation to an internal settlement.[29] McGrady insisted that Unionist-dominated Councils, 'maintained the sectarian attitudes and practices of the former local authorities in spite of the rather innocuous nature of their present powers and functions'. He continued, 'It is evident ... that it would be a disastrous policy for any British Government to allow a return of "majority" devolved government in Northern Ireland under Unionist control. It must be abundantly clear that the substantial powers, which would be then devolved to Northern Ireland, would be exercised in a sectarian and discriminatory manner; that the same disregard for the rights of the minority in housing, jobs and recreation would apply at governmental level....Only the participation of the minority in executive government can safeguard their rights in a devolved administration'.[30]

The SDLP considered local councils would indicate what would emerge from a devolved administration based on an internal framework in Northern Ireland. The Party expressed the fear that Unionists would continue to act in a sectarian and discriminatory manner against the minority community if powers were devolved back to local bodies and wanted to steer the Government away from an internal settlement to the Northern Ireland conflict.

Departure of Gerry Fitt from the SDLP

Gerry Fitt played a prominent role in the foundation of the SDLP in

1970. He was in a key position, having won a seat at Westminster in the General Election of 1966. Fitt as an activist in the Civil Rights Movement was successful in getting Northern Ireland debated in the House of Commons. At a time when a Labour administration was in power, Fitt focused the attention of the 'broad-Left' in the British Parliament to injustice in Northern Ireland. This created the necessary conditioning for the British left-wing establishment to act purposefully on the grievances demonstrated by the Civil Rights campaign. Fitt had cut quite a figure in the Westminster Parliament constructing the Campaign for Democracy in Ulster – a London-based group – in the late 1960s and he had encouraged support from over one-hundred Labour back-benchers, among whom were Stanley Orme, Paul Rose and Kevin McNamara.

In reality, the SDLP could not have been formed without Fitt. He was essential to the SDLP to give it the necessary limelight to advance its policies and to justify its existence. It was through his contacts with trade unionists and the British Labour Party that the SDLP obtained credibility during its formative years. Fitt, with the backing of Devlin, established contacts with the Irish Labour Party through its General Secretary, Brendan Halligan. A combination of Fitt's efforts and the good-will of his associates admitted the SDLP to membership of the Socialist International. Fitt's overall value to the SDLP was his ability to promote their cause beyond the borders of Northern Ireland.

However, Fitt's function within the SDLP seriously diminished because he was ill-suited to the role of Leader. Like Devlin, Fitt had a very distinct individualistic style. His greatest weakness was his failure to create an organisational structure for the Party in West Belfast. Another shortcoming was his inability to contribute to policy formulation within the SDLP. Austin Currie has maintained that, from early on, it was apparent Hume was the driving force in articulating policy, and, indeed, in representing the face of the SDLP. Currie recalled, 'For quite a while that Hume was deputy leader, he was effectively Leader of the Party in thinking and strategic terms, because that wasn't Gerry's forte. Gerry made up things as he went along and didn't articulate well thought out objectives'.[31] Fitt and Devlin joined the SDLP in 1970, coming from a background of trade union and street politics very much associated with the 1940s and 1950s. Fitt and Devlin understood Socialism more in a British-framework as opposed to a European context. While middle-class people joining the SDLP would have been conscious of the left-of-centre dimension within the Party, they were, nevertheless, more anxious to affiliate as Social Democrats rather than

Labour members. Socialism for people like Hume and his followers was basically Social Democracy within a European context and Brian Feeney has argued that the SDLP was not a Labour Party in the traditional sense of its meaning.[32]

Fitt's motives for joining the SDLP in 1970 reflect to a large degree Paddy Devlin's objectives and long-term plans for the Party. When asked in an interview why he joined the Party, he maintained,

> 'I thought I was going to form a Party that would have links with the trade unions and talk to Protestants to try to bring about a Northern Ireland situation were we would work at some internal arrangement. The others were Nationalists. While it was in my blood to be a Labour man – it was in their blood to be Nationalists. There is no Labour standing within the SDLP. It is not a Labour Party and never was.'[33]

With hindsight, Fitt expressed regret in joining the SDLP. Although elected its first Party Leader, Fitt recalled never feeling in control of the SDLP. He claimed he became disillusioned with the Party once it was taken over by rural Nationalists. He believed the SDLP was primarily a Nationalist Party and recalled a conversation he had with Paddy Devlin at his home in Belfast prior to the Party's formation.

> 'Paddy, you know the history of the Nationalist Party here. There are only us from Belfast. If we go in with that crowd they will annihilate us. They are all up from the country and they will smother us. We agreed about that. The pressure was on. Irish News editorials, etc. – people were saying that we should get together, and that we needed a new cohesion. Eventually I agreed, but I was very reluctant about it.'[34]

Fitt denied ever being a Nationalist himself, but rather, his involvement with the SDLP swamped him with Nationalism. He was a leader of a Party whose political philosophy did not express his own political aspirations. However, Ivan Cooper pointed out that one has only to look at Fitt in his former political career with Republican Labour to note the sectarian tone of that Party which was certainly not lacking in Nationalist sentiment.[35]

Until the European Elections held in June 1979, Fitt had been the SDLP's sole MP. In reality, the SDLP needed Fitt more than he needed them, simply because he had already created his political niche at Westminster. Unlike his former Party colleagues, Fitt was going into the SDLP with a political career, behind him. With Hume's success in the European elections, Fitt's leadership was seriously undermined. In essence, Hume deposed Fitt 'as the real leader of nationalist opinion in the North.'[36]

Hume was elected with 140,622 first-preference votes, 'adding 14,297 votes to the total SDLP poll in May and pushing the Party's share of the vote to a record 24.6 per cent'.[37] Unlike the majority of his comrades in the SDLP, Fitt held a strong dislike for Southern politics. He was much happier in the political arena of Westminster and British Labour Party politics. Like Paddy Devlin's departure from the SDLP, it was not any one incident, but rather a culmination of factors which led to his exit.

On 20 November 1979, Gerry Fitt misinterpreted the SDLP understanding of Atkins' constitutional proposals for Northern Ireland saying,

'At a quick reading I find some of the proposals are very interesting so far as they go out of their way to give protection to the minority in Northern Ireland. I believe the proposals are worthy of the deepest consideration and that is certainly what my Party will be doing at the earliest opportunity.'[38]

Michael Murphy pointed out that Fitt's comments were another example of his impulsive individualism since he was not representing the Party by them.

The negative reaction of the SDLP to Atkins' Constitutional Conference was due to the absence of the Irish dimension in the Government proposals. It was for this reason that Fitt apparently resigned from the SDLP. He announced he '...was cutting all links with the Party because of its unanimous decision not to attend the proposed constitutional conference on its present terms of reference'.[39] He believed that a power-sharing settlement could be agreed within the parameters of Akins' proposed Conference. He accused the SDLP of becoming Republican in the absence of any political initiative and maintained, 'The IRA and the SDLP do have something in common even up to the present moment. I didn't. They wanted an United Ireland – by different means and different methods'.[40]

This was a phenomenal charge for Fitt to have levelled at the SDLP. After all, one had only to refer to his speech as SDLP Leader at the 1978 Annual Conference to find his endorsement of the Irish dimension. Fitt said, '...the SDLP stands for the unification of this country. The SDLP wants to unite people of all religions and outlooks, not only in Northern Ireland, but the whole of Ireland, so that we can eventually bring about the reunification of this country by consent, not coercion'.[41] During an interview with Fitt, he made reference to two factors which led to his despondency in relation to Northern Ireland politics. The first of these was the failure of the Pope's appeal in Drogheda in 1979, directed specifically at the Provisional IRA, to end violence. The negative response to that plea left Fitt feeling disconsolate. Secondly, the death of Lord Mountbatten and of eighteen British soldiers at Warrenpoint reinforced for him the futility of the Northern Ireland conflict. Fitt did not intend to resign over Atkins' Constitutional Conference. It was a mixture of the hard-line reaction he received at an emergency meeting of the SDLP held in Dungannon, and quite significantly, the toll it was all exacting on his wife.[42]

Since the failure of the Constitutional Convention, and the implementation of the British Government criminalisation and Ulsterisation strategy, the SDLP felt disillusioned with London's shift from its stance at Sunningdale which had been in favour of power-sharing and an Irish dimension. This had the effect of maintaining the Unionist veto on political change in Northern Ireland. For the SDLP, the reality of such a position meant that Unionists never had to negotiate a settlement with the Nationalist community. Also, the Unionists' hard-line position made it virtually impossible to reach any form of accommodation within the parameters of Northern Ireland. In a practical sense, inter-party talks were a futile exercise.

For the remainder of the 1970s, the SDLP continued to try to legitimise the Irish dimension as a permanent basis for resolving the Northern Ireland conflict. They recognised that power-sharing was no longer an attainable goal. Their priorities were to give new impetus to the Irish dimension, as well as to maintain the principle of power-sharing in the event of devolution. The SDLP acknowledged that the British and Irish Governments would have to override the Unionist veto – a view expressed by Seamus Mallon in particular. In order to obtain a political endorsement for new Northern Ireland institutions, the SDLP recommended that two separate referendums take place, one in the North and one in the South. Devlin and Fitt gave the impression that, during their time with the SDLP, they specifically sought an internal political solution to the Northern Ireland conflict. In retrospect, this demonstrates an inverse position to their earlier political careers. The internal solution did not reflect the majority consensus in the SDLP which endorsed some formal expression of the Irish dimension.

By the end of 1978, the SDLP was seeking a joint Nationalist strategy with the main constitutional parties in the Republic in relation to Northern Ireland and to their relationship with the Unionists. While federalism was a favourite option of the SDLP, the reality was that Unionists would not differentiate a federal option from the concept of a traditional united Ireland. To get political momentum into Northern Ireland politics, the SDLP wanted both Governments to draw up a political framework which addressed the rights and aspirations of both communities in Northern Ireland. The SDLP recommended that political development take place by means of side-stepping the Unionist veto on political initiatives.

John Hume and the Leadership

Following Gerry Fitt's resignation from the SDLP, John Hume was formally elected Leader by the Party on 28 November 1979. As Richard Davis has argued, Hume represented 'the new tertiary-educated Catholic politician' whereas Fitt 'typified the older working-class activist'.[43] While Fitt had, initially, enormous influence at Westminster, Hume on the other hand had established close contact with senior political circles in Dublin and also 'influential Irish Americans, including Senator Edward Kennedy'.[44] Before Hume assumed the leadership he had spent several years of high-profile political activity in Westminster and Brussels. Unlike other contemporary Northern Ireland politicians, Hume's political personality had a distinct sense of 'internationalism'.[45]

From the beginning of Hume's leadership of the SDLP, the British were wary of dealing with him. The departure of Fitt, and Hume's subsequent elevation to the leadership of the Party caused some concern in British circles generally and the Northern Ireland Office (NIO) in particular. During Fitt's tenure as SDLP Leader, British Officials knew where they stood in Northern Ireland. Fitt's resignation was a demonstration of his inability to maintain his conviction that the SDLP would accept the principles of Atkins' Constitutional Conference.[46] James Prior, Northern Ireland Secretary of State from September 1981 to September 1984, has argued that Fitt and Devlin 'were working to remedy injustice rather than to peddle traditional Nationalist views'. Prior doubted Hume's abilities 'to be a strong leader'.[47] Hume's election to the European Parliament and his international experience with senior American politicians encouraged him to move outside the insular domains of Northern Ireland.

O'Leary and McGarry have argued that Hume 'despaired of an internal settlement, and began to build an international constituency to support his Party's position'.[48] Subsequently, as Rolston has pointed out, Hume mobilised 'support from political parties in the South' rather than negotiating directly with the NIO.[49] By the end of the 1970s, Hume had built up a considerable reputation in America and Europe as well as with the main constitutional parties in the Republic.[50] He became the 'sole conduit between the Northern Catholics and the major parties in the South' as Donald Akenson has pointed out, and if Hume 'does not approve of something, no Southern Government will touch it'.[51]

Some have described Hume as 'being less pliant and more Nationalistic' than Fitt;[52] others have disparaged his elevation to the level of 'Statesman' and they believe that Hume 'was completely incapable however of doing more than produce superficially new and attractive versions of what were in fact traditional nationalist notions'.[53] Hume felt that the British guarantee and the Unionist dependence on it were crucial problems in resolving the Northern Ireland conflict. Accordingly, he believed Unionists should 'believe in themselves as their own best guarantors in a future shared with the other people of the island of Ireland'. For the Unionists to ascertain the conditions for Irish unity, Hume encouraged the constitutional parties in the Republic to outline their definition and commitment towards unity.[54]

The Northern Ireland problem, according to Hume, was much deeper than a religious conflict. The core of the problem was identity. Hume defined unity as agreement between the people on the island of Ireland, diverted from the traditional interpretation of unity which emphasised geographical unity. Hume argued:

> '...Unionists define unity as the South taking over the North. Our definition has always been an agreed Ireland. What is the problem we are trying to solve? The problem is relationships. Until Unionists settle their relationship with the rest of the island to their satisfaction nothing is going to be stable. That is central to my philosophy throughout the last 25 years.'[55]

The mechanism for attaining Hume's definition of unity entailed a process of reform, reconciliation and reunification. Hence, the first priority in this process was to be the introduction of equality of treatment between both communities within Northern Ireland. Once this was established, it was argued, reconciliation between both parts of the island could take place, enabling a new Ireland to evolve.

Only through an Anglo-Irish strategy adopted by both British and Irish Governments could, the SDLP believed, this 'New Ireland' model be fashioned. In an article in *Foreign Affairs* Hume outlined what the Anglo-Irish strategy should be.

'[The Goverments] should first make it clear that there are no longer any unconditional guarantees for any section of the Northern community. There is only a commitment to achieving a situation which there are guarantees for all. Second, they should make it clear that there is in fact no particular solution as such, but only a process that will lead to a solution. They should declare themselves committed to such a process, a process designed to lead an agreed Ireland with positive roles for all. They should invite all parties to participate in this process, the process of building a new Ireland. Some groups will undoubtedly react with an initial refusal, but the process should continue without them, leaving the door always open for their participation at any stage.'[56]

By the end of 1979, Hume's experience in the international arena of America and Europe gave him a wider vision of how the Northern Ireland problem might be resolved. Of American politics, Hume claimed:

'In the United States, in spite of a deep difference of origin and background, they have formed a constitution which is able to harness great differences for the common good. Yet the Italians remain Italian, the Blacks are still black, and the Irish still parade on St Patrick's Day. They have created a unity in diversity.'[57]

Referring to Europe, Hume argued:

'Europe itself has suffered centuries of bloody conflict....Yet thirty-four years after the Second World War, as a result of an agreed process, they have been able to create one parliament to represent them, one community – and the Germans are still Germans, the French are still French. They, too, have a unity in diversity. Is it too much to ask that we on this small island do precisely the same thing? Is it too much to ask that these two responsible Governments begin to declare themselves now in favour of such a process? Can we too build a unity in diversity?'[58]

Hume was greatly impressed by European politics and the manner in which European institutions were evolving. John Duffy has pointed out, 'If a problem becomes irresolvable, change the context of the problem. That would have been how Hume viewed the Northern Ireland situation. It was irresolvable within its own boundaries, even within the boundaries of the whole island'.[59]

The essence of Hume's political philosophy was that the distinctness of the Unionist tradition could be accommodated in a 'New Ireland'. Hume argued that if Europe was able to accommodate ethnic minorities, a small island such as Ireland could successfully embrace its two traditions. He maintained that the removal of the British guarantee to the Unionists would engage that section of the community in genuine dialogue with the Nationalist community concerning future relationships within the island, thus allowing the diversity of both traditions to be accommodated. In 1988 he told the BBC,

'What the withdrawal [of the guarantee] means is that Unionists must negotiate their own future with the people in the North and the rest of Ireland. As long as Unionists have that guarantee, genuine dialogue will not take place because Unionists are going into the unknown. Genuine dialogue has never taken place between the two sections of the community here. It will only take place when that guarantee is gone. The goodwill which would generate from such dialogue would produce the type of Ireland we would all want to see – an Ireland with no one dominating.'[60]

Despite Hume's status of 'Statesman' in the Irish and international field of politics, he was not without his critics. Ivan Cooper has argued:

'In order for us to move forward politically within Northern Ireland, we need courageous men who will take courageous decisions and cross divide. John is not that way. John is not a leader in a divided society. He sticks too closely to the Church. He sticks too closely to the traditional line. He doesn't break new ice. He is not a leader.'[61]

For Cooper, Hume was more involved with the Irish dimension than with reaching out to the Unionist community in Northern Ireland. He criticised Hume for concentrating too much on the international scene rather than on domestic politics. As the 1980s unfolded, Cooper argued the SDLP became too closely aligned with Hume and lacked organisational democracy and pointed out, 'Hume likes to control everything. He always delegates to relatively safe lieutenants'. By the time he took over the SDLP at the end of 1979, Chris McGimpsey, an Ulster Unionist Councillor, believed Hume found local politics a waste of time. McGimpsey believed Hume's influence on the thinking of the SDLP was comparable to Paisley's predominance in the DUP, maintaining, 'A lot of the successes and prestige of the SDLP is built exclusively on the success and procedures of John Hume'.[62]

III

The Anglo-Irish Process

1980-1985

CHAPTER FIVE

Anglo-Irish Progress and Obstacles

By the beginning of 1980, the SDLP wanted to have the Northern Ireland conflict analysed as an 'Irish' problem. Since the collapse of Sunningdale, successive Government policies in Northern Ireland tended toward minimum involvement. The SDLP adopted a strategy of becoming 'persuaders' to get the Government to introduce an Irish dimension as part of an overall settlement: they strove for the two Governments to co-operate within an Anglo-Irish context with the objective of setting up a quadripartite conference which would involve both communities and the British and Irish Governments.

A major obstacle to establishing such a conference lay with the Unionist population. Austin Currie has claimed:

'Of the four parties, the Unionists would have the most to gain from participation in such a conference. Their lack of security, their crisis of identity is the kernel of the Northern Ireland problem. And who can blame them for that lack of confidence when, among other things, the basis of their cherished constitutional position rests on an Act of the British Parliament and is subject to party political bargaining at Westminster and elsewhere? The strength and durability of such commitments and guarantees can be gauged by the action of Ted Heath in 1972 in stripping them of their Stormont Parliament almost overnight.'[1]

Unionists felt their sense of identity was best protected by the British Government constitutional guarantee that Northern Ireland would remain a part of the United Kingdom as long as the majority of its citizens wished it. To the SDLP, this guarantee to the Unionists impeded any constructive political progress. Only when this veto was removed would Unionists be willing to negotiate as equal partners in resolving the Northern Ireland problem. Removing the Unionist veto, the SDLP reasoned, would make the way was clear for creating a 'New Ireland' with new institutions and increased cross-border development and co-operation.

Further, the Government support for the *status quo* in Northern Ireland was seriously contributing to lack of progress. Consequently, the SDLP sought external help from the Republic of Ireland, the EEC and the United States in its task of persuading the British Government to forego its support for the Unionist veto in Northern Ireland affairs. Also, they sought the setting up of a framework for a joint approach by the two Governments to resolve the crisis.

In the Republic, Jack Lynch resigned as Taoiseach on 5 December 1979 and was succeeded by Charles Haughey. Initially, Haughey's elevation led Fianna Fáil to revert to its 1975 hard-line position in relation to Northern Ireland. Haughey stated:

'We must face the reality that Northern Ireland, as a political entity, has failed and that a new beginning is needed. The time has surely come for the two sovereign Governments to work together to find a formula and lift the situation on to a new plane, that will bring permanent peace and stability to the people of these islands.'[2]

It was a position which re-stated the SDLP stance in relation to Northern Ireland.

Haughey/Thatcher Summits

On 21 May 1980, Charles Haughey and the British Prime Minister, Margaret Thatcher, held their first-full scale meeting in which Northern Ireland was discussed in depth. This initial meeting between the heads of two Governments was significant in that it focused the Northern Ireland problem at inter-governmental level. Also, it was consistent with the SDLP strategy that the Northern Ireland problem be resolved within an Anglo-Irish framework. The SDLP was delighted at Haughey's public identification of the British guarantee to the Unionists 'as the stumbling block' and 'immov[e]able object' in the Northern Ireland conflict.[3]

Seamus Mallon developed a close rapport with Haughey which had an influence on Fianna Fáil's Northern Ireland policy during the early 1980s. Mallon acknowledged that he did have some clout with Haughey. Mallon claimed:

'You had their [Fianna Fáil's] basic position which hadn't really been thought out. It started with Jack Lynch in 1973. They were working against substantial forces in their own party. It was essential that they were given a focal point in the North through the

SDLP to validate their changing position. Yes, I would have thought I had substantial influence on their thinking at that time.'[4]

Mallon echoed Haughey's strong attack on the British Government constitutional guarantee to the Unionist community in Northern Ireland, saying:

'The reality is that the Unionists will not move politically, or even enter into realistic discussion, while they have the prop of an assurance on their constitutional future. They must be told without any equivocation that Northern Ireland is not a viable entity. Consequently, the relationship between the North and South must be redefined as part of the process of creating stability within Ireland and producing harmonious relationships between both sovereign governments.'[5]

Although only at an embryonic stage, the Anglo-Irish process was beginning and five years later it crystallized in the signing of the *Anglo-Irish Agreement*.

The Anglo-Irish Summit held in Dublin on 8 December 1980 was a landmark in the Anglo-Irish process. The most important development from this Summit was the commissioning of 'joint studies covering a range of issues including possible new institutional structures, security matters, economic co-operation and measures to encourage mutual understanding'.[6] Hume described the Summit, 'as a significant advance and the framework within which a solution could be found'.[7] He regularly insisted that the Northern Ireland problem was not only about relationships within Northern Ireland, but also about relationships within the whole island of Ireland and between Britain and Ireland.

The initiation of a Commission for Joint Studies reflected the parallel developing strategy which the SDLP set out in its policy document *Towards a New Ireland*, endorsed at the 1979 Annual Conference. The document called for a joint British and Irish approach to Northern Ireland to resolve the conflict. A motion at the 1979 Conference was overwhelmingly passed stating:

'Conference...calls on the British and Irish Governments to agree to and promote a joint Anglo-Irish process of political, social and economic development within which the representatives of the two traditions in Northern Ireland would work in partnership towards the creation of peace, stability and lasting unity within Ireland.'[8]

Hume described the 1980 Summit as a 'significant and important milestone' on the road to a solution to Northern Ireland's problems.[9] He believed the summit provided the mechanism in which 'a framework within which a progressive process towards a solution could begin'.[10]

By the end of 1980, the SDLP was happy that its Anglo-Irish strategy to overcome the political impasse in Northern Ireland was finding some expression through the Haughey/Thatcher Summits. But the Party was disappointed with the outcome of Atkins' Constitutional Conference which demonstrated that the Government was still trying to resolve the Northern Ireland problem within the parameters of the Province itself. Despite this setback, the start of the Anglo-Irish process in 1980 placed the SDLP in a stronger position than it had occupied since the collapse of Sunningdale. In addition, the Party now had support from a Fianna Fáil administration in the Republic which boosted its morale and largely promoted its analysis and assessment of the Northern Ireland problem.

In contrast to the Unionist perception, the SDLP believed the Unionist identity could be more securely maintained within an all-Ireland framework than in a purely British context. Accordingly, any Unionist tradition would, in the main, be guaranteed if it was endorsed in an Anglo-Irish context by the two Governments. From the SDLP perspective, therefore, the Anglo-Irish framework was the only formula for attaining political momentum and getting the Unionists to abandon their political trenches. Sean Farren pointed out:

'The State's establishment as a product, in the first instance, of British colonialism in Ireland and, in the second, as a product of a form of Irish Nationalism which failed to adequately acknowledge a plurality of cultural traditions in Ireland, emerges as the basic issue in seeking a settlement....The one option which Britain is refusing at present to consider is that which goes to the core of the crisis, the colonial nature of the Northern Ireland state as presently constituted.'[11]

Sean Farren was one of the main authors of the policy document, *Northern Ireland – A Strategy for Peace* which was endorsed at the SDLP 1980 Annual Conference. The core of the document examined the British Government constitutional guarantee to the citizens of Northern Ireland. It pointed out that: 'It must be clear that for the British Government to claim that it has no longer any interest in remaining in Ireland while constantly reiterating and underwriting a guarantee which effectively blocks meaningful reform is a position which contributes nothing to achieving a settlement'.[12] The policy document reiterated the SDLP position that the responsibility for creating political progress lay with the British and the Irish Governments. A vital element to this new framework, for the SDLP, was a proper examination of the three sets of relationships at the centre of the conflict. These were between the two communities of Northern Ireland and between Northern Ireland and the Republic. The other important relationship was between Britain and Ireland.

Northern Ireland – A Strategy for Peace, sought a Constitutional Conference in which the two Governments could address the constitutional issue and possible structures for Anglo-Irish relationships. The SDLP envisaged a single unitary state, or a federal or confederal state, as the likely structures which would accommodate the two traditions. The document placed more weight on the federal system of government stating:

> 'The existence for sixty years of two political entities in Ireland, each with its own institutions and legal system, presents a strong case for considering a federal, or confederal constitution, based on these entities. Also, within a federal, or confederal arrangement the means whereby the estranged parts of Ireland could gradually learn to work together in partnership might be seen to be most effectively provided.'[13]

The joint studies commissioned by the two Governments at the December 1980 Summit in Dublin, included 'possible new institutional structures, citizenship rights, security matters, economic co-operation and measures to encourage mutual co-operation'.[14] However, the constitutional issue of Northern Ireland was not going to be part of that agenda. The Joint Studies set up under the December Summit were about institutional, not constitutional, matters. In effect, the constitutional issue still remained the business of the British Government alone. Nevertheless, the SDLP warmly welcomed joint studies, but felt that the scope of the new relationship between the United Kingdom and the Republic had a long way to go. Despite their limitations, they sat comfortably in the overall framework of SDLP policy.[15] However, the hunger-strikes throughout 1981 were a considerable setback to SDLP hopes of attaining their political objectives through joint London–Dublin co-operation.

The Hunger-Strikes: the Rise of Sinn Feín
The Republican prisoners at the Maze, formerly Long Kesh, were demanding political status. Political status had been granted to

Republican prisoners at Crumlin Road jail in 1972. The Labour Government had implemented a strategy of criminalisation which effectively meant that all such prisoners in Northern Ireland convicted after 1 March 1976 were to be treated as ordinary criminals without political status. Republican prisoners were unable to achieve their demands via the 'dirty protest'.[16] They adopted the new method of the hunger-strike to attain their objectives.[17]

The SDLP had been successful through its leader, John Hume, during the late 1970s, at placing international pressure on Britain to devote its efforts and resources to resolve the Northern Ireland conflict. The first hunger-strike started a decade later on 27 October 1980. The Government then made conciliatory overtures, and one of the prisoners was close to death, so the strike was called off. The prisoners believed that the Government, acting through an intermediary, was about to grant concessions to the prisoners; it was on this understanding that the strike was cancelled on 18 December 1980.[18]

The 1980s demonstrated that the SDLP was no longer going to support any political initiative purely within the parameters of Northern Ireland. A second hunger-strike initiated by Bobby Sands in March 1981 proved to be a major setback for the SDLP's initial enthusiasm towards the evolving Anglo-Irish process. Sean Farren, SDLP Chairman 1981-1986, recalled:

'The [second] hunger-strike derailed the Anglo-Irish process. We lost valuable time then. The hunger-strike had overtaken in a sense a process we were already engaged in. Although the hunger-strikes had started in the late [19]70s, they only reached their climax at the time we were articulating the principles on which we wanted to move things forward politically within the North. They created tension within the SDLP in terms of whether we should fight or not fight various by-elections. But nonetheless, we kept our eye on the ball in terms of what we felt needed to be done at inter-governmental level.'[19]

The hunger-strikes succeeded in generating intense emotion in the Nationalist community. The image of Irishmen dying of hunger in British prisons aroused instinctive traditional Irish sympathies. Denis Haughey, criticised Government policy on the hunger-strikes, and alleged, 'Had the British Government pressed on with that kind of arrogant insensitive policy there was a real danger of emotions taking over. We were conscious that the British attitude to the hunger-strike was creating an electoral base for movement in Nationalism'.[20] Alex Maskey of Sinn Féin recalled, 'There was a view within Sinn Féin towards the end of the [19]70s, that we needed to broaden the struggle as we saw it. One way of doing that was electoral politics, but it was a minority view. The hunger-strike jettisoned the thought process on that. We had to enter electoral politics whether we liked it or not. It was no longer an issue for discussion, it had to be dealt with'.[21]

The hunger-strikes raised major difficulties for the SDLP which were the first direct challenge to their control of the minority community vote; they brought the Party into competition with Sinn Féin, which became politically active from the start of the second hunger strike on the 1 March 1981. Austin Currie believed the hunger-strikes gave Sinn Féin support it would not otherwise have obtained.[22]

During the first hunger-strike, Hume had played a major role as a mediator between the Republican prisoners and the Government. Hume has said:

'I assumed I was the only person that was talking to them. I had spoken to the spokesperson for the hunger strikers and he told me specifically what would settle it. That is what I specifically put to Mr Atkins which conformed with a specific proposal I had been making for some time out of the situation. I rang the Secretary of State and he told me, I'm sorry, but we couldn't accept your proposals. Although in my discussions I had with him, I had the clear impression he accepted them. But I then discovered when I turned on the news that someone else had gone into the prison.'[23]

This duality of strategy by the Government towards the hunger-strike damaged SDLP faith in the Government.

The two by-elections in Fermanagh-South Tyrone in April and August 1981 following the death of Independent Socialist, Frank Maguire and the death of hunger-striker, Bobby Sands, caused immense difficulty and division within the SDLP. In the first by-election on 9 April the SDLP was in a double-bind – wanting to contest the election, but wary of splitting the Nationalist vote. It was left to the Party Executive to decide what strategy to adopt: '...after voting sixteen-to-three to put up a candidate, its decision was reversed by eleven-to-eight a week later, when Noel Maguire, a brother of Frank, promised to oppose Sands as an independent'.[24] Reacting to the SDLP decision in relation to the Fermanagh-South Tyrone elections, Seamus Mallon claimed, 'I accept that it was a bad decision but I feel that to have run would have been much worse...we put our hopes, foolishly perhaps, in Maguire, with whom we had come to an agreement, that if he stood we would step down'.[25]

In the 1979 General Election, the SDLP decided not to put forward a candidate in the Fermanagh-South Tyrone constituency. The Party felt that, were it to put up a candidate alongside an Independent, then a safe Nationalist seat would fall to the Unionists. But Austin Currie defied the Party executive decision not to forward a nomination for the area. He decided to run as an Independent against the outgoing MP, Frank Maguire. Currie lost to Maguire and resigned his position as Chief Whip of the SDLP. In addition, the Party removed Currie from the post of Party Spokesman on Housing and Constitutional Matters.[26] Currie paid for his actions in 1979: he was not even considered as a nominee for Leader, Deputy Leader, or Chief Whip in the SDLP when Fitt left the Party.

In 1981 Currie, who had originally been nominated to represent the SDLP in case Noel Maguire stepped down from his candidacy, had been prepared to run as an Independent, as he had done in 1979. Without informing Currie of his intentions, Maguire withdrew his nomination as SDLP candidate forty-five minutes into the one-hour limit permitted before candidates could retract their nominations, thereby leaving a clear contest between Bobby Sands and the Unionist candidate, Harry West. Currie was therefore excluded from the contest. It reflected the absence of SDLP abilities to anticipate political moves in their own party.   Another major embarrassment for the Party was that SDLP Fermanagh District Councillor, Tommy Murray, signed the nomination papers of Bobby Sands for the Election. In this instance, the SDLP were indirectly assisting Sinn Féin. This incident caused a lot of chagrin and internal friction in the Party.

Among the key members of the SDLP who were opposed to the Party not entering the contest in Fermanagh-South Tyrone were Austin Currie, Joe Hendron, Sean Farren and Paddy O'Hanlon. Hume defended the Party decision not to put forward an SDLP candidate because Noel Maguire had put himself forward already. There was a groundswell of support for Maguire among the local SDLP grass-roots. Mallon has maintained:

'I felt the Party should not contest the election on the basis of the divisions of the party in the area whether to contest...the vote for Currie was only a narrow victory and many of those who opposed his candidature vowed not to back his election campaign...I felt contesting the seat could split the Party in the area and advocated abstention.'[27]

In addition, the SDLP was aware that the Local District Elections were being held in June 1981. They felt that if they were seen to support the Government stance on the hunger-strike, their electoral support in the minority community could suffer significantly. The final result of the Fermanagh-South Tyrone by-election gave Bobby Sands 30,492 votes and Harry West 29,046 votes, a result which gave the Republican movement a major boost.

On 5 May 1981, Sands died after sixty-six days on hunger-strike. Bobby Sands' funeral was attended by over one-hundred thousand people and was given extensive coverage by the international media. The SDLP knew that Provisional Sinn Féin was beginning to represent the voice of the minority community in Northern Ireland. They had received international sympathy and support for their cause at a level never anticipated by the SDLP. The hunger-strike became the impetus for Sinn Féin to enter the political arena at the expense of the SDLP.

The SDLP withdrawal from the Fermanagh-South Tyrone contest did immense damage to the moderate image of the Party. It portrayed the SDLP as a 'green' Nationalist party in the eyes of the Unionist community. Eddie McGrady felt it was a mistake for the SDLP not to put forward a candidate in the two by-elections in 1981.[28] Mallon has pointed out that the hunger-strikes had a bearing on SDLP decisions at this time. He said 'it was a totally no-win situation. We had to be aware quite literally of the physical safety of people. It wasn't that we all didn't want to fight the election, but the physical safety of those who would have to fight it was an overriding consideration.'[29]

From the Unionist perspective, the SDLP's passive approach towards the by-elections placed the Party in the same camp as Provisional Sinn Féin. The results of the Fermanagh-South Tyrone by-elections demonstrated that the majority of the Catholic population in Northern Ireland, at the very minimum, gave tacit support to the hunger-strike campaign.

Relations between the SDLP and the Government also deteriorated during the period of the hunger-strike. The SDLP had strong allies in the United States and Europe, and with the main constitutional parties in the Republic. Yet the Party felt increasingly marginalized and ineffective in its dealings with the British Government during 1981. Margaret Thatcher, in her memoirs criticised the SDLP and recalled, '...the SDLP was losing ground to the Republicans. This was a reflection not just of the increasing polarisation of opinion in both communities, which it was the IRA's objective to achieve, but also of the general ineffectiveness of the SDLP MPs'.[30]

Despite Thatcher's strong Unionist instincts,[31] Hume met the Prime Minister in London on 13 May 1981 to persuade her to compromise in handling the hunger-strike. He attempted to warn her about the hunger-strikes, and that they, 'could endanger democratic institutions North and South, as well as swelling IRA support in America [but] she played down its importance.[32]

A General Election in the Republic on 11 June 1981 returned two hunger-strikers to the Dáil. While Hume's advice was ignored by the British Prime Minister, the Taoiseach, Garret FitzGerald, was able to persuade Margaret Thatcher of the need to bolster the SDLP position in the Catholic community because of the serious threat Sinn Féin posed to the stability of Ireland as a whole. These were the issues which lay behind the signing of the *Anglo-Irish Agreement* in 1985.[33]

Bobby Sands' death created a second by-election seat on 20 August 1981 which was won by Owen Carron who had worked as Sands' election agent in April. This second by-election caused as much controversy for the SDLP as the first one. According to Seamus Mallon, the SDLP Executive recommended the Fermanagh-South Tyrone seat should be contested. The Party's Constituency Selection Convention opposed this decision.[34] While there was understandable pressure on the SDLP leadership to contest the seat, the democratic machinery built into the Party Constitution meant that the Executive could not overrule the decision taken by the Constituency Selection Convention.

The SDLP gave conflicting signals about the stance it was going to take at the second by-election. Following an SDLP Central Council Meeting after the first controversial by-election, the Party decided it would fight all future elections. Events leading up to nomination day for the April by-election led Hume to comment, it had been 'a crash course for the public in the real meaning of a "unity" candidate' and he also observed, 'It is now clear that never again will there be any pressure on the SDLP to agree to such a candidate. The whole notion of a unity candidate has been an albatross since 1974. However, that albatross has gone now and that has been one positive outcome of the last week'.[35] Despite strong assurances that the Party would put up a candidate at the next by-election, the SDLP reversed its position in the face of the impending election. Dr Brian Turner, one of the minority Protestant members resigned from the SDLP. He wrote to the *Irish Times* stating that thirty-thousand Catholic people were prepared 'to vote for shooting their neighbours in the back' and he felt betrayed by the SDLP decision not to contest the Fermanagh-South Tyrone by-election in August 1981.[36]

Owen Carron won the by-election, increasing Sands' earlier vote by 786, to 31,278, with a higher electorate turn out of 88.6 per cent. Gerry Adams, then Provisional Sinn Féin Vice-President, publicly declared that candidates from his party would contest all seats in Northern Ireland 'to emerge as the undisputed leaders of the Nationalist community'.[37] The SDLP refused to accede to the Sinn Féin demand for the Party to withdraw from local councils as a demonstration of their support for the H-Block campaign. Relations between the SDLP and Sinn Féin were, to put it mildly, pugnacious, during the hunger-strike era. Sean Farren, SDLP Chairman, attacked Sinn Féin for what he described as its 'blatant betrayal of true Republicanism' and stressed: 'Opposition to the Fascism of the Provisionals will be maintained and upheld by the SDLP'.[38] Alternatively, Sinn Féin believed that if John Hume held office, he would have been in favour of promoting internment.[39] Maskey recalled:

'There were people within the SDLP at that time, who would have interned us very quickly. Because there was a lot of political tension and pressure, people were saying we must have some sort of a settlement. As a result of that, I have no doubt, there would have been people within the SDLP who would have been quite prepared to have interned us if they could have got a relationship going with the Unionist party of the day for seats in a Stormont parliament.'[40]

The SDLP had supported the humanitarian dimension of the hunger-strikers' demands. They called on the British Government to display greater flexibility in its attitude to the hunger-strike, a request largely reiterating the position recommended by the European Commission on Human Rights.[41] As the H-Block campaign developed throughout 1981, the SDLP took a firm and condemnatory stance towards the National H-Blocks Committee who were the main organising body working on behalf of Republican prisoners. The SDLP had reasons to suspect the IRA and the INLA were an integral part of the Committee. Hume strongly attacked the Committee stating: 'Lives of human beings, whether their own members or victims of their campaign, are considered to be expendable in the pursuit of political objectives. We disagree with that campaign'.[42]

To damage the credibility of the SDLP Sinn Féin revealed that a series of secret meetings had taken place between senior members of the SDLP and Sinn Féin about the future of Nationalist politics in Northern Ireland. Sinn Féin representation at these talks comprised Danny Morrison and Joe Austin. The SDLP was represented by John McAvoy, Chairman of Newry and Mourne District Council, and Seamus Mallon. Seamus Mallon met Danny Morrison and Joe Austin in early December 1980 to discuss the hunger-strike crisis. In addition, Hume met Danny Morrison and Martin McGuinness on 26 December 1980 for discussions on the general political situation in Northern Ireland. Subsequently in July 1981, Hume met Jimmy Drumm and Eamon McCrory of Sinn Féin in Derry to discuss the deteriorating political situation caused by the hunger-strike.[43] The leak of the SDLP/Sinn Féin talks further discredited the SDLP within the Unionist camp.

By the time the hunger strike was called off on 3 October 1981, the SDLP position as the sole voice of the minority community in Northern Ireland was compromised. Sinn Féin, by storming the political arena, posed difficulties about voting patterns among the minority community for the SDLP. But in another sense the SDLP was in a less vulnerable position than it had been since its genesis in 1970. It was successful during the 1980s in forging cohesive links with the main constitutional parties in the Republic and promoting the Anglo-Irish process.

By the beginning of the 1980s, Hume had been successful in mobilising international support in favour of SDLP policies. In Britain too, there had been a major shift in British Labour Party policy towards Northern Ireland. At its 1981 Annual Conference, the British Labour Party accepted its National Executive Committee decision to accept Irish unity as a long-term objective. The National Executive called for a power-sharing arrangement as an interim measure and also for closer co-operation between Britain and the Republic of Ireland,[44] effectively ending the bipartisan roles in Northern Ireland which had existed under the Conservatives. This shift in Labour Party Northern Ireland policy heralded a parallel approach to the SDLP strategy in Northern Ireland. No doubt, Hume's close rapport with Kevin McNamara, a member of the Parliamentary Labour Northern Ireland Committee from 1974–1979, had considerable influence on Labour Party Northern Ireland policy.

Prior and Rolling Devolution Proposals

On 2 July 1981, Secretary of State, Humphrey Atkins proposed an Advisory Council made up of currently elected representatives. The

Council was to be composed of fifty representatives from Westminster, the European Parliament and District Councillors.[45] The Council was to scrutinise Government departments and proposed legislation. It was also to evaluate Government political initiatives on the future of Northern Ireland.[46] Atkins' proposals were rejected by the SDLP. As the hunger-strikes had exacerbated the polarisation between the two communities in Northern Ireland it was now virtually impossible for the political parties to agree to any model of an interim settlement.

Atkins was replaced by Jim Prior as Secretary of State on 13 September 1981. In his initial appraisal of the political situation in Northern Ireland, he wrote in his autobiography,

'The Unionist parties, both OUP and DUP alike, made it equally clear to me that they were not prepared to accept the form of "power-sharing" which had been introduced in 1973. They did not believe that it was possible to run an effective Government in which some members were unsympathetic to remaining part of the UK. And the Nationalists made it equally plain that they required both a form of power-sharing and a much closer relationship with the Republic of Ireland, often referred to as the "Irish dimension". '[47]

Prior's initial talks with the SDLP about his plans for devolution in Northern Ireland stimulated some optimism within the Party. During these deliberations with the SDLP, reference was made to an American-style executive having distinct and separate powers from an Assembly. Hume has explained:

'The executive would initially be led by the Secretary of State and he would appoint from inside and outside the Assembly a broad-based administration. The Assembly itself would have separate powers and would be constructed along congressional lines with strong committees and powers of investigation....I think Mr Prior is considering getting rid of junior ministers and replacing them with Northern Ireland people, but doing it in such a way that it cannot be vetoed by any party....The proposal is that he can appoint ministers from inside or outside the Assembly so that if a party in the Assembly says it will not serve, this would not bring down the assembly, as happened in 1974.... He would simply replace them with other people from outside the Assembly. These people could, of course, be British Ministers, but they could also be Northern Ireland citizens who were not elected to the Assembly'.[48]

Such proposals could only be welcomed by the SDLP as they meant in essence that a power-sharing executive could not be boycotted or brought down as had happened in the 1974 experiment. In theory, perhaps, the British Government could have used this mechanism to reverse the SDLP decision that an internal solution for Northern Ireland was no longer attainable. Subsequent developments brought about by the British Government throughout 1982 however, confirmed the SDLP view that an internal solution to the Northern Ireland conflict was obsolete.

As early as February 1982, it became clear to the SDLP that Prior was abandoning the concept of a US-style cabinet or executive and opting for 'rolling devolution'.[49] Prior remarked:

> 'A problem with the SDLP was that at one point during my talks I had said that I was considering my approach more akin to the American Cabinet system, whereby Ministers would not need to be members of the legislature. The Secretary of State might choose his own Ministers: they would be part of the Secretary of State's executive and, as such, answerable to the Assembly, although not necessarily members of it....I think this together with the committee system in the Assembly, might have proved acceptable to the SDLP....Unfortunately, when I told the SDLP at my next meeting with them that I had to drop this idea, they appeared to be tremendously upset and virtually accused me of having acted in bad faith.'[50]

As Prior's proposals unfolded during 1982, the SDLP interpreted the Government initiative as only vindicating the Unionist position and dismissing the legitimacy of the Irish dimension. The abandonment of an Irish dimension in Prior's *White Paper* in April 1982 had been due to the direct intervention of Margaret Thatcher, as Prior recorded in his autobiography,

> '... although the suggestions which I made for greater co-operation with the Republic of Ireland fell well short of the arrangements which had been agreed at Sunningdale between the British and Irish Governments in 1973, they were too much for her. She insisted that the separate chapter on Anglo-Irish relations in my draft should be scrapped, and a less positive version incorporated at the end of the chapter on "The Two Identities" in Northern Ireland.'[51]

He also claimed that Thatcher, 'relied almost entirely upon Ian Gow, who gave her hard-line Unionist advice, which was utterly disastrous'. Thatcher professed in her autobiography, 'My own instincts are profoundly Unionist'. Of Prior's devolution proposals, she recalled, 'Before publication, I had the text of the *White Paper* substantially changed in order to cut out a chapter dealing with relations with the Irish Republic and I hoped, minimise Unionist objections'.52

To the SDLP, Prior's 'rolling devolution' proposals were evading the heart of the Northern Ireland conflict and consolidating the innate sectarianism which was already embedded in the Northern Ireland State. Sean Farren pointed out the substance of the SDLP position as to Prior's initiative:

'What Mr Prior and his advisers at Stormont and Westminster wilfully ignore is that remedies built upon the essentially undemocratic foundations on which Northern Ireland itself rests will merely perpetuate instability and frustrate genuine efforts at reconciliation....When successive British Governments reiterate the so-called constitutional guarantee to Northern Ireland they are simply reinforcing these undemocratic foundations and underscoring their own partisan involvement in the crisis. They do so because despite claims that this guarantee simply respects the democratic wishes of the majority, they ignore how this majority was contrived at in the first place. So however much Britain may wish to deny that its involvement in Northern Ireland is "neutral" so long as this position is maintained, so long will real progress be retarded. Unionist parties can continue, as they are clearly doing now, to reject with impunity all attempts to establish partnership Government.'53

Prior's devolution proposals were adumbrated in a Government *White Paper* published on 5 April 1982. The SDLP welcomed part three of the proposals which acknowledged the nucleus of the Northern Ireland conflict. Paragraph 17 of the *White Paper* stated, 'The difference in identity and aspiration lies at the heart of the "problem" of Northern Ireland; it cannot be ignored or wished away'.54 As far as the SDLP was concerned, the extent of the initiative went no further in accommodating the Irish dimension of the conflict. The *White Paper* did not contain any practical guidelines as to how the Irish dimension was going to be integrated into the overall initiative. The Irish dimension was not going to be facilitated through Prior's internal devolution proposals for Northern Ireland. Prior suggested that the Irish dimension for the non-Unionist section of the Northern Ireland community would be administered through a parliamentary tier of the Anglo-Irish Council. However, any administration would be on the basis that both Governments agreed to proceed with the Anglo-Irish Council at parliamentary level.

The SDLP rejected Prior's proposals largely because they were an exclusively internal initiative that failed to give the Irish Government an essential role along with the British Government to create the necessary framework for a political settlement in Northern Ireland. The British Government still viewed the Anglo-Irish process as a framework only for fostering co-operation in areas of mutual interest between the Republic and Northern Ireland. The constitutional issue of Northern Ireland was perceived as an internal matter for the United Kingdom Government only. The way forward politically, to the SDLP, was for both Governments to unite in drawing up a framework in which the political parties within Northern Ireland could secure agreement. It was only through the development of an Anglo-Irish process that the SDLP thought the constitutional conundrum could be solved.

John Hume issued a press release on 26 April 1982 vehemently attacking Prior's *White Paper*. He quoted the Secretary of State's distinct integrationist comments in the House of Commons on 5 April 1982. Prior had said, 'I believe that our proposals are the most likely to tie Northern Ireland into the United Kingdom'.[55] Again there was nothing to assure the SDLP that the Irish dimension was going to receive equal recognition by the British Government. Hume said, 'I think it quite amazing that the said proposals, which are virtually for the Government of a particular area, should go through without searching public discussion, either in Britain or any part of Ireland'.[56] Hume maintained that the Assembly was not addressing the overall problem and would be just the same as all the previous British initiatives.[57]

The SDLP saw the proposals as a move to integrate Northern Ireland with the United Kingdom to appease the Unionist community. Government policy was therefore a contradiction in terms. It acknowledged that the nature of the Northern Ireland conflict lay with differences in identity and aspiration. Yet the Secretary of State proclaimed integration in the House of Commons. Prior maintained:

'I have always acknowledged the problem of those in the North who have an identity with and a desire for an all-Ireland arrangement. As long as they work for that peacefully, they are perfectly entitled to do so. However, we must make it clear that they are part of

Northern Ireland and any parliamentary body which the House might decide to have must be seen within the context of Northern Ireland as part of the United Kingdom.'[58]

The SDLP was unenthusiastic with Prior's scheme for devolution. It viewed the rolling devolution proposals as an indication that the Government was reducing its level of commitment to the Anglo-Irish process. Both the SDLP and the Irish Government believed that Prior's devolution plans for Northern Ireland were doomed to failure. An internal solution to the Northern Ireland conflict without an Irish dimension was totally unacceptable to the SDLP. Seamus Mallon, speaking to the Irish National Council, stated:

'As in the Northern Ireland Convention and the Atkins'[s] Conference, Mr Prior's plan now asks us to submerge our political conviction that a lasting solution can only be found in an Irish context and in doing so to reinforce the reality and consequences of partition to which we are fundamentally opposed. We are being asked to give our consent to be governed in a constitutional framework which by definition is exclusively British and by yet another administrative system which is based on Unionist majority rule.'[59]

Mallon had already stated a case for the need for effective co-operation at an earlier date:

'The British Government attempt to find a solution could fail if Anglo-Irish developments were not pursued and if the claims of the non-Unionist and non-British section of the community were not recognised.'[60]

Prior announced on 14 July 1982, that elections to the new Assembly would take place on 20 October 1982.[61] There was considerable anger in the SDLP as to which strategy was best suited to the Assembly Election challenge. The SDLP believed Prior's rolling devolution proposals were so devised that there was a real danger of a majority rule system of government returning to Northern Ireland. The *Irish Times* indicated that Austin Currie, Paddy O'Hanlon, Joe Hendron, Sean Farren, Eddie McGrady, Denis Haughey and Frank Feeley were initially in favour of participating in the Assembly to show up the intransigence of the Unionist position. In an interview Austin Currie recalled that, 'the SDLP had been formed to fight elections...' and said,

'That is not to say that anybody in the Party looks forward to participating in the Assembly. We would prefer that it was not there, but we have to face reality. ... It would be impossible to overestimate the dangers inherent in the Assembly to all of the Nationalist tradition in the island and to the minority in Northern Ireland. The Unionists of all shades will ensure that it will provide a vehicle towards turning back the clock to prior to 1969 and 1972. We could have a situation where all the gains of the Civil Rights Movement and the SDLP over the years are in jeopardy. That is why the Assembly elections are so important.'[62]

From Currie's perspective, for the SDLP to contest the election on an abstentionist position 'would be to revive the very principle of old-time Nationalism that the SDLP was set up to repudiate'.[63] He suggested, 'We should have fought the election and gone into the Assembly at an early stage and put down a motion in favour of power-sharing. If we had been defeated on that, to have withdrawn. If we had have withdrawn [*sic*] we could perhaps have brought the thing down!'[64] Correspondingly, Joe Hendron maintained, 'We made a mistake. We fought the elections, but didn't take our seats. I calculated that at the time we lost one million pounds. There was definitely division over whether you stand and fight the election, and after that, whether you took your seat or not. We should have taken our seats in the Assembly, and put down a motion on power-sharing which undoubtedly would have been chucked out. Then you could have walked out with some dignity Also, you could have been on salaries without going near the place.'[65]

By contrast, Denis Haughey recalled, 'We were not going to participate in an Assembly where mechanisms existed which could have led to a restoration of majority rule. Once done it could not be undone. Those were the rules that Prior devised. We were not going to lend validity to that by participating in it.'[66] Hume's personal preference was 'to go into the Assembly, challenge the Unionists on power-sharing right away and walk out'.[67] The ultimate vote of the Executive and the Constituency Representatives came to twenty-five votes in favour contesting the elections, but not taking their seats in the Assembly, while fourteen people voted for a total boycott. Paddy Duffy, Michael Canavan, and Hugh Logue along with Seamus Mallon supported a total boycott of the Assembly.[68] Paddy Duffy and Michael Canavan representing the extreme 'green' section of the Party refused to stand as SDLP candidates in the election, and stood down from the Party Front Bench.

Seamus Mallon argued:

'Since 1978, we had been calling for moves on the Anglo-Irish front and these had made a tentative beginning in 1980. ...I wanted to encourage these talks rather than legitimise Prior's plan. ...I felt that a total Nationalist boycott by our party, the IIP and Sinn Féin would embarrass the British Government and show up the plan for what it was, a failure.'[69]

Seamus Mallon's decision to back the democratic wishes of the Party was an important factor in maintaining the unity of the party. With Mallon's support, Hume was able to sustain a concerted and unified strategy by the SDLP towards the Assembly elections.

The SDLP had its first direct political challenge from Sinn Féin which had decided to fight the Assembly elections too. Richard McAuley, a leading member of Sinn Féin, said, 'We intend to negate the SDLP claim that it represents the Nationalist population'.[70] Sinn Féin have argued that if their party had decided not to fight the 1982 Assembly elections, the SDLP would still have participated in Prior's Assembly. Sinn Féin considered the SDLP a subservient political organisation, forever willing to engage in talks with the Government and participate in its internal initiatives. Maskey has suggested that Prior's Assembly:

'...could have endangered stabilising the North of Ireland. We went into the Assembly elections on the basis that we would not take our seat, and that no Nationalist should take their seat. The SDLP adopted the same position. We believe that basically scuttled the Assembly. In other words, it scuttled an internal Northern Ireland solution....Sinn Féin have criticised the SDLP for entering every political initiative for talks and discussions. That would be our biggest criticism with the SDLP over the years. Our view was that unless those talks were all-inclusive, they were destined to fail. We believe SDLP participation was giving encouragement to the British Government. They were able to say on the one hand, that they were negotiating with Nationalists, whilst at the same time, in our view, putting quite a repressive regime in place for the rest of us. Therefore, we criticised the SDLP for being involved in those initiatives.'[71]

Eddie McGrady has disputed the Sinn Féin assertion that it influenced the SDLP decision not to take their seats in Prior's Assembly. He has insisted:

> 'What happened there had nothing to do with Sinn Féin or any-body else. Having had the experience of the Assembly and the Convention, we said this scenario is going to be more of the same. It won't work because it is not addressing the real problems. Its going to be another barking/talking shop. We didn't want anything to do with it. I think Prior thought we were bluffing. He made his announcement irrespective of our representation. In fact, contrary to our representation.'[72]

Following this line of argument, the SDLP absence from Prior's Assembly was not influenced by Sinn Féin strategy. Rather, it reflected a SDLP frustration with Prior. The SDLP might have been enticed to attend the Assembly, if the Government had set up the parliamentary tier of the Anglo-Irish Council. With no sign of an Anglo-Irish dimension to Prior's initiative however, the SDLP adopted a hard-line position against the 'rolling devolution' proposals. Hume asserted:

> 'We are saying to the British Government it is time you faced the real problem if we are ever to get a real solution. ... Northern Ireland was created for the Unionists. They are the only people who can make it work. There are only two ways for them to do so. Majority rule, which they have discredited, and partnership, which they reject. All British Government solutions have been based on an attempt to make Unionism work.'[73]

Hume said British Government strategy and Unionist intransigence continued to be the main impediments to any political progress in Northern Ireland. Regarding Prior's devolution proposals, he argued, 'In 1973 they were firmly for power-sharing and a real Irish dimension. Then they quietly tried to drop the Irish dimension. Now they are offering, not power-sharing, as of right, but power-sharing only on the basis of it being guaranteed by Unionists.'[74] Brendan McAllister, a member of the SDLP Newry branch who had been newly elected to the Party Executive, resigned from the SDLP over its Assembly Election Manifesto:

> 'Since the end of the 1976 Constitutional Convention, our Party has undergone a process of conversion such that its credibility as a

moderate political party has been undermined. This process of 'greening' has been embodied in the call for a British declaration of intent to withdraw, a call for the removal of the constitutional guarantee to unionists and most recently by the publication of the SDLP's Manifesto for the Assembly elections. In demanding a quick end to the proposed Assembly the party is abdicating its responsibility as set out in its constitution to pursue its objectives within a Northern Ireland context ...' .[75]

While 1981 was perhaps the most challenging year for the SDLP since its formation in 1970, the year 1982 proved to be an arduous and turbulent period for the Party. The SDLP had placed much hope in the Anglo-Irish process as a strategy to have their policies adopted by the British and Irish Governments. Two Anglo-Irish Summits, in May and December 1980, demonstrated to the SDLP that the issue of Northern Ireland was at last being addressed in an Anglo-Irish framework.

The SDLP eagerly anticipated another Anglo-Irish Summit scheduled for November 1981. On 11 June 1981 Garret FitzGerald took up the position of Taoiseach of a new Fine Gael and Labour Coalition Government in the Republic. On 6 November 1981, FitzGerald met Margaret Thatcher at a Summit in London. This was a momentous meeting at which it was formally announced that an Anglo-Irish Inter-Governmental Council was to be established. Both leaders 'agreed that it would be for the Parliaments concerned to consider at an appropriate time whether there should be an Anglo-Irish body at parliamentary level ...'.[76] FitzGerald, like his predecessor Charles Haughey, believed that the Northern Ireland problem could best be resolved within an Anglo-Irish context. FitzGerald told the Dáil on 10 November 1981:

'... with respect to new Anglo-Irish institutional arrangements, I should like to recall the genesis of this concept. The view that the problem which all of us in Ireland face must be resolved in the context of progress in the wider arena of Anglo-Irish relations was made explicit in 1979 both by my own party in its policy document, "Ireland-Our Future Together" and in the SDLP document *Towards a New Ireland – A Policy Review*.

Be it said to the credit of the SDLP, a Party too frequently criticised nowadays for narrowness of approach, that they presented the concept primarily as a method designed to resolve the anxieties of the Unionists rather than as a means to advance their own political priorities. In fact they conceived of the Anglo-Irish institutions as a network of dialogues through which North-South exchanges would be conducted, as it were, across a United Kingdom table....The intention, in short, was to create confidence and thus over time to facilitate dialogue; it was not to create institutions which would in themselves produce constitutional change.'[77]

The constitutional issue of Northern Ireland was not officially within the terms of reference for the Joint Studies initiated at the 1980 Summit. The Anglo-Irish Council established by the November 1981 Summit in London provided the blueprint for potential Dublin involvement concerning the affairs of Northern Ireland, through an envisaged Anglo-Irish inter-parliamentary body.

Political developments in the Republic had immense consequences for SDLP strategy towards Prior's devolution plans during 1982. The entire Anglo-Irish process suffered a considerable setback when the Government in the Republic collapsed unexpectedly on 27 January 1982 over the issue of a controversial tax on children's clothing set out in the Government budget proposals. In the subsequent General Election in the Irish Republic, a Fianna Fáil administration was returned to power on 18 February 1982 with Charles Haughey re-elected as Taoiseach. Barry White has commented that the, '...Anglo-Irish initiative provided a lifeline, as Hume had hoped when he helped launch it, suggesting that constitutional politics could still deliver the goods. Haughey's tendency to oversell its implications for unity was a constant worry, but the potential for growth was there.'[78] If FitzGerald had remained in office his administration would probably have encouraged the SDLP to take part in Prior's Assembly. FitzGerald recorded:

'...it seemed to me that it was not for us in Dublin to sabotage this honest, if somewhat unimaginative, attempt to get the political process in Northern Ireland restarted. Accordingly I issued a statement describing it as the first attempt in many years to tackle the fundamental problem of bringing about devolved Government in Northern Ireland on a basis that would secure the interests of both sections of the community there...'. [79]

This was in sharp contrast to the stance taken by Haughey's Fianna Fáil administration from February 1982. Fianna Fáil circles felt that Prior took advantage of the political instability in the Republic during the period between the collapse of FitzGerald's Government on 27 January 1982 and the new Fianna Fáil administration on 9 March 1982 to steam ahead with his proposals, using the time to draw up a British Government initiative which embodied no direct input from political circles in the Republic.[80] In the event, from the SDLP point of view, the *White Paper* which was published on 5 April 1982 was predisposed to the Unionist position and did not embrace the Irish dimension.

When the new Irish administration took over office in March 1982, the final seal of Prior's initiative was almost complete without any role left for participation from the Irish Government. In reaction, the SDLP secured a hard-line stance from the Fianna Fáil administration which vehemently opposed the Assembly proposals. The SDLP lobbied for Anglo-Irish structures to go into operation parallel to the seventy-eight-seat Assembly, as well as a 'meaningful' role for the minority.[81] A statement issued after a meeting between the Taoiseach, Charles Haughey, and senior members of the SDLP in Dublin on 22 March 1982, illustrated how Fianna Fáil policy towards Northern Ireland echoed the SDLP position. It stated that:

'Both sides considered that the proposals as they were emerging were unworkable. They found them deficient in that they concentrated on the details of an administration for Northern Ireland, without due regard for the broader dimensions of the problem. ...They shared the conviction that...progress should be pursued in present circumstances through the further development of the Anglo-Irish process initiated between the Taoiseach and the British Prime Minister at their meeting in December 1980.'[82]

Crisis in the Falkland Islands on 2 April 1982 contributed to deteriorating relations between the British and Irish Governments. After the sinking of the *Belgrano* by a British submarine with the loss of three-hundred and sixty-eight lives, the Haughey administration withdrew their co-operation from EC Member States who were implementing economic sanctions against Argentina. This caused strong anti-Irish feeling in Britain. If anything developed from the Falklands' War, it was a strengthening of the Unionist position. Prior recorded that the Unionists 'were not slow to point out that if we could send troops to protect one-thousand four-hundred Falkland Islanders, who wished to remain part of the United Kingdom, we should certainly do absolutely everything we could to help the million or so Unionists in Northern Ireland, who also wished to stay in the United Kingdom'.[83]

Britain declared that matters in Northern Ireland were the internal responsibility of the United Kingdom Government. In July 1982

Margaret Thatcher re-asserted, '...that no commitment exists for Her Majesty's Government to consult the Irish Government on matters affecting Northern Ireland. That has always been our position'.[84]

CHAPTER SIX

The New Ireland Forum Report

Council for a New Ireland: the SDLP Vision

By the middle of 1982, the Anglo-Irish process initiated by both Governments was in tatters. For the SDLP, 1982 marked the dismantling of the Anglo-Irish process, rather than a step in its evolution. The British Government withdrawal of its level of commitment to Anglo-Irish relations was greeted with alarm in SDLP circles. The impetus to introduce what became known as the New Ireland Forum arose as a consequence of the breakdown in the Anglo-Irish process. Relations between both countries remained sour as a result of the Falklands' Crisis.

The other important factor which blocked SDLP strategy towards the end of 1982 was the forthcoming Assembly elections on 20 October. The SDLP plan for developing the concept of a council for a 'New Ireland' was an ingenious strategy, at a time when Anglo-Irish relations was at an all-time low. It enabled the SDLP to exercise their influence with the political élite in the Republic and the Party were able to fashion SDLP philosophy and ideology to integrate it in the political mainstream in the Republic.

In the Republic Fianna Fáil sources in the Republic would claim that the idea for a Council of Ireland was originally their inspiration, identifying a meeting between the Irish Independence Party and Fianna Fáil in May 1982 as the origin of that plan. Fianna Fáil informed Hume of their idea so that he could use this formula as a focal point for the Assembly elections in October 1982.[1] Fianna Fáil envisaged the Council as a progressive Nationalist vehicle to establish the basis for negotiating a final settlement to the conflict with the British Government and the Unionists. The Council was also intended as a tool facilitating the SDLP role in a more proactive sense than ever before, as well as an alternative to the Assembly.[2]

Once the Assembly elections concluded in October 1982, the SDLP wanted the Anglo-Irish process to recommence as this was the best means to have their policy of a new Ireland realised by both Governments. For the SDLP 'rolling devolution' was never going to be a reality, as Unionists were opposed to the principle of power-sharing at executive level. Subsequently, the Assembly was based on an internal framework in Northern Ireland, which over-ruled the SDLP position that the conflict could only be resolved on an Anglo-Irish basis.

Rather than proceed with the Assembly elections on an abstentionist ticket, the SDLP focused on seeking a mandate from the electorate to introduce a Council for a New Ireland. Hume recalled that it was a scheme to make Irish Nationalists in the South reconsider their opinions; 'Up to then it was just the usual slogans'.[3] The SDLP Manifesto for Prior's Assembly elections stated:

'The Anglo-Irish framework is therefore the proper framework for a solution. It is long past the time when the British Government should allow its policies to be dictated by the intransigence of Unionism. It is also for those who believe in a New Ireland to spell out their proposals in some detail. Towards that end it is the intention of the SDLP following the election to propose to the Irish Government the setting up of a Council for a New Ireland made up of members of the Dáil and those mandated in this election. The Council should have a limited life and have the specific task of examining the obstacles to the creation of a New Ireland and producing for the first time on behalf of all the elected democratic parties in this country who believe in a New Ireland, an agreed blueprint so that a debate on real alternatives can begin within the Anglo-Irish framework.'[4]

Subsequently, by the end of 1982, SDLP efforts were concentrated on eliciting support from the main constitutional parties in the Republic for an all-party Council specifically addressing the issue of the North. The SDLP wanted all the constitutional Nationalists on the island of Ireland to consider how the Unionist tradition would be preserved in a New Ireland. The Council was to act as a preparatory forum in which the two Governments could draw up the necessary framework for this 'New Agreed Ireland'. Following another sudden General Election in the Republic, on 25 November 1982, Garret FitzGerald was returned as Taoiseach, leading another Fine Gael and Labour administration.

At the SDLP Annual Conference in 1983, delegates reaffirmed the Anglo-Irish framework as the basis for finding a solution to the Northern Ireland problem.[5] Another conference motion censured the Assembly and demonstrated the Party's determination not to take part in what they described as a 'meaningless charade'.[6] Hume wanted the

Council to be an arena in which the SDLP, along with the main constitutional parties in the Republic, could define an Irish identity which would incorporate the Unionist tradition in some way. Hume acknowledged that: 'This means that democrats in the South and in the SDLP must find the humility to acknowledge that we have so far failed to conceive of and to define an Irish identity which adequately accommodates all traditions of this island'.[7]

The SDLP had emphatically reiterated their opposition to an internal solution to the Northern Ireland problem by the beginning of 1983. From the SDLP viewpoint, Northern Ireland was not a 'geographical, natural or socio-political entity' and as Sean Farren believed, 'Northern Ireland has never had the social and political cohesion necessary to make it a viable entity'. He has added:

'... Nationalists favour power-sharing because, in the short-term it is their only guarantee of a meaningful role in political decision-making in their own land. In the longer-term they see it as a way of building trust between both communities in order to ensure a peaceful evolution towards some form of Irish unity. Therefore, it was through the Anglo-Irish process that the SDLP believed that the identities and aspirations of both traditions could be properly accommodated. In particular, this framework assimilates the sovereignty of both communities within Northern Ireland which lies at the heart of the problem. In addition, the SDLP wished to see the New Ireland Forum as the basis of a negotiating document which the British Government could use for resolving the Northern Ireland conflict.'[8]

SDLP internal documents influence Forum Conclusions
The main purpose of the Forum was to make a major impact on British thinking and to reinvigorate the Anglo-Irish process. The launch of the Forum on 11 March 1983 stemmed from the zeal of John Hume in his efforts to present the first major reappraisal since partition of the Nationalist position within the thirty-two-counties. It had the potential to be radical in that it sought to establish an all-Ireland framework which would embrace the Unionist tradition. The SDLP Executive and Constituency Representatives Group met in Gweedore, County Donegal, on the weekend of 9–10 April 1983 to discuss the Party's formal negotiating position for the Forum proceedings. The Party prepared three discussion papers prior to their final report.

The first paper, 'The Anglo-Irish Dimension of the Forum' was prepared by Denis Haughey. He argued that from the outset that the SDLP should view the Forum as a mechanism to 'make a major impact on British thinking'. The biggest dilemma for the SDLP was how to get the British Government to act on, 'the outcome of the Forum's work'. Haughey suggested that the report should include 'a fundamental critique' of the British position on the Northern Ireland question and give 'an unapologetic exposition of its weakness'. He added, '...we must see to it, that the Forum presents a constructive challenge to the validity of the 1920 settlement itself'. He set out five prime objectives for the Forum to expose:

1. The discriminatory implementation of partition and its social, economic and political consequences.

2. The futile repercussions of partition on British financial and security resources.

3. A direct challenge over the British guarantee to the Unionists 'on the basis that its apparent democratic nature is a sham'.

4. The reality that Northern Ireland is not a purely internal United Kingdom concern.

5. The 'advantages to Britain of a settlement which would achieve unity and harmony in Ireland'.[9]

These principles were fundamental to the main body of the report.

In a second paper from the Gweedore weekend, Sean Farren drew up a list of questions for the Party to address the conflicting issues of pluralism and protection for minority communities in Ireland and their constitutional implications in a new 'agreed' Ireland. The Party's task was to identify what kind of constitutional recognition and protection could be given to minority communities in Ireland. In a New Ireland the SDLP had to determine whether 'constitutional provisions' of 'basic Human Rights' had to be directed under the moral guidance of the main Churches in Ireland or based on a 'secular framework' such as the United Nations *Declaration of Human Rights* or the *European Convention on Human Rights*.[10]

Again, in a third paper written in July 1983 Sean Farren pointed out that the proposals presented at the Forum would form the basis for future discussion with the British Government and the Unionist parties.

Farren spelt out that Britain was not neutral in its presence in Northern Ireland and was, '...in fact supporting a sectarian state' by only recognising the wishes of one of the two communities within Northern Ireland. He argued that 'Britain's presence is part of the problem' and there could be no resolution until this problem was addressed. Farren acknowledged that the *Forum Report* would not bring about an immediate solution but would '... provide a new and more realistic basis for progress than anything that has been done since 1973–74'.[11]

Hugh Logue, a member of the SDLP Forum Study Group prepared a fourth paper entitled *The New Ireland as a Unitary State*. The 'New Ireland' had to embrace a new consciousness of unity reflecting 'maximum flexibility and negotiation'. He argued that unity was not 'an assimilation of the North into existing structures' or a dilution of respect for 'Unionist apprehensions' but that Unionists 'remaining as a single political force would have diminished'. He proposed that the constitution should 'grant all rights under the United Nations Charter of Human Rights....All other provisions for family, moral, social rights [were] to be provided for in State law'. In his proposals harmonisation between North and South was to take place in different spheres over different time-scales. Financial, legal and key service areas were to converge within a five-year time-scale. The new State was to retain membership of the European Economic Community and the United Nations. An Anglo-Irish Council was to be created dealing with 'matters of mutual interest'. The paper recommended the amalgamation of the Royal Ulster Constabulary and the Garda Siochana as a single police force.[12]

One of the central difficulties with Logue's paper was his failure to outline the specific role of the Anglo-Irish Council. If Unionists were to accept a unitary state they would have to maintain a significant institutional link with Britain and the Anglo-Irish Council would have to play an essential role between them. The difficulty with Logue's unitary proposals – as with any put forward for a single state – was the assumption that Unionists would accept this constitutional scenario. Naturally the *raison d'être* for the existence of Unionism would have disappeared so the Unionist 'need to assert and defend their separateness would have dissolved'. However, throughout the course of SDLP history, the Party identified Irish unity in the short-term as an unrealistic objective.

A fifth internal paper for the Forum negotiations examined SDLP views on *Joint Sovereignty*. The new paper was based on *Towards a*

New Ireland previously prepared in 1972. A fundamental change from the 1972 document was the exclusion of a National Senate of Ireland whose formal role was one of facilitating harmonisation between North and South with the prime objective of Irish unity. Creation of a National Senate made 'the 1972 scheme essentially an interim one'. The SDLP acknowledged in the fifth discussion document that interim plans were 'inherently unstable'; in this document the Party had moved from its position of calling for an interim settlement to arguing that joint authority could be a permanent solution. It reinforced the principle of power-sharing by avoiding any return to the former system of Stormont majority rule. The other change from the Party position on joint sovereignty as outlined in 1972 was that security was not to remain solely with the sovereign powers. A power-sharing government would not enable any one 'national group' to dominate security measures. The document stated 'there seems little point in depriving the Northern Ireland Government of policies that some might call essential to any institution that could be called a Government'.[13]

A sixth discussion document examining overall SDLP strategy to the Forum pointed out that the main purpose of the Forum was to induce the British away from their current policy 'of political non-intervention' and a military maintenance of the *status quo* and to move them towards, 'dialogue...political movement [and] change'. The SDLP strategically saw the report as having three objectives: '[First to] describe a range of options which could be adopted to meet the needs of the situation. Second, to describe a range of options but plump for one as the "preferred option". Third, to describe the broad principle which must be the basis for any settlement and leave the form unspecified.'[14]

The Forum was a platform for the SDLP and the other main Nationalist parties in Ireland to discuss what shape Irish Unity should take in a 'New Ireland'. It was to provide the basis from which to move forward in North-South and in Anglo-Irish relations. Hume saw the Forum as an opportunity to construct a cohesive Northern Ireland policy between Fianna Fáil and the coalition parties of Fine Gael and Labour. Such an achievement would be vital given the long-standing animosities between FitzGerald and Haughey. Fianna Fáil favoured a British withdrawal from Ireland as the dominant priority for the British strategy to resolve the Northern Ireland conflict. However, the coalition parties stressed the necessity for reconciliation within Ireland as the initial prerequisite for any solution. From the SDLP perspective, the Forum was attempting to get the British to address sectarianism in

Northern Ireland. Farren remarked, 'It will serve no purpose for the British Government to pretend that its presence in Northern Ireland is simply a "peace-keeping" one. Britain's presence is part of the problem and there will be no solution if Britain fails to acknowledge this fact.'[15]

A seventh SDLP pamphlet *The Fundamental Problems* was leaked to the press during the summer of 1983: 'The publicity was unintentional, but the response was good, and Hume's analysis was to form the basis of the future work of the Forum, being carried over into the final report'.[16] In this discussion document, the SDLP believed that there were four areas of agreement between the main parties of the Forum:

- First, the British Government needed to reassess its history of involvement in the conflict, and the practice of sectarianism within the Northern Ireland State. Also, it needed to address its failure 'to accommodate the Nationalist position'.

- Second, the Nationalists needed to appraise their inability 'to convince the Unionist population and the British Government of the merits of the Nationalist aspiration'.

- Third, the paper noted that 'the principal reasons why the structures of Northern Ireland do not work is the fact that they deny to the Nationalist section of the community within Northern Ireland an adequate involvement in decision-making and an adequate symbolic and administration expression of their Irish identity and aspiration'.

- Fourth, the SDLP paper addressed the need to acknowledge 'the problems posed by Loyalists in any new structures'.

According to the SDLP, these four principles were at the hub of the crisis and provided the basis from which the Forum should embark. All options had to be open to resolving the conflict. Significantly, this marked a departure from the traditional Nationalist concept of negotiating a purely unitary state. The initial question which the Forum had to address was: 'why...constitutional Nationalist politicians have hitherto not succeeded in persuading Britain to reassess its own position adequately'?

The same paper discussed the need for constitutional Nationalists to attempt to understand the Unionist tradition. It acknowledged that Nationalists would have to spell out in financial terms how much the 'New Ireland' would cost the present Irish Republic. Also, the Forum would have to address the ways in which necessary adjustments to the Irish constitution regarding moral and religious matters could take place. A large section of the paper addressed the complexity of Unionism and its resistance to inclusion in an Irish State:

> 'Loyalism, as a self-proclaimed repository of Protestant values and experience in Ireland, claims to embody a particular set of moral and philosophical values epitomised by the notion of liberty and individual conscience. This, is set against a Protestant view of the Roman Catholic tradition as being authoritarian and centralist and as valuing individual judgement as far less than is the case under the criteria that emerged from the Reformation. The Loyalists therefore claim that their heritage comprises elements of political loyalty to Britain and a system of philosophical and moral principles both of which are incompatible with their perception of the identity, heritage and aspiration of nationalist Ireland.'[17]

The task for the Forum, therefore, was to redefine the traditional idea of 'Irishness' which would accommodate both the British and Protestant constituents of the Unionist tradition. The paper suggested that the Forum should aim to measure Irish unity 'ideologically, symbolically, economically, politically and socially'. It specified that Irish unity from the SDLP perspective implied 'agreement freely arrived at by the two traditions in Ireland'. This radical approach initiated by the Forum prompted the question: is there an inclusive sense of Irishness which accommodates both the Unionist and Nationalist viewpoints? Another question raised by the paper was what role would Britain play 'in sustaining these structures'?

In an eighth discussion paper towards the Forum negotiations the SDLP considered a settlement based on three models; a United Ireland; Federal Ireland; or a Confederal Ireland. Any one of the three models had to be based on the geographical political divisions created by partition in Ireland. The main reason for examining a settlement on a geographical basis was the sense of 'reassurance that the values, beliefs and way of life which partition was intended to protect would still be afforded' to the Unionists. From the Nationalist viewpoint, a 'change in the framework of relationships with the rest of Ireland' would encourage this community 'to give its allegiance to the Northern State then seen as no longer an alien imposition'. The paper addressed some of the difficulties involved in the continuation of the two States in Ireland. To maintain Northern Ireland as a separate State 'without provision for power-sharing in some form, safeguards in the all-Ireland Parliament and administration might not be sufficient to prevent a continuation of the kind of socio-political tensions experienced in the fifty years of Stormont rule'.[18]

A United Ireland, the first option outlined in this paper, would allow devolved powers to a local administration within Northern Ireland under the control of a local assembly. 'Westminster powers over Northern Ireland would be "transferred" to Dublin and Northern Ireland representation in an all-Ireland Parliament determined on an agreed basis commensurate with the degree of autonomy to the Northern State.' It was envisaged that an all-Ireland Parliament, as already conducted in the Republic, would govern the twenty-six counties 'with the additional responsibilities for the defence, security and external relations of the whole country'. Legislation would be introduced to provide a separate assembly for maintaining Northern Ireland. In addition, provision would be made to safeguard minority rights. An Anglo-Irish Council would provide the necessary institutional framework to express the 'British heritage' of the Protestant tradition. Harmonisation of particular services would be implemented in an all-Ireland context. But, no 'formal relationship between Church and State in either part of the country' would take place.

The second option discussed in this paper was a Federal Ireland. 'The main case for this model would appear to rest in the equal status which it would confer on the two States in Ireland.' The powers contained within the old Stormont Government would provide the basis for negotiating the system of government for Northern Ireland. New central Government powers 'would be those with a clear all-Ireland function, defence, foreign affairs, taxation, customs and excise, external communications, all-Ireland security and court system.' The structure and composition of the central Parliament and Government were still problems to be addressed. For instance, should the Parliament be bicameral or unicameral? The paper suggested that the Head of State in a federal settlement should be 'chosen alternatively from within each state, possibly by its assembly'.

As a third option, the SDLP argued that a Confederal State would have strong parallels to that of a Federal Ireland. The essential difference would be the high level of autonomy and independence each State would have. 'The attraction of such a basis to a settlement must be greatest to those of the Unionist-Protestant tradition who desire the least possible contact with the rest of Ireland. Its attraction to the Nationalist community would only be in the degree of representation which it could achieve in the all-Ireland Parliament/Council and Government. Power-sharing within Northern Ireland in this arrangement would seem to be highly desirable if not essential.' This paper noted that: 'All-Ireland structures and their powers would be severely limited in a confederal arrangement. A Council of Ireland might be a more appropriate title than Parliament...'. The Council's powers would be restricted to external defence, foreign affairs, customs and excise, limited aspects of all-Ireland security and the provision of an all-Ireland court, again with limited jurisdiction: 'The emphasis which the other models would place on integration and harmonisation would be considerably less in this arrangement.'

The Forum Report: a move away from traditional Nationalism or SDLP Rhetoric?

Garret FitzGerald, re-elected as Taoiseach in November 1982, was originally opposed to Hume's Council of Ireland proposals as simply a Nationalist forum. FitzGerald wanted the Unionist tradition integrated into the Council of Ireland proposals. Terms of reference were changed in order to attract the Unionists into the discussions. 'From Hume's perspective, the agenda drawn up for the Forum was more-or-less what Hume wanted to achieve.'[19]

Despite FitzGerald's desire to ensure Unionist involvement in the Forum, he felt the emergence of Sinn Féin into the political arena had to be immediately countered. In his autobiography he recorded:

'I had come to the conclusion that I must now give priority to heading off the growth of support for the IRA in Northern Ireland by seeking a new understanding with the British Government, even at the expense of my cherished, but for the time being at least clearly unachievable, objective of seeking a solution through negotiations with the Unionists.'[20]

In addition, Peter Barry, Minister for Irish Foreign Affairs, openly conceded that he wanted to:

'... defend the interests of the Northern Ireland minority and in particular to support the elected representatives of the minority who reject violence as a means of achieving political progress...The SDLP has been consistently supported by the Northern Ireland minority over the last ten years and deserve all the support and encouragement we can give them.'[21]

By June 1983 FitzGerald had been able to persuade Margaret Thatcher of the possible demise of the SDLP. She noted:

> 'I had a meeting with Dr FitzGerald at the European Council at Stuttgart in June 1983. I shared the worry he expressed about the erosion of SDLP support by Sinn Féin. However uninspiring SDLP politicians might be—at least since the departure of the courageous Gerry Fitt—they were the minority's main representative and an alternative to the IRA. They had to be wooed.'[22]

The political threat that Sinn Féin might eclipse the SDLP was not taken seriously by the British Government until the end of 1983. Secretary of State, Jim Prior, expressed concern as to whether the SDLP could stop the advance of Sinn Féin. He said that, at worst, the Provisionals might turn Ireland into 'a Cuba off our Western coasts' and expressed concern that Sinn Féin could render the SDLP obsolete in the next Local Government Elections; '...that is why we must do all we can to strengthen constitutional Nationalism in the meanwhile'.[23] The Ulster Unionist Leader, Jim Molyneaux said that no-one could rescue the SDLP from 'the results of their own mistaken policies' or arrest the slide within the Nationalist community from the SDLP to Sinn Féin.[24]

The year 1983 was a difficult one for the SDLP as it attempted to defend its political position against the rising tide of popularity for Sinn Féin. At the SDLP Annual Conference in January 1983 delegates recommended fighting all seventeen Westminster seats. This denoted a reversal in their position from the former Fermanagh-South Tyrone by-elections, but this strategy enabled Unionists to win seats where the Catholic vote was split between the SDLP and Sinn Féin. Acrimony between Sinn Féin and the SDLP was too great to set about any electoral pact between the two parties in areas with a Nationalist majority. Sinn Féin was confident that it could displace the SDLP as the main political voice of northern Nationalists and described the SDLP as a 'party in decline'.[25]

The SDLP used the British General Election on 9 June 1983 as an opportunity to focus the attention of the electorate on the New Ireland Forum discussions. Seamus Mallon said: 'Our aim is to rescue the name of Irish unity from those who have sullied it....that is the battle going on in this election'.[26] The Party manifesto repeated earlier SDLP statements that the British Government and Unionist politicians 'lie at the root of the deadlock which has paralysed politics in the North of

Ireland'.[27] It rededicated Party efforts to the Forum as the best means of providing a blueprint for peace and stability in Ireland. During the election campaign, there were several ugly attacks on the homes of SDLP members and Party Offices in the Falls Road which, according to media reports, were traced to Sinn Féin supporters.[28] The four SDLP candidates for Belfast in the Westminster elections strongly challenged the Provisional IRA and Sinn Féin, pronouncing that: 'Sinn Féin and the Provisionals were Fascists and Mafia who had undermined the fabric of society in Belfast'.[29]

In the General Election on 9 June 1983 John Hume won the Foyle seat. Eddie McGrady was defeated by Enoch Powell in South Down by 548 votes. Seamus Mallon lost Newry and Armagh to Jim Nicholson by 1,554 votes. Gerry Adams with 16,379 votes and a majority of 5,445 over SDLP candidate Joe Hendron won the West Belfast seat. Danny Morrison for Sinn Féin was narrowly defeated in Mid-Ulster by the William McCrea of the Democratic Unionist Party. Overall the SDLP obtained 17.9 per cent of the poll, gaining 137,012 votes. This was down from 18.8 per cent of the poll which it held at the 1982 Assembly Elections with a total of 118,891 first-preference votes. The worrying factor for the SDLP was the increase in Sinn Féin's share of the vote which increased from 64,191 first-preference votes representing 10.1 per cent of the poll in the 1982 Assembly Elections, to 102,701 votes or 13.4 per cent in the General Elections.[30]

In a sense, the Irish Government came to the rescue of the SDLP through the New Ireland Forum. Padraig O'Malley has argued that 'the Forum became a political tool to undermine support for Sinn Féin'.[31] Farren has also insisted:

'I think a democratic government had a duty to arrest the rise of Sinn Féin, given that they were very committed to the armalite and the ballot box at the time. The danger of subversion in the South was very real. However, they were responding to policies which we had articulated. The Forum gave us in the short-term a boost in terms of being seen to be delivering on our mandate. We had gone into the 1982 elections asking for a Council for a New Ireland. FitzGerald claims credit for being instrumental in establishing the Forum, but the idea had come from us. He was the immediate cause if you like of the Forum, but the idea had come from us. Our concept of it was an exclusively Nationalist Forum and always was. We justified it by saying that Nationalist Ireland had to get its act together.'[32]

For FitzGerald's Coalition Government, the New Ireland Forum was a preparation for the *Anglo-Irish Agreement* which was designed to arrest the growth of Sinn Féin. The SDLP had already drawn up their own policies in the late 1970s for a joint cohesive Nationalist strategy to establish a proper framework for resolving the Northern Ireland conflict and the Southern parties in 1983 were merely responding to this.

The final *New Ireland Forum Report* was a compendium of earlier SDLP discussion documents and represented the SDLP analysis of the Northern Ireland problem. To the SDLP this report represented a consensus among constitutional Nationalists for the right of Unionists to be and remain Unionist and stay British. It recognised that Nationalism could only succeed through its readiness to respect and accommodate the British identity of the Unionists and their links with Britain. Some sections of the report appeared to represent a shift from traditional Nationalism in an openness to a pluralist society in a new Ireland: new social democracy within a new future Ireland would accommodate the Protestant tradition, so that '...their cultural, political and religious belief can be freely expressed and practised'.[33] This signified considerable progress in Nationalist thinking. The Irish nation was no longer being defined as a Catholic nation. Sections of the report dealing with 'plurality' and changes to the Irish constitution had definite strains of SDLP philosophy; the report mentioned that 'a new Ireland will require a new constitution which will ensure that the needs of all traditions are fully met'.[34]

The themes set out in Chapter Three of the *Forum Report* which examined the origins of the Northern Ireland problem had already been set out by the SDLP in its paper *The Anglo-Irish Dimension of the Conflict* in April 1983. This was a traditional Nationalist analysis of the Irish problem. It highlighted the ways in which Nationalists in Northern Ireland had been denied their identity since partition. The report traced the evolution of the Unionist power bloc in Northern Ireland and how it deliberately discriminated economically and socially against the Nationalist community. British Governments had been blamed for creating the structures in Northern Ireland which denied Nationalists the opportunity to express their Irishness. Indeed, the origin of Ireland's trouble, according to the *Forum Report* had been the result of 'imposed division of Ireland which created an artificial political majority in the North'.[35]

As Kevin Boyle and Tom Hadden have maintained:

'The credibility of the *Forum Report* would have been greatly increased by an honest acknowledgement that, allowing for the different size and circumstances of the minorities in both parts of Ireland after 1920, the record of intolerance and disregard for other than the majority interest was broadly similar both North and South of the border.'[36]

The constitutional Nationalist interpretation of who was to blame for the Irish problem remained unchanged. The report failed to move away from traditional Nationalist grievances against Britain. A more impartial historical account showing the shortcomings of the Republic towards Northern Ireland since partition would have given the Forum more credibility. Nevertheless, the whole concept of joint authority was a departure from traditional Nationalism. For the first time since partition, constitutional Nationalists were willing to recognise the British identity in Northern Ireland of the Unionist tradition. Although it was not an entirely democratic solution, it nonetheless heralded a radical rethinking of traditional Nationalism.

The Forum appeared, at first reading, to be a radical attempt to present a new wave of Nationalism. There were, however, many difficulties with its attempt to accommodate the Unionist tradition because it emphasised the Unitary State option. The authors of the report claimed to recognise the difference between Protestants and Catholics but, in essence, still called for a break in the links with Britain. Although the general tone of the report appeared modern, social trends in the Republic during the 1980s were largely conservative and influenced by the power Catholicism still wielded in the Republic. Divorce and abortion referendums in the Republic demonstrated the influence of the Catholic Church on social and moral issues. Brendan McGarry and John O'Leary pointed out that 'if Nationalism can equally accommodate other traditions, and if it allows for a composite ideology, then it will no longer be the exclusivist ideology of the past'.[37]

At the launch of the final *Forum Report* Garret FitzGerald stated that the 'Unitary State' was merely the preferred option of the parties to the Forum. He said that all the parties were willing to discuss the other two options and indeed any other proposals that emerged as the framework for an institutional arrangement for a new Ireland. A short time later Charles Haughey was in the same seat saying that the 'Unitary State' proposal was not an 'option but a conclusion', that the proposals on joint sovereignty and federation had no status at all, and would not lead to peace and stability.[38]

Haughey represented the face of traditional Nationalism in the stance he took on the unitary option. It was only a matter of time before

Haughey demonstrated that he did not respect the Unionist position. Despite guarantees to the Unionists in the *New Ireland Forum Report* stating, 'that the new Ireland which the Forum seeks can only come about through agreement and must have a democratic basis'[38] Haughey stressed at a press conference after the launch of the report that Unionist consent only applied 'to the particular structures of unity, not to the principle itself'.[39] Such comments did irreparable damage to the status of the Forum as a new force in Nationalist thinking.

Democracy, consent and respect for the Unionist position seemed to be irrelevant to Haughey. Padraig O'Malley maintained that Haughey believed it was a British duty 'to coerce the Unionists to the negotiating table, even if that meant going behind their backs'.[40] For Brian Girvin the *Forum Report* was, 'notable for its failure to deal with the concept of Britishness in any fundamental way. By emphasising traditional Nationalist fundamentalism the forum clearly lost an opportunity to face up to its own myths'.[41] To Arthur Aughey, 'constitutional Nationalism is revealed once again as discounting all that Unionism means, and as understanding democracy in a way which takes account only in passing of the majority in Northern Ireland'.[42] Often the report has been interpreted as a defence of traditional Nationalism simply because of the emphasis on the 'Unitary State' as the preferred option. On the other hand Paul Arthur has pointed out that the unitary state option was preferred, 'partly as a gesture to traditional Fianna Fáil policy but actually in obeisance to the aspirational rather than the operational'.[43]

Fine Gael, the Irish Labour Party and the SDLP were willing to discuss the concepts of a federal and confederal state, or joint authority with the British Government. Moreover Boyle and Hadden argued that FitzGerald, Spring and Hume 'repeatedly stressed the open-minded nature of the report and laid emphasis more on the list of "realities and requirements" – notably the need to accommodate both traditions – that were identified as essential to any lasting settlement than on any single option'.[44]

From the Unionist position, Chris McGimpsey has maintained:

'The way the Forum was set up did not entice Unionists. You were going to have what was going to appear to be Unionist parties going down to Dublin with no involvement through the UK Government; Dublin, the SDLP and the Unionist parties sitting down to negotiate the future of Ireland. There was no way that was going to happen!

The report itself I thought was extremely disappointing. My

brother and I were the only two members of the party who went down to Dublin and gave evidence. Really, we felt they just ignored everything we said. We found that a severe disappointment.'⁴⁵

The publication of the *Forum Report* presented difficulties for the SDLP in that the 'Unitary State' option was credited to all the Forum parties. Ironically, Sinn Féin generally welcomed the overall recommendations of the report. Alex Maskey of Sinn Féin has recalled:

'The Forum itself came out with the Unitary State as the preferred option. We could not object to that. We would have supported the unitary state model undoubtedly. Our position was we would basically have looked at anything. We actually took a lot of succour from the fact that even although we were excluded, that the preferred option was for a "Unitary State". The one criticism we had of the Forum was that it went nowhere. No one acted upon it which was the difficulty.'⁴⁶

The underlying SDLP motivation for the New Ireland Forum was to articulate a coherent constitutional Nationalist argument in relation to Northern Ireland with the objective of engaging British attention. Denis Haughey maintained, 'The Forum was a means of getting a consensus view on the Irish Nationalist side and presenting it to the British in such a way that it was impossible to ignore it'.⁴⁷ Assessing the *Forum Report* in the House of Commons on 2 July 1984, John Hume said, 'The most important aspect of the report is not the three options, but the views of the Irish Nationalists about the ways in which realities must be faced if there is to be a solution. We also say that we are willing to examine other ways of accommodating those realities and requirements.'⁴⁸ For Hume, as for the SDLP, the Forum's task was to elucidate the realities of the Northern Ireland problem and regarded chapter five of the report as the central basis of requirements to enable political progress to evolve. Hume felt that Charles Haughey had misrepresented the *Forum Report* by his emphasis on the Unitary State.⁴⁹

The *Forum Report* illustrated the British Government crisis-management strategy as the contributing factor to the sense of alienation experienced by the minority community in Northern Ireland. There were expectations in the SDLP that the *Forum Report* might stimulate the British Government to develop new structures and institutions in an Anglo-Irish framework. In particular, the SDLP hoped for progress on the Anglo-Irish front after the London Summit between the two Heads of Government in November 1984. Hume argued, 'It [i]s impossible for the parties of Northern Ireland to reach agreement in the context in which they are operating because they are in a strait-jacket. The Northern Ireland problem represents the failure of Britain and Ireland to sort out their relationships. They have been backed into a corner and that corner is called Northern Ireland.'[50] He anticipated the London Summit between FitzGerald and Thatcher in November 1984 would advance the Anglo-Irish process and pointed out, 'I do not expect anything dramatic to happen at the Summit. But I would expect either the beginning of a new process or a considerable development of the Anglo-Irish process initiated in 1980 by Mr Haughey.'[51]

The Brighton bombing of 12 October 1984 in which the Provisional IRA almost murdered the entire Thatcher Cabinet at the Conservative Party Conference hardened the Government stance against the Nationalists' alleged sense of alienation in Northern Ireland. The initial British response to the *Forum Report* after the Anglo-Irish Summit at Chequers on 19 November 1984, was a serious blow to the SDLP. It was here that Margaret Thatcher made her famous comment, 'out, out, out' to all three options proposed by the *Forum Report*, and this posed a potentially disastrous setback to Anglo-Irish relations. To the SDLP, British rejection of the report had the capacity to fuel Sinn Féin's popularity with the minority electorate, since the SDLP Forum proposals could be interpreted as having failed to change the British Government position on Northern Ireland. Yet, the Anglo-Irish Inter-Governmental Council was still in place. This meant that Anglo-Irish relations could still work through the machinery of the Council.

Seamus Mallon responded angrily to the famous press conference in which Margaret Thatcher made her comments, describing her remarks as 'insulting, provocative and offensive to all Irish people' and claimed:

'Alienation which is a lack of consensus and perception that the institutions of the State were created and are for the benefit of only one community, is a cancer which pervades every facet of life in Northern Ireland. The very concept of Northern Ireland is based on alienation and on the subjugation of those of the Irish tradition to those of the British tradition. Every single available indicator – from election results to opinion polls showed that the communities were further apart than at any time in Irish history. Northern Ireland is simply not viable and is sick onto [*sic*] death.'[52]

Hume was equally hostile to the British Government in the immediate aftermath of Thatcher's rejection of the Forum proposals. Hume retorted:

> 'There is now no credible, political force on the Unionist side in Northern Ireland which will accept anything short of majority rule or which will agree to any form of political recognition of the Irish identity of the minority. We may yet be driven to the conclusion that no serious business can be done with this particular British Government. The Nationalist minority in the North has outgrown the Northern State. The British Government may still prevail over us. But they should bear this in mind: You do not have our consent. You have never had our consent. All your military might cannot force our consent.'[53]

Overlooking SDLP anger towards the British Government the Ulster Unionist, Harold McCusker, described the Forum as 'dead and buried'.[54]

Unionists initially held out hopes that the SDLP would take their seats in the Assembly even after Thatcher had dismissed the *Forum Report*. In the Republic, Charles Haughey took advantage of FitzGerald's humiliation. He alleged that the *Communiqué* issued after the Summit 'reflected an abject capitulation to a new British intransigence and craven desertion of the principles of the Forum report.'[55] Like the SDLP, Haughey believed the British Government attitude towards the *Forum Report* demonstrated its support of the Unionist veto over political progress in Northern Ireland.

Despite this grave setback to Anglo-Irish relations, the SDLP remained totally opposed to any British Government initiative which did not encompass direct Irish Government involvement. Consequently by the end of 1984 the prospects for political progress in Northern Ireland looked bleak. The SDLP believed that a federal solution was an unrealistic solution in the short-term: they fixed their sights on the possibility of a 'joint authority'. The best outcome the SDLP could hope for was one hinted at by the new Secretary of State, Douglas Hurd, that the Irish Government, at best, could have a consultative role in Northern Ireland affairs.[56] Hurd rejected the alienation thesis put forward by the SDLP.

At the European Council in Dublin Castle on 3 December 1984, the Taoiseach, Garret FitzGerald and the British Prime Minister, Margaret Thatcher agreed that Anglo-Irish relations would resume on a firm basis through the Anglo-Irish Inter-Governmental Council.[57] It was through this mechanism that both Governments were committed to search for a new political framework acceptable to all sides in Northern Ireland. Although damage had been inflicted by Margaret Thatcher at the press conference on 19 November, at the end of 1984 Anglo-Irish co-operation was still on course.

The importance of the Forum was not what it attained by the end of 1984 but rather what it achieved in laying the foundations for the signing of the *Anglo-Irish Agreement* in 1985. As Paul Arthur has explained, the Forum 'has to be seen as a negotiating document in the ongoing Anglo-Irish process'.[58] Both Arthur and Jeffery have concluded, 'the Forum exercise was a brilliant piece of public relations which commanded international attention, made much of the effort of the Assembly appear redundant, ensured that the SDLP continued to hog the limelight, and, as a corollary halted the onward march of Sinn Féin'.[59]

Paddy O'Hanlon was critical that there had been no direct Southern involvement in the Northern Ireland question since partition. He was pleased that the proceedings of the New Ireland Forum took place at all. As to the position of the Republic, he maintained:

'It was the first sign of genuine coherent interest in the problem. The fact that they had come in from the cold was enough for me. I just wanted them to address this problem regarding the conflict. Symbolically, it [the *New Ireland Forum Report*] was a very important document, and really committed them [parties both North and South] to what has become a much more urgent process where they feel there is something in it for them too. Therefore, I do not think its merit lay with anything within its pages. The fact there was a report at all, that's the miracle of it.'[60]

The Forum proved an invaluable learning process for the three participating parties in the Republic regarding the Northern Ireland situation. The SDLP played a key role in providing direct educational input from their Southern colleagues in relation to the North. It denoted a stage in proceedings in which an Irish government and opposition parties in the Republic really appreciated the complexity of the Northern Ireland situation. The report outlined and defined the basis on which subsequent Irish Governments got to grips with the Northern Ireland problem.

While the final outcome of the *Forum Report* recommended a Unitary State as the preferred option, in practical terms the SDLP believed joint sovereignty was a more viable option. Seamus Mallon was opposed to joint authority and in the end supported the unitary stance, maintaining:

'I would have sided with the Fianna Fáil position, in so far if you are going to make joint authority an objective in a *Forum Report* , why not call it unity and go that further step? The whole question of federalism is one which I would have much preferred to explore. Joint authority has a nominalistic ring about it. Federalism is somewhere I think it will end anyhow, and one which might have been pursued.'[61]

Mallon had a private desire for some type of federal solution yet he backed Haughey to support the unitary position throughout the Forum discussions which displeased the other SDLP delegates at the Forum. Ironically, however, Mallon played a vital role with the support of Wally Kirwan, from the Department of the Taoiseach, in preventing the breakdown of the entire Forum proceedings. Fianna Fáil was opposed to joint authority and insisted on a unitary state as 'the only constitutional model for a new Ireland'.[62] But Mallon and Kirwan produced a compromise formula which recommended the unitary state as the preferred type of political unity which the Forum desired. Their formula enabled the other federal/confederal option and joint authority option to be included in the overall final report.[63]

The SDLP resisted Haughey's insistence that solutions be put into the final *Forum Report* . However, the Party allowed Haughey to continue with his emphasis on the unitary state and the report retained the statement that: 'The Parties in the Forum also remain open to discuss other views which may contribute to political development.'[64] Hume feelt the tragedy of the Forum was the public reaction to its proposals rather than to the underlying philosophy of its report. He recalled: 'The Forum said there are two sets of legitimate rights. The challenge is how to accommodate them both. That was all negatised [sic] by producing the so-called solutions. That's Southern Nationalism in its simplistic form.'[65] After its final publication the SDLP was able to say that the *Forum Report* successfully represented overall Party strategy.

CHAPTER SEVEN

The Anglo-Irish Agreement

Inter-Governmental Negotiations based on the Principles of The New Ireland Forum Report

Anglo-Irish relations were back on course by the start of 1985, despite the initial damage done by Mrs Thatcher's famous 'out, out, out' protest at the Press Conference following the Chequers Summit on 19 November 1984. Underlying the media hype of Thatcher's reaction to the *Forum Report*, quiet diplomatic negotiations were continuing between senior British and Irish officials. Thatcher's comments overshadowed the contents of the *Communiqué* issued immediately after the Summit. Most significantly it stated, 'the identities of both the majority and the minority communities in Northern Ireland should be recognised and respected, and reflected in the structures and processes of Northern Ireland in ways acceptable to both communities'.[1] The fact that less than a year later the *Anglo-Irish Agreement* was signed was a clear indication that a strong Anglo-Irish negotiating mechanism and relationship was in place between both Governments, despite the discord.

Sean Farren recalled the immediate aftermath of the Chequer's episode:

'It was one of the minor miracles of recent Irish history. You had to pay a lot of tribute in this instance to the Irish Government. The tribute must go to FitzGerald and his officials in foreign affairs. They decided to take this setback on the chin, and then put it behind them. They said right, we have received a fairly severe setback here. If we go around nursing our grievances we are going to get nowhere. Within twelve months they had turned things around.

It seemed to be a time when Nationalists could have come together in a great outpouring of grievances and anti-British sentiment. Had we played on that, and just used that, it was not going to get you anywhere. It was only going to annoy the British more. They could then feel justified not doing anything because the Irish were just ganging up on them. FitzGerald, being much more far seeing, along with his officials, began a concerted process of wooing

British Tories and presenting their position in the Foreign Office. They devoted a lot of personal resources to that. We did not have the clout to do that. You are looking at what was the ball game here. The ball game was an inter-Governmental one.

From the SDLP perspective, we had made all the points we wanted to make through the New Ireland Forum. The *Report* had articulated our principles. We kept our eye in terms of what we felt needed to be done at inter-Governmental level. We felt we had laid the basis for that in a very concrete and determined way through the outcome of the New Ireland Forum. The *New Ireland Forum Report* was the negotiating document in terms of principle, not in terms of actual structures which the Irish Government adopted over the next twelve months to talk to the [British] Government about. The principles were there – clear condemnation of violence, recognition both that there had to be equality or parity of esteem for both traditions within the North. Also, that any change could only come about on the basis of consent. The *Agreement* was taking that a step forward creating new structures at inter-Governmental level and giving the Irish Government a voice in the affairs of Northern Ireland.'[2]

FitzGerald's sense of urgency in checking the momentum of the move in support from the SDLP to Sinn Féin led to the impetus of the New Ireland Forum and, subsequently the *Anglo-Irish Agreement*.[3] Paradoxically, as Gerry Adams put it, 'the political leverage of the SDLP...has been unwittingly enhanced by the armed struggle of the IRA'.[4] In the immediate aftermath of Thatcher's rejection of the *Forum Report*, Padraig O'Malley argued that the outlook for the SDLP was 'ominous' unless the British Government responded in a favourable manner to the *Report* in advance of the May 1985 Local Government Elections. O'Malley claimed that without a strong Government response to the Forum the authorities would have, 'vindicated Sinn Féin's contention that constitutional politics alone have failed to convince either the Unionist majority or the Government to accommodate the minority'.[5]

There had been initial optimism in Unionist circles that Thatcher's rejection of the *Forum Report* would subsequently pressurise the SDLP back into inter-party talks. The SDLP was not going to be enticed into the Assembly by the Unionists, as to do so would be to revert to resolving the conflict in an internal framework. Throughout 1985, the starting point for any inter-party talks from the SDLP viewpoint had to be based on the findings and recommendations of the *Forum Report*.[6] As to the Northern Ireland Assembly, Hume stated, 'We said that going to such a conference table would in fact be a waste of time.'[7] For the SDLP, the context for talks with Unionists had to embrace not just representatives of the communities in Northern Ireland, but the Irish and British Governments as well.[8]

At the SDLP Fourteenth Annual Conference from 25-7 January 1985, delegates passed a motion endorsing the principles of the *Forum Report*. The motion addressed the central issue of the report. It acknowledged that the existing structures within Northern Ireland contributed to the sense of, 'alienation' felt among the minority population. It stressed that the majority ethos in both parts of Ireland permeated the society in each State. In addition, the motion again offered the SDLP an opportunity to assail the British guarantee and its 'effects of inhibiting the dialogue necessary for political progress'.[9]

In particular, the SDLP wanted to see Anglo-Irish negotiations develop on the basis of Paragraph 4.15 of the *Forum Report*. Hume referred to Paragraphs 4.15 and 4.16 of the *Forum Report* in his Leader's Speech at the Annual Conference. These two paragraphs were the crux of the entire report. Subsequently, they became the foundation of the inter-Governmental negotiations which led to the signing of the *Anglo-Irish Agreement*.

Firstly, they emphasised that new political structures and institutions were required to, 'accommodate together two sets of legitimate rights: the right of Nationalists to effective political, symbolic and administrative expression of their identity; and the right of Unionists to effective political, symbolic and administrative expression of their identity, their ethos and their way of life'.[10]

Secondly, in line with SDLP thinking, recognition of these rights, 'had to transcend the context of Northern Ireland'.[11] John Hume claimed, 'There were four proposals in the *Forum Report*, not three. The fourth one was there because some of us foresaw she [Margaret Thatcher] might say "out, out, out". The fourth one was if people refused our proposals, we would like to know what theirs were...We would listen to any proposals that would lead to political development and progress.'[12] Further, Hume clarified, 'Our position was you could not have options. We should meet and discuss the problem. Then on the basis of that let a solution emerge. That has been our consistent position.'[13]

Therefore, in the opinion of the SDLP, the objective of the *Forum Report* was to furnish the British Government with a fuller or more informed understanding of the central issues at the heart of the Northern Ireland conflict. Having grasped the nub of the problem, the next stage of the Anglo-Irish process was for both British and Irish Governments to establish a proper framework for resolving the conflict. Hume believed the Forum, 'set out the principles and realities that should govern any solution and it became a basis for real dialogue between the two Governments'.[14]

Prior to the publication of the *Anglo-Irish Agreement*, Eddie McGrady explained:

'The SDLP on behalf of the minority in Northern Ireland are seeking some way that they can express themselves fully, politically, institutionally and symbolically. That is the thrust of our campaign for these many years. We have tried many methods within Northern Ireland. We found that within Northern Ireland nothing was seen to work....Therefore, the dimension was broadened into the Anglo-Irish Forum. I cannot comment as yet whether the negotiations between the two Governments will bear sufficient fruit to achieve that objective. But it would be against that background that the proposed *Agreement* will be judged as to whether it is meaningful progress or sufficient progress towards that objective...The minority in Northern Ireland have got aspirations towards a united Ireland...they want to be able legitimately, democratically and peacefully pursue that objective in any new dimension or any new structure which may arise. That is why we think the participation of the Irish Government is a necessary balancing factor to that participation or methods of administration should I say, that was previously carried by the Unionist administration...'.[15]

McGrady believed the Irish Government was conducting the negotiations with the British Government on behalf of the New Ireland Forum in which the SDLP played a major role.

The *Forum Report* played a pivotal role in engineering movement within the Anglo-Irish sphere. As 1985 unfolded, it became apparent that the *Report* achieved its objective from the SDLP viewpoint. It provided a negotiating document between the two Governments which the British largely accepted as the nature of the Northern Ireland problem.[16] Further, it enabled both Governments to devise forthwith a framework which addressed the core principles of the *Forum Report*. Specifically, the Forum helped set the terms of reference for the high-level Anglo-Irish negotiations throughout 1985.

The inter-Governmental talks gave urgent attention to the sense of 'alienation' felt by the minority community. The *Forum Report* concluded that this sense of alienation was attributable to the Government strategy of 'crisis management' and in particular its containment measures within Northern Ireland.[17] Strong emphasis on security measures demonstrated, 'the absence of political consensus' in the minority community.[18] Significantly, the *Forum Report* called for new security structures which which both traditions could identify, 'on the basis of political consensus'.[19]

Reference to self-determination in the *Forum Report* reiterated the SDLP position on this controversial issue. It stated, 'political arrangements for a new and sovereign Ireland would have to be freely negotiated and agreed to by the people of the North and by the people of the South'.[20] This was a departure from traditional Nationalism which formerly defined self-determination purely in the context of the thirty-two counties. Self-determination was to become an important demarcation line separating Sinn Féin and the SDLP on the constitutional issue of Northern Ireland during the Hume/Adams talks in 1988.

The Forum, 'served as a catalyst, provided an agenda and helped to prepare the ground for a phase in Anglo-Irish relations when the "Irish dimension" was again regarded as an essential part of any new political initiative by the British'.[21] It augmented the Irish Government negotiating position with the British in its attempts to create a framework to resolve the conflict. Therefore, it was in the best interests of the SDLP to concentrate their energies throughout 1985 on these important inter-Governmental negotiations. Hume wanted to guarantee that the underlying principles of the *Forum Report* would become the basis of the negotiations between the two Governments. He argued, 'We were involved in the initiation of the New Ireland Forum to move the talking into what we regard[ed] would be the proper framework, because of all the failures which had taken place within the Northern Ireland framework. Having done that, we have to await the outcome because the two Governments are doing the talking now.'[22]

SDLP Expectations: the impending Anglo Irish Agreement

Following a brief period of disappointing Anglo-Irish relations in the aftermath of the Chequers Summit, contact radically improved during 1985. In January the Irish Government started to consider British draft proposals on Northern Ireland 'based on the idea of consultation rather than joint authority'.[23] Mrs Thatcher was initially more concerned with obtaining stronger security co-operation with the Irish Republic than addressing the issue of Nationalist grievances within Northern Ireland. She indicated, 'The real question now was whether the agreement would result in better security... Above all, however, we hoped for a more co-operative attitude from the Irish Government, security forces and courts. If we got this the agreement would be successful.'[24] FitzGerald put forward the concept of a power-sharing executive which no-one would be able to boycott to the British, 'which Jim Prior had floated but not proceeded with in early 1982'.[25] The Irish Government was not going to reach any final agreement with the British without securing the approval of the SDLP. The SDLP wanted both Governments to move beyond some cosmetic exercise in reconciling nationalist grievances and urged that any new political package which addressed Nationalist grievances should embrace the *Forum Report*.

Ideally, the SDLP wanted the Irish Government to play an executive role in the affairs of Northern Ireland as part of the final package being negotiated between the two Governments. They sought the Anglo-Irish package to include, 'alterations to the legal system, including a name change for the RUC and the dropping of references to the Queen in Northern Ireland's courts'.[26] Delegates at the SDLP Fourteenth Annual Conference in early 1985 passed motions demanding that the Tricolour should, 'have the same right to be displayed as the Union Flag' and also called for a phasing-out of the UDR.[27] The disbandment of the UDR was regularly demanded by Seamus Mallon, SDLP the Party Spokesman on justice.

An SDLP policy document *Justice in Northern Ireland* was published on 18 August 1985 and criticised the manner in which the *Emergency Provisions Act* operated. In particular, it focused attention of the issues of the 'Supergrass' trials, the use of plastic bullets and the shortcomings of complaints procedures.[28] These issues reflected the range of internal measures which the SDLP sought to rectify at the forthcoming Anglo-Irish Summit. The document was highly critical of the British so-called 'shoot to kill' policy. The acquittal of members of the security forces for several controversial killings brought the judicial process into disrepute and caused anger in the SDLP. The Party expected the Irish Government to address the problem of unacceptable standards of Government in Northern Ireland as part of its negotiating stance with the British.

Seamus Mallon was concerned the Irish Government might accede to a simplistic joint British/Irish strategy which failed to address the complexity of Nationalist grievances. Mallon argued that the expectation that improvements in security and the administration of justice would lead to Nationalist integration in Northern Ireland were ill-founded, maintaining, 'This assumption is erroneous. Nationalist alien-ation can only be ended by fundamental changes in the political and constitutional structures which have isolated them from the rest of the island as well as by far-reaching changes in security, justice and other administrative policies. Any attempt to reform those policies, however far-reaching, in isolation from fundamental political changes, would be to walk into a dangerously counter-productive cul-de-sac.' Beyond this, Mallon stressed the importance of a constitutional change in the status of Northern Ireland as essential to correcting the failure of partition. He argued that no amount of reform within Northern Ireland could appease Nationalist grievances. He wanted to see a new political order evolve in Ireland which would lay the foundations for a 'Unitary State'.[29] At the SDLP Annual Conference in November 1985 Seamus Mallon opposed any deviation from Irish unity as a result of the forth-coming *Anglo-Irish Agreement*. Mobilising towards unity was 'the bea-con light we must keep flashing' he told the Conference. He stressed, 'We cannot and will not put this aspiration on the back burner.'[30] FitzGerald recorded, '...in John Hume's absence in the United States Seamus Mallon had come close to coming out against the negotia-tions...'.[31]

Hume saw the forthcoming Anglo-Irish Summit not as a final set-tlement, but rather as an interim exercise to establish equality between the communities within Northern Ireland:

'The first stage in the process must be the creation of absolute equality of treatment of all people in the North. Based on that equality we begin the reconciliation process and the breaking down of barriers and prejudice, distrust and hatred: that is a long-term process but is the only one that will lead to the real unity of the people of Ireland, because it would be a unity based on the accep-tance of diversity. If you ask any united country in the world why they are united, the answer is a contradiction. They are united because they accept diversity.'[32]

John Hume made it clear there was no instant solution to the Northern Ireland conflict. He believed the two Governments needed to establish a process which addressed the grievances of the minority community and assuaged the fears of the Unionist tradition. Such a process addressing the core of the Northern Ireland conflict had to be an open-ended measure which would evolve to heal the wounds of the past.

Hume believed the seriousness of the division between the two communities made it impossible to quantify the time-limit or costs of a final settlement .

The *Anglo-Irish Agreement* was formally signed as an international contract by Margaret Thatcher and Garret FitzGerald at Hillsborough Castle on 15 November 1985. There are different theories as to why the *Agreement* was engineered. Ultimately, it was an attempt by both Governments to create a framework for resolving the Northern Ireland conundrum. Claire Palley believed it was the first step towards the creation of an all-Ireland Federal State.[33] Some observers have claimed the *Agreement* was, in effect, the exercise of joint authority by the British and Irish Governments over Northern Ireland. In the absence of political consensus within Northern Ireland, the *Anglo-Irish Agreement* was a device to implement a devolved system of Government acceptable to both communities. There is some validity in the contention that the Agreement was about the containment of Sinn Féin and the IRA. Garret FitzGerald was perturbed by the increasing electoral popularity of Sinn Féin during the early 1980s. The threat that Sinn Féin would eclipse the SDLP prompted FitzGerald to take counteractive measures.

One section of the *Agreement* committed both Governments to establish a devolved Government based on the 'co-operation of constitutional representatives within Northern Ireland'.[34] The objective of the *Agreement* was to initiate a political process which addressed the problem of inequality between the two communities in Northern Ireland. From the minority perspective, the central role of the Irish Government was to protect its interests on Human Rights issues and to prevent discrimination.[35] The two Governments pledged themselves to review political,[36] legal [37] and internal security matters.[38] They were committed to develop cross-border co-operation on security, economic, social and cultural matters.[39] Nationalist grievances could be processed through a new Anglo-Irish Secretariat located at Maryfield, near Belfast.

What was significant in the *Agreement* was the enervation of the Unionist status within Northern Ireland. While Article 1 (b) of the *Anglo-Irish Agreement* recognised, 'that the present wish of a majority of the people of Northern Ireland is for no change in the status of Northern Ireland' and the Unionist identity was safeguarded it nevertheless, in theory, downgraded the Unionist status to mere equality with that of the Nationalist. The *Anglo-Irish Agreement* gave implicit official recognition from the British Government that direct rule had failed to effect the necessary reforms demanded by the minority community. It empowered The Irish Government to examine the work of the Standing Advisory Commission on Human Rights (SACHR), the Fair Employment Agency (FEA), the Equal Opportunities Commission (EOC), the Police Authority for Northern Ireland (PANI) and the Police Complaints Board (PCB).[40] This was an admission that reform and parity in Northern Ireland could not be won by British efforts alone. The Irish Government's consultative role in Northern Ireland affairs was a formal recognition of the 'Irish dimension'.

Article 1 (a) of the *Anglo–Irish Agreement* confirmed that, 'any change in the status of Northern Ireland would come about with the consent of a majority of the people of Northern Ireland'. Irish unification could not be imposed on the Unionist community without their consent. However, O'Leary and McGarry have argued that the *Agreement* did not demonstrate any relinquishment of irredentist claims on Northern Ireland but, rather, marked the formalisation of, 'inter-state co-operation in conflict-management'.[41]

The *Agreement* was largely a response to the alienation thesis presented in the *New Ireland Forum Report*. Its implementation was a strategy by both Irish and British Governments to guarantee Nationalists equal status to the Unionist community. Garret FitzGerald stressed that his priority during negotiations with the British was to obtain a political package which could reverse the sense of alienation experienced in the minority community in some way.[42] He acknowledged that, 'If we were to make serious progress in tackling the alienation of the minority there would have to be a radical change in the security arrangements in Northern Ireland.' But FitzGerald conceded the final outcome of the negotiations fell short of his objective, 'of achieving a full identification by the minority with the policing system in Northern Ireland'. He wrote, 'The form the *Agreement* eventually took was less helpful than we had originally hoped in terms of ending Nationalist alienation and securing Nationalist acceptance of the institutions and security structure in Northern Ireland.' Nonetheless, he was optimistic the *Agreement*, 'would significantly enhance support among the Nationalist community for constitutional politics, and would have a significant adverse effect on support for and tolerance of the IRA within this community'.[43] Irish officials, on the other hand, were somewhat disappointed when the British declined their proposals for some form of joint-authority in Northern Ireland.[44] The British were concerned that the implementation of joint-authority would derogate British sovereignty over Northern Ireland.[45] The final political package between the Governments displayed a marked retreat from the joint-authority concept.

The signing of the *Anglo-Irish Agreement* on 15 November 1985 was warmly welcomed by the SDLP. Its implementation could be described as a major coup for the Party. In effect, the *Agreement* contained the principles of the *New Ireland Forum Report* which largely reflected the SDLP diagnosis for resolving the Northern Ireland conflict. It provided an acceptable framework in which the SDLP would participate in a devolved system of government. The British Government reverted to its position as stated in 1974 at Sunningdale, therefore it recognised the right of the Republic to play a major role in Northern Ireland as the political caretaker of the Nationalist community.

The SDLP believed that power-sharing had to be a fundamental principle in any acceptable devolution arrangement in Northern Ireland. Shortly after the publication of the *Anglo-Irish Agreement*, Hume remarked, 'The sort of devolution that we would be talking about quite clearly would be a power sharing devolution. One of the values that I see in this *Agreement* [is that]...it creates the framework for real reconciliation based on equality – and that's what I think we want to get engaged in'.[46] O'Leary has argued, 'The Accord explicitly recognises that an Irish dimension and agreed devolution (Article 4) are necessary to complete the reform of Northern Ireland. Since these arguments have been dominant in the SDLP from its inception, it is plain why the Accord symbolically establishes the constitutional equality of the Northern Ireland minority.'[47]

The *Agreement* enshrined the legitimacy of the minority sense of 'Irishness'. To the SDLP this was a major advance by the British Government towards an understanding of the minority community. It was official recognition from the British that there were two distinct traditions in Northern Ireland. Further, the *Agreement* removed the Unionist veto which formerly impeded political development and which the SDLP constantly campaigned against. Hume believed one of the successes of the *Agreement* was the end of this impediment to political development. He maintained:

'I think that there aren't any unconditional guarantees anymore. I think it has been made clear to the Unionists that they don't have a veto over British policy in Northern Ireland. It is quite correct they shouldn't have. The veto is now being confronted. That's what's happening at the moment. I think that is what is very significant. In many ways it might turn out to be more significant than the *Agreement* itself. The guarantee is no longer an unconditional guarantee.'[48]

Ideally, the SDLP would have liked the *Agreement* to have given the Irish Government executive powers over Northern Ireland in concert with London. Despite its shortcomings, the SDLP welcomed the new role of the Irish Government in the affairs of Northern Ireland. On a cautious note Seamus Mallon warned:

'...if the Anglo/Irish Conference and the [Maryfield] Secretariat starts to show concrete results of its deliberations in relation to how Nationalists on the ground live, the environment in which they live, the type of justice with which they deal, the way in which they are treated by the administration and by the Police, the UDR and the Army...if that changes I think you will see a response from people in the Nationalist community, but they will not respond simply to a document which has been written. They will respond to the net results of that document. That is where the results will be found.'[49]

John Hume hoped the *Agreement* would remove the justification for violence. In theory, the *Anglo-Irish Agreement* put into operation the political machinery of the Anglo-Irish Secretariat through which Nationalists in Northern Ireland could have their identity protected and grievances redressed by the Irish Government. With such a mechanism in operation, the Nationalist community could ideally pursue the goal of Irish unity peacefully. The ethos of the *Agreement* was to provide equality of treatment for both traditions in Northern Ireland. Hume argued, 'This *Agreement* is not a solution. This *Agreement* is only an opportunity.'[50]

The *Anglo-Irish Agreement* was an endorsement of SDLP views as to how the two Governments should set about resolving the Northern Ireland conflict in a proper framework. It represented the first part of the SDLP three-stage process in resolving the problem. It laid the basis for providing equality between the two traditions within Northern Ireland. The reconciliation of 'difference' between the two communities could be accommodated. This was the core of the SDLP political philosophy. It was not territorial unity which concerned the SDLP; the problem was to create a political process which could unite the *people* on the island of Ireland who were divided.[51] Once an acceptable degree of equality between both communities was established over a period of time, the SDLP proposed that the foundations were laid for progressing towards a new constitutional settlement. The SDLP acknowledged that an instant solution to the Northern Ireland conflict was unattainable.

Accordingly, the SDLP objective of attaining a new 'agreed' Ireland was a long-term strategy in an evolving process. Unlike traditional Nationalists, the SDLP accepted that Unionists had to be part of the process of any long-term constitutional settlement affecting Northern Ireland. The removal of the Unionist veto was to enable the foundations of equality to be laid. It was the underlying reason why both Governments had to be involved in bringing about any long-term settlement. The SDLP believed the *Agreement* outlined the proper context for resolving the conflict. It addressed the relations between the Republic of Ireland and Britain, between North and South, and internally between the two communities.

Impact of the Accord on the Catholic Community and Unionist Reaction

For the SDLP the immediate consequence of the *Anglo-Irish Agreement* was that it gave the minority community recognition of their Irish legacy. It provided the proper British/Irish framework for resolving the conflict, as part of the SDLP three-strand approach. The SDLP believed the *Agreement* cancelled the Unionist veto and marked a significant shift in the British Government position towards the Unionist community. Hume felt the *Agreement* was creating a situation in which the Government was telling the Unionist community they were not going to be blackmailed anymore.[52]

Seamus Mallon held the opinion that Irish Government support in the Anglo-Irish Secretariat at Maryfield was more than symbolic. It was a practical measure which worked on a daily basis to address issues affecting the minority community. The demolition of Divis Flats in Belfast and Rossville Flats in Derry were particular examples of the efficiency with which the Anglo-Irish Secretariat dealt with social problems actively. Mallon also gave the example of the 'Go-ahead' for the Dundalk/Newry Road, which people in his constituency had been campaigning to achieve for years, as further evidence that the Secretariat at Maryfield was working. He felt that in comparison to the speed with which District Councils in Northern Ireland worked and compared to the effectiveness of Northern Ireland legislation which has gone through Westminster, the role of the Anglo-Irish Secretariat has been very effective.[53] Mallon was nevertheless critical of the slow pace at which the Secretariat implemented reforms in the areas of social justice and law and order. He agreed with Charles Haughey that the *Agreement* failed to attain its objectives in relation to the position of Nationalists in Northern Ireland.[54]

Mallon also acknowledged that he was disappointed with its success in connection with the quality of justice and how it affected Nationalists *vis-à-vis* the security forces. For Mallon, the *Anglo-Irish Agreement* brought an all-Ireland dimension to the Northern Ireland problem through the Secretariat. The acid-test for Mallon was to ask Nationalists if they wanted to go back to the situation before 15 November 1985. He had no doubt whatsoever that Nationalists would respond positively to the *Agreement* at that level. Mallon believed another positive element of the *Agreement* was at a political level in its effect on the Unionists. He felt it had, 'forced Unionism and the Unionist political parties to try to redefine what Unionism means.' Mallon felt the British Government relationship with the Unionists would never be the same again and said, 'That is the type of catharsis which had to take place if there ever was to be a rethink of the Unionist entrenched position in the North of Ireland.'[55]

The SDLP was happy that the Secretariat at Maryfield had addressed many grievances by the end of 1986. In particular, the Secretariat reviewed the implications of a variety of proscriptions which affected the minority community. It reviewed the legal aspects and implications of the *Flags and Emblems Act* which was subsequently repealed. The law against *Incitement to Hatred* was strengthened under the auspices of the Secretariat[56] and they raised questions over RUC handling of Orange Parades during the marching season. New guidelines on 'Fair Employment' practices were produced at their instigation and an International Fund to help areas of high unemployment was established.[57] The Secretariat worked for improved representation of Catholics on a range of Public Bodies. They also sought permission to use Irish script for place names on public notices.

The SDLP entered the 1987 General Election fully endorsing the *Anglo-Irish Agreement*. In its election manifesto, they restated the *Agreement* was a framework which laid the basis for 'final peace and stability'.[58] They gained another MP at Westminster with the success of Eddie McGrady in South Down. McGrady beat Enoch Powell by a narrow majority of 731 votes. Seamus Mallon gained a majority of 5,325 votes in Newry and Mourne over Ulster Unionist, Jim Nicholson. Hume topped the poll in the Foyle constituency with a 9,860 lead over DUP candidate Gregory Campbell. Overall, the SDLP share of the poll was up by 3.2 per cent from the 1983 elections.[59] McGrady's electoral victory for the SDLP appeared to be further confirmation that the *Anglo-Irish Agreement* had been the correct strategy to pursue.

The *Anglo-Irish Agreement* dispelled any urgency on the part of the SDLP to reach agreement on devolution with the Unionists. The Party had secured an agreement which implemented their analysis of the Northern Ireland conflict. It committed both Governments to accepting the principle of power-sharing. Irish Government presence at Maryfield through the Anglo-Irish Secretariat fulfilled the Irish dimension for the SDLP. Also, the Party believed the *Agreement* removed the Unionist veto which, it argued, had blocked political progress and a political solution within Northern Ireland. Therefore 1986 was a year in which the SDLP felt it did not need to fight its corner. It had attained its objective of moving the Anglo-Irish process to the next stage in which both Governments held joint responsibility over Northern Ireland.

In the short-term, the *Anglo-Irish Agreement* had the effect of further polarising the two communities within Northern Ireland. If anything, it illustrated the degree of division which existed between the two communities and also among Nationalist groups themselves. The probability of a devolved system of government arising during 1986 was extremely remote. The SDLP was not prepared to agree to a suspension of the *Anglo-Irish Agreement* as a prerequisite for engaging in serious talks with Unionists.

Unionists felt the SDLP and, in particular, John Hume, represented the antithesis of reconciliation between the two communities. They felt bitter that Hume had been actively involved with the Irish Government in the negotiations which culminated to the signing of the *Agreement* in November, 1985. In relation to the *Anglo-Irish Agreement*, Chris McGimpsey recollected:

'The *Anglo-Irish Agreement* had really a bad effect on those of us who were pushing for the Party to be more accommodating Personally, it made me more hard-line at the time. The *Anglo-Irish Agreement* cost us about four years. I would say we were in 1988/89 where we were at in early 1985. The [19]80s were a decade of deterioration in relationships between the SDLP and the Ulster Unionists. It was only really coming out of the [19]80s things started to improve.'[60]

The immediate reaction to the *Anglo-Irish Agreement* by the Unionists was to call on the British Government to hold a Referendum: when they were unsuccessful in persuading the Government to do so, the fifteen Unionist MPs resigned their Westminster seats. Their anger was vented as strongly on the Government as it was on the SDLP. Martin Smyth argued that Unionists were angry that the SDLP had been consulted about the *Agreement* and that Unionists had been sidelined in the negotiations. In an interview he recalled, 'We were deliberately lied to in the House. We had to make the only form of protest that we could make, and that was to abstain from the political scene and resign our seats.'[61]

Most Unionists viewed the by-elections on 23 January 1986 as a discrete form of Northern Ireland referendum on the *Anglo-Irish Agreement*. For the SDLP, the elections demonstrated an opportunity for the minority community to give Party backing of the *Anglo-Irish Agreement*. Any dilution of the Sinn Féin vote would be an outward manifestation of the success of the *Agreement*. The SDLP only contested four constituencies feeling that to contest all fifteen would simply give further credit to the Unionist contention that the by-elections represented a referendum on the *Anglo-Irish Agreement*. They fought the marginal constituencies of Newry and Armagh, South Down, Mid-Ulster and Fermanagh-South Tyrone and were successful in getting Seamus Mallon elected in Newry and Armagh with a 2,583 majority over Jim Nicholson of the UUP. Martin Smyth felt that Unionists knew the Newry and Armagh Constituency had, in the previous few years, only been on loan to the Unionists.

Eddie McGrady, SDLP candidate for South Down was defeated by the UUP sitting candidate Enoch Powell by 1,842 votes. In both these constituencies, Sinn Féin polls were low. In Newry and Armagh Sinn Féin gained 6,609 votes and in South Down they received only 2,936 votes. In Mid-Ulster and Fermanagh-South Tyrone however, the SDLP took second place to Sinn Féin. In Mid-Ulster, Adrian Colton of the SDLP was narrowly defeated by 967 votes with a vote of 13,021 to Danny Morrison of Sinn Féin, who obtained 13,998 votes. In Fermanagh-South Tyrone, Austin Currie for the SDLP polled 13,021 votes. The seat was won by Ken Maginnis of the Ulster Unionists and Sinn Féin candidate Owen Carron came in second place with 15,278 votes. Overall, the SDLP won 70,917 votes representing a total of 12.1 per cent of the poll. This represented a rise of 6 per cent for the SDLP, but there was a decline of 5.4 per cent in Sinn Féin support.[62]

Generally the SDLP had little sympathy for the plight of Unionism in the post-Hillsborough era. The SDLP believed the Unionists had no choice but to accept the conditions of the *Agreement*. At the SDLP Annual Conference in 1986, Hume maintained the *Anglo-Irish Agreement* was based on the consensus of the fifty-nine million people living on the islands of Ireland and Britain, rather than the veto of one-and-a-half million citizens.[63] For the SDLP, the *Agreement* was a quantum leap from the days of Stormont mismanagement and provided a better system of government than Direct Rule. Hume blamed the extreme right-wing Unionism of the past for the use of the veto over more liberal leaders such as Terence O'Neill and Brian Faulkner.[64]

When referring to their past performance, Hume recollected that Unionists, 'threw out Brian Faulkner' and argued that both the SDLP and Faulkner predicted, 'The next offer would be worse from a Unionist point of view. It was inevitable therefore that the Government would take action'.[65] Hume maintained, 'It was necessary that those leaders of Unionism who believe in the veto style approach...should learn that it doesn't work any more and that Governments don't let that happen any more.'[66]

The *Agreement* was a significant political landmark for the SDLP because it instituted a proper framework for the process of ensuring equality between the two communities and confirmed Hume's contention that there was no instant blueprint for resolving the Northern Ireland conflict. There could only be a process and the first stage had to be based on equality. He argued:

> 'The *Agreement* says very clearly that unity can only take place if those who want it can persuade those who don't. That has always been the case and is still the case. Unionists say it is around the corner and on the other hand, the IRA say Irish unity has been sold out. Neither of those positions are accurate. The accurate position is that the division of Ireland is a division of people. Sovereignty isn't about maps, its about people.'[67]

Hume felt the *Agreement* put into action the SDLP strategy to establish unity and equality in a framework negotiated between Irish and British Governments as the best approach to solving the Northern Ireland conflict. Sentiments towards the *Agreement* have perhaps been summed up by Patsy McGlone, former Secretary of the SDLP. He has maintained that one of the greatest achievements of the *Anglo-Irish Agreement*, 'has been to face down the Unionist veto for the first time in Irish history. As a result, Unionist leaders have for the first time been forced to think about their relations with the rest of Ireland and to think about relations with their Nationalist neighbour.'[68]

IV

Hume/Adams Dialogue and the
Path to Peace
1986–1997

CHAPTER EIGHT

Hume/Adams Dialogue:
New Beginnings?

Delegates to the SDLP Annual Conference in 1985 called on the Party to avoid entering, 'into any pact, alliance or understanding with any group or party which supports or condones the use of violence to further its aims'.[1] The majority of delegates did not want any electoral arrangement with Sinn Féin in the forthcoming Local Government Elections. Relations between the SDLP and Sinn Féin were still sour as a consequence of the hunger-strike era. Sinn Féin association with the military campaign of the IRA was the crucial barrier to any serious co-operation between the two parties. Hume maintained:

> 'Our differences are fundamental, very, very fundamental, so fundamental that it would be impossible to enter into electoral arrangements. I would think if the Republican Movement believe in what they say it to be their policies, that they would think the differences are fundamental as well. The differences relate to methods...They believe that politics cannot and peaceful means cannot solve the problems of Ireland. They believe that violence or what they term the armed struggle is the only way forward.'[2]

Despite solid SDLP opposition to electoral pacts with Sinn Féin, their President, Gerry Adams, publicly called for the support of the SDLP on social and economic issues at local government level. Broadcast in the BBC programme *Up Front* on 3 September 1985 Adams announced:

> 'It is worthwhile acknowledging the fact that Sinn Féin and Republicans made a mistake in not contesting elections and in not being involved in electoral politics. That is an honest assessment of the last fifteen years....I think it is in the general interest – I have said this on numerous occasions. There needs to be a united Nationalist approach to the whole question of the British involvement in this country.'

As part of the same discussion, John Hume rejected any pact with Sinn Féin at local level and responded:

'For most of the past fifteen years, Sinn Féin and the Republican Movement (in what they said was a matter of principle), took no part whatsoever in elections, encouraged people not to cast their votes and on some occasions told them to burn their votes. That meant they did not care who took control of local councils or who represented people – whether Unionists represented them or not. Therefore, this seems a major change in attitude if in fact they are seeking a pact.'

Gerry Adams' comments sustained his earlier efforts via the help of the Redemptorist Priest Alex Reid to form an alliance with the SDLP and the Dublin Government in developing a joint comprehensive strategy.[3] During the BBC radio programme, *Behind the Headlines* , on 31 January 1985 Adams said he would be asking the Sinn Féin Ard Chomhairle (the Sinn Féin National Executive) to invite the SDLP to take part in talks on what he termed 'pan-Nationalist interests'.

In September, matters were once again discussed in the media by Sinn Féin and SDLP Leaders. Adams said, 'I have down for our National Executive Meeting very soon, the issue of an invitation from Sinn Féin to the SDLP to talk about pan-Nationalist interests.' The SDLP totally opposed the armed conflict of the IRA and Hume felt it was meaningless to have talks with Adams and Sinn Féin who, he argued, were merely subordinate to the Army Council of the IRA. Hume declared:

'If I am being asked to talk to the Provisional Republican Movement, then it is the Provisional Republican Movement that I want to talk to. As I understand the Provisional Republican Movement, Sinn Féin are subject on all matters to the Army Council....I want to talk to the people who are making the decisions. What I want to talk to them about is my belief that violence cannot achieve anything in this country and my wish that they would cease...'.

Adams defended the Sinn Féin position and argued:

'...The people who make the decisions for Sinn Féin are the National Executive, the Ard Chomhairle of Sinn Féin....Sinn Féin is involved in a political struggle and the IRA is involved in an armed struggle. If John Hume wants to talk with the IRA about the armed struggle let him go ahead. If John Hume wants to talk about a political struggle...let him talk to Sinn Féin.'⁴

The IRA Army Council made an official statement on 1 February 1985 to confirm that it was willing to have talks with the SDLP leader. In its statement inviting Hume to have talks with them the Army Council said, 'We believe that for years the weakness of the SDLP position on the British presence, the Loyalist veto and Irish unification, has allowed Britain to continue to examine internal accommodations and that this has prolonged the suffering and postponed a resolution of the problem of partition.'⁵

Hume accepted the opportunity to talk to the IRA, as otherwise, with the District Elections looming in May 1985, Sinn Féin could use his refusal for propaganda purposes. Determined to press ahead with the IRA talks despite the strong disapproval of the British and Irish Governments, Hume reflected a purposefulness in his objectives. Basically, the cause of the Northern Ireland conflict had been interpreted differently by the SDLP and Sinn Féin and their approach to resolving the problem was essentially different. For instance, Adams believed, 'There are two problems. Firstly, there is the problem of decolonising Ireland. Further, there is the problem of uniting the Irish people and building a just society.' From the SDLP perspective, Hume explained in response:

> 'What we want to do by political means is to create a basis of equality in this society, then reconciliation, which can only take place on the basis of equality. Once reconciliation between the two traditions takes place, then you are on the way to a genuine unity. We want the [British] Government to adopt that as a policy. To be partners in bringing that unity about. That is the way you do it by political means. That is a very clearly distinct philosophy from the philosophy put forward by Gerry Adams and the Provisional movement.'⁶

While there was an initial danger that the Chequers episode could have led to the demise of the Anglo-Irish process, Hume's proposed talks with the IRA exerted an additional strain on these negotiations. The possibility of a major split between the Coalition Government in the Republic and the SDLP was growing. Without caution, these talks might have diminished the initial impetus needed to pursue a joint Government approach throughout 1985.

Garret FitzGerald avoided a public confrontation with Hume over his proposed talks with the IRA Army Council. He was astute enough, in the wake of the Chequers catastrophe, to resist any public denouncement of the SDLP leader. A serious split between the SDLP and Dublin could have led the British Government to abandon the principles of the *Forum Report*. Had such a situation arisen, the Irish Government negotiating position with the British would have been severely eroded. Margaret Thatcher could have proceeded with another internal solution to the Northern Ireland conflict, nullifying any further Anglo-Irish development.

The meeting between Hume and representatives of the IRA Army Council took place on 23 February 1985. It only lasted several minutes because the IRA insisted that the proceedings should be filmed: they claimed Hume had a disproportionate advantage over them because of his public political profile in the media. Hume was somewhat apprehensive that the IRA would use a video-recording for propaganda purposes. Instead he suggested he make a joint statement with the IRA Army Council as an acceptable compromise. To conclude, Hume maintained that he was kept waiting for twenty-eight hours. At no stage did he meet senior IRA officials who were to participate in the talks.

Unionists viewed the meeting between Hume and the IRA Army Council as a gambit by Hume to opt out of any inter-party talks.[7] Despite the breakdown in the talks, both the DUP and the Ulster Unionists vociferously condemned Hume's actions and linked them to the abstentionist policy of the SDLP towards Prior's Assembly as a demonstration that the Party took an increasingly entrenched position, refusing to work within the accepted boundaries of Northern Ireland. In essence, Unionists claimed there was no distinction between SDLP and Sinn Féin policy.

It could be argued that the offer of talks by Adams was a deliberate tactic by Sinn Féin to drive a wedge between FitzGerald and Hume for electoral purposes. Such a tactic might have produced short-term gains but it is more probable that Sinn Féin was looking for a strategy to enhance its political profile among the minority electorate.

The public offer of talks marked an important step by Sinn Féin towards full involvement in constitutional politics. However, the significance of their offer was overshadowed by the serious negotiations taking place between the British and Irish Governments prior to signing the *Anglo-Irish Agreement*. Hume was kept informed by the Irish Government on the progress of Anglo-Irish negotiations throughout 1985. He played a key role in the negotiations, often advising Garret

FitzGerald and his senior officials what policies would be acceptable to the Nationalist community in Northern Ireland.[8]

British and Irish Governments anticipated that Sinn Féin would enjoy increased electoral support at the expense of the SDLP. By the end of January 1985, FitzGerald recorded:

'... it was clear that the fear that Sinn Féin might defeat the SDLP at the local elections in May no longer concerned us or the British as much as it had done; the Provisionals were not now expected to threaten the SDLP's position as had been feared in 1983 and 1984....the joint fear of Sinn Féin electoral success had gradually been replaced on both sides by a positive hope of seriously undermining its existing minority support within the nationalist community.'[9]

The SDLP retained its leading position in the May 1985 Local Government Elections. There was no drastic fall in SDLP popularity as had been forecast originally by FitzGerald. The SDLP fought the elections on the basis of the *New Ireland Forum Report* and its Anglo-Irish strategy. They attained 17.8 per cent of the total electorate, compared to 17.5 per cent of votes, in the 1981 local government elections. Sinn Féin obtained 11.8 per cent. This was the first time Sinn Féin contested Local Government Elections. The SDLP realised that Sinn Féin was becoming a permanent fixture in the electoral system in Northern Ireland.

With the proper political framework in place through the implementation of the *Anglo-Irish Agreement* Hume hoped that Sinn Féin would abandon its support for IRA violence. He was committed to the view that no lasting political solution could be achieved in the midst of violence. He was open to supporting whatever initiatives might be taken to try and secure an end to violence. He was looking for a strategy to develop the political process to the next stage of taking violence out of the political arena. There was also a growing concern in the Provisional movement that IRA violence was not actually going to achieve the desired effect of reunification.

The Sinn Féin desire to abandon the IRA armed struggle during 1987 coincided with Hume's search for the gradual integration of the Republican Movement into mainstream politics.[10] Gerry Adams enlisted the help of his close friend Father Alex Reid, a Redemptorist Priest from Tipperary who was based at Clonard Monastery in West Belfast, to open up dialogue between Sinn Féin and the SDLP. Reid became convinced, during 1987, that there was enough common ground between the two parties to enter into formal dialogue on reunification. He made direct contact with John Hume and arranged a meeting with Adams and Hume.[11] Both Adams and Reid shared the same dream of a United Ireland. Yet their methods of attaining this goal were different. Father Reid had been trying for a number of years to persuade Republicans to forsake violence.[12] His 'reputedly strong but anti-violent Nationalist views gave him a natural entrée into the Republican world'.[13] Not until January 1988 did the SDLP and Sinn Féin enter into what became officially known as the Hume/Adams dialogue. Reid encouraged both leaders to establish formal dialogue between their parties and to identify the emerging consensus that lay between them.

During 1987 John Hume called on the IRA to cease their campaign of violence. Hume felt that Unionists would view an IRA cessation of violence as a gesture of goodwill and a commitment to real peace and would still fully respect their tradition.[14] He argued that the IRA should lay down its arms and, 'search for self-determination on the basis of the *Anglo-Irish Agreement*.'[15] He repeatedly stated that the *Anglo-Irish Agreement* provided the basis for equality to exist between the two traditions. He argued Sinn Féin should abandon its support for the armed struggle and embrace democratic politics.

Meanwhile Sinn Féin was aware that the *Anglo-Irish Agreement* was a device used to undermine their electoral strength among the minority community and to consolidate the SDLP as a political entity. Both Governments were satisfied that the *Agreement* influenced the results of the January 1986 by-elections. This was acknowledged by Garret FitzGerald[16] and the Secretary of State for Northern Ireland, Tom King.[17] The biggest threat to the survival of Sinn Féin following the *Anglo-Irish Agreement* could have come from the Unionists if they had opted to work towards devolution alongside the SDLP. Sinn Féin prevailed because there was a lack of a cohesive body of Unionist opinion in favour of pursuing Article 4 of the *Agreement* leading towards devolution. If devolution had materialised during 1986 it would have left the SDLP in an increasingly fortified position, able to ignore Sinn Féin.

The SDLP, and especially Hume, hoped that the *Anglo-Irish Agreement* would force through a new pragmatic Unionist leadership. Article 4 of the *Agreement* which contained the conditions for devolution in Northern Ireland, if implemented, fitted into the SDLP idea of partnership-government and anchored it in a proper framework. The SDLP never envisaged the *Anglo-Irish Agreement* would lead to the demise of Sinn Féin. They accepted Sinn Féin was now a permanent feature of the Northern Ireland political landscape.

The SDLP sought an end to the justification for IRA violence and for Sinn Féin to work towards its objectives by peaceful constitutional means. In the absence of the likelihood that Sinn Féin would abandon their support for the armed struggle and become a constitutional political party, the SDLP maintained its focus on the Anglo-Irish framework. The SDLP believed that if the two Governments, under the auspices of the Accord, were able to get the Unionists to agree to a devolved system of government in Northern Ireland to make serious inroads to address Nationalist grievances, this would render the necessity for the IRA campaign of armed struggle obsolete.

As 1986 passed, Unionist opposition to the *Agreement* calcified. The Loyalist 'Day of Action' on 3 March 1986 and Unionist withdrawal from local council business indicated the degree of Unionist hostility to the *Agreement*. While the *Agreement* moved the political process along the lines prescribed by the SDLP, it did not appear to coax Unionists to enter into serious negotiations about devolution. The message was clear. While the *Agreement* was in place, serious political discussion would not take place between Unionists and the SDLP.

Despite Unionist community opposition to the *Anglo-Irish Agreement* throughout 1986 the SDLP was confident that the correct framework had been created for solving the Northern Ireland conflict. Seamus Mallon claimed that the *Anglo-Irish Agreement* came in the wake of a period of political upheaval and violence that lasted four times as long as Second World War. In that context the conflict would not be resolved in one year. In Mallon's opinion the *Agreement* was not a failure because there had not been enough time to evaluate its success.[18]

The Unionist opposition to the *Agreement* was viewed by the SDLP as a natural consequence of the removal of their veto by the Government. It had forced Unionists to think for the first time about their relations with Britain, with the rest of Ireland and with the minority community in Northern Ireland. Unionists resented the success with which the SDLP had persuaded the British and Irish Governments to accept their analysis of the Northern Ireland conflict. Unionists argued the *Anglo-Irish Agreement* was nothing more than a device of the SDLP and the Irish Government to bring them into a United Ireland. They quite clearly did not want to be part of the Irish political nation or defined as part of one nation state.[19]

The problem faced by Unionists in 1987 was how to put the brakes on the Anglo-Irish framework established by the 1985 agreement. The *Anglo-Irish Agreement* made it increasingly difficult for Unionists to persuade the minority community to abandon their objective of evolving an Irish dimension, or to get involved with them in reforming Northern Ireland. For the SDLP, the very existence of the *Agreement* was an admission by the British Government that it had hitherto failed to reform the North of Ireland. It also signified that an internal solution solely between the two communities would never work.

The *Agreement* left the Unionists in a no-win situation. They felt it weakened their links with Britain and instituted a process to push them out of the Union. The DUP wanted to render Northern Ireland ungovernable, as in 1974. There was no focal point or institution of state in Northern Ireland which epitomised the *Anglo-Irish Agreement*. The UUP wanted to work along more democratic lines by opposing the *Agreement*, and were afraid that if conditions reverted to those of 1974, the Union could be destroyed. During the 1980s the Unionist community was angry at what they felt was the hypocrisy of SDLP strategy to accommodate Unionists. They felt the SDLP attempt to negotiate accommodation with them was a complete failure. Anger among the Unionists was directed towards John Hume. Chris McGimpsey noted, 'Hume talks about peace, reconciliation and understanding, while all his political actions are all about undermining Unionism and Northern Ireland and getting the British and Irish Government to do it for him.'[20] Unionists severely criticised Hume for being out-of-touch with Unionist grassroots opinion and for spending too much time abroad, outside the political arena of Northern Ireland.

Despite the lack of progress on the political front from the Ulster Unionist Party and the Democratic Unionist Party during 1987 the UDA, in a surprise move, published a forward-reaching document, *Common Sense*. The Ulster Political Research Group, the UDA think-tank, issued proposals for breaking the stalemate in local Ulster politics. It proposed that the Secretary of State should invite local political parties to discuss the principles of a new constitution and a devolved legislative Government for Northern Ireland. This denoted an important political movement from the Unionist tradition, as the UDA is the largest Loyalist paramilitary organisation in Northern Ireland. An important aspect of the document was its recognition 'that Northern Ireland will never realise political and social stability until there is consensus on how it will be governed'.[21]

Common Sense was, in effect, endorsing institutionalised power-sharing. The UDA Chairman, John McMichael, felt the *Anglo-Irish Agreement* had shifted fundamental Unionist thinking. It forced Unionists to come to terms with the fact that a minority community within Northern Ireland must be integrated into Northern Ireland society. This was the sort of movement or recognition that the SDLP hoped to see from Unionists as a result of the *Anglo-Irish Agreement*. Hume argued that *Common Sense* accepted the reality that Northern Ireland was a divided society, and to unite it a solution had to be based on the principle of mutual accommodation which reflected that differences existed within it.

However welcome these proposals were in SDLP circles, the reality was that the UDA did not have a political mandate to implement them. There was some optimism in the SDLP that this moderate thinking from the UDA – traditionally perceived as the most intransigent part of the Unionist community – might prevail over the rest of the Unionist community. But the UDA document was based on an internal solution to the Northern Ireland problem. Hume welcomed the notion of a round table conference and SDLP participation with such a conference.[22]

While the SDLP accepted the new Unionist document as a basis for discussion with other parties, there was no way the Party would abandon the political machinery of the *Anglo-Irish Agreement*. Seamus Mallon felt the UDA document concentrated on resolving the Northern Ireland conflict on an internal basis. It ignored the reality that the conflict was also an Irish and a British problem.[23]

If Sinn Féin was pleased that the *Anglo-Irish Agreement* failed to engineer co-operation and unity between the Unionists and the SDLP, they nevertheless questioned the purpose of continuing the armed struggle. The *Anglo-Irish Agreement* instilled a degree of confidence within Sinn Féin that they could not be defeated. Gerry Adams noted, 'There was a military and political stalemate. While Republicans could prevent a settlement on Government terms, we lacked the political strength to bring the struggle to a decisive conclusion.'[24] The *Agreement* contributed to the fact that Sinn Féin reappraised its position on the armed struggle. Michael Lillis, a former senior Irish Civil Servant who drafted the *Agreement* for the Irish Government, noted from private talks he had with Adams that the treatise had a considerable impact on Sinn Féin, particularly Article 1(c) of the *Agreement* which was drafted as follows:

'[1] The two Governments: (c) declare that, if in the future a majority of the people of Northern Ireland clearly wish for and formally consent to the establishment of a united Ireland, they will introduce and support in the respective Parliaments' legislation to give effect to that wish...'.

Lillis, along with Hume, believed this offered Sinn Féin the strongest signal so far from the British, that they had no objection to a united Ireland if a majority in Northern Ireland so wished it to take place. Lillis noted, 'It led to a process of reflection within Sinn Féin which was beginning to take seriously the proposition that the British did not have a fundamental and immovable desire to hang on to Northern Ireland.'[25]

Adams made it clear to Father Reid that he was willing to, 'open up discussions with the Dublin Government and the SDLP'.[26] The implementation of the *Anglo-Irish Agreement* in the short-term slowed down Alex Reid's attempts to bring Sinn Féin into the mainstream of constitutional politics. The two Governments saw the *Agreement* as a vehicle to buttress the SDLP and isolate Sinn Féin. The Irish Government and the SDLP were preoccupied with the implementation of the *Agreement*. The SDLP and in particular John Hume, focused on pressurising the two Governments to implement the *Agreement* to its fullest potential for the benefit of the minority community. Fianna Fáil was sympathetic to the Sinn Féin demand for a British withdrawal from Northern Ireland and therefore, Alex Reid decided to open a channel of communication between Fianna Fáil leader, Charles Haughey and Sinn Féin. In 1986, Fianna Fáil and Sinn Féin were united in their opposition to the *Anglo-Irish Agreement*. Fianna Fáil felt the *Agreement* gave constitutional *de jure* recognition to Northern Ireland. They also thought it did not contain sufficient commitment to the necessary reform of Northern Ireland as espoused by Nationalists.[27]

Despite Sinn Féin misgivings about the *Anglo-Irish Agreement*, there was visible support for it among Northern Nationalists. Brendan O'Brien believed this contributed to Sinn Féin broadening its base of support South of the border.[28] Sinn Féin delegates voted at their Ard Fheis in November 1985 to end abstentionist policy from the Dáil.[29] Under Haughey's leadership, Fianna Fáil articulated a pure Republican philosophy. Haughey wanted to accommodate Sinn Féin in 1986 but feared that Sinn Féin might erode traditional Fianna Fáil electoral support in the next General Election in the Republic. Haughey co-operated with Alex Reid largely in order to safeguard Fianna Fáil electoral territory. By the time Haughey was elected to office in 1987 there was no Republican challenge to Fianna Fáil in the South.

Alex Reid was fully conversant with the Sinn Féin position on how to bring about a lasting settlement in the Northern Ireland conflict. Like Fianna Fáil, Sinn Féin envisaged a democratic solution which entailed an end to British rule. Both parties viewed Article 4 of the

Agreement as acquiescence from the Irish Government and the SDLP to an internal solution to the conflict. Reid attempted to involve a senior member of the SDLP in his deliberations. [30] But the SDLP was holding out for the *Anglo-Irish Agreement* as the 'mechanism' to deal effectively with Nationalist grievances. Unlike Sinn Féin, the SDLP opposed an immediate British withdrawal from Northern Ireland. George Drower noted:

> 'Having written to Tom King to ascertain what would be the Northern Ireland Office's reaction to talks with Sinn Féin, Reid recruited Hume to be the intermediary between Adams and King. Keen to generate a political dialogue, he then contacted Adams and Hume to ask if they would be willing to meet.'[31]

From 1986 Gerry Adams benefited from the presence of Alex Reid as an intermediary to relay the Sinn Féin position pertaining to a-cessation of IRA violence to Charles Haughey. He informed Haughey, through Reid, that he would consider calling on the IRA to implement a cease-fire if the Irish Government would pursue the issue of Irish unification.[32] Adams, along with other senior Sinn Féin strategists engaged in a serious internal debate as to the value of the armed struggle. So Sinn Féin examined ways in which it could enhance its political standing without abandoning its aim of British withdrawal from Northern Ireland and its goal of Irish unity. Sinn Féin realised it could not pursue a strategy for peace alone.

Through Alex Reid, Sinn Féin sought the support of the SDLP and Southern political parties to draw up a joint strategy which would culminate in a constitutional settlement. However, 1986 proved premature for assistance to be afforded to Sinn Féin. The Coalition Government in the Republic and the SDLP were not going to abandon the *Anglo-Irish Agreement*. Neither the SDLP nor John Hume were prepared to enter into any new joint strategy with Sinn Féin which deviated from the *Anglo-Irish Agreement*. By the end of 1986 there was no indication of any focused uniform political co-operation between the Nationalist and Republican parties in Ireland. Fianna Fáil and Sinn Féin felt the *Agreement*, 'copper fastened' partition.[33] Relations between the SDLP and Fianna Fáil deteriorated during 1986 as a result of the *Anglo-Irish Agreement*.[34]

Initially there were fears in the SDLP that a change of Government in the Republic could affect the implementation of the *Anglo-Irish Agreement*. Haughey had spoken in Limerick on 12 September 1986, hinting that he would re-negotiate the terms of the *Agreement* if elected to power.[35] When he took over as Taoiseach on 10 March 1987 with a new minority Fianna Fáil administration, he accepted that the *Agreement*, 'entered into by an Irish Government'[36] was binding. Continuity in the administration of the *Anglo-Irish Agreement* thus prevailed despite the fact that it would be conducted by a Government led by Fianna Fáil.

But from the outset Fianna Fáil opposed the constitutional implications of the *Agreement*.[37] While it would administer and implement the *Anglo-Irish Agreement*, it did not accept any system of Government in Northern Ireland which backed an internal arrangement. They felt the *Agreement* was a revised version of the Summit philosophy of the early 1980s. It was a formal mechanism without any formal right to consult. In this context Fianna Fáil opened dialogue with Sinn Féin on a common understanding.[38] Relations between the SDLP and Fianna Fáil were poor prior to their re-election. Meanwhile, both Mallon[39] and Hume[40] were confident that the newly-elected Fianna Fáil administration led by Haughey in the Republic would continue to implement the *Anglo-Irish Agreement*.

Hume hoped that the *Agreement* would eventually convince Sinn Féin that the British were neutral in relation to their presence in Northern Ireland. This became the centre-piece of the SDLP position when the Hume/Adams dialogue began in 1988. The SDLP had already suffered its own casualties as a consequence of the *Agreement*. Pascal O'Hare resigned from the Party on 3 January 1986 because he felt that the *Agreement* was imposing an internal solution on the Northern Ireland conflict which supported the Fianna Fáil contention that the Irish Government was permitting a settlement in a Northern Ireland context only.

With the proper framework in place to facilitate change *via* the implementation of the *Anglo-Irish Agreement*, Hume hoped that Sinn Féin would forsake its support for IRA violence. He was committed to the view that no lasting political solution could be achieved in the midst of violence. He was looking for a strategy to develop the political process to the next stage where violence would be taken out of the political equation. There was also a growing belief in the Provisional movement that IRA violence in isolation would not in itself achieve the aim of reunification. Fresh approaches necessitated a radical reappraisal of entrenched beliefs.

The dilemma for Hume was how to create the circumstances in which Sinn Féin could enter democratic constitutional politics. The reality was that Sinn Féin was almost trapped into supporting the armed struggle. After more than sixteen years of violence Sinn Féin had become conditioned into feeling alienated and to believing that the armed struggle was the only method of attaining its objectives. The fact that Sinn Féin was reappraising its strategy for supporting the armed struggle – as a consequence of the *Anglo-Irish Agreement* – was, from the SDLP perspective, a significant development. It affirmed Michael Lillis' thesis that the *Anglo-Irish Agreement* had a profound effect upon Sinn Féin.[41]

Sinn Féin published *A Scenario for Peace* in May 1987. This discussion paper was endorsed by Sinn Féin Ard Chomhairle at their Ard Fheis in November and was a watershed in the Sinn Féin attitude towards the armed struggle. Sinn Féin realised it needed a process which would win the support of a wide range of Irish, British and international opinion. Adams maintained, 'Such a process would have to contain the necessary mechanics of a settlement: the framework, time scale and the dynamic necessary to bring about an inclusive, negotiated and democratic settlement.'[42] The recognition in the document that Sinn Féin, 'seeks to create conditions which will lead to a permanent cessation of hostilities [and] an end to our long war'[43] was significant. To the SDLP this was also a welcome development. It represented the direction that the Party wanted Sinn Féin to take.

The major difficulty between the two parties was how each interpreted the *Anglo-Irish Agreement*. The SDLP felt the *Anglo-Irish Agreement* was a lesson for Sinn Féin on how democratic politics could bring about results.[44] Sinn Féin was afraid the *Agreement* would lead to a new 'pragmatic leadership' with Unionists who in turn would 'do an internal deal with the SDLP'.[45] As well as Sinn Féin reappraising the usefulness of the armed struggle, it was also engaged in reviewing the consensus which existed among Northern Nationalists on the constitutional issue.

The debate within Sinn Féin and Hume's search for moving the political process into a new era of non-violence took place simultaneously during 1987. These factors, in turn, set the scene for the Hume/Adams dialogue. Yet there were still marked differences between the two parties. Sinn Féin still saw the political problem in terms of British colonialism and the need for immediate British withdrawal. They wanted an end to British rule in Ireland within a given time-scale. They defined the Unionist community in Northern Ireland as a 'National minority in Ireland'.[46] In other words, the Unionists were defined as part of the Irish nation, which they vehemently opposed. In any national settlement Sinn Féin wanted the Unionists to be included as part of the Irish people as a whole.

Unlike Sinn Féin, the SDLP felt that the British were neutral in their position towards Northern Ireland. The 1984 *Forum Report* (see Chapter Six) acknowledged the distinct nature of the Unionist tradition. Therefore, the SDLP would have to view the Unionist community as having a separate identity and ethos from the rest of the people in the island of Ireland. They had to argue that in any new constitutional settlement, the Unionist community would have to be assured of an absolute right to self-determination.

The main difficulty the SDLP envisaged for moving the political process forward was how to make a model of self-determination which also embraced the reality of the Unionist position. By contrast Sinn Féin simply declared that the Unionists were part of the Irish nation and as such could take part in national self-determination. Another salient distinguishing feature between the parties was that the SDLP did not believe that the British should withdraw immediately from Northern Ireland. While a lot of common ground existed between both parties in their overall objective of attaining Irish unity, their method and diagnosis of the conflict differed considerably.

Eddie McGrady argued that the bomb at Enniskillen Cenotaph in November 1987 which did irreparable damage to Sinn Féin support for the armed struggle. International publicity surrounding this bombing brought the IRA terrorist campaign to an all-time low. McGrady viewed the invitation by Father Alex Reid at the end of 1987 to Hume and Adams to commence talks as a ploy by Sinn Féin to get off the hook in the aftermath of the Enniskillen massacre. He felt Sinn Féin was looking for a way out, a means to break the impasse. He would have liked to have seen an SDLP strategy of working with Sinn Féin towards a declaration of peace which would not have estranged the Unionists or jeopardised the Party's moderate position in Northern Ireland politics.[47] Ideally, McGrady and those who supported him in the SDLP would like to have seen power-sharing devolution with a strong Irish dimension as the way forward politically in Northern Ireland – in other words, the full implementation of the *Anglo-Irish Agreement*. Nevertheless, Alex Reid was confident during 1987 that Sinn Féin was genuine in its search for a peaceful settlement.

During 1987 John Hume called on the IRA to cease its campaign of violence. He argued that the IRA should lay down its arms and, 'search for self-determination on the basis of the *Anglo-Irish Agreement*'.[48] He repeatedly stated that the *Anglo-Irish Agreement* provided the basis for equality between the two traditions and from this premise he argued that Sinn Féin should abandon its support for the armed struggle and enter democratic politics.

By 1988 the *Anglo-Irish Agreement* had been in place for over two years. There was general acceptance in the SDLP circles that it had failed to end the sense of alienation in the Catholic ghettos of Belfast and Derry.[49] The laborious pace of bringing about reform and ending IRA violence had been the intrinsic flaw of the *Agreement* but it had been successful in bringing Sinn Féin to reconsider their views in relation to the armed struggle.

Formal Dialogue between the SDLP and Sinn Féin

John Hume and Gerry Adams held their first private discussions on 11 January 1988 at the instigation of Alex Reid. The meeting lasted more than two hours and encompassed a wide range of issues, enabling the two leaders to put forward their own analyses of the political deadlock. After the meeting, they both agreed to report to their parties and engage in further dialogue if they deemed it would be productive. The talks signified a remarkable *volte face* between the SDLP and Sinn Féin. Bitter animosity between the two parties gave way to a surprising tone of moderation demonstrated by the amicable rapport between the two political leaders.

Meetings between the SDLP and Sinn Féin continued to take place in the wake of events which stirred animosities against the British and against the Nationalists. On the one hand, the Gibraltar killings when the SAS shot dead three members of the Provisional IRA on 6 March 1988, illustrated a sinister vigilance on the part of the British authorities. On the other hand two British Army Corporals were murdered shortly afterwards on 19 March 1988 at a funeral of one of the Gibraltar three and illustrated that violence was still in currency. Eddie McGrady, with a sizeable Protestant vote in South Down, [50] was the most prominent dissident from the SDLP towards the Hume/Adams dialogue. He was opposed to the SDLP talks with Sinn Féin while IRA violence continued. He also felt that these talks, 'might jeopardise the prospect of fruitful dialogue with the Unionists'.[51]

Other senior members of the SDLP also opposed the Hume/Adams dialogue. It was felt that Sinn Féin had more to gain from the dialogue than the SDLP. Incidents such as the Enniskillen massacre when eleven people were killed on 8 November 1987 after a Provisional IRA bomb went off at a Remembrance Day ceremony showed that violence was still on the agenda. An arms haul in which one hundred and fifty tons of arms and ammunition for the Provisional IRA were seized on the French coaster Eksund on 1 November 1987 was further evidence of aggressive activity. Again, John O'Grady, a Dublin dentist, was kidnapped in the Republic on 14 October 1986 by the 'Border Fox' Dessie O'Hare and ransomed for one-and-a-half million Irish pounds, was also an incident which left Sinn Féin morale at a very low ebb.[52] Furthermore Fianna Fáil was successfully able to prevent Sinn Féin from gaining political momentum with the electorate in the Republic. This rendered Sinn Féin weak in terms of justifying their position to continue of the 'armed struggle'. Therefore, they had everything to gain from the hype around the talks.

The formal Hume/Adams dialogue took place in January 1988 with SDLP Constituency Representatives and at a later stage the Party Executive body who endorsed the continuation of the talks at Hume's discretion. Alex Reid initiated the talks between the two party leaders, not with the short-term objective of attaining an IRA cease-fire, but to explore the possibilities for a political settlement. The main difficulty between the two parties was finding agreement on the issue of self-determination. The dialogue between the SDLP and Sinn Féin increasingly drew in other senior party figures.

Along with John Hume were SDLP Deputy Leader, Seamus Mallon as well as Austin Currie and Sean Farren. Gerry Adams was accompanied by Mitchel McLaughlin, Danny Morrison and Tom Hartley. The absence of Martin McGuinness[53] at these talks indicated the difficulty the SDLP faced in convincing Sinn Féin to pressurise the IRA to call off its military campaign. Unlike Gerry Adams, McGuinness believed that the IRA could not be defeated and had the capacity to win the war against the British.[54]

The core of the Sinn Féin thesis was that the British were the cause of the conflict. Hume argued throughout the talks that although the IRA perceived themselves as attacking the British, in effect, the people being attacked were the Unionist community. One of the central disputes between the two parties during the talks concerned British interests in Northern Ireland.[55] Hume placed the onus for the suffering of the minority community represented by the SDLP and Sinn Féin on the IRA armed struggle.[56] As a consequence the British justified their security policy as a reaction to the IRA violence. In such circumstances Hume argued that the British were not the cause of all the oppression. He also pointed out that even if the goal of a British intent to withdraw from Northern Ireland was attained it would lead to greater chaos and danger for the Catholic community. As a result Hume said that the IRA needed to review its strategy and methods and accept that the British military departure in the short-term was an unrealistic objective.[57]

Throughout their history the SDLP argued that the Unionists had a veto on British policy to which they had no right. The, 'veto was exercised in that British policy denied Irish unity'.[58] Since the signing of the *Anglo-Irish Agreement*, the SDLP believed that Britain was neutral in its policy towards Northern Ireland. From the SDLP viewpoint, the Unionists had to be included in the whole area of self-determination. This was at the heart of the search for peace. Hume put five questions to Sinn Féin which he felt were the basis for justifying an end to all violence.

'1. Do you accept the right of the Irish people to self-determination?

2. Do you accept that the Irish people are at present deeply divided on the question of how to exercise self-determination?

3. Do you accept that in practice agreement on exercising that right means agreement of both the Unionist and Nationalist traditions in Ireland?

4. If you accept 1, 2 and 3 would you then agree that the best way forward would be to attempt to create a conference table, convened by an Irish Government, at which all parties in the North with an electoral mandate would attend. The purpose of such a conference would be to try to reach agreement on the exercise of self-determination in Ireland and on how the people of our diverse traditions can live together in peace, harmony and agreement. It would be understood that if this conference were to happen that the IRA would have ceased its campaign. It would also be understood in advance that if such a conference were to reach agreement, it would be endorsed by the British Government?

5. In the event of the representatives of the Unionist people refusing to participate in such a conference, would you join with the Irish Government and other Nationalist participants in preparing a peaceful and comprehensive approach to achieving agreement on self-determination in Ireland? Would we in fact and in practice take up the challenge laid down by Tone?'[59]

The SDLP position during its negotiations with Sinn Féin started from the premise that unity was the goal of Republicans and Nationalists. In these circumstances, in order to move towards this objective, they had to find a political process which was acceptable to the Unionists. In essence, this meant that a form of agreement had to be reached by the SDLP and Sinn Féin over the exercise of self-determination.

The SDLP believed that the Unionists had, 'a natural veto since they live on the island of Ireland and since their agreement is essential if unity is to be achieved'. The SDLP wanted the talks with Sinn Féin to focus on how to bring to an end 'the British presence in Ireland'. However, they wanted this process to take place in a manner in which stability and peace would prevail. To do so they needed to persuade Britain to assist them in 'achieving that objective'.[60]

If Sinn Féin adopted the SDLP analysis of the Northern Ireland conflict the SDLP envisaged, 'concerted political action, nationally and internationally', to pressurise the British Government to adopt a policy to persuade the Unionists that their interests could be best served in a new Ireland. It fell to both parties to put all their energies into persuading the Unionists to adopt a strategy of, 'building a new Ireland'.[61]

It was apparent from the discussions that Sinn Féin would not accept an internal arrangement as a basis for any new long-term or interim settlement. Sinn Féin held the view that SDLP support for devolution encouraged Britain to believe that an internal solution was possible.[62] Gerry Adams argued that it was, 'futile to rehabilitate the six-county state' and consistently attacked the SDLP, 'sponsorship of various British experiments to internalise' the partition of Northern Ireland.[63] Austin Currie, one of the SDLP negotiators at the talks argued that the SDLP had no ideological or historical commitment to devolution. Currie argued that if devolution became part of an overall permanent solution the SDLP would support it.[64]

The SDLP put forward two proposals at the SDLP/Sinn Féin talks. The first was for an all-party, all-Ireland Conference convened by an Irish Government. The purpose of this Conference would be to reach agreement on the issue of self-determination. The SDLP communicated to Sinn Féin that the IRA campaign had to end before their entry to such a Conference. The SDLP also argued that any British declaration with a hint of withdrawal would, 'lead to permanent division and bloodshed in Ireland'.[65] The second proposal was for a Conference of all Nationalist parties to agree on a common strategy in relation to Northern Ireland.[66] Sinn Féin accepted the SDLP proposal that the Dublin Government should convene a round-table Conference of all the political parties in Ireland.[67]

So the SDLP had challenged 'the theology of Republicanism' during its exchange of talks with Sinn Féin in order to challenge the central contradiction of the IRA armed struggle. Internal discussions extensively reviewed British motives for remaining in Northern Ireland. The SDLP believed that Britain would leave Northern Ireland given the right circumstances.[68] This was the key factor which could affect the IRA attitude to their terrorist campaign.

Talks broke down; Sinn Féin was not convinced by the SDLP that the British were neutral on the issues of their presence in Ireland. Sinn Féin felt that Britain was itself the problem and wanted the SDLP to precipitate a British withdrawal. In their analysis Sinn Féin argued that the British Government must change its policy of partition and relinquish power to a government elected by all the people of Ireland. Sinn Féin held the position that Britain had a responsibility to persuade the Unionists along that line of argument. The two parties differed completely on the issue of British withdrawal. The SDLP believed that Britain should remain in Northern Ireland until Sinn Féin and the SDLP could persuade the Unionists to adopt their policy towards a new Ireland.[69] Central to the continuation of 1988 talks was the fact that Hume did not allow Republicans to be stereotyped as criminals and gangsters. Despite pressure from Unionists to cast Republicans in the role of criminals and gangsters, Hume sustained a respect for the Republican ideology.[70]

The SDLP believed that the people of Ireland as a whole had a right to self-determination; agreement on, 'the exercise of that right' was the fundamental basis of the real search for peace. Unionists had to be taken on board. The SDLP also admitted a 'fundamental disagreement' with Sinn Féin on the British Government role, responsibilities, motives and duties in Northern Ireland.[71]

When the *Anglo-Irish Agreement* was signed, the SDLP felt it moved Britain into the position of the 'honest broker' on its Northern Ireland policy. The SDLP, unlike Sinn Féin, accepted the reality that it was not simply British influence which made the Unionists want to live separately from the rest of the people of Ireland. The SDLP acknowledged that it was a *status quo* which the Unionists desired for themselves.[72] The division of Ireland was a more complex phenomenon than simply allocating blame to Britain for all Ireland's ills.

During the talks, the SDLP accepted the Sinn Féin contention that the IRA was politically motivated, they were not prepared however, to confer legitimacy on their activities. The SDLP wanted the British Government to act negotiators on behalf of the Unionists. According to the SDLP thesis, since Britain was neutral by its presence in Northern Ireland, then the British should, 'use all their considerable influence and resources to persuade the Unionist people that their best interests are served by a new Ireland'. The SDLP wanted national and international pressure placed on Westminster to adopt a policy which committed them, 'towards progressively breaking down the barriers between both parts of Ireland that have developed since partition'.[73]

After the talks with Sinn Féin in September 1988 the SDLP conceded there were difficulties involved in persuading the Unionists to move towards the concept of a new agreed Ireland. They claimed that an end to the IRA campaign and, 'the subsequent demilitarisation of the North' would introduce Unionists to the idea of a new Ireland. Once this had taken place a Conference could be established along the lines advocated by the former Taoiseach, Charles Haughey. This would necessitate a strategy to bring about this new Ireland by all recognised parties with a mandate in Ireland.[74]

At the end of the talks the SDLP left Sinn Féin in no doubt about the paradox of the IRA armed struggle. From the SDLP viewpoint Sinn Féin was supporting an armed struggle which was not logical. The IRA campaign made a mockery of the Sinn Féin objective of a pan-Nationalist consensus to persuade the Unionists to move towards a new agreed Ireland.[75] Ultimately SDLP wanted to persuade the British Government to pursue a pro-Irish unity policy. Also, it wanted the British to persuade the Unionists of the advantages of such a plan.[76] The basic differences which prevented the two parties agreeing on a political way forward were on the issues of Irish self-determination[77] and British neutrality over Irish unity.[78]

There was disappointment in the SDLP when the talks did not lead to a cessation of IRA violence. It was unrealistic to assume that this would happen in the short-term given the complexity of the Northern Ireland conflict. The talks signified a process of maturation which took place within Sinn Féin in its relationship with the SDLP. That the talks took place at all indicated a move away from Sinn Féin's traditional view that the SDLP were collaborators with the British. Mark Ryan has demonstrated the extent to which Sinn Féin had moved in its attitude to the SDLP, arguing:

'During the hunger-strikes and the subsequent electoral contests, Sinn Féin activists had denounced the SDLP as right-wing and

middle-class, as well as accommodating towards Britain. In the conservative climate of the late 'eighties, Sinn Féin leaders sought to
retreat from what they regarded as a "Leftist" or even "ultra-
Leftist" stance in favour of emphasising their common Nationalist
outlook.[79]

Drower noted that Hume was pleased the talks led to a debate on the
causes of the Northern Ireland conflict rather than its symptoms.[80]
When the talks ended in September 1988 Hume continued the debate
with Sinn Féin openly in public dialogue at venues such as the SDLP
Annual Conference. The talks between Hume and Adams continued in
private with the help of Father Alex Reid despite their official termina-
tion.

News of the talks provoked a predictable reaction from Unionist
parties. They felt that Hume was seriously damaging his credentials as
a leader of a party committed to non-violence.[81] Unionists viewed the
SDLP/Sinn Féin talks as a 'pan-Nationalist front' combining
Nationalist and Republican forces to attain their ultimate objective of a
united Ireland. The Alliance Party which called for an internal solution
to the Northern Ireland conflict attacked SDLP policy for not moving
towards a devolved government. Dan McGuinness, the Alliance
Chairman, stressed that the SDLP was only interested in setting up an
all-Ireland constitutional forum which could only recommend an all-
Ireland solution.

'Alienation' still an unresolved issue for Catholics – Hume
moves SDLP towards Sinn Féin

Relations between the British and Irish Governments were at a low ebb
as a result of British handling of the Stalker Affair. The Taoiseach,
Charles Haughey, spoke of his Government's dismay at the British
authorities' handling of the matter.[82] John Stalker was removed from an
official British inquiry into the circumstances surrounding the deaths of
six unarmed Catholic men in County Armagh on 11 November 1982.
Britain refused to prosecute any member of the RUC in connection
with the incident. Other issues became linked to the affair. Added to
the controversy were the SAS killings of three IRA members in
Gibraltar in disputed circumstances. Also, on the British mainland, the
Court of Appeal in London rejected a submission to review of the case
of The Birmingham Six and it refused to consider appeals against their
convictions.

Former Tanaiste, Dick Spring, told the Dáil that Anglo-Irish relations were perhaps at their most serious since the early 1970s. He spoke of the, 'willingness of the British Government to sanction the perversion of justice' and, 'the increasing authoritarianism of the British establishment'.[83] His comments reflected the anger felt within political circles in the Republic at the administration of justice in Northern Ireland. The Irish Government role in Northern Ireland – under the auspices of the *Anglo-Irish Agreement* – as the guardian of minority interests was undermined by these controversial incidents. From the minority viewpoint, these incidents did little to confirm the SDLP contention that the *Anglo-Irish Agreement* meant that Britain was now neutral in relation to the two communities in Northern Ireland.

Political tension heightened in Northern Ireland after the killing of Mairead Farrell, Sean Savage and Danny McCann in Gibraltar on 6 March 1988. A grenade and gun attack at Milltown Cemetery on 16 March 1988 added to the violence. Then the murder of two British Army Corporals on the Andersonstown Road in Belfast on 19 March 1988 was witnessed on television news-bulletins across the world. The horror and revulsion felt in all political circles gave what Secretary of State Tom King called a 'new impetus' to relations between Britain and the Republic. He pledged to use the indignation unleashed by the atrocities of the Andersonstown incident in particular to try for a new political initiative.

The traumatic events which took place at that time led to renewed determination by the British and Irish Governments to co-operate fully within the *Anglo-Irish Agreement*. There are strong grounds for arguing that the atrocities in March 1988 contributed towards expediting an economic initiative for the Republican stronghold of West Belfast. After a meeting of the Inter-Governmental Conference on 25 March 1988 Gerry Collins, Minister for Irish Justice said, '...there was now an acceptance by the British Government, that the problem of Northern Ireland was not just a security one, and that the dissatisfaction of the Nationalist population had to be addressed'.[84] The Northern Ireland Office used the SDLP and Catholic Church officials as representatives for community groups in areas such as West Belfast. The British Government believed it could marginalise Sinn Féin at community level with the help of the SDLP and the Catholic Church in their administration of community projects and schemes. They hoped they could use the SDLP and Catholic Church officials to take control of community-based activity in staunchly Republican areas. The Government also believed that some community groups had close links with paramilitary organisations such as Sinn Féin, and, 'to give support to those groups would have the effect of improving the standing and furthering the aims of a paramilitary organisation'.[85]

Sir Kenneth Bloomfield, Head of the Northern Ireland Civil Service and his working-group of senior Civil Servants met with the SDLP on 8 April 1988 at Stormont. The purpose of this meeting was to discuss a comprehensive strategy for social and economic regeneration of the greater West Belfast area, including Poleglass and Twinbrook.[86] Both the Irish Government and the SDLP played a consultative role in drawing up the *Making Belfast Work* (MBW) programme. The British Government used the MBW initiative as part of an *ad hoc* experiment to tackle the social and economic deprivation in West Belfast with the objective of minimising terrorism.[87] The possibility of embracing Sinn Féin in the realm of democracy was far from any British Government mind.

After talks between the SDLP and Sinn Féin broke down in September 1980, John Hume's priority was to establish an initiative which could take Sinn Féin into the political process. He realised that a devolved settlement with the Unionists as outlined in Article 4 of the *Anglo-Irish Agreement* was no longer desirable. Hume knew that to continue along these lines would be interpreted by Sinn Féin as supporting an internal solution to the Northern Ireland conflict. Hume had to appease Sinn Féin by publicly denying support for a devolved arrangement for Northern Ireland.

The Hume/Adams dialogue provoked change in the SDLP strategy on devolution. It was no longer a case of merely attaining devolution within the framework of the *Anglo-Irish Agreement*. The SDLP no longer concentrated on the immediate issue of inter-party talks to attain devolution within Northern Ireland. This created tensions between some senior members of the Party. For instance, Currie felt it was unfortunate that certain elements within the SDLP were not as keen on the concept of devolution as he had been.[88] He did not directly include John Hume in that category for diplomatic reasons. Eddie McGrady felt that if the Party resumed talks with Gerry Adams they would only restore Sinn Féin credibility and by doing so the SDLP sacrificed any chance of dialogue with Unionist politicians on the issue of devolution. Seamus Mallon wanted a time-limit imposed on the talks between the SDLP and Sinn Féin.[89] *The Independent* [90] reported that an estimated sixty-five per cent of SDLP activists supported the talks with Sinn Féin. Yet some senior members of the SDLP feared that the talks could increase Sinn Féin's status and empower it as the Nationalist political party at their expense.

At the SDLP Seventeenth Annual Conference from 6 to 8

November 1987, delegates passed a motion seeking 'inter-party negotiations, as soon as possible with a view to establishing a devolved part-
nership-administration in Northern Ireland'.[91] Seamus Mallon, a member of the new Working-Committee set up to examine the SDLP position on devolution in Northern Ireland promised that the group would
leave 'no stone un-turned' in its examination of the problem. Austin
Currie stressed to delegates that devolution could not be allowed to
weaken or undermine the *Anglo-Irish Agreement*. Eddie McGrady urged
that devolution would not be an end in itself and should be capable of
allowing a new Ireland to evolve.[92] Currie wanted a devolved system of
power-sharing in Northern Ireland and argued that the *Agreement* was
'an incentive to the SDLP to get involved in a devolved power-sharing
situation'.[93] The *Anglo-Irish Agreement* from Currie's viewpoint acted as
a guarantee to the minority community call for equality. Should any
devolved arrangements which the SDLP entered into fail, there would
be the protection of Irish Government intervention under the terms of
the *Anglo-Irish Agreement*.

Currie, McGrady, Hendron and, more cautiously, Mallon of the
SDLP wanted to see a devolved power-sharing Government in
Northern Ireland on the basis of Article 4 of the *Agreement*. A
Working-Committee which included Austin Currie, Seamus Mallon
and Sean Farren was set up to prepare the SDLP's best strategy for
attaining a devolved settlement along with the other main political parties.[94] From the SDLP perspective, the difficulty in moving towards a
devolved settlement in the post-*Agreement* era was to get Unionists to
accept the view that Northern Ireland was a divided society in which
there had to be accommodation of differences. Hume argued that when
Unionists referred to Northern Ireland they were only talking about
their own tradition.[95] He felt that if they continued to refuse to accept
the fact that both sections of Northern Ireland society needed to be
accommodated in any settlement, they would isolate themselves from
the Government and the rest of the international community.[96]

Informal and secret exploratory talks took place between the four
main constitutional political parties of Northern Ireland at Duisburg in
West Germany on 14 and 15 October 1988 at the invitation of
Eberhard Spiecher a lawyer and Lutheran ecumenist who had a keen
interest in Irish affairs. The talks developed into discussions which
focused on the obstacles to inter-party talks. They became tentative
talks between the parties about possible devolution, but only if the
Anglo-Irish Agreement could be put on ice to accommodate the
Unionists. The SDLP was represented by Austin Currie, the Alliance

Party by Gordon Mawhinney, the UUP by Jack Allen and the DUP by Peter Robinson.[97] Currie would argue that the Unionists' willingness to hold informal talks with the representatives of the SDLP at Duisburg was a significant development – especially with the presence of Peter Robinson of the DUP – at a time when Unionists officially refused to hold inter-party talks with the SDLP because the *Anglo-Irish Agreement* was in operation.

The objectives of the Duisburg talks were about exploring the possibility of starting formal inter-party talks. In the final instance, the Unionists wanted to suspend of the *Anglo-Irish Agreement*.[98] A sufficient time-lapse was to take place to enable inter-party talks. Unionists sought private reassurances from the Secretary of State, Tom King, that the Maryfield Secretariat was only run on a skeleton basis. This would have fulfilled the Unionist mandate to challenge the conditions of the *Anglo-Irish Agreement*, thus enabling inter-party talks to take place.[99]

Some SDLP members such as Currie and McGrady were prepared to meet the Unionist agenda which, in effect, signified a suspension of the *Anglo-Irish Agreement*. From their viewpoint, a suspension of the *Agreement* was a major shift in the Unionist position from calling for its total abolition. If inter-party talks were going nowhere there was always the safety mechanism of the resumption of the Anglo-Irish political machinery. Mary Holland observed that Hume, as Party Leader, saw little point in pursuing an internal structure for Northern Ireland until the Unionists had established a new relationship with Dublin.[100] For Hume, once that relationship was in place, then there was a basis for proper government in the North.

Hume feared that Unionists might use the agenda for inter-party talks agreed at Duisburg – namely the suspension of the *Anglo-Irish Agreement* – as a means to revert to an internal settlement of the Northern Ireland conflict. The SDLP was not going to support any new arrangement which did not embrace an active role for the Republic. The SDLP had no objection to inter-party talks between meetings of the Inter-Governmental Conference, but their official reply to Unionist leaders stated that they, 'would not want to give any impression that the *Anglo-Irish Agreement* and its workings had been suspended'.[101]

What was evident to the SDLP by the end of 1988 was the lack of cohesion in strategy between the constitutional Nationalists in solving the Northern Ireland problem. Ideally the SDLP wanted to see a bipartisan policy from the main constitutional parties in the Republic. Fine Gael, Labour and the Progressive Democrats favoured an interim settlement based on power-sharing in Northern Ireland.[102] The SDLP, strongly influenced by Hume, held out hopes that a Fianna Fáil administration, led by Haughey, could reach a new settlement embracing Sinn Féin.

Both former Taoiseach, Garret FitzGerald and Tanaiste, Dick Spring who were key negotiators of the *Anglo-Irish Agreement*, supported Currie rather than Hume for the suspension of the *Agreement*. Spring was open to the idea of running-down the Maryfield Secretariat as suggested by the Unionists to allow inter-party talks to take place[103] although he did not view this as a suspension of the *Anglo-Irish Agreement*.[104] Also, Spring did not approve of Hume taking part in talks with Gerry Adams in January 1988: he remained unconvinced that Sinn Féin had moved away from hard-line support for the IRA 'armed struggle'.[105] FitzGerald was less generous in the number of concessions to Unionists and felt that a defined period with no meetings of the Anglo-Irish Conference would enable talks to take place between the political parties in Northern Ireland. However he opposed the temporary reduction or removal of the Secretariat at Maryfield.[106]

The Duisburg discussions were about finding a formula of words to allow inter-party talks to take place against the background of the *Anglo-Irish Agreement*. According to Currie a formula was found which would have led to inter-party discussions. He recommended to Hume that it was worth considering the suspension of the meetings of the Inter-Governmental Conference for a specified period[107] to facilitate dialogue between the major political parties in Northern Ireland. This was never followed up by Hume or any other Unionist leader. The Duisburg talks, from Currie's viewpoint, were undermined because of the Hume/Adams dialogue. From the outset of the dialogue between Hume and Adams it became apparent that both leaders agreed that a political formula had to be found which embraced an all-Ireland dimension. The SDLP was divided over what it wanted to talk about – devolution or some kind of all-Ireland conference? Currie's negotiating stance was weakened in that the terms of reference for a political settlement had now to incorporate Sinn Féin. By the time the Hume/Adams talks broke down in September 1988, both leaders had established certain principles for the attainment of a political settlement in Northern Ireland. While there might have been personal differences between senior SDLP colleagues who supported Currie's viewpoint and other members who backed Hume's position concerning the suspension of the *Anglo-Irish Agreement*, the Duisburg talks did not signify any serious challenge to Hume's strategy for the political future of the Party.

CHAPTER NINE

Towards a Permanent Settlement

The Continuation of the Hume/Adams Process

The 1988 Hume/Adams dialogue signified the embryonic stages of drawing Sinn Féin into the mainstream political process. The substance of these talks laid the basis for the later Hume/Adams dialogue in 1993 which were of paramount importance in that they led to the IRA cease-fire in August 1994.[1] If talks had not taken place during 1988, the SDLP probably would have settled for some type of devolution with Unionists as outlined in Article 4 of the *Anglo-Irish Agreement*. The political reality for the SDLP was that the *Anglo-Irish Agreement* had failed to convince Sinn Féin that the British viewed the legitimacy of the Nationalist and Republican identity on an equal footing to that of the Unionist tradition.

Sinn Féin realised that, regardless of the international interest surrounding any particular incidents during the troubles, it never materialised into political interest towards their overall goal of Irish unity. Sinn Féin had to look pragmatically at the political reality and the futility of the IRA armed struggle in attaining a united Ireland. Sinn Féin realised that to continue along this road would increase its position of isolation among the rest of the constitutional Nationalist parties in Ireland. From the Sinn Féin perspective, the object of the Hume/Adams dialogue was an attempt to unite Irish Nationalist opinion in Ireland on a strategy for moving towards Irish unity.[2] The SDLP adopted a strategy that the British Government should join, 'the ranks of the persuaders' in helping Unionists see the, 'value and safety' of agreeing to a new relationship with the rest of Ireland. This was a strategy Sinn Féin adopted reluctantly and in time learned from the SDLP.

Sinn Féin needed the help of John Hume and the SDLP to support its efforts to find a broadly-based cohesive Nationalist solution to the Northern Ireland conflict. Hume's political standing within Ireland and beyond it on the wider international scene would go a long way to moving the political process along the lines Sinn Féin desired. When the talks broke down in September 1988, Sinn Féin was happy that the

SDLP supported a strategy of finding a framework for resolving the Northern Ireland conflict outside a six-county basis and in a broader all-Ireland context. Unlike the SDLP, Sinn Féin believed that the British and Irish Governments were working towards an internal solution to the Northern Ireland conflict through the implementation of the *Anglo-Irish Agreement*. Thus the party was unable to support the initiative.

The Northern Ireland Office felt the Hume/Adams talks were a deliberate ploy by Sinn Féin to jeopardise dialogue with Unionists. The SDLP recognised both the limitations of the *Anglo-Irish Agreement* and the necessity to move the political process forward. The SDLP conceived the *Anglo-Irish Agreement* as a mechanism which would lead Sinn Féin to abandon support for the armed struggle. By 1988, it was evident that the *Agreement* had failed to achieve this objective.

Although official dialogue between SDLP and Sinn Féin delegations ceased by the end of 1988 nevertheless from 1989 onwards Hume persisted with this strategy despite the disapproval by some of his Party colleagues. Hume concentrated his efforts on establishing a political process leading to an agreed Ireland which would be supported by Sinn Féin. The ingredients needed for such a political formula meant creating all-inclusive negotiations between the two Governments and political parties in Ireland in the hope that round-table negotiations could be established. Hume knew such a framework was the only format Sinn Féin might support and perhaps it would lead to an eventual cessation of IRA violence.

While the SDLP – and Hume in particular – were committed to continuing to persuade Sinn Féin of the counter-productive effects of the IRA strategy in attaining Irish unity, there was another major problem. How could the SDLP and Sinn Féin agree to a process of self-determination between themselves and then again between the two traditions in Northern Ireland? The SDLP position on self-determination was relatively clear. It could only be achieved, according to Sean Farren, 'through a process of joint determination on the part of representatives of both political traditions'. Firstly, it meant rejecting the traditional notion of majority rule within Northern Ireland. Secondly, it called for all to respect and acknowledge the identities and traditions of the two communities. Thirdly, it meant going into discussions, 'on a basis of equality in order to agree the political institutions most appropriate' to the reality of the situation within Northern Ireland. For such a process to take place, there had to be a complete cessation of violence to enable the construction of a, 'democratic base for such dialogue'.[3] If nothing else came out of the joint party talks, the SDLP was successful in bringing about a gradual sense of realism to Sinn Féin. The difficulty for both parties was how to agree on a strategy which enabled Unionists to exercise their right to self-determination in relation to a political settlement within Northern Ireland. The SDLP promoted the principle of self-determination with consent. The right of the Irish people to national self-determination was agreed, but the exercise of that right was for the people of the North and South to express that right in separate referendums.

In his address as Leader to SDLP delegates at the 1988 Conference, Hume was vehement in his criticism of Sinn Féin. He felt the IRA reasons for violence were no longer appropriate. He produced detailed statistics which showed that the IRA killed 'Six times more people than the British Army, 30 times as many as the RUC and 250 times as many as the UDR'. He described IRA methods as having, 'all the hallmarks of undiluted Fascism'. In one of his strongest attacks on the IRA campaign he said, 'If I were to lead a civil rights campaign in Northern Ireland today the major target of that campaign would be the IRA. It is they who carry out the greatest infringement of human and civil rights.'[4] When the talks broke down between the SDLP and Sinn Féin in September 1988, it was by no means the end of the search for peace between the two parties. Hume believed the SDLP's top priority was to persist in persuading Sinn Féin that the IRA armed struggle was wrong, '...and that it must be ended so that political progress can be made'. In the same SDLP statement presented at the end of the talks he stressed that constitutional politicians had, '[a] duty to change the political climate away from violence and towards a peaceful accommodation of our differences'.[5]

Brooke/Mayhew Talks

When Margaret Thatcher left Downing Street and John Major was elected Prime Minister in November 1990 the absence of political movement in Northern Ireland towards the end of the 1980s resumed. Nevertheless, Peter Brooke, Secretary of State at that time, played a vital role in sowing the seeds that led to the first IRA cessation of violence in August 1994. In an interview on the 3 November 1989 Brooke confirmed that the Provisional IRA could not be defeated militarily but only contained. Significantly, he said that if violence ended he would not rule out talks with Provisional Sinn Féin.[6] Later in November 1990, Brooke told his Constituency Party that Britain had no selfish, economic or strategic interest in Northern Ireland and would accept unification by consent. This was a major clarification of British interests in Northern Ireland by a Secretary of State. In particular, from the SDLP viewpoint, it made the Sinn Féin contention that Britain had economic and strategic interests in Northern Ireland obsolete. Hume argued that Brooke, 'played a significant part in putting over that idea' adding, 'When history is written it will be seen to be the first major step by the British in the peace process.'[7]

An 'Inter-Party Talks' formula was established by Peter Brooke and continued after the appointment of his successor Sir Patrick Mayhew on 11 April 1992. The 1991 talks commenced between the British Government and the four Northern Ireland parties representing Unionist and Nationalist communities, and in 1992 the Irish Government formally participated in the discussions. Before Unionists would get involved in these talks they demanded a suspension of the workings of the Anglo-Irish Conference in order that negotiations proceed.[8] This framework has remained the basis for the current all-party negotiations. In line with the SDLP analysis of the situation all the participants to the talks agreed that a settlement must address the three sets of relationships: *Strand One* – Northern Ireland; *Strand Two* – North-South relations; and *Strand Three* relations between the British and Irish Governments. Unfortunately, the round table talks ended in November 1992 without reaching overall agreement. The British Government continued discussions mainly on a bilateral basis with the Northern Ireland parties and separately with the Irish Government on matters of mutual interest, under the auspices of the Anglo-Irish Inter-Governmental Conference.

The SDLP had every reason to endorse the basic structure of the three relationship approach which the Brooke/Mayhew talks were to follow. It was, after all, an SDLP analysis of the situation. This formula had been endorsed at party conference, and within the party's hierarchy represented through the constituency representatives and executive committee. Also, enshrined in this formulae was an SDLP concept that the outcome of any talks should be put to the people in a joint referenda, north and south.[9]

The 1991-1992 inter party talks broke down as a result of two different agendas. The Unionists went into the talks to replace the *Anglo Irish Agreement* and to end or at least dilute the role of the Irish government in Northern Ireland. The SDLP were steadfast on preserving what they had achieved through the *Anglo-Irish Agreement* until an even stronger Irish dimension could be attained. With hindsight, it was obvious that Hume had his sights set on bringing Sinn Féin into mainstream politics rather than concentrating on Unionist concerns over inter-party talks. Talks collapsed in view of the impending Anglo-Irish Conference Meeting and the Irish General Election on the 25 November 1992.

The SDLP's European proposal in Strand One of the Brooke/Mayhew talks was a grandiose scheme by Hume to extend the Northern Ireland problem into the international arena. The SDLP proposed a six-member Commission, 'with each Commissioner heading one of the six traditional Departments of Government in Northern Ireland, while exercising certain responsibilities collectively (e.g. security and judicial matters, civil, human and communal rights, fiscal and budgetary matters, European and external relations)...' who would appoint a cabinet to run the various Northern Ireland departments. Alternatively, the Commissioners could appoint a cabinet to run the various departments as Ministers of State.[10] Three of the Commissioners were to be elected by a single transferable vote 'for a three-seat Northern Ireland constituency'. The other three Commissioners were to be elected by the British Government, the Irish Government and the European Community. Overall, it was an absurd and impractical proposal in relation to the parameters of Strand One of the talks. At the time, European Commission President Jacques Delors, was asked by the *Irish News* about the SDLP plan for devolution in Northern Ireland. He stated, '... I don't feel the European Commission has a duty to interfere in the internal problem of a country, of a province'.[11]

The majority of the SDLP would have preferred strengthening the role of the Secretariat at Maryfield and, overall, the *Anglo Irish Agreement*. Tom Kelly, SDLP member and former Election Agent for Joe Hendron has maintained:

'Hume having won the battle to get the Secretariat up and running I don't think he won the battle in getting it teeth. That is the route they should have gone down. Unionists learned to live with the Secretariat; Mallon and McGrady's view would have been the route to go was to strengthen Anglo-Irish relations and everything else would have fallen into place. That was the big stumbling block for Sunningdale was that they didn't get a Secretariat like that established. Now that they had it established they should have tried to get it pushed out in the public role and after a while it would wear people down. It is already there ten years.'[12]

It could be argued that Hume never had any interest in the Brooke/Mayhew talks because without Sinn Féin they were a, 'dead duck'. Hume privately believed the framework for the talks over the Brooke/Mayhew period was designed to exclude a significant body of Nationalist opinion without which no progress towards lasting peace was possible. Whatever the shortcomings of the Brooke/Mayhew talks announced in early 1991, from the SDLP perspective, they signified movement towards a British-Irish context for resolving the conflict rather than one within Northern Ireland itself. The British Government adopted the thesis put forward by the SDLP on the three central relationships at the core of the problem.

The SDLP took a considerable amount of criticism from Unionists for allegedly obstructing the efforts of Peter Brooke and subsequently, Sir Patrick Mayhew, in bringing the main constitutional parties to the conference table. In the final submission document by Unionists at the end of the Brooke talks, unionists were prepared to make major concessions to the SDLP in the hope of saving the process and establishing an interim agreement. There were three elements addressed for the SDLP:

1. Minority rights guaranteed by providing a Bill of Rights.
2. Nationalists would have a meaningful role in the administration of Northern Ireland in a new Northern Ireland Assembly.
3. A recognition of the desire for Nationalists to forge more visible links with the Irish Republic through an Inter-Irish Relations Committee.

The SDLP branded Unionists as, 'insincere' and more concerned with inflicting damage on the *Anglo-Irish Agreement* than seeking accommodation. Much SDLP cynicism towards Unionist proposals was somewhat understandable given that the policy documents were delivered on the 9 November 1992. It was the eve of the completion of talks, to make way for a forthcoming Anglo-Irish Inter-Governmental Conference. The final round of inter-party talks in the Brooke/Mayhew process recommenced on the understanding that meetings of the Inter-Governmental Conference would be suspended for a three-month period. The collapse of the talks in November 1992 dashed any hopes within the SDLP of building upon the *Anglo-Irish Agreement*. Denis Haughey, SDLP International Secretary, had severe reservations from the beginning about the Brooke/Mayhew process initiative, believing it to be premature. The British Government was still giving out hopeful signals to Sinn Féin of its place in democratic politics. On the 16 December 1992, Sir Patrick Mayhew gave a speech at the University of Ulster, Coleraine, which praised the richness of the

Nationalist tradition and added, if there was a cessation of violence, then Sinn Féin could be admitted to talks and there would be significant changes if violence ended.[13]

Despite negative reaction from Unionists towards SDLP participation in the Brooke/Mayhew talks during 1992, Mark Durkan, Party Chairman at the time, defended the positive role of the SDLP in the talks. He recalled:

> 'We did make the point in our opening presentation regardless, if Unionists had an academic right to a veto, the fact was in terms of demography; in terms of geography no new Ireland could be created without the actual consent of the Unionist people....Our proposals address specifically matters pertaining to Northern Ireland (Northern Ireland within the UK). We respect the position that if a majority wish to remain in the UK we remain in the UK. We also have the position if a majority wish to change that position then that should happen. Its other parties who seem to have the position who only want to have one type of majority conclusion on the constitutional status of Northern Ireland. We are prepared to leave the constitutional question up to the wishes of a majority and then create political structures accordingly.'[14]

In the 1992 British General Elections the SDLP registered its highest vote since its foundation. The party won 184,445 votes representing 23.5 per cent of the total poll, reflecting an increase of some 30,000 votes on the 1987 election results. Eddie McGrady increased a 700 majority into one of 6,000 in South Down. Joe Hendron took the West Belfast seat from the Sinn Féin leader, Gerry Adams. There is consensus among both Unionists and Nationalists that the SDLP won the seat due to tactical voting by up to 3,500 Protestants living in the Shankhill Road in Belfast.[15] The SDLP widened the gap with Sinn Féin in the vital Mid-Ulster seat and more significantly overtook Sinn Féin in Fermanagh-South Tyrone by a small margin of 206 votes. Both seats came to be held by Unionists due to a split in the Nationalist camp.

Overall the SDLP vote rose from 154,087 first-preference votes or 21.1 per cent of the valid poll in the 1987 General Election, to 184,455 votes representing 23.5 per cent of the poll in the 1992 General Election, thereby demonstrating a rise of 30,368 votes for the SDLP. The overall Sinn Féin vote fell by 5,098 votes between the 1987 and 1992 elections. In the 1989 European Elections the SDLP increased its overall percentage of the valid poll from 22.1 per cent in 1984 to 25.5

per cent in 1989. The Sinn Féin overall percentage dropped from 13.3 in 1984 to 9.1 in 1989.

The 1994 European Election results were a resounding achievement for the SDLP with John Hume attaining 28.9 per cent of the valid vote. It marked the highest recorded vote for the SDLP in its entire history. Sinn Fein's overall percentage of the valid poll rose slightly to 9.9 per cent. In the 1993 Local Government Elections the SDLP increased its overall number of councillors from 121 in 1989 to 127 in 1993. This represented a small percentage increase from 21.0 in 1989 to 22.0 in 1993. Sinn Féin also polled well in the 1993 Local Government Elections, increasing its number of councillors from 43 in 1989 to 51 in 1993, showing a percentage increase from 11.2 in 12.4.

Part of main problem for the SDLP from 1992 onwards was complacency. From 1983 to 1992 the Party increased its representative number of MPs from one to four. Tom Kelly has maintained:

'The European Elections demonstrated that electorally Hume could do no wrong. If anything he galvanised Nationalist opinion at this stage. There was no analysis how he got that vote out. In the past the Party would have looked to see, do they need an extra six votes here or there? It was fairly scientific between 1985 and 1992. When things are going well people do not feel any need to remedy anything organisationally. There was a very close look at key constituencies and vote management. It all went to the wayside because after 1992 you had the high of the Local Government Elections; the high of Hume's personal vote at the European Elections. People then thought there is no need to analyse voting patterns because we have won the electoral battle. They obviously hadn't.'[16]

In 1993 Hume and Adams met on at least four occasions to mark out how a settlement could be attained and to discuss how an end to Republican violence could be achieved. It was obvious from their dialogue that in order to appease Sinn Féin, a public statement released in April 1993 outlined the view that an internal solution to the Northern Ireland problem could not be considered.[17] In the Hume/Adams Press Release of 26-7 September 1993 in which a report of their position was submitted to Dublin, it stated, 'We agreed to forward a *Report* on the position reached to date to Dublin for consideration. We recognise that the broad principles involved will be for wider consideration between the two Governments.'[18] The statement added that their talks had made, 'considerable progress' and that a joint report aimed at starting peace negotiations would be delivered to the Irish Government by Hume in Dublin on 26 September 1993.[19]

Throughout the Hume/Adams episode, Hume always took total responsibility for entering into dialogue with Sinn Féin. He maintained, 'It is I who am doing it. I take full responsibility for what I am doing and for the decisions that I have taken to enter into this dialogue.'[20] In a sense it could be argued that Hume was protecting the SDLP from any damage or political fall-out. Notwithstanding Hume's audacity, it was a process that could not have taken place without SDLP organisational machinery behind him. If Hume has gone solo to continue the process and left the Party, he would not necessarily have had any support. Eddie McGrady has observed:

'The whole process was one of explanation and not negotiations. Delegations would have made the whole thing different. People accompanying Hume would have been there to explain the SDLP position and challenge the concept of Sinn Fein use of violence. Sinn Fein are now using almost totally SDLP language. It was a Hume/Adams process rather than a SDLP process.[21]

Mallon and McGrady were in effect excluded from the Hume/Adams process making it a John Hume master-plan.

Within the SDLP Eddie McGrady was perhaps the main private critic of the Hume/Adams initiative. He questioned Sinn Féin's sincerity at the 1993 Annual Conference.[22] Likewise the West Belfast MP during the talks, Joe Hendron, originally would not have questioned Hume's integrity, but the sincerity of the Republican leadership.[23] But criticism changed once Adams regained the seat from McGrady in the 1997 General Election. Although Hendron has always said, '...my position is unimportant in the pursuit of peace' [24] he nevertheless remained bitter that the process lost him his West Belfast seat. In *John Hume A Profile*, Hendron discussed the SDLP Leader and his role: 'I pose the question did he overdo the meetings with Gerry Adams in a political context? Did he have to go into bed with Gerry Adams on the number of times that he did?'[25] Alternatively, a *Sunday Tribune* survey of SDLP councillors representing just over 36 per cent or 46 of 127 of their full number in September 1993, demonstrated that 98 per cent of those councillors canvassed backed the Hume/Adams process.[26] Put in its proper context this is significant given the brunt of Loyalist attacks against the Party were aimed at SDLP councillors to force an end of the talks.

The question is often asked, in retrospect, if Hume was deceived by Adams' involvement in the peace process? Did Adams have ulterior motives to oust the SDLP from the political arena? Tom Kelly has suggested:

> 'That was Sinn Féin strategy; I don't know if it was Gerry Adams' strategy. I would credit Adams with enough sense to know that if he could undermine the SDLP and Hume and the fact he is four-teen years younger than Hume would leave him in an impivotal [*sic*] position to lead Irish Nationalism. Hendron sped up the peace process because Adams had nowhere else to go. The very fact they tackled the elections in the way they did proved that they wanted an electoral mandate. Hume bought into what he saw as the bona fides of Sinn Féin wanting to go democratic. I think Hume is too shrewd to be duped. He invested in a personal relationship with Adams and he didn't really invest in a relationship with Sinn Féin.'[27]

Mark Durkan has offered a different perspective on the Hume/Adams process arguing:

> 'A decision was taken in April 1993 at a Constituency Representatives meeting not to hold party delegations, but rather to leave it as a John Hume and Gerry Adams process. Hume would have consulted other Party representatives about content of state-ments. It was definitely wasn't John Hume just on his own. Its not the absolute solo-me-alone-type enterprise. Yes, we did take a deci-sion in 1993 – one of the points that John Hume took at that time was that if the thing fall [*sic*] apart the blame would be attached to him rather than to the Party. Some of the strongest support would have come from Seamus Mallon.'[28]

From within Unionism, Gary McMichael of the UDP stated:

> '...the Loyalist people feel very disheartened with the SDLP/Sinn Féin talks. They perceive the joint statements by Hume/Adams rul-ing out an internal settlement in Northern Ireland as negating any chance of democracy within Northern Ireland. The talks back up what Loyalists fear is a pan-Nationalist front. The different ends of Nationalism are working towards the same end by ruling out an internal settlement. They are stating there can be no democratic solution in Northern Ireland.'[29]

However, Mark Durkan has explained:

> 'We do not believe the problem is a purely internal Northern
> Ireland problem. There is obviously a deep British dimension to the
> problem and a very strong Irish dimension to the problem. We want
> to accommodate both. We are criticised within the Nationalist com-
> munity for our recognition:
> 1. the particular position of the Unionist population.
> 2. our adherence that the constitutional status of Northern Ireland
>   can only change with the consent of a majority. We do not wish
>   to exclude or deny the British dimension nor are we prepared to
>   accept the Irish dimension should be excluded.'[30]

It has not only been Unionists who have critical of Hume. Southern politicians have equally been outspoken about him. In the Republic, the SDLP
leader John Hume was not without his critics, at the Workers' Party Ard
Fheis in April 1989 Proinsias De Rossa said, 'We the Workers' Party can
assist the South in its slow and shocked reappraisal of John Hume who
once had the status of a Saint in the South but is now exposed as another
tribal leader whose main asset is that he says tribal things very slowly and
very quietly.'[31] De Rossa became leader of the newly created New Agenda
and subsequently the Democratic Left in February 1992 and later he was
also to become one of the leaders of the Rainbow Coalition. He accused
Hume of a 'monumental error of judgement' and urged him not to have
talks with Adams until Sinn Féin clearly unequivocally rejected terrorism.[32]
Speaking at the launch of his party's Local Government Election manifesto
in Belfast De Rossa argued, 'I would have hoped that all democrats would
accept that it is not possible to achieve political arrangements on Northern
Ireland over the heads of one million Unionists and that any attempt to
by-pass them is simply a recipe for disaster. Unfortunately, this lesson
seems to be lost on John Hume.'[33]

Michael McDowell, Progressive Democrat Spokesman on Northern
Ireland said, 'The publication of a joint statement retards the process
of rapprochement between constitutional Nationalism and moderate
Unionists'.[34] At the same time Tanaiste, Dick Spring was not as keen
on John Hume having a major input into Northern Ireland politics as
he had been under previous administrations. On balance sources in
Foreign Affairs did not want to alienate Hume as they saw him as a
key figure in the Republic's attitudes towards Northern Ireland.
Therefore, Government figures in the south will still not publicly criticise Hume despite their private opinions.

Perhaps the best compromise on arguments for and against the Hume/Adams process in the SDLP comes from the current Party Chairman Jonathan Stephenson who suggests:

'Hume holds cards very close to [his] chest. There was unease within the Party because they didn't know enough about the process. Arguably they couldn't be told about the process because it would have invalidated [its privacy]. It would have been prone to leaks. The consensus was never at any time to do anything other than back Hume and Hume's judgement. There were concerns most notably in the months leading up to the August 1994 cease-fire. That cease-fire justified Hume's approach.'[35]

The Downing Street Declaration

A joint declaration known as *The Downing Street Declaration* was formally signed by British Prime Minister John Major and Taoiseach Albert Reynolds on the 15 December 1993. The *Declaration* was greeted in the SDLP with enthusiasm as a proper framework for creating a permanent settlement within Northern Ireland. In particular, the SDLP identified parts of Paragraph 2 of the *Declaration* which stated that, '...the ending of divisions can come about only through the agreement and co-operation of the people, North and South, representing both traditions in Ireland'. Paragraph 3 which declared that, 'the development of Europe will, of itself, require new approaches to serve interests common to both parts of the island of Ireland, and to Ireland and the United Kingdom as partners in the European Union' was a welcome sanction of the SDLP's strong European prescription for resolving the conflict.

Also, from the SDLP viewpoint, Paragraph 4 was perhaps the most striking. It contained Party demands consistent with its earliest recommendations set out in unpublished policy documents in 1971 whereby both Governments should take on the role of 'persuaders' implementing interim measures North and South which had an in-built evolving mechanism towards reaching a final settlement. As already mentioned the SDLP set out its position on self-determination at the 1975 Constitutional Convention discussions. They advocated separate referendums for North and South in any agreed settlement. This concept was implicitly endorsed by the two governments in Paragraph 4 of the joint declaration. Nevertheless, Eddie McGrady complained that Unionists had received assurances about the veto, 'no less than seven times' in the document while, 'democratic Nationalists' had not even merited a mention.[36]

The *Declaration* contained the principles which Hume and Adams set out in their first joint statement in April 1993 in relation to self-determination. The *Declaration* was also a premeditated strategy by both Governments to address the stated reasons for armed struggle given by the IRA. Peter Brooke's earlier clarification that Britain had no selfish, economic or strategic interest in Northern Ireland again was spelt out. A concept that was used repeatedly in the *Declaration* exposed to the Republican movement their archaic reasoning for supporting the, 'armed struggle'.[37]. Hume publicly played down the similarities between *The Downing Street Declaration* and the Hume/Adams document so as not to cause problems for Adams. However, on the 28 January 1994, Seamus Mallon told House of Commons there was no difference between the Hume-Adams document and *The Downing Street Declaration* on the issue of self-determination.[38] The Hume/Adams document was made available to SDLP constituency representatives for perusal and wider debate. Joe Hendron as Chairman of the Constituency Representatives recollected that the original Hume/Adams document was shorter than the joint declaration. Hendron has maintained the two premiers, Major and Reynolds, included their own paragraphs specifically in the final joint declaration.[39]

The main points set out in *The Downing Street Declaration* dealing with self-determination, British interests in Northern Ireland and the concept of a conference held by the Irish government following an IRA cease-fire originated in the SDLP/Sinn Féin talks of 1988. The Unionists embraced an understanding of the Northern Ireland conflict as set out in *The Downing Street Declaration* but opposed the practical process of implementing the North-South bodies which it would install.[40]

Hume has argued that *The Downing Street Declaration* addressed the traditional reasons for Republican violence and made evident, 'These reasons [for violence] no longer exist; the British are not here defending their interests by force as in the past; not preventing the people of this island exercising their right to self-determination; what does remain is a legacy of a deeply divided people that can only be resolved by agreement to face up to that realisation : that's the challenge of the *Declaration*.'[41] Albert Reynolds, former Taoiseach in the Republic, described *The Downing Street Declaration* as, 'a first step in a process that a cessation of violence can evolve into a full democratic dialogue for agreement.'[42]

John Hume consistently confronted Republicans maintaining, 'Republicans are facing a challenge which amounts to one of the greatest acts of moral courage this century. The past reasons for the republican armed struggle no longer exists.'[43]

The Long Road to Peace

During the run up to the first IRA cease-fire on 31 August 1994, Unionist leader at the time, James Molyneaux, reacted to the Hume/Adams process stating, 'It is quite disgusting to see the SDLP leader, Mr Hume, selling his soul to the devil and joining in a sordid attempt to blackmail the British, American and Irish Governments into giving the Armalite supremacy over the ballot box.'[44] When asked, in the autumn of 1993 after a meeting with John Major, if he had been advised not to continue dialogue with Gerry Adams, Hume replied that he, '...didn't give two balls of roasted snow what anyone advises me. I will continue these meetings'.[45] In the weeks leading up to the first cease-fire Seamus Mallon warned it was make-or-break time for Sinn Fein.[46] The *Hume/Adams Statement* of 29 August 1994, boosted hopes of an imminent IRA cease-fire. In the *Statement* both leaders made it clear that an internal settlement was not a solution to the Northern Ireland conflict. They added, 'Both Governments and all parties have already agreed that all relationships must be settled. It is our informed opinion that the peace process remains firmly on course. We are, indeed, optimistic that the situation can be moved tangibly forward.'[47] On the 31 August 1994 the IRA officially called a cessation of its military operations. In its statement the IRA announced:

'Recognising the potential of the current situation and in order to enhance the democratic process and underlying our definitive commitment to its success, the leadership of Oglaigh na hEireann have decided that as of midnight, August 31, there will be a complete cessation of military operations. All our units have been instructed accordingly.'[48]

Hume was convinced that the IRA cease-fire meant a permanent end to the IRA violence. He said, 'The IRA has totally and absolutely ended its campaign and has totally and absolutely committed itself to the democratic and peaceful process. I am absolutely convinced because I have been engaged in this more than anyone else ...'.[49] On 13 October 1994 the Combined Loyalist Military Command comprising the Ulster Defence Association, The Ulster Volunteer Force and the Red Hand Commandos also announced a cease-fire.

The peace process suffered a severe setback on the 17 November

1994. The Taoiseach, Albert Reynolds resigned after the Irish Labour leader and Tanaiste, Dick Spring, withdrew his Labour Party from Government with Fianna Fáil over the Attorney General's handling of the extradition of the paedophile priest Fr Brendan Smyth. Subsequently, Spring formed a new Coalition Government in the Irish Republic with Fine Gael whose leader John Bruton became Taoiseach, and the Democratic Left led by Proinsias De Rossa, without having to hold a General Election. During his fifteen months as Taoiseach, Bruton tried to appease Unionists and diluted Reynold's previous role of representing the interests of Nationalists in political talks. Bruton's aspiration to act as a 'neutral referee' was evident when he refused to meet Hume and Adams together in October 1994.[50] The British Government failed to deliver on its commitment in terms of Nationalist aspirations once the IRA called a cease-fire. Bruton's dilution of Nationalist consensus and attempts to appease Unionists contributed to the collapse of the IRA cessation of violence. The British Government demonstrated bad faith in the tortuously slow pace of the peace process.

Framework Documents were signed between British and Irish Governments on 22 February 1995. They outlined proposals for North-South bodies with executive and harmonising functions not dissimilar to earlier SDLP documents. Like the earlier *Downing Street Declaration* the *Framework Documents* largely represented SDLP philosophy. From a SDLP viewpoint, the *Documents* signified an even playing field for the two communities within Northern Ireland. In fact the sub-headings of the negotiating documents had been part of other SDLP policy documents for some time. Despite Sinn Féin's reservation about the *Framework Documents* Gerry Adams remarked, 'The ethos of the document[s] and the political framework envisaged is clearly an all-Ireland one.'[51] Mark Durkan accused Unionists of treating the *Framework Documents* as if they had a 'texually transmitted disease'.[52]

The SDLP felt John Major was pandering to the Unionists to keep his Government in power. McGrady believed the British Government had destroyed the trust needed for the peace process to succeed. He claimed, 'The British Government rejected the Irish dimension and by that rejected all of us who are of that tradition.' He argued that the SDLP was opposed to elections before all-party talks. McGrady believed the Government was sacrificing everything including the joint approach by the two Governments, the three strand formula and, 'the twin-track approach for transient Parliamentary expediency'.[53] Sir

Patrick Mayhew, during a trip to Washington introduced another obstacle to Sinn Féin and the fringe Loyalist involvement in all-party negotiations by insisting on decommissioning of some arms as a tangible confidence-building measure in advance of talks. This new precondition became known as 'Washington 3'.

McGrady has argued that the SDLP favoured any arms decommissioning issue being dealt with by a, '...separate but simultaneous conference table....chaired by an independent negotiator'.[54] The SDLP put proposals to Westminster and Dublin asking Senator George Mitchell, assisted by two other figures of international standing, to head an international body which would advise the two Governments on dealing with the arms question committing political parties to the removal of all weapons from Irish politics.[55] McGrady was viewed as the more moderate of the three standing SDLP MPs but he could be scathing in his attacks of Unionists. He referred to Unionist 'not-an-inch-mentality' as offering nothing to either the peace process or political movement.[56]

The peace process reached a desperate stage by the end of November 1995 because British and Unionists insisted on arms surrender before talks rather than as a result of them. The two Governments made a dramatic breakthrough in the arms decommissioning issue by holding a midnight summit on 28 November 1995 on the eve of President Clinton's visit to Northern Ireland. Both Governments agreed to launch a 'twin-track' process so that the decommissioning issue and all-party negotiations could run simultaneously. They issued a joint communiqué to establish a date for all-party talks by the end of February 1996. An international body established by the two Governments was set up to provide an independent assessment of the decommissioning issue. The body chaired by George Mitchell was to submit its report by mid-January 1996. It was only to be an advisory body. Paragraph 12 of the *Downing Street Communiqué* dated 28 November 1995 stated that, 'to review progress in preparatory talks for all-party negotiations, the two Governments plan to meet again by mid-February 1996'.[57]

The IRA exploded a large bomb at Canary Wharf in London killing two people on 28 February 1996 marking the end of the IRA cessation of violence. Hume, as far back as the SDLP 1994 Annual Conference, had called on the British Government to convince Unionists that they had no veto over political progress in Northern Ireland. This fell on deaf ears.[58]

With a General Election and a Local Government Election looming in Northern Ireland within a time span of a year, Sinn Féin wanted to undertake an election pact or joint strategy with the SDLP. From the SDLP point of view, for the two parties to undertake a joint electoral strategy the Party Chairman, Jonathan Stephenson, pointed out that Sinn Féin would have to abandon its policy of not taking Westminster seats. He stated, 'Any agreement with any party would have to involve a joint commitment on policy, not just an agreement on candidates.'[59]

The SDLP 1995 Annual Conference, demonstrated the acrimonious nature of the quarrel about whether the Party would have an electoral pact with Sinn Féin. Three SDLP MPs Hendron, McGrady and Mallon came out in strong opposition to a tactical move backed by allies of John Hume which effectively left open the option of electoral pacts in the constituency of West Tyrone and also in Mid-Ulster. A motion calling for the SDLP to reassert its policy of rejecting electoral pacts with other parties in any circumstances was diplomatically referred back to the Party Executive. This left the possibility of a deal between the two parties in the winnable seats of Mid-Ulster and West Tyrone.[60] Eddie McGrady said opposition to electoral pacts was, '...fundamental to the integrity of the SDLP'. Mallon argued a pact with Sinn Féin would be contrary to the 'heart and soul' of the Party.[61] The proposals for electoral pacts with Sinn Féin split the Party down the centre.

Elections to the proposed Northern Ireland Forum and all-party negotiations were held across Northern Ireland on 30 May 1996. The SDLP received a total of 160,786 votes signifying 21.36 per cent of the valid vote. Sinn Fein attracted a resounding 116,377 votes representing 15.47 per cent of the total vote.

On the 10 June 1996 all-party negotiations began in Stormont against a backdrop of violence. The Manchester bombings on the 15 June 1996 destroyed a large part of the city centre and injured 200 people. The political fall-out of the first infamous Drumcree stand-off between Portadown Orangemen from entering from Drumcree Church via the Nationalist Garvaghy Road led to serious protests and road-blocks across Northern Ireland. Consequently, when the Forum resumed for business in Belfast after the summer recess on the 6 September 1996, the SDLP and Sinn Féin did not attend. The two Drumcree situations of July 1996 and July 1997 left many in the nationalist side wondering, did the so called 'orange card' still dictate political authority in Northern Ireland?

Expectations in the SDLP that Sinn Féin would sustain electoral success at the Forum elections – as in the short term Catholics might encourage Sinn Féin to abandon the 'armed struggle' to take their place in democratic politics – were, in time, proved to be flawed. However, the 1997 Westminster General Election results saw Gerry Adams win his former West Belfast seat from Joe Hendron of the SDLP. More striking, from a Sinn Féin viewpoint, was Martin McGuinness' success in Mid-Ulster taking the seat from the DUP candidate Willie McCrea. Overall Sinn Féin attained 16.1 per cent of the total valid vote with 126,921 votes. Despite the SDLP losing one of its MPs, the Party vote held up within an overall vote of 190,844, representing 24.1 per cent of the valid poll. Sinn Fein's performance at the 1997 Local Government Elections was even more impressive. They increased their number of councillors by 23 from a 1993 total of 51 to an overall number of 74 in 1997. This represented 16.9 per cent of the valid poll. The Local Government Elections were very disappointing for the SDLP. They had 120 councillors elected, seven fewer than the 1993 Local Government Elections. The SDLP recorded 129,942 first-preference votes or 22.6 per cent of the valid poll.

Whatever rapport there might be between Adams and Hume when it has come to elections, tribal fights have come to the fore. In and *Irish News* article on 20 February 1997, Hume threatened Sinn Féin that he would look elsewhere, 'for political progress if Republicans do not deliver peace'. Hume also stated that an electoral pact with Sinn Féin without a cease-fire would be asking SDLP voters to 'support the killing of innocent human beings by the IRA'.[62] Even Hume must have been taken aback at the surge in Sinn Féin support among the electorate. In a pre-election call he warned people against trusting Sinn Féin. 'In a last-ditch attempt to persuade Nationalists not to vote for Gerry Adams' party, Mr Hume said the election had boiled down to the issue of trust. He said Nationalists had been conned by Sinn Féin and knew what was at stake: "People can see through the inconsistency of people talking peace but justifying violence", he insisted.'[63]

Jonathan Stephenson has reflected on the consequences of the Hume/Adams process:

'The price has been paid in terms of the electoral performance of Sinn Fein. The price is worth paying to get the Republican movement to understand that politics is the way forward. That does not mean what John Hume did was the only way to open that door to them. They would have reached that decision themselves. John Hume got them to realise that sooner. It was extremely worthwhile. It is generally accepted that the Republican movement are now on the road to political involvement; Hume with his discussion with

Gerry Adams has helped that process on the way. Clearly as Sinn Féin moved down the road of political involvement and used SDLP language they would eat into SDLP territory.'[64]

The reinstatement of the IRA cease-fire until the 22 July 1997 was a deliberate ploy by the Republican movement to wait until elections in Northern Ireland, the United Kingdom and the Republic of Ireland were out of the way. The General Election in the Republic of Ireland on the 6 June 1997 led to a Fianna Fáil/Progressive Democratic Coalition. This was a much more satisfactory outcome for those of a Republican mindset who attributed the conditions of the first cease-fire to Ahern's predecessor, Albert Reynolds. Bruton never won the confidence of the Republican movement, and in many ways acted as a novice in his handling of the peace process. The innate intricacy of bringing the Republican movement into democratic politics which Reynolds, along with Hume and others, had carefully cultivated in the creation of the peace process was lacking in Bruton. In the original negotiations which led the Republican movement to abandon the 'armed struggle', Sinn Féin had been given assurances by the SDLP, Irish Government and Irish American Senior Officials that they would not be alienated by Unionist or British Government moves in the peace process. That guarantee did not hold under Bruton's leadership. He attempted to create a balanced Northern Ireland policy reflecting the interests of Unionists as well as Nationalists. It was a noble crusade, but unfortunately John Major's minority-led Government depended on Unionist support in the House of Commons and it failed miserably to move the peace process forward in Northern Ireland. That Hume condemned British Government Northern Ireland policy at the SDLP 1993 Annual Conference suggests an admissible conclusion that John Major led a weak Government. Hume said:

'Every British Government this century, except that of Mr Heath, chose the easiest option when it came to Northern Ireland. Their only policy was maintenance of the Unionist veto which was central to the mess that Northern Ireland is in. The unionist mindset – the classic Afrik[a]aner mindset is that the only way to protect their identity, ethos and way of life is to hold all power in their hands and exclude everyone else.'[65]

The establishment of a North-South Council of Ministers has been the SDLP aim in any overall or interim peace settlement within Northern

Ireland. At the 1992 SDLP Annual Conference Hume reaffirmed this commitment. He told delegates that cross-border structures would be an important element in the healing process. These structures would have the capacity to represent both the Nationalist and Unionist identities. He repeated the earlier SDLP desire to have strands one and two of a three-stranded settlement endorsed in a joint referendum.[66]

The SDLP submission paper to the Forum For Peace and Reconciliation established by the Irish Government after the IRA cease-fire in August 1994 concluded that the establishment of acceptable cross-border bodies would be among the most difficult challenges facing all parties and both Governments.[67]

The arrival of the Government of Tony Blair and reinstatement of the IRA cease-fire in 1997 signified that the commitments and promises which led to the IRA cessation in 1994 might be delivered under the management of Mo Mowlam as Northern Ireland Secretary of State. The expectation that the Blair Government will not repeat the inactivity on Northern Ireland as demonstrated by John Major's Government has continued. The political process, based on dialogue and in a peaceful environment, might allow reconciliation to take place, creating a new basis of trust between the two communities within Northern Ireland. Was eighteen months of an IRA cease-fire a lost opportunity to make Sinn Féin face up to its political responsibilities?

V

International Dimension and
Party Organisation

CHAPTER TEN

Mobilising Europe and America

The SDLP Promotes the European Dimension from its Origins

The SDLP first policy document, *Towards a New Ireland*, contained a federal framework and recommended joint sovereignty or condominium as the most effective political structure to accommodate the Nationalist and Unionist identities in Northern Ireland. This meant Northern Ireland needed direct links with both the Republic of Ireland and Britain. Richard Jay has argued that federation provided Britain with, 'a mechanism of by-passing its own guarantee [to the Unionists] on the constitutional status of the North'. To the SDLP federation also provided a means of stronger cross-border co-operation between Northern Ireland and the Republic and thereby side-stepped the controversial issue of the Unionist veto over political progress in Northern Ireland. Federation would set in motion an evolving movement towards all-Ireland institutions. 'The central virtue of federation, it is claimed, is that within its two states each "tradition" can be assured of effective representation and security, leading thereby to greater tolerance, understanding and harmony.'[1]

The essence of a European dimension in Northern Ireland affairs from the SDLP perspective implied cross-border regional development in social and economic matters. This was the bedrock of SDLP thinking since its earliest policy discussion papers during 1971 and was not an original SDLP proposal, but originated in the *1920 Government of Ireland Act*. The Council of Ireland enshrined in the *1920 Act* – and in the subsequent *1973 Sunningdale Agreement* – was to act as a body composed of members from the Southern and Northern Ireland Parliaments to discuss matters affecting the whole of Ireland. O'Leary has argued that if a Council of Ireland, as contemplated in the 1973 proposals at Sunningdale, were revived Northern Ireland would probably fare better in its share of EC funds than is currently the case. It would 'bring the two political systems closer without impinging on the vexed question of sovereignty'.[2]

The SDLP analysis of the Northern Ireland problem has always recognise the divided identities and loyalties between the two communities. In any new constitutional settlement, therefore, political structures would have to be created which would incorporate the minority community. The SDLP recognised that one could not advocate a unitary state arrangement as an overall political settlement because of Unionist resistance. Therefore, as Ben Caraher has indicated, the Party believed that Northern Ireland should be governed by the United Kingdom and the Republic of Ireland. This was the doctrine reflected in *Towards a New Ireland* which has remained SDLP policy ever since.[3]

There was some degree of confusion in SDLP strategy as to a federal solution however. As Daniel Elazar has pointed out, '...there are those who see federalism and federal arrangements as [the] means to attain ends external to them, such as political unification ...They are not particularly interested in federalism as such but in the utility of federal arrangements to achieve what to them are larger ends'.[4] So the underlying question in relation to the SDLP definition of federalism has been, can federalism simply mean political unification in the traditional sense, or is it an open-ended device used by the party to accept an overall political settlement democratically agreed between all sections of the political divide within Northern Ireland? After the publication of the *New Ireland Forum Report* in 1984, a MORI survey for the *Irish Times* discovered conflicting views in the SDLP. Sixty-two per cent of SDLP voters supported a unitary state, while 73 per cent also supported federation.[5]

The SDLP is a full member of the Socialist International which is a combination of political parties and organisations of Democratic-Socialist inspiration. It defines Democratic Socialism as an, 'international movement for freedom, social justice and solidarity. Its goal is to achieve a peaceful world where these innate values can be enhanced and where each individual can live a meaningful life with the full development of his or her personality and talents and with the guarantee of Human and Civil Rights in a democratic framework of society'. The Socialist International defines the profile of its members as 'Socialist, Social Democratic and Labour Parties'.[6] The SDLP is also a member of the Confederation of European Socialist Parties, a structure for co-operation between the European Socialist parties. In the absence of a political forum in Northern Ireland, the SDLP co-operated with the Socialist International successfully to organise conferences on economic and social development, regional development and other subjects.

Hume as MEP and Post-Nationalist Philosophy
Dick Burke, Irish EEC Commissioner for Transport, Trade and Administration from 1977 to 1980 was invaluable in providing Hume

with experience of the European political setting. Hume told George Drower in an interview:

> 'Dick Burke offered me a part-time job as his special adviser in the European Commission. That of course was very valuable to me, in addition to helping me in a difficult financial time. I built a lot of major contacts in Europe and I got to know the European scene inside out. That's been valuable to me ever since.'[7]

Hume believed that the only way to close the gap between the affluent and poorer countries was to strengthen the central institutions within the European community. From his entry into Europe, he sought to lobby for a more constructive regional policy between member states. Hume took his seat with the Social Democrats, the largest parliamentary block within the European Parliament. As White has illustrated, 'Hume had found himself a political niche, as Fitt had done at Westminster.'[8] Hume's 'fluency in French and the experience he had gained of Brussels bureaucracy while Richard Burke's adviser proved to be invaluable in the manoeuvres he needed to engage in to win EC grants'.[9] Hume was successful in getting substantial EC funding needed to build the new bridge across the Foyle (£25 million sterling). He was also the main campaigner to obtain EC funding to develop Derry harbour and airport.

Hume attempted to focus the community in drawing up a financial package for Northern Ireland. He lobbied European Socialists to investigate how the EEC could assist the Northern Ireland economy. He successfully tabled a motion concerning community regional policy and Northern Ireland.[10] Through this motion, Hume asked the Commission to review the outlook for the economy of Northern Ireland and to assess the policies and resources required to bring the region up to the Community average as regards living standards and employment. Also, Hume argued the Community should put forward proposals as to how the necessary resources should be made available. Hume believed that membership of the EEC entitled Northern Ireland to parity of living standards. In an address to the European Parliament he said, 'If there is idealism in this Community and if there is a human face, then here is an area which is troubled today and which this Community can step in and help.'[11]

Through the Motion seeking direct European involvement in Northern Ireland, Hume repeated the principles contained in Article Two of the *Treaty of Rome*, signed on 25 March 1957, which stressed

the Community should, '...promote throughout the Community a harmonious development of economic activities, a continuous and balanced
expansion, an increased stability, an accelerated raising of the standard
of living and closer relations between its Member States.' He also
referred back to a Heads of State meeting in Paris in 1972, which
established that the goal of reducing economic imbalances within the
Community was a 'high priority'. Hume argued that the search for
peace in Northern Ireland was connected to the provision of jobs and
decent living standards. He maintained the European Community had
the financial means to reduce regional imbalances. Hume recalled that
the Heads of Government meeting in 1972 recommended the establishment of the European Regional Development Fund (ERDF). Also, he
argued that this was not the only financial instrument capable of exert-
ing a considerable effect at regional level. There was the European
Agricultural Guidance and Guarantee Fund (EAGGF), the Social
Fund and the European Investment Bank. That is why Hume asked
the Commission, 'to present a report on the impact of community
membership on Northern Ireland'.[12]

The European Socialists elected Hume as Treasurer in the summer
of 1979. He played a major role within this group in relation to matters
affecting Northern Ireland. Consequently, following the motion passed
by Hume and other members of the Socialist group, the *Martin Report*
was prepared by Madame Simone Martin after she visited Northern
Ireland in September 1980 and submitted to the European Parliament
in June 1981. The European Commission accepted the broad outline of
the *Martin Report* and approved a package (worth £63 million) originally targeting housing in Belfast. Hume had to negotiate with German
and Danish officials who blocked the original proposals to enable the
release of funds to Belfast. In the end, the Council of Ministers
released the money on the understanding that it would be spent on
redevelopment work in Belfast. The British Government agreed to
reallocate funds specifically for housing.[13]

Hume who always keen to obtain direct European involvement in
the Northern Ireland problem was successful in having the Political
Affairs Committee within the European Community chaired by the
Danish Liberal Neils Haagerup. Its role was to investigate the political
situation within Northern Ireland. A report to the European Parliament
by Haagerup in 1984 concluded that consensus must be found for the,
'legitimate and visible expression' of the Irish dimension to the
Northern Ireland conflict. This should include, 'the establishment of
joint British-Irish responsibilities in a number of specified fields, politi-

cally, legally and otherwise'.[14] This recommendation bolstered the SDLP contention of the legitimacy of the Irish dimension and for a joint British and Irish Government strategy in addressing minority alienation within Northern Ireland.

The *Haagerup Report* called on the European Community to undertake, 'greater responsibility for the economic and social development of the province; it encouraged closer Anglo-Irish co-operation and a power-sharing form of Government in Northern Ireland'.[15] The timing of the *Haagerup Report* in March 1984 was significant, coming before the publication of the *New Ireland Forum Report* and the signing of the *Anglo-Irish Agreement*. Guelke has argued that the *Haagerup Report* also marked a particular success for Hume, 'The significant political result of the debate was to put added pressure on the Government to reach agreement with the Republic of Ireland through the Anglo-Irish process.'[16] In tandem with American international assistance, the *Anglo-Irish Agreement* was also the culmination of intensive lobbying through the institutions and member states within the European Community, as conducted by John Hume and the Irish Government.

Denis Kennedy has shown that Haagerup and his committee were strongly influenced by the work of the New Ireland Forum. Their report supported the principles contained in the New Ireland Forum – and the SDLP emphasis – for a joint Anglo-Irish approach to the problem. Recommendations for joint British/Irish responsibilities in a number of areas were later echoed in the *Anglo-Irish Agreement*. Kennedy has noted that, '...the real significance of [the]*Haagerup* [*Report*] was that it showed the extent to which an essentially Nationalist analysis of the problem was being accepted by external neutrals, as was the idea that progress towards a solution lay in the broader Anglo-Irish context, and possibly in joint sovereignty'. Kennedy also expressed the view that the *Haagerup Report* played a definitive role in persuading the Thatcher Government to reach a similar conclusion between 1983 and 1985. The European Parliament and Commission fully endorsed the recommendations of the *Anglo-Irish Agreement* through the president, Jacques Delors.[17]

More recently, Hume's influence at Strasbourg was demonstrated when the Committee on Culture, Youth, Education and the Media in Strasbourg included a motion for resolution[18] on minority languages in the *Killilea Report* [19] at his request. Additionally, as a consequence of the IRA cease-fire in 1994 Hume was able to rally the support of Northern Ireland's two other MEPs Ian Paisley and Jim Nicholson, and influence his close confidant, Commission President Jacques

Delors, to create a special 'Task Force'. As a result, an EU Task Force was created which undertook a 'Special Support Programme for Peace and Reconciliation for Northern Ireland and the border counties of Ireland'. The European Commission has subsequently endorsed the work of the Programme For Peace and Reconciliation by funding the scheme (some £240 million pounds) over the last three years.[20]

The SDLP has utilised its position in Europe to promote a European information campaign locally on social and economic issues. Seminars have been held on a number of issues ranging from disability, employment, minority languages and women's rights to rural development. It has been easier for interest groups in Northern Ireland to work under the auspices of European Socialist groups than in a purely SDLP forum.

John Hume has consistently presented a thesis that the nation state is, 'no longer a sufficient political entity to allow people to have adequate control over the economic and technological forces that affect people's opportunities and circumstances': he has referred to the Single Market which has made the Irish border, 'a county boundary as goods, people, and services move freely across it'. Also, for Hume, British membership of the EU undermines the Republican argument that Britain has strategic and economic reasons for remaining in Northern Ireland – one of the key objections which led to the breakdown of the Hume/Adams talks in 1988. The SDLP European *credo* emphasises that membership of the EU distinguishes the British presence as non-Imperial, non-Colonial and assists in realising the objectives of greater harmonisation of services between Northern Ireland and the Republic even if Sinn Féin maintain a contrary view. Hume believes that the, 'nation-state is not the last word in polity creation'. He argues that the nation-state restricts the scope of a country's economic and technological capabilities: the only way to address the reality of, 'wider economic and technological forces [is by] shared sovereignty and interdependence'. The nation-state, traditionally based on territorial claims of one state over another, is not the basis for resolving the Northern Ireland conflict. The way forward is by moving towards the European objective of greater integration between Member States. The co-operation between Britain and the Republic of Ireland initiated by the 1980 Dublin Summit between Margaret Thatcher and Charles Haughey was, to Hume and the SDLP, to unite different forms of sovereignty as part of overall European co-operation between Member States.[21]

Hume's success in winning a European seat at Strasbourg enabled the SDLP to start building, 'an international constituency'[22] which was a mechanism for developing the Party policies. Hume stood for the European Elections taking an emphatically pro-European stance, totally contrary to the views held by Paddy Devlin in 1979.[23] Hume associated the unification of Ireland, '...and the removal of the border, with the wider concept of unification in Europe and the removal of economic and social barriers'. His post-Nationalist philosophy promotes the idea of unifying the people of Ireland thereby replacing the outmoded premise of territorial unification. It revises, or from the SDLP view-point, it overrides traditional Nationalism which was essentially an, 'outdated territorial Nationalism'.[24] The SDLP believes that Irish unity is increasingly advanced by Britain and the Republic of Ireland being members of the EU. It creates the evolving process of the demise of economic, social and judicial discrepancies between Northern Ireland and the Republic.

Hume directs SDLP thinking that Irish unity can be engineered in the context of a European nation-state. Both parts Ireland share common social and economic interests that can be best served in a European context. Therefore it would serve both parts of Ireland well to be treated as one clear geographical unit or region within Europe. It is in the area of tradition and culture that irreconcilable differences permeate the Northern Ireland conflict. Hume promotes the European dimension as a vehicle for surmounting these difficulties and does not support the traditional Nationalist argument that British occupation of Northern Ireland or the partition of Ireland has been the cause of the conflict. His analysis is based on the premise that the root of the problem is attributable to the division of the people within the island of Ireland. Hume argues that European integration is a mechanism to address areas of conflict. It is a process that allows differences and identity to be retained as between the French and the Germans.[25] Hume focuses on the Unionist thesis that the Protestant ethos and identity cannot be accommodated in all-Ireland political structures. Hume believes the European dimension is an example of how the Protestant identity of the Unionist community can be maintained in all-Ireland institutions.

Connected to Hume's argument for post-Nationalism is how to overcome the problem of Northern Ireland and the Republic being cat-egorised as a single region for the purposes of EC bureaucracy. This is unlikely to be solved in the foreseeable future as it is Britain which is the member state which represents Northern Ireland at Strasbourg. Paul Arthur notes that British caution in relation to EC membership has contributed to 'Euroscepticism' in sections of the Ulster Unionist

Party.[26] Kennedy also argues that, 'In very general terms Ireland is pro-integrationist, while Britain has a minimalist approach to integration.'[27]

There has been considerable improvement in relations between the United Kingdom and the Republic of Ireland since both countries formally joined the European Economic Community in 1973. Regular contact between both Governments at meetings of the Council of Ministers has helped to counteract traditionally strained relationships. Boyle and Hadden have referred to the introduction to the *Anglo-Irish Agreement* which has stressed the desire of both states, 'to develop the unique relationship between their peoples and the close co-operation between their countries as friendly neighbours and as partners in the European Community'.[28]

Arthur and Jeffery have pointed out the importance of the European dimension to the Northern Ireland conflict in a debate which took place before the Council of Europe in 1976 and which was approved by the Political Affairs Committee.[29] 'The Document came down unequivocally in favour of "strong coalition government" which should develop "technical, social and economic" co-operation between North and South...'.[30] It illustrated that membership of the Council implied the principle of democracy and human rights had to be applied throughout the Community. Also, the Council of Europe had an interest in legislative, administrative and judicial practices in Northern Ireland. The document set out the view that British and Irish membership of the EC implied, 'an even higher degree of obligation to co-operate than is the case between sovereign states in general'.[31]

Summit meetings between Margaret Thatcher and Charles Haughey in May and December 1980 officially incorporated the European dimension into the Northern conflict. Both Governments decided in December in Dublin, 'to undertake joint-studies covering possible new institutional structures, citizenship rights, security matters, economic co-operation and measures to encourage mutual understanding'.[32] As Arthur has indicated, this process was taken further by the establishment of an Anglo-Irish Council by Garret FitzGerald following an Anglo-Irish Summit on 6 November 1981. The evolving Anglo-Irish process from December 1980 and the establishment of the Anglo-Irish Council placed the Northern Ireland problem in an EC context. Hume has compared the institutions of the European Community to those of the *Anglo-Irish Agreement*. He has argued that the Ministerial Conference was modelled on the Council of Ministers and the Anglo-Irish Secretariat on the European Commission.[33]

For Hume the European dimension was more than just cross-border co-operation. It undermined the Unionist premise that Northern Ireland was just another part of the United Kingdom and reinforced the SDLP argument for an Irish dimension. Unlike the rest of Britain, Proportional Representation (PR) was introduced to Northern Ireland as the system of voting, 'at a time when the Government was stoutly defending the simple majority system'.[34] Taoiseach at that time, Liam Cosgrave, and the Minister of Foreign Affairs, Garret FitzGerald, were the main lobbyists for securing PR for the European Elections in Northern Ireland, thereby securing a seat in the European Parliament for the SDLP.

The SDLP proposals to Strand One of the 1992 inter-party talks had a specifically European dimension. The Party drafted plans for a Northern Ireland Executive Commission with three members elected in Northern Ireland, in addition to a further three nominated independently by the British, Irish and EC. Commissioners would be equivalent to a Cabinet with a Northern Ireland Assembly modelled on the European Parliament. The proposals supported a stronger role for the Irish Government. The SDLP envisaged six Commissioners heading Northern Ireland's Civil Service Departments with collective responsibility for security, judicial and budgetary matters. The proposals included a North-South Council of Ministers based on the European model. Overall, the SDLP plans replaced Direct Rule from Westminster with an inept consortium of British, Irish and European control over Northern Ireland.

The Euro-style Council of Ministers proposals from the SDLP for Strand Two of the 1997/98 talks process have dealt with North-South co-operation. These proposals have been based on the Party's 'European Model Proposals' set out in the Brooke/Mayhew 1992 talks. The SDLP has recommended a North-South Council based on the European model to cover, 'economic development, including industrial investment; agriculture and rural development; tourism and transport; security and legal affairs, including matters relating to human, civil and communal rights; environment, health and social welfare; culture and educational matters.'[35] The Council of Ministers would oversee that cross-border institutions with executive powers implement agreed decisions between both jurisdictions in Ireland.

North-South co-operation according to SDLP philosophy is thus nothing more than both parts of the island co-ordinating a cohesive policy for the island as a whole, for vital services such as agriculture and industry, for maximising funding to such sectors which would benefit from a joint cross-border applications for assistance from Europe, rather than operating with separate status.

Defending the SDLP position on Europe at the 1992 talks Hume has argued:

> 'Northern Ireland is not a natural political entity and therefore you cannot have a normal democracy. Experience has shown us that normal majority rule simply does not work in Northern Ireland because [of] its Government by one side over another. Therefore, we argue also we need a completely new approach. The approach we adopted is a separation of powers. We feel experience has shown us that if an Assembly controls the Government of Northern Ireland whether it is power-sharing or not it will not work because any one party, by walking out, can wreck the whole thing. We have proposed a separation of powers which is what the American system did. The American system was designed by Ulster Presbyterians. They elect a President separately from an Assembly called Congress. The President then appoints his Cabinet and the Congress can question them or have their own power but the Cabinet administers the country. Because we are a divided society what we have proposed is that we elect three Presidents or Commissioners or whatever you want to call them and that they appoint a Cabinet of six people – either three others with themselves or appoint six people to run the different departments. The Assembly would be able to question them or put proposals to them – all that to be worked out – that's the basic proposition. Because of the identity situation we proposed that there be a British Commissioner and an Irish Commissioner and more importantly a European Commissioner. We thought that if we asked the European Commission to nominate a Commissioner, that would ensure that Northern Ireland got major attention in that the European Community would do all in its power to make up for the major economic loses of the last twenty years.'[36]

The ingredients of the *Framework Documents* in February 1995 proposing cross-border institutions and greater harmonisation between both parts of the island, taking the entire island as a single unit for EU economic policies and funding, was largely attributable Hume's European thinking.

Parliamentary aide and close confidant to John Hume, Mark Durkan, supports this European philosophy. As a potential future

leader and representative of the next generation of senior party personnel soon to come to the fore in the SDLP, European thinking will
clearly still dominate the Party policies when Hume steps down as
Leader. Hume has successfully imprinted his European ethos in the
SDLP rank-and-file as offering the best analysis in dealing with the
Northern Ireland problem. It provides a political context in which to
overcome the traditional orthodoxies of nineteenth-century Nationalism
based on the principles of absolutist notions of sovereignty and territorial indivisibility.[37] Hume has always maintained the European
Community has a significant role to play in resolving the Northern
Ireland conflict. Cross-border co-operation and the removal of economic and social barriers has eased the lack of trust between the two States.
It has not been a solution to the conflict, but has been at least a mechanism for moving forward. The European ingredients of co-operation
and shared sovereignty are still, according to Hume, the way forward
for settling the troubles.

Unionists view Hume's strong pro-European stance in the SDLP
simply as a camouflaged mechanism for developing their traditional
objective of a United Ireland. Kennedy has argued that, 'the Party was
still seeking to associate the whole territory of Northern Ireland with
the Republic as a means of satisfying Nationalist aspirations'.[38] The
Cadogan Group, formed in 1991 by a small group of academics with a
strong pro-Union position, adopt the stance that the, 'European
Community is based on its Member States, and is an embryonic Union
of those States...'. The Group claims that there are no plans for the
EU to subsume organised states within newly-created regions. 'There is
no uniformity of "regionality" across the Community, so a prerequisite
of a Europe of Regions would be a radical reorganisation of the internal
administration of Member States...' and they contend that a Europe of
the Regions 'is a myth and likely to remain one'.[39] They emphasise the
limitations of what can be attained at European level in relation to the
Northern Ireland problem.

Hume has led the SDLP to accept the European context as the only
means to resolve a conflict which is otherwise irreconcilable. Kennedy
has suggested that Hume's post-Nationalism is in fact a Nationalist
demand. He has pointed out, 'The weight of post-Nationalist thinking,
as reflected in the United Nations, the Conference on Security and Co-
operation in Europe, and in the European Union, is that the cultural,
religious, linguistic and all civil rights of minorities must be fully protected within their countries of residence by the authorities there.'[40]

The SDLP understand the European dimension is based on the

concept of a Europe of the Regions.[41] The *Hume Report* was adopted
by the European Parliament in 1987.[42] The Member State on which
Hume focused in producing the document was the Republic of Ireland.
Kennedy criticises this report for dealing only with the regional problems within the Republic. He believes it lacks a constructive recommendation on creating, 'an enhanced role for the regions in the institutions of the Community'.[43] The problem of the SDLP vision for a
'Europe of the Regions' is therefore, how do you facilitate Northern
Ireland's integration with the Republic as one region? This is the main
limitation to the SDLP, and in particular Hume's, concept of moving
towards a Europe of Regions. The European dimension presents itself
as a model for resolving the Northern Ireland conflict but it does not
remove the obstacles to the conflict. Britain is the sovereign state in
which Northern Ireland is represented at Strasbourg.

Gerard Delanty argues that the movement towards European unification might be the best context in which to proceed with Northern
Ireland. Such a model could provide the foundation for new institutions acceptable to both traditions and remove 'sectarianism and the
war-psychosis that has now penetrated the entire fabric of the society...'; he believes that a European dimension creates, 'new terms of
debate' over the 'insolvable [*sic*] question of national sovereignty'. Like
Hume, he would argue that, 'the age of the territorial nation-state in
now irreversibly in decline'.[44] The way forward could be for Northern
Ireland to optimise its regional identity of Ulster as a distinct European
region, but retain present territorial arrangements within the United
Kingdom. Paul Hainsworth writes that SDLP strategy towards
European integration, 'tends to end at the shoreline of a united
Ireland....At this crucial political level the SDLP is no less parochial
and no less tradition-bound in its arguments than the Ulster
Unionists.'[45] Significantly, Ruane and Todd point out that overall the
'[European] Parliament's resolutions have supported the demands of
constitutional Nationalists for reform and an institutionalised Irish
dimension rather than the Unionist demand for a stabilising of existing
structures.'[46]

In line with the SDLP thesis on movement towards a new, 'agreed
Ireland' Delanty argues, 'Before unification with the Republic is put on
the political agenda, it is far more important to establish the socio-cul-
tural, and economic, foundations upon which a mature political culture
can be built capable of dealing with the complex normative issues that
would be involved.'[47] So, in spite of faults in the SDLP promotion of a
European dimension as a basis for solving the Northern Ireland problem,

the current peace process may depend on Community structures. Hume maintains, 'I believe that we should follow the European example of evolution....I hope that we can achieve something similar in Ireland....The challenge facing us is not to find an instant package to solve the Irish problem but to create a framework that will facilitate a healing process, leading invariably and surely to a new Ireland.'[48]

Despite the general enthusiasm for Hume's ethos of social democracy in the SDLP, the Mallon camp in the Party are concerned that using the Social Democratic label might displace their Nationalist ideals. Seamus Mallon takes a more resolute position in relation to the nation-state. He is an apologist for Nationalism, arguing that it will always be a vibrant and legitimate political philosophy on the island of Ireland. Mallon believes that it will always be a major motivating force within the SDLP. He does not espouse Hume's post-Nationalist ideology and asserts:

'I don't know of a date which the SDLP will cease to be Nationalist and become something else. Nationalism will always be there. Nationalism is a positive factor. It's a legitimate political philosophy. It is only Nationalism in political terms that can provide the outlet to people who would have otherwise favoured the use of violence.'[49]

Whatever different interpretations are given to Hume's post-Nationalist philosophy the European dimension has nevertheless been an important model for acceptable cross-border institutions to the SDLP in their negotiating stance in the 1997/98 peace talks at Stormont. Sean Farren a senior party negotiator at these talks, addressing the SDLP student support group at Trinity College in Dublin said:

'Since the overwhelming desire of the majority of people within the Nationalist tradition throughout Ireland is for partnership, not domination, it is clear that co-operation based on mutual respect will be the goal of such arrangements. In practical evidence of this goal will be a requirement that all decisions in a North-South body be consensually based. This is the same basis for decision-making followed within the European Council of Ministers upon which the SDLP has based its model for North-South institutions.'[50]

American Involvement in the Northern Ireland Conflict

By 1976, the collapse of Sunningdale and the failure of the Constitutional Convention created a sense of hopelessness and stagnation in northern Irish politics. For the remainder of the 1970s, the British Government lacked the incentive to introduce any new political initiative. The gradual enervation of power-sharing as enshrined in the *1973 Northern Ireland Constitution Act* alarmed many members of the SDLP. The pact between the Unionists and the Labour Party at Westminster during the late 1970s did little to espouse SDLP faith in progressive Government policy towards Northern Ireland.

The SDLP was left in the political wilderness from the mid-1970s onwards. Having attained the heights of participation in Government during the Sunningdale era, they were demoted to almost political irrelevance for the remainder of the decade. The Party had extreme difficulty in keeping their policy of power-sharing and an Irish dimension alive in a climate of political indifference from the British Government and deliberate intransigence from the Unionists. It left the Party feeling vulnerable in contrast to Unionists whose morale was buoyant during the mid-1970s.

John Hume's connection with American politics was motivated by two considerations. Firstly, there was the reality that John Hume might face unemployment in the mid-1970s. It was a matter of some urgency for him to develop his career in America. As Barry White has commented, Hume and his connections with America acted, 'as a lever to create political movement in Northern Ireland'.[51] These connections created a political vehicle for the SDLP to network and court political allies abroad to allow the Party to crusade for the Nationalist political position outside Northern Ireland. White has also maintained that Hume built up a good relationship with Irish-American political leaders, both from his early television appearances as a Civil Rights activist, and later, as a Government Minister during the period of the Sunningdale administration.

Hume had already entered into direct communication with influential American circles in 1972 when he first met Edward (Ted) Kennedy. Following the death of thirteen civilians in Derry on 'Bloody Sunday' on 30 January 1972 a Congressional Sub-committee was established under the Chairmanship of Hugh Carey, who subsequently became Governor of New York. Delegations from Northern Ireland went to the United States in 1972 to give evidence to that Sub-committee. During the early 1970s, Kennedy consistently attacked British policy towards Northern Ireland. After 'Bloody Sunday' Kennedy supported the demands from Irish-American groups for British withdrawal from Northern Ireland and the reunification of Ireland. Hume felt at the time that Kennedy was acting out of genuine desire to help the situation, but that nevertheless, his comments were inopportune and somewhat naive.[52]

Bloody Sunday generated intense interest on Capitol Hill concerning the Northern Ireland conflict. In the aftermath of Bloody Sunday, Ted Kennedy decided that the next time he went to Europe he would talk directly to political activists in Northern Ireland. Seán Donlon, former Irish Ambassador in the United States and Head of The Anglo-Irish Division of the Department of Foreign Affairs in Dublin, recalled that, as Kennedy had no immediate plans to visit Ireland, he sent a message asking if John Hume could meet him during his travels to the Continent. Sean Ronan, Irish Ambassador in Bonn, arranged a meeting between Hume and Kennedy in the Irish Embassy at Bonn.[53] From this initial meeting, Hume and Kennedy built up a close rapport.

Hume's subsequent influence was to prove vital in moderating Kennedy in his approach to Irish issues. There is no doubt that Hume did influence Kennedy in promoting constitutional Nationalist politics in the United States. Michael McKinley has observed that Kennedy came to be guided almost entirely on Northern Ireland issues by Hume. Kennedy later described Hume as, '...one of the finest and most creative political leaders of our generation, a man of extraordinary courage and wisdom and understanding'.[54]

Many Catholic Irish-Americans have entertained romantic notions of the eventual reunification of Ireland. Many descendants of Irish emigrants who found refuge in America after the Great Famine in 1845 still hold bitter feelings towards Britain for one of the worst plights in Irish history. This archaic thinking among Irish-Americans towards Britain was still evident in the United States until the mid-1970s. When the troubles broke out in 1969 the older generation of Irish-Americans blamed Britain for the outbreak of the violence. Nostalgia among Irish-Americans led many to Revolutionary Nationalism. Andrew Wilson has commented that, 'These militants believed the Provisionals were the direct heirs of the heroes of 1916, guided by the same principles and objectives.'[55]

The outbreak of the troubles in 1969 enabled Irish-American Republicans to rekindle their militant attitudes towards Britain. Thus, the Provisional IRA garnered a considerable amount of indirect support for their campaign of violence from the Irish-American community. The Provisionals' lifeline was coming largely from funds and arms supplied indirectly through Irish-American support. There was considerable apprehension within the SDLP during the mid-1970s, that the continuing political vacuum might lead to Nationalists to abandon constitutional politics and support militant republicanism. It was vital for the SDLP to cut off this lifeline to the Provisional IRA.

From the mid-1960s onwards, the Irish diplomatic service had focused on obtaining Ireland's membership of the European Economic Community. Donlon has said, 'All available resources were marshalled for that particular purpose, with the result offices in the States were run down. This in effect gave the British a free run in the States and it gave militant republicanism a free run.'[56] Donlon has also maintained the Irish-American community was hostile towards the Irish Government when the emigration laws were changed in the United States during the early 1960s. Instead of lobbying for liberal legislation to permit Irish exit visas, the Irish Government actually lobbied the United States Government to close the American door on Irish emigration. Sean Lemass, Minister for Industry and Commerce under De Valera's Fianna Fáil-led Government in the Republic, was extremely nervous about the serious decline in the population of the Republic. He believed that unless emigration was curtailed in Ireland, the Republic would never be able to build up an economy. Donlon has claimed this infuriated Irish-Americans at a time when Hispanic emigration was just beginning and the black population was beginning to assert itself in the United States.

When the troubles broke out in Northern Ireland in 1969, the Irish Government's ability to influence Irish-Americans was severely hampered. Donlon believed, 'That is why the IRA particularly, in the early 'seventies, had such a significant success.'[57] FitzGerald pointed out that the initial approach to meeting the challenge of the IRA campaign could be traced back to Jack Lynch and his Minister of Justice, Des O'Malley, in 1972.[58] Jack Lynch, as Leader of Fianna Fáil took a more moderate position in relation to Northern Ireland in contrast to some of the hard-line thinking on the issue within Fianna Fáil. After he assumed power in the Republic from Liam Cosgrave on 16 June 1977, he upheld the former Coalition strategy in relation to the Irish-American lobby in the US. Subsequently, successive Irish Governments (with the support of the SDLP) have attempted to steal Irish-American support away from traditional sympathy for the IRA. From the mid-seventies onwards, the Irish Government, with the vital support of John Hume, made significant inroads into the traditional Irish-American support for militant Irish Republicanism. By the end of the 1970s, the success of Hume, Michael Lillis and Seán Donlon led to the isolation of the Republican lobby in the United States.

From 1970 onwards, Irish-American groups in the United States became highly organised in lobbying support within their own

Republican Party against British injustices in Northern Ireland. The Irish Northern Aid Committee, known as NORAID, was founded in 1970. NORAID was established largely as a fund-raising body for dependants of Irish Republican prisoners with close links to the Provisional IRA. British, Irish, United States and SDLP sources viewed the organisation as a pro-terrorist group. Jack Holland has written that, within sixteen months of its formation, there were some seventy branches of NORAID throughout the United States. The greatest support was concentrated in the New York area, where the Committee claimed two-thousand members. The organisation had a very strong pro-IRA ethos among its members. According to Holland, NORAID had frequent contacts with IRA activists and political spokesmen such as Ruairí O'Brádaigh and Joe Cahill.[59] The SDLP believed that NORAID was a discrete front-organisation for the Provisional IRA with particular hostility towards their Party and the Irish Government.

While NORAID had little success in securing substantial American diplomatic support over Northern Ireland, the Irish National Caucus[60] proved better at infiltrating American diplomatic circles. It set out to campaign against British injustice and for the provision of human rights in Northern Ireland representing militant republicanism. Rigorous British security policy in Nationalist areas during the 1970s and the, reputedly, inhumane treatment of suspected terrorists in Police Interrogation Centres in Northern Ireland, gave the Caucus the necessary propaganda it needed for its survival. The Caucus initiated the setting up of the Ad Hoc Committee on Irish Affairs in September 1977. Although it was an informal body without any status or locus stand in Congress, it nevertheless had recruited over one-hundred Congressmen. The fear among constitutional Nationalists regarding this new body was that the majority of its members were Democrats. From the SDLP perspective, there was the danger that constitutional Nationalism might become overshadowed by militant Irish Republicanism.

As early as 1976, it became evident that one objective of the SDLP and Irish foreign affairs officials was to preclude Irish-American groups from taking over the Northern Ireland issue from outside the orbit of the constitutional Nationalists. Their other key objective was to persuade the British Government to bring the political parties in Northern Ireland together again in order to form some type of power-sharing administration. Holland has commented that:

'In spite of the many links between Ireland and America, no United

States Government in this century had shown any willingness to involve itself directly in the dispute with Britain. Two World Wars and a host of common global interests have fastened the Anglo-American partnership with stronger bonds than most Irish or Irish-Americans care to admit.'[61]

There was a great deal of apprehension among Irish constitutional Nationalists that Irish-American groups such as NORAID and the Irish National Caucus would influence American foreign policy on Northern Ireland. This fear became a reality when the National Caucus staged a publicity coup during the American Presidential Election in 1976. The Irish National Caucus focused on the election strategy of the Democratic Party to secure Jimmy Carter as President. One of the leaders of the Irish National Caucus, Father Sean McManus, persuaded Carter's aides of the importance of the Irish-American vote to win the prize of the White House. Carter flew to a conference at Pittsburgh to meet with delegates from eighteen Irish-American political groups as a consequence of McManus' intervention with the Democratic Party election officials.

An introductory speech at the Conference from McManus contained a vehement condemnation of British Human Rights violations. Wilson has said that McManus spiked aspects of the Democratic Party manifesto with words of his own, stating, '...The United States should encourage the formation of a United Ireland...'. Carter, suffering from fatigue after an intensive election campaign, 'overlooked the inflammatory sentence and said he supported McManus's [sic] statement'.[62] This incident alarmed John Hume and senior Irish Government officials in the United States to such an extent that they consolidated their efforts in Washington to counteract the relative success of the Irish National Caucus' lobbying in the Democratic Party. Hume, with the aid of Donlon and Lillis, convinced the White House to adopt the Carter initiative which was launched in July 1977.

Hume promotes Constitutional Nationalism in the United States with the aid of Senior Irish Government Officials

Hume became an important figure in the crusade against militant Irish Republicanism in the United States. He was an invaluable asset to the Irish Government on this issue. Hume had accepted a Fellowship at Harvard University in 1976. This opportunity gave him access to a wide network of influential Americans. In particular, it gave Hume the chance to rekindle his close friendship with Ted Kennedy and to promote constitutional Nationalism in the States. Although Hume joined ranks with Irish Government officials in the battle against NORAID and the Irish National Caucus, it was nevertheless Hume who success-fully converted Kennedy from promoting the objectives of militant Irish Republicanism to those of constitutional Nationalism. This was a major blow to NORAID and the Irish National Caucus.

In 1976, Garret FitzGerald, as Minister for Foreign Affairs in Dublin, shared a similar philosophy and viewpoint on Northern Ireland as Hume. Like Hume, he wanted to stem the flow of funds to the Provisional IRA and also open up the American connection to enable pressure to be placed on Britain to revive the political process in Northern Ireland. Traditionally, relations between Irish Embassy officials and Irish-American Congress politicians in Washington were distant. White has pointed out that Hume helped to foster relations between the Irish Government and Irish officials working in the United States with leading Irish-American politicians in Washington. Hume succeeded in having SDLP philosophy incorporated, 'into major statements from Washington and Dublin...'. Also, White has observed, 'It also helped counter the British Embassy's recurrent theme that Northern Ireland was Britain's problem alone, and proof of Hume's effectiveness was the succession of British Ministers and Civil Servants sent to drown his message.'[63] FitzGerald joined forces with Hume to co-ordinate a joint policy of obtaining the support of leading Irish-American leaders to rally behind constitutional Nationalists. Two other key players in this team were Seán Donlon and Michael Lillis. Both these senior civil servants worked for the Irish Foreign Affairs Department in Washington. 'They hoped that closer co-operation with politicians like Edward Kennedy and Tip O'Neill could nourish a strong support network which would be used to crush [militant Irish] Republicans.'[64] It was this combination of force which eventually counteracted the influence of militant Republicanism within the Democratic Party.

Donlon was the second civil servant from the Irish Department of Foreign Affairs in Dublin since the outbreak of the troubles in 1969 to be appointed to Northern Ireland in August 1971. His first assignment had been to collect information relating to the introduction of intern-ment. Eamon Gallagher, Donlon's predecessor, tutored Donlon in who to contact in Northern Ireland. Subsequently, when Donlon visited Derry, one of his first meetings was with John Hume. Donlon had known Hume since their student days together at Maynooth College. From August 1971, he began to know Hume professionally. Gallagher had initially introduced Hume to officials in the Department of

Foreign Affairs, but it was Donlon who became the main point of contact for Hume in the department. Hume also developed a close working relationship with Michael Lillis.

Hume's earlier discussions with Edward Kennedy had led to his introduction to some of the most influential Irish-American Democrats, in particular, Tip O'Neill, Speaker of the House, Senator Daniel Moynihan and Governor Hugh Carey of New York. 'Together with the Irish diplomatic corps in Washington, Hume began to champion the idea that these "Four Horsemen" [O'Neill, Moynihan, Carey and Kennedy] should co-ordinate their efforts on Ireland and issue a joint condemnation of IRA supporters in America.'[65]

Carey, O'Neill and Moynihan had all supported American Irish-Republicans in the past to pursue their own political careers.[66] With the combined efforts of Hume, Donlon and Lillis, the 'Four Horsemen' were strongly influenced by the persuasive arguments put forward by this joint Irish delegation. Towards the end of 1976, Wilson has commented that Hume and Michael Lillis set out to persuade the 'Four Horsemen' to issue a joint statement condemning both violence and Irish-American support for the IRA.[67]

Wilson has also maintained the failure of the Loyalist General Strike in May 1977 led to Hume becoming more optimistic about the prospects of agreement between the SDLP and moderate Unionist opinion at this time.[68] John Hume and Michael Lillis were behind the 'Four Horsemen' releasing a statement categorically condemning Irish-American support for the IRA on St Patrick's Day 1977. Hume drafted an outline of the statement for the 'Four Horsemen' to endorse.[69] The exact timing of the release of the statement had also been Hume's suggestion. It was a direct appeal for constitutional politics rather than discredited paramilitary methods. The 1977 St Patrick's Day statement galvanised American foreign policy on Northern Ireland. McKinley has indicated that the joint statement was testimony to Hume and to his, 'profound influence upon the attitudes of leading Americans'.[70] Edward Kennedy acknowledged, in an interview for *Magill* magazine in October 1997, the influence of John Hume in showing him the non-violent way forward in Northern Ireland.[71]

Adrian Guelke has argued that the origins of the Friends of Ireland can be traced back to the 1977 St Patrick's Day joint statement by the 'Four Horsemen'.

'The main features of the Friends [of Ireland] position on Northern Ireland are opposition to fund-raising for the Provisionals in the

United States, support for constitutional Nationalism as represented by the SDLP and the Irish Government, and a commitment that the United States Government should provide generous economic aid for Northern Ireland after a political settlement.'[72]

This was the first time that senior Irish-American officials joined together publicly to denounce the Provisional IRA. Also it signified the first public awareness exercise in the United States to contend that funding the Provisionals was not the proper vehicle for peace within Northern Ireland. John Hume along with the 'Four Horsemen', Seán Donlon, Michael Lillis, Jim Sharkey the Irish Embassy's Political Counsellor in the United States, and Tony O'Reilly, President of Heinz and a prominent Irish businessman in America, were the motive forces supporting 'Friends of Ireland'. From March 1976 onwards, Ireland Fund dinners were regularly arranged in order to raise money for cultural and charitable events in Northern Ireland. It was a forum for advocating the principles of constitutional Nationalism, draining American dollars away from the Provisional IRA campaign in Northern Ireland.

The Ad Hoc Committee in Congress headed by Mario Biaggi essentially adopted the Provisional IRA line. Hume, along with the 'Four Horsemen', did not want two groups in Congress dealing with Northern Ireland, namely, one backing the Irish Government and the other militant Irish Republicanism. Therefore, Tip O'Neill was the main instigator of the Friends of Ireland and were formally constituted in that they derived their authority from the Speaker. Biaggi's group had no formal authority – hence its title the 'Ad Hoc' Committee on Irish affairs. In effect, it had no status at all, obtaining neither finance nor administrative facilities.[73]

During the mid-1970s Hume successfully cultivated an American connection to the Northern Ireland problem. He saw his efforts rewarded by the statement of the 'Four Horsemen' on St Patrick's Day, 1977. From the Spring of 1977, a major shift in the American assessment of the problem developed. A fresh wave of thinking was starting to emerge among leading Irish-Americans. This was an important breakthrough for constitutional Nationalists in the fight against militant Irish Republicans in America. Aware of the stalemate in Northern Ireland politics, Hume planned to use his influence with the 'Four Horsemen' and Irish officials in Washington to prompt the British Government to pursue political progress again in the province.

The political vacuum in Northern Ireland during the mid-1970s left the SDLP unable to make any progress in local politics. These were the worst years that the Party had encountered in its short history as a political organisation. There were fears in SDLP circles that they might become politically marginal to the Catholic community they represented in the absence of political progress. Their initial dread that militant Republicanism would overtake constitutional Nationalist politics were exaggerated during this period. It was not until after the success of the hunger-strikes in the early 1980s that Republicanism proved to be a real threat to the SDLP. Joint efforts by the Irish Government and Hume were to reduce the financial, political and moral support for the IRA.

Hume was effective in converting a large percentage of Irish-Americans to the cause of constitutional Nationalism. This gave him the impetus to place American pressure on the British Government to force Unionists to reach some form of political compromise. 'Hume suggested to the Four Horsemen that Carter could offer the inducement of large American financial aid and industrial investment if a political agreement was reached.'[74] Traditional American policy towards Northern Ireland viewed the crisis as an internal issue for the British Government over its own affairs. But Wilson outlined in his thesis that Hume's suggestion of a Presidential Statement on the Northern Ireland issue was received enthusiastically by the Four Horsemen. 'Hume also believed that an initiative from Carter would have influence with Unionists. He hoped they would be more inclined to listen because Carter was a fundamentalist Protestant from the Bible belt'.[75]

The Carter initiative in August 1977 meant that American foreign policy on Northern Ireland was no longer neutral. Mary Holland has remarked that British officials at the Foreign Office were opposed to the first draft of the proposed Presidential Statement. In particular, they were against any Irish Government involvement in any political process in Northern Ireland. American aid for Northern Ireland was also another bone of contention for the British authorities.[76] External financial assistance for Northern Ireland implied direct rule had failed to reform the Northern Ireland State. However, in July 1977 the appointment of Peter Jay as new British Ambassador in Washington created a more conciliatory stance between Westminster and America.

White has argued that Hume, '...knew it was unrealistic to expect President Carter to come out and publicly attack Britain. He suggested that Carter could use a carrot to interest the British, offering American economic assistance in the event of political agreement being reached...'. Michael Lillis wrote the first draft of Carter's speech on Northern Ireland which was delivered on 30 August 1977. It took eight months of tough negotiating between the British, Irish and United States Government officials before the final speech was agreed. 'Hume's role was crucial at this point, advising how far to go and when the timing would be right, but always he knew he had a trump card in Tip O'Neill's support.'[77] Tip O'Neill wanted the endorsement of John Hume on all issues.[78]

When the Carter initiative was eventually launched in August 1977, it was a modified form of the original first draft. Yet it did have direct input from Hume, although this was never publicly admitted as it might have antagonised the Unionist tradition in Northern Ireland. Carter's statement supported an internal solution based on some form of political agreement among the political parties in Northern Ireland. The relevant part of the speech was its reference to the Irish Government having a role to play in a solution to the Northern Ireland problem. The initiative was a major coup for Hume and the Irish Government. Partnership-government and an Irish dimension were current SDLP policy during this period. The Carter initiative was the final seal of approval from Washington for constitutional Nationalism. It confirmed that the strategy taken by Hume and the Irish Government Officials in America during this period had eventually paid off. The intervention by the Irish-American lobby during the Carter Presidency was a milestone in American foreign policy towards Northern Ireland and from 1977 onwards, American administrations have played a more direct role in Northern Ireland's affairs.

The success of Carter's statement in August 1977 was a clear sign to Irish Republicans in the United States that constitutional Nationalism now dictated American foreign policy towards Northern Ireland. In reaction to the constitutionalists' success, NORAID and the Irish National Caucus, set out to establish a formal group of supporters in Congress. The Ancient Order of Hibernians and the National Caucus approached Congress Officials who championed the Irish Republican cause. Mario Biaggi formed the Ad Hoc Committee for Irish Affairs on 27 September 1977. American Irish Republicans hailed the Committee as a major breakthrough for their cause. The Ad Hoc Committee was basically concerned with Human Rights violations in Northern Ireland.

From 1978 onwards, it was apparent that the 'Four Horsemen' were no longer just going to criticise Irish Republicans in America who supported the armed struggle. Their joint St Patrick's Day statement in 1978, while criticising Irish-Americans who supported the Provisional IRA, also criticised the British Government and Unionists for causing the political impasse in Northern Ireland. Edward Kennedy hinted, 'that the efforts and impact of those in Northern Ireland were, to a very great extent, determined by active British support for power-sharing'.[79]

The release in August 1978 of an Amnesty International inquiry into Police harassment of suspected terrorists in Northern Ireland gave the Four Horsemen some ammunition to use against the British Government. Their change in attitude towards Westminster was to some degree to counteract the influence of the Ad Hoc Committee in promoting the Irish Republican cause. It also indicated their frustration at not being able to persuade the British to bring about a new political initiative in Northern Ireland.

The 1979 St Patrick's Day statement was critical of British Government Northern Ireland policy and, 'identified...drift...delay and neglect...and...conspicuous tilt in favour of the majority and to the detriment of the minority'.[80] Hume encouraged the 'Four Horsemen' to step up their pressure on the British to bring about a new political initiative within Northern Ireland. Hume also persuaded Tip O'Neill to lead a political delegation to Ireland to coincide with the British General Election in April 1979. This, '...could convince both the Conservative and Labour parties to give more consideration to a political solution in Northern Ireland'.[81]

O'Neill listened to Hume's advice and subsequently travelled to Northern Ireland with a delegation of leading Congressional Republicans and Democrats in the spring of 1979. After discussions with the SDLP and Unionist parties in Northern Ireland, he went to London to meet the leaders of the other main British political parties. After his meeting with Prime Minister James Callaghan, O'Neill realised that the British Government was ambivalent about reintroducing the political process to Northern Ireland. He accused the main political parties in Britain of using Northern Ireland as a 'political football'.[82]

The election of a Conservative Government led by Margaret Thatcher in April 1979 raised expectations that some new political initiative would be taken towards Northern Ireland. Edward Kennedy, in an interview given to the *Belfast Telegraph* , stressed that if the opportunity was missed to bring about a political initiative within Northern Ireland, the Four Horsemen's ability to block funding for the IRA would suffer a serious setback. It would appear that SDLP policy was the basis of his philosophy. He said, '...that the British should consider the withdrawal of the guarantee unless the Protestants agreed to some form of power-sharing'.[83] This line of argument ran parallel to SDLP thinking during the late 1970s.

Matters came to a head in relations between America and Britain when O'Neill supported the Irish National Caucus' ban on the sale of arms to the RUC in August 1979. O'Neill had the backing of constitutional Nationalists to support this ban. It was a sign of the anger of constitutional Nationalism towards British policy in Northern Ireland. Wilson has argued that O'Neill played a vital role in supporting Biaggi's amendment to the *State Department Appropriations Bill* and succeeded in bringing the amendment through Congress. From early August 1979, the State Department announced it would suspend its licence for arms sales to the RUC pending a review of policy.[84]

This incident made the Thatcher Government realise how powerful an influence the Four Horsemen were in Washington. To appease American pressure, the new Secretary of State, Humphrey Atkins, announced on 25 October 1979 that he would be calling a conference to discuss the possibility of drawing up some form of devolution in Northern Ireland. Hume believed that the British were about to launch an important initiative. As time passed, Guelke has argued that it became apparent that the Atkins' initiative was nothing more than an attempt to convince the Americans that the British Government had a definite policy towards Northern Ireland. Despite the weakness of Atkins' political initiative, American pressure on Britain did contribute to, 'overcoming British inertia and encouraging the British [to] grasp the nettle of the Loyalist veto on political progress'.[85]

Neil Blaney, Independent Fianna Fáil Teachta Dala for Donegal, visited the United States in December 1979. He condemned Irish Government policy under Jack Lynch to the Irish-American lobby. In a sense, he was setting the tone for the new Haughey administration in the Republic of Ireland. There was delight among Irish-American Republican circles at Charles Haughey's election as Taoiseach in December 1979. They felt his Government would be more supportive of the Ad Hoc Committee.[86] FitzGerald noted that this lobby looked to Haughey, 'to vindicate their cause'[87] and encouraged him to get rid of Seán Donlon as Irish Ambassador in the United States during 1980.

Donlon had been one of the key players in diminishing financial and political support for militant Irish Republicanism in the United States. Haughey gave into Irish-American Republican pressure for Donlon to be transferred to the post of Permanent Representative to the United Nations in New York. But Haughey reversed his decision to remove Donlon after strong public condemnation from Hume. More

importantly, the Four Horsemen warned Haughey they would withdraw their co-operation with the Irish Government if Donlon was
removed from his post.[88]

Hume was opposed to Haughey's tacit support for Biaggi during the
early 1980s which indirectly provided a bulwark for the position of
NORAID and the Irish National Caucus. Hume insisted that Haughey
make a public statement denouncing militant Irish Republicanism in
the United States.[89] Haughey made a speech in Cork on 23 July 1980
where he named and denounced NORAID and the Irish National
Caucus. Nevertheless, there still remained a degree of ambivalence in
his attitude towards Biaggi.

The Reagan Administration adopted a more neutral position to
Northern Ireland when it took office in January 1981. There was the
expectation that United States policy would radically change under
Reagan. The anticipated casualty was the abandonment of the strategy
initiated by Hume, Lillis and the Four Horsemen promoting the constitutional Nationalist position in the United States.[90] This strategy was
aimed at getting the White House to pressurise the government into
taking action to resolve the Northern Ireland problem. The tactic had
achieved considerable success. President Carter had twice asked
Thatcher about her policy towards Northern Ireland.

Reagan's Presidency began with a commitment to non-interference
in Anglo-Irish affairs. Until Carter's initiative in 1977, the United
States administration had taken a strategy of regarding the Northern
Ireland problem as an internal United Kingdom concern. President
Reagan stressed that the United States could not intervene or interfere
in the affairs of Northern Ireland.[91] Even throughout the hunger-strike
era, the American administration sustained a policy of non-involvement
in the issue, maintaining it was British responsibility.[92]

In March 1982 Charles Haughey travelled to the United States
seeking Reagan Administration support for the Irish Government negotiating position with Westminster.[93] He tried to persuade the Reagan
administration to include a statement favouring unity as part of official
United States policy on Northern Ireland. Reagan outlined that, 'The
United States cannot chart a course for the people of Northern
Ireland...[and]...If endurable solutions are to come they must be from
the people themselves. United States policy will continue to urge the
parties in Northern Ireland to come together for a just solution.'[94]

Haughey's association with Teddy Glesson, the President of the
Loughshoremen's Association – who had purported links with organisations supporting the Provisional IRA – tainted his June 1982 trip to the

United States.[95] Haughey always sought American support for negotiations between the British and Irish Governments to concentrate purely on Irish unity. He wanted, 'to have this aim incorporated as a goal of United States foreign policy'.[96] Haughey counteracted the advancement of constitutional Nationalism in the United States during the 1980s by undermining the work of Hume, Donlon, Lillis and the Four Horsemen. During an address to the Fianna Fáil Ard Fheis in 1984, Haughey criticised the American Government for failing to include, 'the re-establishment of the historic unity of Ireland as a major objective of her foreign policy'.[97]

In May 1984[98] and again later in March 1985[99] Haughey called on the United States administration to persuade the British Government to support the proposal in the *Forum Report* which called for a constitutional conference. The conference was to be convened by both the British and Irish Governments with the objective of agreement as to new structures for a new unitary Irish state. Haughey felt that FitzGerald's negotiations with the British during 1985 were moving towards endorsing an internal settlement for Northern Ireland. From his viewpoint, the *Anglo-Irish Agreement* negotiations attempted to restructure society in Northern Ireland. Haughey was afraid that signing the *Anglo-Irish Agreement* would, 'enable Britain to turn to Ireland's friends around the world...and claim that Ireland's problems were resolved'.[100] Therefore, the international forum would no longer have to be concerned about British policy towards Northern Ireland. Haughey opposed the *Anglo-Irish Agreement* calling for American support of the Fianna Fáil objective of Irish unity.

British fears of continuing American influence in the Northern Ireland conflict abated when Ronald Reagan led a new American Republican administration in the United States. But the hunger strikes of 1980-81 resuscitated nostalgic American support for militant Irish Republicanism. Most notably, it boosted the NORAID fund-raising campaign.[101]

After Margaret Thatcher made her famous 'Out, Out, Out' comments in November 1984 the outlook for developing the Anglo-Irish process was extremely gloomy. Mrs Thatcher had planned an official visit to the United States for January 1985. During her visit, she was to address a joint session of the House and Senate. Tip O'Neill made it known to Thatcher that it would be very difficult for him to offer this prestigious platform in the light of the deteriorating Anglo-Irish situation. It is now known that Bill Clarke, a close friend of Seán Donlon, persuaded President Reagan to phone Thatcher about the Forum episode. From that time onwards, her tone was much more moderate in relation to Northern Ireland.[102] FitzGerald has noted that this, 'must have been a factor contributing to the more positive approach the British adopted a month or so later'.[103] Donlon claimed, 'We needed the backing of people like President Reagan to achieve what became the *Anglo-Irish Agreement*. We might not have achieved that without American backing.'[104] Following a European Summit meeting in Dublin, FitzGerald and Thatcher held a bilateral meeting which placed Anglo-Irish negotiations back on-course. Thatcher was subsequently able to go to Washington and have her ceremonial lap of honour. Indirectly the hard work which the SDLP put into the *Forum Report* could have been seriously jeopardised if the Irish Government had focused all its attention on Thatcher's remarks. It could have echoed the Falklands era when Anglo-Irish relations deteriorated markedly in 1982.

The Irish Government was able to use United States' intervention to get British support for the principles contained in the *Forum Report*. President Reagan praised, '...the courageous and forthright efforts by those directly involved in the *Report* of the New Ireland Forum'.[105] One of the main difficulties for the SDLP during the run up to the *Anglo-Irish Agreement* was dealing with the lack of coherent policy by Fine Gael and Fianna Fáil on Northern Ireland. It led to, 'persistent divisions among Irish-American organisations, preventing the development of a united front'.[106] United States backing for the *Anglo-Irish Agreement* was vital in the aftermath of Thatcher's strong rebuke to the Forum's findings because it reinforced the SDLP policy of establishing a strong Anglo-Irish framework based on the principles of the *New Ireland Forum Report*.

By 1980 Hume had capitalised on bringing an American dimension to the Northern Ireland conflict. The British were made aware that their Northern Ireland policy was now outside the domain of the British Isles. There was now an international audience to monitor their progress. The Northern Ireland problem was no longer just an internal problem between the two communities. Hume, with the help of Irish officials, was responsible for extending the remit of the Northern Ireland problem to an international sphere from 1977 onwards.

This international dimension later played a role in the making of the *Anglo-Irish Agreement*. While Hume was successful in marginalising American support for militant Irish Republicanism by 1980 he also managed to promote his political policies with the help of American allies, despite the political vacuum in Northern Ireland during the late

1970s. Hume felt it was important to re-educate Irish Americans concerning the essence of conflict in Northern Ireland. He felt the problem was more complex than the simple Irish-American formula to, 'get the British out and the problem will be solved'.[107] Much of his time was spent trying to instil the philosophy of constitutional Nationalism among senior Irish-American politicians.

In practical terms, Hume devoted a lot of his energy to pursuing economic assistance for Northern Ireland. His task was made all the more difficult by the IRA bombing campaign in Northern Ireland which was frequently directed at foreign industrial targets in Northern Ireland. In 1978, The Ancient Order of Hibernians in the United States had written to top American industrialists and major companies warning of the dangers of investing in Northern Ireland.[108] Hume had difficulties in counteracting the scaremongering of militant Irish-American extremists in his efforts to obtain foreign investment for Northern Ireland.

With the help of the Irish Government Hume actively campaigned in the United States against the MacBride Principles which attempted to ensure that American companies who invested in the Province increased the participation of Catholics in the Northern Ireland workforce. Hume felt that rather than eliminating discrimination the MacBride Principles only acted to discourage new investment for jobs. He also undermined the Sinn Féin drive for exit visas to the United States from the mid-1970s and throughout the 1980s in support of Irish Government policy. Hence the SDLP and its constitutional Nationalist position was successfully promoted in the United States almost single-handedly through John Hume as the legitimate and sole representative of the Northern minority from the mid-1970s onwards.

However, the rise of another Irish American lobbying group with considerable influence has diluted the Hume monopoly over Northern Ireland matters in America during the 1990s. During Bill Clinton's Presidential Election Campaign in 1992 Niall O'Dowd, publisher of *Irish Voice* in New York, helped set up an Irish-American pro-Clinton group to rally significant Irish-American support for the prospective Democratic President. Bruce Morrison a former Congressman was appointed Head of the new group along with Raymond Flynn, Mayor of Boston. In the first meeting between Clinton and the new group initially named 'Irish Americans for Clinton', Clinton promised that, on election, he would assign a 'special envoy' to Northern Ireland and provide a visa for Gerry Adams who had been banned from the United States since the 1970s.[109] This group, led by O'Dowd and Morrison equally, played a significant role with the SDLP and others involved in gaining the trust of the Irish Republican leadership, to achieve the IRA cessation of violence in August 1994. This Irish-American group has not been popular with the SDLP. Bruce Morrison has recalled, 'I was always a minor player with Hume because I wasn't Foley and I wasn't Kennedy.'[110] The SDLP felt the group identified too much with Sinn Féin and was caught up in its political agenda to the detriment of other parties.[111] O'Dowd and others took over the role of influencing senior American officials which formerly had been carried out by Hume and the Irish Government.

The 1990s have been years of a dramatic turn-around in American involvement in the Northern Ireland problem. Figures such as Senator Edward Kennedy who adopted SDLP policy and remained resolute opponents of militant Irish Republicanism since the mid-1970s, surprisingly supported Gerry Adams, Sinn Féin President, in his move to obtain a visa to enter the United States before the first cessation of violence in August 1994.[112] Edward Kennedy's own change of mind has depended largely on Hume's regular up-to-date advice following the Hume/Adams initiative; this initiative sent out signs to the Clinton Administration that Hume's frequent contact with Adams made it less unsavoury to deal directly with Sinn Féin. Despite the erosion of the influence of the 'Four Horsemen' during the 1990s Kennedy has, if anything, increased in prominence in the Clinton administration. The Kennedy influence has not stopped with Senator Edward Kennedy, but the appointment of his sister Jean Kennedy Smith as United States Ambassador to Ireland has made the family an American force to be reckoned with.

Jean Kennedy Smith has played an active role in the peace talks largely to the benefit of the Nationalist community in Northern Ireland, much to the hostility of the British Government who have traditionally dictated Northern Ireland policy to former United States administrations, most recently through, 'the influential British Ambassador to Washington, Sir Robin Renwick'.[113] With strong support from John Hume, the two Kennedys, among others, played a vital role in getting Gerry Adams a visa to the United States despite total opposition from the British Government. Hume persuaded the Irish Ambassador that Adams was sincere in his search for peace and that the visa would bring the dividend of an end to the IRA campaign of violence. The granting of a visa to Gerry Adams was a rebuff to London and a clear sign that American foreign policy towards Northern Ireland under the Clinton Administration was largely autonomous from British interference. Conor O'Clery has claimed, 'The visa decision indicated that Mr Clinton's National Security Council headed by Mr Anthony Lake was now in the ascendancy over the traditionally pro-British State Department on the Irish question'.[114] The fall-out from the Adams visit left the 'special relationship' between the United States and the Major-led Conservative administration in Britain and at very low ebb.

The Clinton Administration took its lead not only from the SDLP leader John Hume, but also from the Irish Government under the Taoiseach at that time, Albert Reynolds, who came into power in February 1992. Ironically this meant that Irish Government support for constitutional Nationalism in Northern Ireland represented traditionally by the SDLP took a back-seat during the 1990s. This reversal in Irish Government Northern Ireland policy was implemented under the direction of Séan O hUiginn, Head of the Anglo-Irish division of the Department of Foreign Affairs in Dublin, and Martin Mansergh, the Taoiseach's adviser on Northern Ireland, who both became instrumental in engaging Sinn Féin in mainstream constitutional politics.[115]

Although Clinton's lifting of the visa ban on Gerry Adams was a significant determinant in bringing the 1994 cease-fire it meant that SDLP access to the highest echelons of American power was now also available to Sinn Féin too. This was perhaps the biggest sacrifice that the SDLP and Hume made to Sinn Féin in the peace process. They opened the doors of the White House to Adams. Once Adams obtained access to Irish-American groups, he would achieve, 'political stature' at Hume's expense.[116] In fact after the announcement of the first IRA cessation of violence in August 1994, it became clear that access to the White House was not only a SDLP privilege but available to all of Northern Ireland's political parties including the fringe Loyalist parties. Acknowledging the role played by all involved in bringing about the current peace process, the Clinton administration would regard John Hume as its chief architect. In the aftermath of the August 1994 IRA cease-fire – and its subsequent renewal – the SDLP leader has also been credited with the achievement of harnessing the economic influence of Irish America to invest and create growth in Northern Ireland through private funds and in the International Fund For Ireland.

CHAPTER ELEVEN

Party Organisation

American Assistance for improving the SDLP Organisational Base
The 1983 General Election marked a downturn in SDLP fortunes.
Towards the end of 1984, John Hume wanted to broaden the political
base of the SDLP. He decided to develop this concept by contacting
the leadership of the Democratic Party in the United States. The
Democratic Party suggested that the SDLP communicate with its
National Democratic Institute for International Affairs (NDI).[1] The
Friends of Ireland in Congress (of whom the 'Four Horsemen' were all
Democratic members, would vehemently have sought assistance for the
SDLP through the NDI.[2]

The SDLP solicited NDI assistance 'in developing a program [*sic*]
to strengthen the Party's capacity to contribute to democratic development within Northern Ireland'.[3] The NDI made it clear to the SDLP
leadership that it could not give any support to the Party in their election campaigns. Its support was basically by way of an insight to technical services, rather than of a political nature. Such support services
were in the areas of 'organizational [*sic*] development, constituent services, civic education, and financial management'.[4] The NDI recommended that a feasibility study should be undertaken after the
Northern Ireland local elections in May, 1985, to identify the exact
areas in which the Institute could offer assistance to the SDLP. The
NDI intended to concentrate its efforts on 'the organizational weakness
of the SDLP'.[5]

Therefore, the NDI's initial remit was to build up the Party machine.
Membership of the SDLP was falling and electoral techniques were outmoded.[6] Participants in the NDI seminars included the deputy leader,
Seamus Mallon and various other lower-ranking members. The NDI
thought it was totally impractical that some of the brightest and best calibre candidates within the SDLP were not receiving training. Tom Kelly
recalled, 'The NDI were insisting that the SDLP choose the brightest
and best candidates for training. However, the Party leadership selected
people for personal reasons rather than out of merit.'[7]

The SDLP's American delegation which attended the NDI seminar in 1984, made detailed recommendations to the Party Executive on methods of gaining greater efficiency in the Party organisation. The SDLP group tried to draw up a plan or strategy which would best translate their American experience to the practical benefit of the Party. It was felt that there was no sense of communication from the Party leadership down to the grass-roots members. It was particularly at grass-roots levels that members of the SDLP needed a sense of belonging.

The group felt that the Party should increase its strength by developing electoral strategies for a forthcoming Westminster Election in 1987 as well as for subsequent Local Government and European Elections. The review group believed the basic organisational objective in the SDLP should be to disseminate information about what each unit of the party was doing to the greatest extent possible. Consequently, two benefits would accrue. Firstly, there would be a greater sense of involvement for the membership; secondly, the work of individuals and groups within the Party might improve. In particular, it was suggested that consideration should be given to scientific and professional analysis of election results and available political surveys Also, campaigning preparation should be undertaken by SDLP headquarters by way of training candidates and branches in the techniques of electioneering. Any new comprehensive approach in SDLP strategy was also to include a complete reorganisation of Party Headquarters.

The executive needed to give better assistance to Party Councillors and representatives in briefing and assisting them on contentious issues. There was a need for better conduct of internal meetings at all levels of the Party ranging from branch level through to the Executive Committee. Also, greater professionalism had to be given to budgeting and finance by the internal Party organisation.[8]

The Formation of the Social Democratic Group
The establishment of the Social Democratic Group (SDG) marked a major departure for the NDI who traditionally operated non-partisan programmes. Northern Ireland was the single country where they made an exception by working solely with the SDLP. It was a unique relationship between Hume and the Chairman of the Democratic National Committee (DNC) Paul Kirk and other senior Democrats at that time.[9] To some degree, Sinn Fein's entry into electoral politics within Northern Ireland would have contributed to the formation of the SDG with the objective of strengthening the SDLP organisationally.[10] The Party urgently needed to motivate itself to contest elections in a serious and systematic way.

The National Democratic Institute (NDI) was funded initially by the National Endowment for Democracy (NED) which was associated with the Democratic Party in the United States. The NDI states that its main objective is 'to foster and support democratic institutions and pluralistic values overseas'.[11] It was envisaged that the SDLP institute would be a separate entity from the NDI. The SDLP would appoint its own personnel to the proposed Institute and it would be responsible to the Party in its requirements. The NDI would fund the new Institute 'for agreed upon programmes of development.[12]

It was recommended that the Institute was to be invested as a Company, limited by guarantee. The shareholders, three in number, would be 'nominated by the Central Executive of the SDLP and act as Trustee Shareholders on its behalf'.[13] The Trustee Shareholders could be appointed to the Board of Directors if warranted. The Institute would be under the direct control of the SDLP executive. Consequently, the SDLP Institute would be expected to pursue any selected programmes as requested by the SDLP. Formal agreement between the NDI and the SDLP was officially sanctioned by Eddie McGrady on behalf of the SDLP on 12 April 1986. Tom Kelly recalled, 'Eddie McGrady was the first Chairman of SDG. That was significant not only because he was an accountant, but also because organisationally McGrady is probably the best of the SDLP'.[14]

The SDLP Institute was officially given the title, The Social Democratic Group Limited (SDG). It was inscribed by the Register of Companies for Northern Ireland on 28 May 1986. The Board of Directors consisted of Berna McIvor, Michael Boyd, Peter Gibson and Donovan McClelland, all carefully hand-picked by John Hume. Eddie McGrady was appointed Chairman, Pat Brannigan (Treasurer) and Alban Maguinness (Secretary of the Board). Tom Kelly was appointed second Executive Director of the SDG, after his predecessor, John Kennedy, left after some six months.[15] Kelly was Mallon's Westminster assistant until 1987. The first Board of Directors meeting was held on 14 June 1986. Grants of $20,000 and $10,000 each from the NDI were recorded by the Chairman ($20,000 National Endowment Funds and $10,000 raised privately). The initial expenditure of the SDG for the first quarter of its existence was £600. This included the registration of the new organisation, and press advertising for the Executive Director's position.[16]

The SDG was thus established as a formal training and development organisation for the SDLP with direct links with the NDI. It dealt with the training needs of key figures within the SDLP, one example of which was on their media techniques. In particular, it focused on the needs of the Chair, Secretaries and Branch Treasurers of the SDLP. In its objectives, it set out to provide technical assistance and training for branch development, campaigning and electioneering techniques, communications, fund-raising, policy research and political education.[17]

The main objective of the NDI in helping the SDLP establish the SDG was to broaden the base of support for constitutional non-violent politics within Northern Ireland. The SDG set out objectives in three main areas focusing on its training to advance their ultimate goal.

1. **The civic education and recruitment of young people**.
   To design outreach programmes that would educate young people in the value to society that their participation in democratic politics would make.

2. **Designing the substance and delivery mechanisms for the message of democratic participation**.
   Training workshops to concentrate on using the media as an instrument to demonstrate to the community the benefits of participating within the democratic process.

3. **Leadership development**.
   Training to be used in defining organisational portfolios within the SDLP. Also, individuals within the Party should be assisted 'to utilize [*sic*] their experience in other areas to strengthen the political process'.[18]

The NDI sent three Democratic Party consultants to Northern Ireland as part of a survey team during the summer of 1985 and spring of 1986. This allowed the NDI to assess the political context of Northern Ireland and to identify the precise training needs of the SDLP. 'In addition, an advisory committee comprising twelve prominent Democratic Party activists from the academic, political and labor [*sic*] fields...contributed its expertise in developing NDI's program with the SDLP.'[19] A selected SDLP delegation attended seminars on democratic development in Northern Ireland from 13-23 July 1986 at Harvard Institute of Politics and at the McCormack Institute, University of Massachusetts.[20] The seminars provided the delegates with practical training and input in relation to organisation, strategic planning and media techniques.

In June 1987, a third survey team was sent to Northern Ireland by the NDI to review the progress of the SDG. Patricia Keefer, NDI Senior Consultant and Les Francis, a Democratic Party Consultant, spent ten days in Northern Ireland; Brian Atwood, NDI President, also joined the group for four days.[21] The purpose of their visit was to assess the SDG accomplishments during its first year in operation and identify future assistance which the SDG might require.

The NDI survey team expressed concern that erroneous and, in some cases, deliberate, media accounts about the SDLP's American connections could have a detrimental effect on the work of the SDG. The SDG was viewed as a vehicle for providing financial resources for the SDLP by Unionists who alleged that the SDLP grant of $30,000 had come from the CIA.[22] However, there was no substance to these allegations and they did not in any way warrant the final closure of the SDG. Also, Unionists believed the NDI's relationship with the SDLP was, in effect, American aid for the SDLP to promote the *Anglo–Irish Agreement*.[23]

For the period 1 July 1987 to 30 June 1988, the NDI gave the SDG a grant of $50,000 for the purposes of organisational development, civic education and management skills.[24] Funds were not misappropriated by the SDG but, at times, the organisation failed to meet the stringent bureaucratic requirements of the NDI. The NDI as a 'non-profit incorporated entity'[25] was subject to United States' laws and regulations in their use of Government funds. The NDI needed the SDG to provide quarterly reports of activities and expenditure. Before the NDI could approve SDG funds it had to 'gain approval by the NDI Board of Directors before going to the National Endowment for Democracy Board of Directors for NED funding'.[26] The NDI required the SDG to report funding as 'federal' originating either from the NED, or 'non-federal' or non-NED private sources.[27] The NDI was unable to commit itself beyond $30,000 to the SDG for specific proposals in April 1986 . Basically, the SDG had failed to present proposals in time for the NDI and NED boards to approve further assistance.[28] The NDI pointed out that it did not want the SDG to give the appearance that its activities were 'directly related to campaigns or elections'.[29]

The survey team in 1987 found that the SDLP had immense difficulties fully grasping the role and purpose of the SDG. There was an aura of vagueness surrounding its existence. The SDG had to deal with 'its own program [*sic*] and internal decision-making apparatus...and explain its separate identity from that of the party'.[30] Also it had to 'understand the various relationships within and between the NDI and the NED and their respective boards and staff'.[31] It failed to educate the membership of the SDLP 'as to the Foundation's existence and its precise role'.[32]

The objective of the SDG was to echo the role of the NDI as a training institute for non-partisan programmes within Northern Ireland. Yet the NDI realised it was working with the SDG in a very partisan way. Tom Kelly recalled that the NDI told the SDG that it would have to run several non-partisan programmes throughout its life-span. Kelly claimed, 'The SDLP could not live with the fact that they would have to run bi-partisan and non-partisan programmes.'[33]

It was anticipated that the SDG would branch out and become an international institute for the SDLP. However, senior SDLP officials were unhappy at the way it was taking on a life of its own. Mallon saw it as interference in the internal affairs of the SDLP. Some felt that Hume originally regarded it as a way of getting funds into the SDLP. The reality was that interference into the Party from an outside body was going to expose a whole second tier of potential SDLP leaders who demonstrated considerable talent and acumen. This was something which the NDP was keen to cultivate. But it was inconceivable that senior Party figures would subject themselves to a diminution of their powers or control at the hands of a younger generation in the Party.

The bulk of the SDLP members were unable to get their minds around the idea of what an NDI-type institute in Northern Ireland could ideally obtain from service training for other social democratic parties. They certainly did not understand that it was necessary to run non-partisan events to justify its funding for the core activity of organisational training for the SDLP. Kelly claimed,

'The Executive was very split. There were a lot of nodding donkeys at the Executive. The main reason why the SDG fell was because Hume didn't actively support it. Hume could have saved the relationship with NDI. The NDI took the attitude that if you don't run these non-partisan programmes you are not going to get funding. It was already difficult enough for them to find a way of funding us. They decided to pull the plug. They never officially said that. It just went through the grapevine that we were not going to get funded. We had to reach out and get funding from other sources. The reality was the SDLP did not want us to get funding from other sources.'[34]

In the aftermath of the Second Youth Symposium organised by the SDG, the SDLP Executive met and discussed the future role of the SDG. The SDLP was unhappy with the divergent nature of such workshops. The Executive voted in January 1989, by a single vote, for the SDG to continue. Because the SDLP never fully understood the role of the SDG, the organisation did not successfully develop and subsequently, the SDLP relationship with the NDI was badly damaged. Kelly believed the SDG could have grown into a training institute for the SDLP, working with other social democratic parties on a European basis. He believed it could have functioned possibly on the same principles as the Friedrich Ebert Foundation.[35] Kelly recalled,

'Having talked to people in [the] NDI since, they regret in many ways that they came into Northern Ireland on that basis now. I think the history of the relationship proved that it was fairly fraught and things they wanted the SDG to do the SDLP didn't want them to do. I think they had difficulty with that. I think if NDI were to start again they probably would not have come in that route. They would have come in an all-party basis.'[36]

From 1987 until 1989, the SDG successfully conducted two major youth workshops, called the Martin Luther Symposium, representative of the two communities within Northern Ireland. Ironically in 1987, the SDG achieved full participation from all the political parties and all the major churches to join together on one platform. The SDG had obvious potential for bringing people together. Perhaps tragically, their chance was lost. If the SDG could have branched out in a cross-party fashion, it could have developed the SDLP as a pluralist party, mirroring the very definition of its existence as stated in the Party Constitution. The SDG was a unique organisational concept to the United Kingdom and Ireland.[37] However, the difficulty of setting such a precedent within Northern Ireland's political parties led to suspicions about the existence of such an organisation.

The 1987 survey team discovered poor communication existed between the SDG and the SDLP; and among the SDG and the NDI.[38] The team found that the SDG board was reluctant to put plans and activities in writing in case their opponents in the SDLP might distort its proposals, as in the past.[39] A plethora of bureaucratic structures and the confusion engendered by poor communications led to the demise of the SDG. The NDI contact had been important for SDLP organisation at constituency level. However, Tom Kelly argued that there was a down side in the increased efficiency at constituency level by the SDLP; 'For different reasons, the fiefdoms work against each other and the Party centrally stops.'[40]

Despite the demise of the SDG, the NDI has continued to run global projects around the world including projects on Northern Ireland. In June 1994, the board of the National Endowment for Democracy, the umbrella organisation for the NDI, approved a proposal to conduct a series of training programme activities with the constitutional Northern Ireland parties. The programmes operated on the same principles as the former SDG strengthening 'party organization [*sic*] and the practice of politics, while also examining issues of politics in a divided society'.[41] After the IRA and Loyalist cease-fires were put in place in 1994, the NDI widened its training programme to include Sinn Féin and the fringe Loyalist parties, namely the Progressive Unionist Party (PUP) and the Ulster Democratic Party (UDP) not only in organisational training but in the Northern Ireland Peace Process. One of the most successful workshops organised by the NDI was a three-day workshop from 30 May to 2 June 1997 in South Africa. All the participants from all the main Northern Ireland political parties were presented in detail with the details of events that led to the peace negotiations in South Africa.

Internal Organisational Flaws

The SDLP's own internal reviews acknowledged that public perceptions held them to be, 'mediocre, middle-aged, middle-class and muddled', a Party out of touch with its own supporters.[42] Internally, senior party members were criticised for placing more emphasis on securing their own positions than encouraging innovation or expansion in the SDLP.[43] The Party's grass-roots politics was described as 'non-existent' generally and only visible at election time when requiring votes and money.[44] Therefore, throughout the 1980s it would appear that the Party structure was stagnant. Overall, SDLP branches tended to be lacklustre in terms of organisation and member participation. Many branches survived as 'paper' power bases, but in reality there was a marked absence of 'grass-roots political cells'.[45] In relation to branch structure, former General Secretary, Eamon Hanna claimed, 'I tried to get branch organisation going. There was an indifference from the Party leadership. Hume is a great man for setting the vision and has got a massive intellect. He was a visionary – but he was not interested in organisation.'[46] However, SDLP organisational deficits were not simply caused by Hume, they were also symptomatic of the absence of accountable government in Northern Ireland for at least the best part of twenty-five years. There was a lack of discipline among Northern Ireland parties in any competition for power due to the lack of political development in the Province.

The political vacuum created after Sunningdale and the Constitutional Convention in the mid-1970s, led the SDLP to create the Constituency Representatives' Group. It was a means of keeping politics alive within the Party in the absence of devolved politics in Northern Ireland. Frustration existed between the Constituency Representatives' Group, who were often seen as overstepping the limits of the Party guidelines, and the SDLP executive body. This could be attributed to the weakness in the Party Constitution on the specific role of the Constituency Representatives. There was a problem with over-representation of this body on the party executive or, at least, an imbalance of reciprocal representation on both bodies. At the formation of the SDLP, the executive had been the primary political body, but this was now no longer the case. The executive evolved very much into an internal administrative board performing duties more akin to those of the General Secretary and Headquarters administrative staff.

Eamon Hanna maintained that the executive was not really an effective organ within the overall political structure of the Party and had no proper function. 'Executive members...' he claimed '...only voted for sectional interests. They came along to watch but they did not do things. All they did was monitor the work of the small central organisation of two or three people. They didn't have responsibility. Organisationally it was a disaster. You had a degradation of calibre people on the executive.'[47]

The SDLP neglected its organisation during the 1980s. The Party gave priority to constitutional and political issues and was more concerned about strengthening the Party electorally. In the early 1980s the SDLP had no MPs at Westminster after Gerry Fitt had resigned in 1979. It was not until 1983 that John Hume was able to regain a seat for the party. Help from the NDI to the SDLP in 1986 marked the Party's first formal professional training. Mark Durkan employed some of the techniques picked up in the United States and successfully implemented an effective electoral strategy in 1986 and 1987 for Mallon and McGrady. After the SDLP picked up their second seat in Newry and Armagh in 1986 and their third in South Down in 1987, the Party prioritised the electoral targeting of West Belfast, Mid-Ulster and Fermanagh-South Tyrone constituencies for the remainder of the 1980s over and above organisational issues.

Mark Durkan has maintained, 'Electoral expansion would have probably been the dominant theme in Party discussions during the eighties, to that extent the party was successful, particularly the second half of the eighties.'[48] As already mentioned in Chapter Nine, the

SDLP failed to capitalise on its good performance at the 1992 elections and allowed Sinn Féin to use the peace process as a vehicle to reverse its downward spiral of support. As a consequence of the continuing financial crisis in the SDLP towards the end of 1991, the Party had to cut three of its staff at Headquarters. The posts of General Secretary, Press Officer and a clerical position were reduced. According to party sources, the Party owed the bank in excess of £150,000.[49] Former Press Officer Jonathan Stephenson who resigned in August 1991 before the position was abolished, accused the SDLP leadership of reducing the Party to, 'the status of a postal address in South Belfast'.[50] This was against the background of Mr Eddie Lawlor, a London property developer, who offered to donate £50,000 to the SDLP for new premises the Party obtained in Belfast's Mount Charles district. Although Lawlor planned to donate £50,000 a year for three years to help with the upkeep of the new building, its maintenance costs spiralled. Belfast SDLP Councillor Hugh Lewsley said the SDLP was a 'Party living in a palace which could only afford a semi-detached house'.[51] Finances got so bad that in 1992 the Party had to move to more modest premises on Belfast's Lisburn Road. Despite the financial crisis in the SDLP and the reduction of its Headquarters' staff to only two people in 1992, by 1996 the Party managed to turn the downward spiral of cutbacks around to the extent that the Party now employs seven people and has spacious new Headquarters in Belfast.

The SDLP created important changes to its Constitution and Party organs as discussed at a major conference in June 1995.[52] The objective of these changes was to modernise and introduce more democratic mechanisms within the overall Party organisational structure. The Party Constitution (Clause Nine) outlined that the Party Leader and Deputy Leader could be elected each year by secret ballot. The leadership amendment meant any challenger would need to be nominated by at least five branches of the Party. Under the former Constitution, the Party Leader was elected by the constituency representatives group which was then verified at the SDLP annual conference.

The Party also decided to establish a new 'general council' outlined in Clause Six of the Constitution to serve and take responsibility for the overall political leadership of the party between Annual Conferences. This new body has brought together the existing Party Executive, the Constituency Representatives and representatives from the Association of SDLP Councillors. Clause Six(7) of the new Constitution also pledged a motion guaranteeing women 40 per cent representation on the Executive Committee. The Special Delegate

Conference also decided to establish a women's group and a youth section within the Party. The Constitution in Clause Six(6) legislated for these two groups to be nominated to the Executive Committee of the Party. However, the overall principles and aims of the Party remained consistent with the original Constitution. In particular, the Party still sought in Clause Two(4), 'the cause of Irish unity freely negotiated and agreed to by the people of the North and South'. Significantly, a new addition to the Constitution promoted a strong European dimension in Clause Two(7) in order 'to promote unity and harmony among the peoples of Europe, to work to end divisions based upon religion, ethnic origin or perceived national identity and to promote a new international order of peace and justice throughout the world'.

The SDLP lacks a broad Party base particularly in urban areas. Belfast has always been a problem for the SDLP where the Party has failed to off-set the rise of Sinn Féin electoral support. In the formative years of the SDLP faced little competition for the non-Unionist vote. Poor organisation in Belfast was traditionally blamed on Fitt and Devlin. They tended to contain any attempts to strengthen the Party organisation base lest their personal positions were weakened. 'There appears to have been a *"prima donna"* tradition in Belfast, whereby not only Fitt and Devlin but most of the Party's public representation did their own thing with a resultant lack of cohesion.'[53]

Support for Gerry Fitt and Paddy Devlin in Belfast was based on their personal following rather than on the SDLP political machinery. People who owed Fitt and Devlin personal allegiance turned to Sinn Féin after their departure from the SDLP. Fitt was not organised in West Belfast. Although poorly organised in West and North Belfast, the SDLP has continued to work efficiently in South Belfast. A major weakness of the SDLP in West Belfast was its inability to integrate into the community, unlike Sinn Féin. Eamon Hanna has argued, '...looking at some of the SDLP Councillors in West Belfast they are not at the races compared to at least some of the Sinn Féin Councillors'.[54] When Fitt resigned and Joe Hendron took over as the main runner for the West Belfast constituency, it became apparent that organisational skills were not Hendron's forte either. Hanna also maintained that tensions among SDLP Councillors in Belfast City Hall also contributed to poor public confidence in the Party in Belfast.[55]

Outside Belfast, the Party was most efficiently organised in Eddie McGrady's South Down constituency. This constituency escaped the worst of the Northern Ireland troubles. Compared to other parts of the Northern Ireland it enjoyed a relative degree of normality. Eddie

McGrady has argued, 'There is a trust in the constituency [of South Down] which is not present elsewhere in Northern Ireland'.[56] Relations between the local SDLP and Unionist community in South Down is perhaps more open and accommodating than is the norm within Northern Ireland. Potential SDLP voters in the constituency have largely a more moderate Irish identity than, for instance, their Newry and Armagh counterparts.

Like West Belfast, the Newry and Armagh constituency has suffered greatly from the contemporary troubles. In terms of statistics on deaths, the level of security presence and paramilitary activity, the area has incurred the full brunt of the troubles compared to its neighbouring South Down constituency. That has been a crucial factor in the difference between the Newry and Armagh and South Down constituencies. Seamus Mallon realised the importance of a strong organisational base after his electoral defeat in 1983. He had to wait until the 1986 Westminster by-election to win the Newry and Armagh seat.

Since Hume won his Foyle seat in 1983, organisational power for the SDLP has been centred in his Derry office. This has contributed to a centrally-organised deficit at Party Headquarters in Belfast. Financially, the Party was so weak during the 1980s that any fund-raising was dependent almost on Hume's personal charisma.[57] Hanna has argued, 'The Party was virtually being run on a shoe-string. The budget was a joke and the financing was a joke. There has never been money to run a proper organisation.'[58] With the lack of proper resources and necessary strategic planning, SDLP chances of holding a Westminster seat in the Mid-Ulster and Fermanagh-South Tyrone constituencies were quite marginal because strong support for Sinn Féin remained in these areas.

Any organisational and structural development within the SDLP should be given to Belfast. The SDLP fared better in the Greater Belfast area in the European Elections than other elections. It was precisely those Council Districts and towns bordering on Belfast where Alliance were doing unduly well in the absence of proper SDLP organisation. It was basically there that Alliance had grown and developed.

In a peaceful scenario, the SDLP should be able to maintain its present average percentage of the Catholic electorate at around 21.0 per cent of the vote, despite the rise in Sinn Féin popularity. If Sinn Féin support within the Catholic community remains at its current level – recorded at the recent elections at around 15 per cent – then the SDLP's best hope of expansion is in the Greater Belfast area. This would, perhaps, be to the detriment of Independents and more signifi-

cantly to the Alliance share of the electorate. If the minority community in Northern Ireland becomes more integrated into the political fabric
of society, middle-class members of the Catholic community will possibly feel more confident to move away form the establishment Alliance
Party and move towards the SDLP.

Conclusion

Historically, the SDLP is the living embodiment of the Nationalist compromise. The NDP and, subsequently, the SDLP represented an important advance on the politically obsolete position of the absence of recognition for all sections of the community in Northern Ireland. To that extent, the SDLP was revisionist. It revised attitudes to Nationalism within the six counties. It helped the Nationalist tradition to reappraise its position in relation to the constitutional issue. The question raised by the Civil Rights Movement was whether the State formed as Northern Ireland in 1921 was capable of reform? Initially the SDLP attempted to work on the basis that normal political action could provide Nationalists with equal citizenship and a sense of belonging. Once it became clear that Stormont was not open to reform, the SDLP sought an alternative system of Government. Early SDLP documents demonstrate that the Party would have settled for a Sunningdale-type arrangement if the Council of Ireland concept had been properly endorsed by both British and Irish Governments. The SDLP accepted the reality of Northern Ireland and its permanence for as long as a majority wished it to remain that way: However, this never undermined SDLP commitment to Irish unity based on Unionist consent.

The experience of Sunningdale in 1974 and the Constitutional Convention up until 1976 demonstrated that Unionist parties in Northern Ireland were unwilling to accept the principles of power-sharing and an Irish dimension. For the remainder of the 1970s therefore the SDLP campaigned to have the Irish dimension legitimised by the British Government. By 1978, the SDLP had adopted a strategy of seeking a joint Nationalist approach towards the Northern Ireland conflict with the main constitutional parties in the Republic. Realism moved the Party away from federalism in the short-term to a joint authority position. It was on this basis the SDLP sought an Anglo-Irish process in which the Irish and British Governments could draw up a political framework taking account of the equality of the two traditions within Northern Ireland, over the heads of Unionists if necessary.

The SDLP initiative in relation to Northern Ireland was eventually consummated in the Republic with the launch of the New Ireland

Forum in 1983 and by the British Government through the *Anglo-Irish Agreement* in 1985. The dangerous post-Hunger-Strike era led to support for the 'armed struggle' and the emergence for Sinn Féin as a major political force. When Garret FitzGerald took over as Taoiseach in December 1982, he initiated the *New Ireland Forum Report* to halt the leakage of support from the SDLP to Sinn Féin. It was also on this basis that the *Anglo-Irish Agreement* was signed in November 1985. Although the British and Irish Governments came to the rescue of the SDLP during the early 1980s in the hope of removing Sinn Féin and the IRA from the political and military scene, ironically they were adopting strategy established in the 1970s by the SDLP itself to resolve the Northern Ireland conflict.

The SDLP made a decisive impression when the New Ireland Forum brought constitutional Nationalists North and South behind the *Anglo-Irish Agreement*. This gave the Irish Government a role in Northern Ireland which the SDLP had been seeking from the early 1970s. Through the *Anglo-Irish Agreement* the SDLP won considerable ground for attaining parity of esteem for the minority community within Northern Ireland. For the first time legitimacy and focus on an agenda promoting equality was given to Nationalists in Northern Ireland by the British Government. The SDLP achieved institutional concern for an Irish dimension to the Northern Ireland problem. The *Agreement* set in motion a framework in which the two Governments could address the sense of alienation felt by the Nationalist community within Northern Ireland.

The SDLP never viewed the *Anglo-Irish Agreement* as a final settlement, but rather as a mechanism to develop a balanced framework for negotiating a political settlement. It became a forerunner to the *Downing Street Declaration* of December 1993 and the *Framework Documents* of February 1995 which addressed the Irish dimension to the Northern Ireland conflict in considerable detail. Significantly, the *Anglo-Irish Agreement* created one of the mechanisms to get Sinn Féin to reappraise its position in relation to the armed struggle. However, there was some disappointment in the SDLP that the Maryfield Secretariat administered jointly by British and Irish Civil Servants advanced the pace of reform for Nationalist advantage within Northern Ireland at such a slow rate. The *Anglo-Irish Agreement* was the practical expression of principles which the SDLP had formally articulated through the *New Ireland Forum Report*. It endorsed the first step in Hume's 'three-R' strategy – reform, reconciliation and reunification.

One of the SDLP's greatest achievements has been its ability, through its leader John Hume, to win the debate with Sinn Féin in terms of changing the political language and debate over the Northern Ireland issue. In 1988 John Hume and his Party Delegation with Sinn Féin were the main protagonists in getting the peace process off the ground. What then emerged as the Hume/Adams process led to the peace process in its present form. Hume introduced Sinn Féin to the constitutional Nationalist family, legitimising them as a democratic party and giving them the credentials to engage in discussions of mainstream politics. However, a major weakness of the Hume/Adams process was that Hume did not involve his senior Party colleagues. Had Hume done so, this approach would have meant the SDLP rather than just Hume could have received more credit for playing a part in bringing about the IRA cease-fire on the 31 August 1994. Eddie McGrady has argued that a broader formal dialogue between the SDLP and Sinn Féin as in 1988 would have been a much better option than Hume holding individual talks with Adams. If SDLP delegations had been involved in the process, there would have been more participation in the process decelerating the electoral influence of Sinn Féin.[1] Sinn Féin have become fluent in 'Humespeak' using the equality and parity of esteem vocabulary of the SDLP at their expense.

Unionists could have prevented the commencement of the Hume/Adams dialogue in 1988 had they chosen to operate Article 4 of the *Anglo-Irish Agreement* sooner. In such circumstances, Hume would have had to encourage the SDLP to pursue devolution. Yet when the Duisburg Talks took place in 1988, Hume's single-mindedness kept him committed to integrating Sinn Féin into an overall political settlement. Other members of the SDLP, for example Currie and McGrady, would have been more sensitive to the Unionist position and less enthusiastic about abandoning the path of devolution. Significantly, Hume's participation in the 1988 talks with Adams demonstrated an important change in strategy by the SDLP. It meant the Party was more hard-line in relation to the Irish dimension and the operation of Article 4 of the *Anglo-Irish Agreement*. A stronger role for the Secretariat at Maryfield and cross-border institutions created by the *Anglo-Irish Agreement* was secondary to Hume's ultimate objective of getting Sinn Féin to abandon the armed struggle and to enter democratic politics from 1988 onwards. Tom Kelly said Mallon and McGrady believed that if the SDLP had focused on strenthening Anglo-Irish relations through the mechanism of the Maryfield Secretariat, then political events would have fallen into place. Kelly has recalled:

'The SDLP having won the battle to get the Secretariat up and running I don't think won the battle in getting it teeth. That is the route they should have gone down. Unionists had learned to live with the Secretariat. The big stumbling block for Sunningdale was that the SDLP didn't get a Secretariat like that established. Now that they had it established, the SDLP should have tried to get it pushed out in the public role and after a while it would wear people down. It is already there over ten years.'²

This was a major error by the SDLP in terms of an overall political strategic manoeuvre. A greater emphasis on the Secretariat would have increased SDLP clout in the minority community. The Secretariat could have acted to promote an equality agenda for Nationalists, whereas the Hume/Adams process has somewhat hijacked this SDLP advantage.

The Hume/Adams process damaged the chances of Irish Nationalism in the true Republican sense, convincing Protestants that their future could only lie in a united Ireland. In his pursuit of talks with Gerry Adams, Hume forgot that the hand-shake that mattered most in building trust within Northern Ireland was the hand-shake between the leaders of Nationalism and Unionism. Hume's greatest failure was his inability to engage at an intellectual level with Unionist arguments. Hume put the resolution of the Northern Ireland problem and engagement with Sinn Féin above his Party even if that meant sacrificing the SDLP as had happened with the former Nationalist Party. Whatever John Hume's shortcomings, he has been one of contemporary Ireland's most courageous Nationalist leaders in attempting to bring an end to the cycle of violence within Northern Ireland. If the SDLP and, in particular Hume, have moved the entire Irish Nationalist question onto a new level devoid of Irish Republican violence organised by the IRA, their achievement is breathtaking, and the effects incalculable. Its ramifications will be felt beyond the next century.

John Hume is a great statesman in Irish history, but he cannot be described as a Nationalist in the traditional sense because of his post-Nationalist ethos. He is perhaps contemporary Ireland's greatest leader. His qualities in bringing the Northern Ireland conflict to the international forum have proved his statesmanship. Hume realised that to give credibility to the Irish Nationalist position the matter had to be taken beyond the simple boundaries of a local political dispute. Hume's talent has been his ability to mobilise support for SDLP strategy in Dublin, London, Strasbourg, Brussels and Washington. This ability has demonstrated beyond doubt his political powers of persuasion outside

Northern Ireland. It is extraordinary how Hume and such a small Party have influenced both British and Irish policy for Northern Ireland. By the end of the 1980s both British and Irish Governments had adopted the SDLP three-strand approach and general analysis of the Northern Ireland conflict. The peace process has been marked by these SDLP influences.

As to the leadership of the SDLP, Fitt and Hume could be seen to have something in common. Both are individualists and have no interest in Party organisation. On the one hand, Fitt was a street politician; on the other, Hume has tended to take the role of a philosopher, always planning ahead. Hume's lack of interest in Party organisation has led other SDLP MPs to take their cue from him. Consequently, this has led to a disparate Party organisation with no strong central base in Belfast. While Hume has enormous charisma and is well-known and respected throughout the world, this image has not entirely been transferred to the SDLP itself. Gerry Adams' image and persona, on the other hand, have been totally integrated with Sinn Féin. The down-side of Hume's leadership therefore has been the Party's dependence on him for political survival and identity. The SDLP has been inclined to underestimate the intellectual contributions to policy debate of John Duffy, Ivan Cooper, Ben Caraher and Denis Haughey in the early 1970s, and also of Seamus Mallon in the mid-1970s. Sean Farren too played an important role in policy formulation from the beginning of the 1980s.

There is a distinction between the SDLP and Sinn Féin on the constitutional issue of Northern Ireland. Sinn Féin still espouses the need to work towards a thirty-two county unitary sovereign state with no British jurisdiction in Ireland. They will only accept North-South bodies whom they regard as having the will to harmonise both parts of the island into one nation state. The SDLP take a more open-minded position on the future constitutional arrangements for Northern Ireland. In defining its Nationalism by the end of the 1970s the SDLP outlined that it was seeking '... firstly to put the people of Ireland in charge of their own affairs by creating a sovereign Irish state within the island of Ireland'.[3] It did not intend to preserve the sovereignty of the present twenty-six counties, but rather wanted to create a new Irish state throughout the whole island.[4] Once that framework could be established, the SDLP objective was to, 'devise a form of Government that will cater for the diversities within that Nation'.[5] By the mid-1980s onwards they focused more on their former position of accepting some form of joint sovereignty between the British and Irish Governments over Northern Ireland.

While the *Anglo-Irish Agreement* gave a consultative role to the Irish Government it fell short of joint authority. The most recent SDLP position in the talks process has been for a stronger role for the Irish Government in Northern Ireland affairs and as far as possible for movement closer to a joint authority between the Irish and British Governments in Northern Ireland. Cross-border institutions, from the SDLP viewpoint, have presented the potential for moving towards Irish unity but only in terms of democracy, so that the people on the island of Ireland can decide its political fate at some future point in history.

At this moment in history, the SDLP has consciously decided that a thirty-two county republic is not an attainable goal. Inasmuch as the unitary state option is the desired political settlement among certain sections of the SDLP, overall, the Party Leadership is focused on maximising strong executive functions for proposed cross-border bodies. In essence, the party has adopted the views reflected by Ben Caraher that a final agreement between all the parties to the conflict should have no other open-ended agenda. If demographic change in Northern Ireland dictates reunification at some future point the British Government has committed itself to set the necessary legislation in place for withdrawal to take place through the *Downing Street Declaration* and *Framework Documents.*

In the likelihood that Unionists would never accept traditional Irish unity, the SDLP envisage a final settlement by some future generation that might form some type of federal settlement with, perhaps, a constitutional British link remaining. Unionism brought down the *Sunningdale Agreement* in 1974 along with SDLP hopes of compromise. After the Drumcree stand-offs in 1996 and 1997 many middle-class Catholics suffered the sinking sense that the Sinn Féin position on Northern Ireland as irreformable, was perhaps an accurate analysis. The shock of these events, even for Catholics who have rationally understood they have been manipulated, may have been so deep that tribal instincts of fear and intransigence may have taken over any sense of civic attachment to Northern Ireland. The political talks have been and continue to be a vehicle, partly about removing the Nationalist sense of alienation within Northern Ireland and, most importantly, to give Catholics a civic sense of belonging within Northern Ireland. Ironically, the plight of the SDLP rests to some extent with Unionism and its ability to adapt to the reality that the Nationalist community have to be treated with equality in all aspects of Northern Ireland society.

The political survival of the SDLP may be decided by Unionist ability to agree to an Assembly in Northern Ireland which reflects the long-advocated SDLP partnership ethos. This, along with strong cross-border bodies and an avoidance of the mistakes of Sunningdale may be crucial. In the short-term, another Drumcree could undo all SDLP hopes. It would benefit the Sinn Féin analysis that power-sharing with Unionists in a six-county context would be impossible. If Sinn Féin won the argument that Northern Ireland is irreformable over the SDLP contention that all must strive to promote working with Unionists in a Northern Ireland Assembly and with cross-border institutions, what is left is a political vacuum. On the one hand Sinn Féin might gain the hearts of some former SDLP supporters, but on the other, the reverse is also possible. Many middle-class SDLP supporters are just as likely to lose heart, as many Unionists have done already and withdraw from politics entirely. Despite Hume's unpopularity in the Unionist estimation, they would prefer to do business with the SDLP than with Sinn Féin. The demise of Hume's leadership in the SDLP may not be not too far off and the SDLP's greatest chance of survival against the rise of popularity of Sinn Féin may be its ability to negotiate with Unionists.

The SDLP is a social democratic party, more interested in internal reform in Northern Ireland and in working with other political parties than the former Nationalist Party who maintained a position of abstentionist politics fixed on Irish unity. Any Assembly would have to operate power-sharing on the basis of consensus, protecting the rights and identities of both communities. Although the SDLP would prefer to describe itself as social and democratic coming from the Nationalist tradition, in clause 2.4 the Party Constitution clearly establishes a Nationalist agenda. There is a danger the SDLP might use its social democratic label as an apology for any Nationalist credentials, or, simply a device to displace the Nationalist ethos within the Party. The reality is the SDLP gets votes, on the whole, from within the Catholic population in Northern Ireland. It is not an explicitly Catholic organisation, but rather is a secular party.

Nevertheless, the SDLP is opposed to all forms of abortion even when the mother's life is in danger.[6] Ironically after Clare Short, Labour MP for Birmingham, was in Belfast in 1988 to canvass against David Alton's *Anti-abortion Bill*, Eddie McGrady and Joe Hendron shared the same platform as Alton pledging to fight for the success of his Bill. This is an example as to why the 'Campaign For Labour Representation in Northern Ireland' has argued that the SDLP should not be mistaken for a Socialist or even a Social Democratic Party by Labour-supporters in Britain.[7] The SDLP also takes the moral line of the Catholic Church in relation to embryo experimentation.

Despite the SDLP stance against abortion, it is a secular organisation. Also, the Party accept the principle of integrated education without actively endorsing it. The SDLP accept that parents have the choice to send their children to whatever school they choose. This principle was set out by the SDLP in *The Way Forward* in 1988. On other issues the Party fully supported legalising homosexuality in line with the rest of Britain under the *Sexual Offences Act (1967)* at the 1977 Annual Conference. Additionally it endorsed its support for divorce at the 1985 Annual Conference.

Whatever criticisms are levelled at the SDLP, it has provided the minority community with an alternative strategy to the 'armed struggle' of militant Republicanism. It has acted as protagonist for equality for the minority community in Northern Ireland notwithstanding the limitations of its success. Despite the sophistication of the Social Democratic label, the SDLP is a modern Irish constitutional Nationalist party comprising various strands of Nationalism opposed to using violence. In a non-violent Northern Ireland, the minority community would be inclined to be much more strident in its Nationalism, especially among the Catholic middle-classes. In such a scenario, the SDLP could fit very easily under a Fianna Fáil/Irish Labour mantle. However, in the absence of a political forum in Northern Ireland, the SDLP has made effective use of European alliances for a political identity.

Despite Gerry Adams' optimistic forecast for the SDLP in reaction to Catholic voting patterns in the 1997 General Election when he said, 'Let's not be writing the epitaph of the SDLP. It marks a broadening of the Nationalist vote...'[8] the recent elections in Northern Ireland have demonstrated that the Hume/Adams process has seriously undermined the SDLP position as the main political voice of the northern minority community. However, the SDLP has the potential in a peacetime situation to expand in the Greater Belfast area to the detriment of independents and perhaps, more significantly, into the Alliance share of the electorate. As Nationalism in Northern Ireland becomes more integrated into the political fabric of society, members of the Catholic community may feel more confident to move away from the established Alliance Party and perhaps move towards the SDLP. Only time will tell if there is wisdom in Ian Paisley's assertion that, 'It is about time people realised that the SDLP are now reaping what they have sown. They have built up Sinn Fein/IRA and are now an increasing irrelevance and have to kowtow to Sinn Fein/IRA as a result of their misplaced policy.'[9]

Epilogue

The *Good Friday Agreement* signed by the British and Irish Governments on the 10 April 1998 has given Northern Ireland another important opportunity for peace in its otherwise turbulent history. All parties have a chance to prove that the politics of moderation and compromise can win over the voices of extremism. It has taken over twenty years to return to a similar set of circumstances as those of Sunningdale in 1974. The difference between proposals at Sunningdale and those of the current *Good Friday Agreement* is the inclusion of the fringe Loyalists parties and the Republican Movement in the negotiations leading to the final agreement. It was these elements who, back in 1974, by their very exclusion contributed to the downfall of the power-sharing Government at Stormont.

The *Good Friday Agreement* reflects the SDLP impact on contemporary Northern Ireland politics and is a major vindication of Party policy. On close scrutiny it is clear that the SDLP has achieved more of its objectives from this agreement than any other Northern Ireland party. If the *Good Friday Agreement* becomes operational it will be an endorsement of SDLP commitments to cross-community Government and a significant Irish dimension, reflecting the existence of the Nationalist community in Northern Ireland. The SDLP has succeeded in convincing almost all the key players in the current peace process that the three-stranded relationship of Northern Ireland, Britain and the Republic of Ireland is the perspective in which to determine a more worthwhile political future.

The Party has worked vigorously from the Sunningdale era of the seventies, through to the *New Ireland Report* during the early eighties and to the signing of the Anglo-Irish Agreement in 1985, attaining a greater recognition for political rights and equality issues for northern Nationalists and Republicans. The SDLP created the dynamic from its foundation to bring about a realistic Irish dimension on behalf of northern Nationalists. It laid the foundations for replacing the absence of allegiance felt by northern Nationalists to political institutions in Northern Ireland, to one of active participation. If the success of the double referendum - a concept advocated by the SDLP since 1975 - on the *Good Friday Agreement* is endorsed, northern Nationalists will, for the first time in their history, have the potential to give political and institutional allegiance to new structures in Northern Ireland, provided that all elements within the agreement work successfully together.

The SDLP articulates what they believe to be political realism within northern Nationalism, that is, that the creation of a single Irish state is not likely to be achieved in the foreseeable future. If the Irish dimension contained in the *Good Friday Agreement* becomes operational the quest for Irish unity will lose a lot of its dynamic and indeed its attractiveness. The SDLP thesis simply states that if both communities begin to work together at Government level and within institutions which exemplify the aspirations and identities of both traditions, then it will be up to some future generation to negotiate further developments for Northern Ireland's political destiny. In effect the SDLP has thrown down the gauntlet to both Unionist and Republican extremists to decide whether to cross the political threshold of consent and compromise or abandon Northern Ireland to another generation of despair and bloodshed.

John Hume has been an outstanding political visionary. He has been successful in creating the dramatic shift from coercion to democratic politics within the broad nationalist constituency in Northern Ireland. He has been able to use the Hume/Adams process to create the conditions for a peaceful society so that the principles with which the SDLP was created – equality and power-sharing for northern Nationalists – could have the potential of being re-established as in 1974. Hume has succeeded in giving his party the kudos in international political circles for getting nearly all the key players to the Northern Ireland conflict to adopt the SDLP analysis for resolving their political problems. Hume took a significant step back from centre-stage during the recent peace negotiations at Stormont in Belfast. In his place, the SDLP contribution to the talks has been carried out by chief negotiator Seamus Mallon and other senior members of the Party including Sean Farren, Denis Haughey, Mark Durkan and Alex Attwood.

The price of the Hume/Adams process exacted on the SDLP is now the fierce competition for the Nationalist vote between the SDLP and Sinn Féin. However, whether the SDLP continue a dominant role in Northern Ireland politics might perhaps be determined not only by Sinn Féin's strategy and organisational capacity (which should not be underestimated) but also by Unionist support of the *Good Friday Agreement*. It is impossible to gauge at this time if the SDLP will sustain its place as the largest Nationalist party in Northern Ireland. In the short-term, the determining factor will be the degree to which the *Good Friday Agreement* signed by the British and Irish governments on the 10 April 1998 will be accepted or rejected by the Unionist community. The objective of the agreement is to create stability, equality and the sharing of responsibility between the two communities. For the first time since partition, Northern Ireland's institutions through the implementation of a North-South Ministerial Council and a British-Irish Council would reflect the allegiance of its two communities.

The fate of the SDLP in the short-term is dependent on the implementation of the *Good Friday Agreement* and the reaction of Unionists and Republicans If the agreement collapses at some point in the future where does it leave the SDLP? Everything is to be played for between the SDLP and Sinn Féin to win the heart of northern Nationalists. The demise of the SDLP will not take place because the Nationalist constituency in Northern Ireland is large enough to support both parties. The *Good Friday Agreement* represents everything the SDLP has stood and worked for since its formation. It marks what is practicable and what is attainable for northern Nationalists for the current generation.

Appendix 1

SDLP DRAFT PROPOSALS RELATING TO NEGOTIATIONS ON THE PRESENT SITUATION IN NORTHERN IRELAND – SEPTEMBER 1971

Introduction

1. The acute civil unrest which has been a feature of life in Northern Ireland since August 1968 provides clear evidence that the political institutions of the area are in need of drastic revision.

2. This view has been long held by a very large section of the Northern Ireland community. It is now coming to be accepted by many who formerly chose to ignore the evidence pointing in this direction.

3. The evidence in human terms can be found in the experiences of the many people who, three times in their lifetimes, have been evicted from their homes. It can be found in the fact that many citizens have on different occasions been imprisoned for years without trial. It can be recognized in the fact that in each decade community peace in Northern Ireland has been shattered by outbreaks of violence which has disrupted the lives of thousands and cost the lives of hundreds. It is implicit in the phenomenon that since its inception the governing Unionist Party has found it necessary to arrogate to itself arbitrary powers totally at variance with all the traditions of British law.

Instability

4. This condition of chronic instability has been produced by the two dominant conflicting attitudes within the Northern Ireland community. The first and most potent, since it can inspire legislation, is the fear of most Protestants that they might be incorporated into an all-Ireland Republic either by internal and external coercion or by normal democratic process. This has engendered a Policy of repression designed to safeguard against either of these contingencies.

Thus, the Unionist Party has maintained a system of laws and a law enforcement body structured to contain and subdue any subversive activity long before it might become a threat to security. In addition, the Unionist Party has sanctioned at every level a system of discrimination aimed at combating the effects of population trends which might possibly have led in the future to a Catholic majority in Northern Ireland.

5. The reaction to this policy among the Catholic community has bred a resentment of and hostility to what they see as the source of oppression and has led them to look to a united Ireland as offering the only effective guarantee of relief from oppression. Thus, their traditional sense of identity with the aspirations of the Republic have been emphasized by what they see as the injustices of the Northern administration.

Guarantee

6. For all these reasons, any changes directed towards establishing a period of peaceful co-existence leading towards a more integrated community must at one and the same time guarantee the Catholic community against continued or renewed repression while relieving the Protestant community of their apprehension of being coerced into an all-Ireland Republic.

Conditions

7. Such changes could emanate from a Conference held within a framework based on the following conditions:

   (a) That there are four interested parties in the discussions. These are the two principals: The Northern majority and minority; and the two sovereign powers with legitimate interests in the area: the Government of the United Kingdom and the Republic of Ireland.

   (b) That the participants acknowledge that the very necessity for such a Conference implies that the existing structures have proved inadequate.

   (c) That the participants should be free to hear and discuss any proposals relevant to the purposes of the Conference as set out in (6) "*Guarantees*", above.

   (d) That the convening authorities assure themselves that the negotiators for the principals were properly representative.

Changes

8. The areas which such a Conference should examine should include the following:–

    (a) A Bill of Rights guaranteeing due process of law, freedom of association and freedom from political tests. There should be specific constitutional machinery applying to any proposals to amend this Bill of Rights.

    (b) A Fair Practices Act establishing a Commission with investigatory, judicial and executive powers to ensure the application of equitable standards in all areas involving public expenditure.

    (c) Revision of the electoral machinery to ensure that the Northern Ireland parliament is both more representative of the entire spectrum within the community and more conducive to the emergence of new political attitudes and institutions.

    Such revision might include Proportional Representation in all elections and a Senate selected on a vocational basis with extended powers of veto.

    (d) Abandonment of the Westminster model of government in which members are selected by the Prime Minister in favour of a system in which the members of the Government are elected by Proportional Representation and they in turn elect the Prime Minister from among their own numbers.

Underwriting

9. For an changes of the above nature to be acceptable to either of the principals it is necessary that they should be underwritten in legal form by the two sovereign governments. This underwriting should include the following:

    (a) The establishment of a Council of Ireland to promote cross-Border economic and social co-operation; to provide conciliation and arbitration machinery in any cases of alleged infringement of the Bill of Rights; to provide machinery for the creation of a joint security Authority, representative of all three Governments, which would be responsible for adequate Border policing.

    (b) The deletion from the Constitution of the Republic of any claim to jurisdiction over Northern Ireland as being inconsistent with joint membership of the Council of Ireland.

    (c) Financial expenditure in respect of Northern Ireland which is authorized by the United Kingdom Government should become subject to scrutiny by a special Westminster House of Commons committee.

(d) Both sovereign Governments should declare in a binding Protocol their joint commitment to the proposition that the new agreements are envisaged as leading to the emergence of organic political institutions for Ireland and that this emergence will not be inhibited by resort to coercion or threats of coercion.

(e) As a corollary of 9(d) above, a Joint Commission, co-chaired by the United Kingdom and the Republic of Ireland, should keep under continuing review the efficiency of these new arrangements in engendering such new or strengthened organic political and other institutions as the evolving situation may require.

(f) The Government of the Republic should undertake that at the earliest opportunity the Constitution would be amended to delete from it any provisions repugnant to the Northern Bill of Rights and to make provision for increased Northern participation. An example of this might be the creation of machinery whereby Northerners could take part in elections for the President of Ireland.

Interim

10. In the interim period between the successful conclusion of talks and their implementation in statute the area of Northern Ireland should be administered by a Council of State nominated by the Governor after consultation with all the interested parties.

Advantages

11. We fully accept that the principles outlined above may seem complex and costly. We are convinced, however, that the arrangements we suggest have certain overwhelming advantages;

(i) They represent a solution which is geared to the special and local nature of the problem and which takes account of the fundamental inter-dependence of both parts of the island.

(ii) They are sufficiently flexible to permit relatively smooth transition from one phase to another.

(iii) They acknowledge that an extra-ordinary effort at conciliation, education and consultation has to be made on all sides to remedy the damage of the past.

(iv) They contain no element of coercion. Rather, they stress the need for and cater for ample discussion and peaceful persuasion.

(v) They recognise that the Westminster formula of Government and Opposition is quite unworkable in the Northern Ireland context.

(vi) They destroy the classic Unionist Party canard that all shades of non-Unionist opinion seeks merely the immediate creation of a 32-County Republic and the consequent subjugation of Northern Protestants.

(vii) They permit the North an involvement in and partial control over events in the South and they envisage means whereby this involvement and control may be peacefully and gradually expanded.

Proud North

12. We believe this last element to be crucial. It is one which is totally and almost incredibly absent from any other set of proposals. We are Ulster men ourselves, proud to represent an important section of Ulster opinion. Any settlement which diminishes the influence of the North either temporarily or permanently could not enjoy our support. On the contrary, our proposals are carefully designed to increase the stature and influence of all in Northern Ireland – Protestant and Catholic alike.

(PRONI, D. 3072/ 1088)

Appendix 2

Constitution of the Social Democratic and Labour Party as amended at the:-
Seventh Annual Conference, November, 1977
Eight Annual Conference, November, 1978
Ninth Annual Conference, November, 1979
Twelfth Annual Conference, January, 1983
Fourteenth Annual Conference, January, 1985
Sixteenth Annual Conference, November, 1986
Seventeenth Annual Conference, November, 1987
Twentieth Annual Conference, November, 1990
Twenty-second Annual Conference, November, 1992
Twenty-fourth Annual Conference, November 1994
Special Conference, June 1995

SDLP Constitution

CLAUSE ONE: NAME
The Association shall be called The Social Democratic and Labour Party.

CLAUSE TWO: PRINCIPLES AND OBJECTS
The objects of the Party shall be as follows:-

1. To organise and maintain in Northern Ireland a Socialist Party;

2. To promote the policies decided by the Party Conference.

3. To co-operate with the Irish Congress of Trade Unions in joint political or other action;

4. To promote the cause of Irish unity freely negotiated and agreed to by the people of the North and by the people of the South;

5. To co-operate with other Labour Parties and Social Democratic Parties through the Party of European Socialists and the Socialist International;

6. To work for the full participation of women in social, economic and public life on the basis of full equality;

7. To promote unity and harmony among the peoples of Europe, to work to end divisions based upon religion, ethnic origin or perceived national identity and to promote a new international order of peace and justice throughout the world.

8. To contest elections in Northern Ireland with a view to securing the implementation of the following principles:

    (a) The abolition of all forms of discrimination based upon reli-

gion, gender, disability, ethnic origin, class, political belief or
sexual orientation and the promotion of equality amongst all
our citizens.

(b) The promotion of culture and arts with a special responsibility
to cherish and develop all the diverse aspects of our national
cultures.

(c) The public ownership and democratic control of such essential
industries and services as the common good requires.

(d) The protection of the environment with sustainable development and the achievement of social and economic justice for all
our people.

CLAUSE THREE: MEMBERSHIP

1. There shall be three classes of members, namely:

   (a) Individual members;

   (b) Corporate members;

   (c) Associate members.

2. Any member who subscribes to the Principles and Objects of the
   Party and is not a member of any other political party may be
   accepted as an individual member of the Party.

3. An individual member must be accepted into membership by a
   Branch of the Party in the constituency where he resides or for
   which he is registered as an elector.

4. Where there is no branch of the Party in the area in which he resides,
   a member shall be entitled to join the Branch nearest him provided
   that no member shall be a member of more than one Branch.

5. The Executive Committee may expel from the Party any member
   whose activities they consider injurious to the Party or inconsistent
   with its Principles and Objects.

6. A Branch of the Party may refuse into membership any person or
   may expel an existing member, but such persons may appeal to the
   Executive Committee who may confirm or reverse the decision.

7. Corporate members shall consist of Trade Unions affiliated to the

Irish Congress of Trade Unions, Co-operative Societies, Socialist Societies, Professional Associations and Cultural Organisations.

8. A Corporate Member must accept the Principles and Objects of the Party and agree to conform to its Constitution.

9. The Executive Committee may refuse the application of any Organisation for corporate membership and may expel any existing corporate member if they consider its membership would be injurious to or inconsistent with the Principles and Objects of the Party, but such an Organisation may appeal against the decision of the Executive Committee to the Party Conference whose decision shall be final.

10. The Executive Committee shall report to the Party Conference all expulsions of individual or corporate members and all rejections of appeals against expulsion from Branches.

11. Each Corporate Member shall pay to the Executive Committee before 31 March each year an annual subscription of 25p for each member that it wishes to affiliate.

12. Associate Members must accept the Principles and Objects of the Party and agree to conform to its Constitution.

13. The Executive Committee may refuse the application of any person for Associate Membership and may expel any existing Associate Member if they consider its membership would be injurious to or inconsistent with the Principles and Objects of the Party.

14. Each Associate Member shall pay to the Party Headquarters a minimum subscription of £25 per annum.

15. Annual subscriptions shall become due on the first day of January in each year and shall relate to that calendar year.

CLAUSE FOUR: BRANCH, DISTRICT AND CONSTITUENCY ORGANISATION

1. A Branch of the Party shall be formed in any district with the approval of the Executive Committee which shall, if necessary, define the functional area of the Branch.

2. Each Branch shall forward to Headquarters before 31 March each year, the name, address and membership fee for each member and the Branch affiliation fee.

   The amount of the membership shall be determined by Annual Conference. The amount of the Branch affiliation fee shall be determined by the Executive Committee.

3 . Each Branch shall hold an Annual General Meeting before March 31 at which it shall elect the following Branch Officers: Chairperson, Vice-Chairperson, Secretary and Treasurer, and a Committee and at which it shall transact any other relevant business. It shall, in addition, hold at least six business meetings during the year.

4. Each Branch shall promote the policies of the Party, maintain an effective Organisation within its functional area and support Party candidates in local and parliamentary elections.

5. Each Branch shall draw up a set of Branch rules and deposit a copy with the Executive Committee, which shall have the power to declare all or part of a Branch's rules repugnant to the Constitution. Any amendment of or addition to a Branch's rules shall be notified to the Executive Committee.

6. Each Branch shall forward to the Treasurer before 30 September each year a statement of the financial position of the Branch.

7. The functional area of any Branch shall not cross the boundaries of a Constituency.

8. A Constituency Council shall be formed in each Constituency. It shall consist of representatives from each Branch of the Party in the constituency appointed according to the following scale:

Membership	No. of Representatives
10–30	2
31–60	3

and additional representatives in these proportions. Branch representation, at any time, shall be determined by the membership registered at Party Headquarters on the registration date. The registration dates shall be Mar 31, June 30, September 30 and December 31 each year.

9. Each Constituency Council shall hold an Annual Meeting before March 31 at which it will elect the following officers: Chairperson, Vice-Chairperson, Secretary and Treasurer, and transact any other relevant business. it shall, in addition, hold a minimum of three business meetings during the year.

10. The following shall be members of the Constituency Council *ex-officio*:-

    (a) Constituency Representatives for the Constituency;

    (b) The Party's prospective candidates for the Constituency;

    (c) Those members of the Executive Committee who reside in the Constituency;

    (d) District Councillors who are members of the Party and who sit for District Electoral Areas which are wholly or partially within the boundaries of the Constituency.

11. The functions of a Constituency Council shall be as follows:
    (a) To promote, through publicity and other means, the policies of the Party in the Constituency;

    (b) To co-ordinate the work of the Branches in the Constituency;

    (c) To organise, with the approval of the Executive Committee new Branches of the Party in the Constituency where it is deemed necessary;

    (d) To create and maintain in the constituency an effective electoral Organisation.

12. Where there is only one Branch of the Party in a Constituency, the Branch shall perform the functions of a Constituency Council.

13. A District Executive of the Party shall be formed in each District Council Area. It shall be constituted as follows:

    (a) Representatives from each branch in the District Council Area according to the following scale:

Membership	No. of Representatives
10-30	2
31-60	3

and additional representatives in these proportions. Branch representation, at any time, shall be determined by the membership registered at Party Headquarters on the registration date. The registration dates shall be March 31, June 30, September 30 and December 31 each year.

(b) Constituency Representatives who represent constituencies whose boundaries encompass all or part of the District Council Area;

(c) Members of the District Council who are members of the Party;

(d) Members of the Party Executive resident in the District Council Area;

14. Each District Executive shall hold an Annual General Meeting before March 31 at which it shall elect the following officers: Chairperson, Vice-Chairperson, Secretary and Treasurer, and transact any other relevant business. It shall in addition, hold a minimum of three business meetings during the year.

15. The functions of a District Executive shall be as follows:

(a) To co-ordinate the work of the Party's Councillors on the District Council and other public bodies;

(b) To provide a means of communication between the Party's Councillors and the Branches;

(c) To organise, in accordance with Clause Eight, Section 12, meetings to select the Party's candidates in each District Electoral Area of the District Council Areas;

(d) To organise and direct the Party's campaign in local government elections.

CLAUSE FIVE: THE PARTY CONFERENCE

1. The Party Conference shall be the supreme governing authority in the Party. It shall be the duty of each individual member and section of the Party to promote the policies decided by the Conference.

2. The Conference shall normally be held in the period 15 October to 30 November each year on a date to be determined by the Executive Committee.

3. A Special Conference may be held if the Executive Committee so decides or if more than one third of the branches so request the Executive Committee.

4. The Conference shall be constituted as follows:

   (a) Delegates appointed by each Branch in accordance with the following scale:

Membership	No. of Delegates
10-20	2
21-30	3
31-40	4
41-50	5

   and additional delegates in these proportions.

   (b) Delegates appointed by Corporate members in accordance with the following scale:

Membership	No. of Delegates
10-200	1
201-400	2
401-600	3

   and additional delegates in these proportions up to a maximum of 50 delegates.

   (c) Members of the General Council;

   (d) Councillors who are members of the Party.

   (e) Two members selected by the Youth Section of the Party.

   (f) Two members selected by the Women's Group of the Party.

5. Every delegate attending the Conference must be a fully paid-up individual member of the party.

6. Each person attending the Conference by virtue of Section 4 of this clause shall have one vote.

7. Only Branches and Corporate Members who have paid the appropriate membership fees and branch affiliation fees to Headquarters by 31 March shall be entitled to send delegates to the Conference.

8. Motions for the Conference and amendments to motions may be submitted by the Executive Committee, the Constituency Representatives Group, Branches, the Association of SDLP Councillors, the Women's Group, the Youth Section and Corporate Members.

9. Motions shall be received by the Executive Committee not less than seven weeks before the Conference. The Preliminary Agenda shall be circulated to Branches and Corporate Members not less than six weeks before the Conference. Amendments to Motions and the names and addresses of the delegates appointed by the various Branches and Corporate Members shall be received by the Executive Committee not less than four weeks before the Conference. The Conference Agenda, credentials and other documents shall be circulated to those entitled to attend Conference not less than one week before Conference. Emergency Motions may be submitted with the consent of the Conference.

10. The Executive Committee shall submit to the Conference a report of its work since the previous Conference.

11. The General Council and its Committees shall submit to the Conference reports on their work since the previous Conference.

12. The following Party Officers shall be elected at the Conference: Chairperson, two Vice-Chairpersons, International Secretary, Treasurer, and Assistant Treasurer shall be by secret ballot using the Single Transferable Vote.

13. The Conference shall elect ten individual members to serve on the Executive Committee. Delegates will vote by secret ballot using the single Transferable Vote.

14. Candidates for Party Office and for the Executive Committee shall be nominated by Branches or by Corporate Members. The Executive Committee shall be informed in writing of such nominations and receive the written consent of the Candidates at least

seven weeks before the date of the Conference. The names of the candidates shall be circulated along with the preliminary agenda.

15. Representation at the Annual Conference and Selection Conventions may be withheld from those Branches which:

    (a) Do not meet the financial commitments to the Party's central funds as decided by Annual Conference or the Party Executive; or

    (b) Do not submit financial statements as prescribed under Clause Four, Section 6.

16. A Standing Orders Committee of eight members shall be elected at each Conference. The election shall be by secret ballot using the Single Transferable Vote. Members shall be nominated by Branches or Corporate Members. The Executive shall be informed in writing of such nominations and receive written consent of the candidates. The Committee shall elect a Chairperson from among its members.

CLAUSE SIX: THE GENERAL COUNCIL AND THE EXECUTIVE COMMITTEE

1. There shall be a General Council of the Party comprised of: Members of the Party who are members of the European Parliament; the House of Commons and Oireachtas na hEireann; one member elected annually by each Constituency Council; Party Officers and the Executive Committee elected at Annual Conference; and five members elected annually by the Association of SDLP Councillors.

2. The General Council shall serve and take responsibility for the overall political leadership of the Party, between Annual Conferences. The General Council will be responsible for the development, presentation and implementation of policy on behalf of the Party and the Party Leader will appoint Policy Spokespersons from among its members. The General Council shall have the power to delegate tasks and functions.

3. The General Council shall be the main forum for political discussion and decision making within the Party between conferences. It will meet at least five times a year and will be convened and

chaired by the Party Chairperson or Vice Chairperson. The General Council will conduct relations with outside bodies and other political parties on a national and international level and will take decisions on the contesting of elections, and the preparation of manifestos. The Agenda for General Council meetings shall include a report from the Party Leader, Policy Spokespersons, the Executive Committee and the Association of SDLP Councillors.

4. The General Council shall annually elect the Chief Whip of the Party.

5. Of the five members of the General Council elected annually by the Association of SDLP Councillors, at least two shall be women.

6. The Standing Committee of the General Council shall be known as the Executive Committee. The Executive Committee shall consist of the Party Officers and ten ordinary members, elected at Annual Conference; the Leader and Deputy Leader (*ex-officio*); one member nominated by the Women's Group of the Party and one member nominated by the Youth Section of the Party. A Chairperson of the Party who does not seek re-election shall be an *ex-officio* member of the following year's Executive.

7. Where at least 40% of the elected places on the Executive (excluding *ex-officio* members) are not filled by women members, the Executive Committee will co-opt additional women members to achieve such a percentage. Casual vacancies on the Executive Committee will otherwise be filled by co-option.

8. The day-to-day control of the Organisation and administrative affairs of the Party including its financial affairs shall be the responsibility of the Executive Committee. It shall take responsibility for the development of Party Organisation and for the direction of election campaigns, including the ratification of candidates. It shall interpret the Party Constitution and make provision for any matter not contained therein.

9. The Executive Committee shall meet at least nine times a year and shall be chaired by the Party Chairperson or Vice-Chairperson.

10. The Executive Committee shall have power to engage such full-

time administrative and research staff as it deems necessary and shall have the power to determine the remuneration, conditions and tenure of office of such persons.

11. Executive shall have the power to delegate tasks and functions.

12. Trustees may be appointed by Executive to hold on behalf of the Party such premises as the Executive may from time to time decide to acquire and the said Trustees shall be empowered by resolution of the Executive to borrow money on the security of any such premises.

CLAUSE SEVEN: CENTRAL COUNCIL

1. There shall be a Central Council of the Party which shall be constituted as follows:

(a) Members of the General Council;

(b) District Councillors

(c) Representatives of each Branch of the Party appointed according to the following scale:

Membership	No. of Representatives
10-50	2
51-100	3
101-150	4

and additional representatives in these proportions. Branch representation, at any time, shall be determined by the membership registered at Party Headquarters on the registration date. The registration dates shall be March 31, June 30, September 30 and December 31 each year.

(d) Two representatives from each Constituency Council and two representatives from each District Executive

2. The function of the Central Council shall be to provide a means of communication between the membership and the central organs of the Party.

3. The Central Council shall meet at least once a year, in the Spring, and at other times at the discretion of the Executive Committee and shall hear a report from the General Council.

CLAUSE EIGHT: SELECTION OF CANDIDATES

1. The Party's Candidates in any Assembly or United Kingdom or EEC Constituency shall be selected by a Selection Convention called for that purpose.

2. The Selection Convention shall be organised by the Executive Committee which shall have power to determine the procedure to be followed by the Convention.

3. The Selection Convention shall consist of delegates appointed by Branches affiliated to the Constituency Council according to the following scale:

Membership	No. of Delegates
10–20	4
21–30	6
31–40	8
41–50	10

and additional representatives in these proportions. Branch representation, at any time, shall be determined by the membership registered at Party Headquarters on the registration date. The registration dates shall be March 31, June 30, September 30 and December 31 each year.

4. Selection Conventions in Constituencies with three or fewer branches, if Executive so directs, shall consist of all member of these branches.

5. A prospective candidate must an individual member of the Party. He must be proposed and seconded in writing by individual members of the Party and this nomination document must be forwarded to Executive Committee.

6. The Executive Committee shall forward to each Branch affiliated to the Council the names of the prospective candidates at least one week before the meeting of the Convention.

7. The Candidate shall be elected by secret ballot.

8. Only delegates shall have the right to vote and each delegate shall have one vote.

9. The Executive Committee shall appoint the Chairperson of the Convention who shall forward its decisions to the Executive Committee.

10. The decision to contest the election shall be made by the Executive Committee who shall also have the power to ratify or to refuse to ratify the choice of candidates.

11. If there is only one Branch in the Constituency the candidate shall be elected at a full meeting of the Branch called for that purpose by the Executive Committee which shall appoint the Chairperson of the meeting.

12. Candidates for District Council elections in each District Electoral Area shall be selected at a General Meeting of Party members residing in the District Electoral Area called for that purpose. Such selection meetings shall be organised by the appropriate District Executive.

CLAUSE NINE: LEADER AND DEPUTY LEADER

1. There shall be a Leader and Deputy Leader of the Party elected annually at Party Conference by secret ballot, using the single transferable vote.

2. Candidates for the position of Leader and Deputy Leader must be members of the General Council and must be nominated by at least five branches of the Party, such nominations to be forwarded at least seven weeks prior to Annual Conference.

3. In the event of a casual vacancy, between conferences, for the position of Leader, the Deputy Leader shall become Leader. In the event of a vacancy occurring for Deputy Leader, or of a vacancy for both Leader and Deputy Leader occurring simultaneously, the General Council shall elect from its ranks persons to fill the vacancies.

4. The Leader will appoint Policy Spokespersons from the General Council. He/she will prepare a report for the General Council and for the Annual Conference of the Party.

CLAUSE TEN: WOMEN'S GROUP AND YOUTH SECTION

1. There shall be distinct sections of the Party designed to encourage and enhance the involvement of women and young people within the SDLP in line with its aims and objectives.

2. The SDLP Women's Group will promote the involvement of women members at all levels within the Party and in public life. The Group will determine its constitution and its programme of activity consistent with this Constitution and Party policy.

3. The SDLP Youth Section will be comprised of Party members up to the age of 30 and will work to recruit and involve young people in schools, in third level education and those in employment and without work. The Youth Section will determine its constitution and programme of activity consistent with this Constitution and Party policy.

CLAUSE ELEVEN: AMENDMENT

1. Any addition to or amendment of the above Constitution shall only be made at the Party Conference or by a Special Conference properly convened for that purpose as laid down by Clause 5, Section 3 of this Constitution, provided that at least two thirds of those voting support the proposition. Such additions or amendments shall come into force immediately upon the ending of the Conference at which they have been approved.

Notes to Chapters

NOTES TO CHAPTER ONE

1   *Irish Times*, 18 May 1964.
2   Caraher, interview.
3   Duffy, interview.
4   McGrady, interview.
5   NDP File, NIPC, LHL.
6   Ibid.
7   Currie, interview.
8   Caraher, interview.
9   NDP File, NIPC, LHL.
10   Ian McAllister, *The Northern Ireland Social Democratic and Labour Party*, p.34.
11   *Irish News*, 18 Aug 1995.
12   *News Letter*, 2 Mar 1985.
13   Currie, interview.
14   Caraher, interview.
15   Ibid.
16   Currie, interview.
17   *Irish News*, 18 Aug 1995.
18   Ibid., 22 Aug 1994.
19   Ibid., 17 Aug 1995.
20   Paddy Devlin, *The Fall of the Northern Ireland Executive*, p. 63.
21   *Irish Times*, 16 Nov 1995.
22   Cooper, interview.
23   *Irish Times*, 19 May 1964.
24   George Drower, *John Hume Peacemaker*, p.50.
25   Barry White, *John Hume Statesman of the Troubles*, p.74.
26   Haughey, interview.
27   *Irish Times*, 22 Aug 1970
28   O'Hanlon, interview.
29   Cooper, interview.
30   O'Hanlon, interview.
31   Currie, interview.
32   Hume, interview.
33   O'Hanlon, interview.
34   Fitt, interview.
35   Hume, interview.
36   *Irish News*, 17 Aug 1995.
37   Duffy, interview.
38   Ken Bloomfield, *Stormont in Crisis*, p.129.

39 Sabine Wichert, *Northern Ireland Since 1945*, p.153.
40 McAllister, p. 88.
41 Paddy Devlin, *Straight Left*, p. 155.
42 Bloomfield, p. 146.
43 SDLP Discussion Papers, Sept 1971, (PRONI, D. 3072/B/1127).
44 McAllister, p. 96.
45 Pers. Comm.
46 McAllister, p. 95.
47 Wichert, p. 150.
48 Bloomfield, p.155.
49 Devlin, *The Fall of the Northern Ireland Executive*, p. 5.
50 Fitt, interview.
51 Duffy, interview.
52 Haughey, interview.
53 Ibid.
54 Ibid.
55 SDLP Discussion Documents, Sept 1971, (PRONI, D. 3072/B/1127).
56 Ibid.
57 Ibid.
58 Ibid.
59 Ibid.
60 Ibid.
61 SDLP Discussion Documents, Dec 1971, (PRONI, D.3072/1A/22A).
62 Appendix 1, SDLP Draft Proposals, Sept 1971, (PRONI, D. 3072/B/1088).
63 Caraher, interview.
64 Memorandum, 6 Dec 1971, (PRONI, D. 3072/1A/22A).
65 Appendix 1, Sept 1971, (PRONI, D. 3072/B/1088).
66 Duffy, interview.
67 Caraher, interview.
68 Ivan Cooper, 'Northern Ireland—A Condominium', (PRONI, D. 3072/B/1088).
69 Ibid.
70 Condominium papers by Ben Caraher, (PRONI, D. 3072/1A/22A).
71 Ibid.
72 Ibid.
73 Ibid.
74 Duffy, interview.
75 Ibid.
76 Currie, interview.
77 Cooper, interview.
78 Caraher, interview.
79 Ibid.
80 Devlin, *Straight Left*, p. 181.
81 William Whitelaw, *The Whitelaw Memoirs*, pp. 101–2.
82 Ibid., p.93.
83 Ibid., p.93.
84 Paul Bew and Henry Patterson, *The British State and the Ulster Crisis*, p. 53.
85 Ibid., pp. 52 ff.
86 NICP, SDLP Critique, 22 Mar 1973, (PRONI, D. 3072/4/73/7).
87 Ibid.

88   Bew and Patterson, p. 56.
89   Caraher, interview.
90   NICP, SDLP Critique, 22 Mar 1973, (PRONI D. 3072/4/73/7).
91   SDLP Statement, 8 May 1973, (PRONI, D. 3072/4/73/7).
92   Pt 5, Cmnd. 5259.
93   Art. 8, Sunningdale Conference *Communiqué*, 9 Dec 1973.
94   Pt 6, para 116, Cmnd. 5259.
95   Brigid Hadfield, *The Constitution of Northern Ireland*, p. 112.
96   Art 7, Sunningdale Conference *Communiqué*, 9 Dec 1973.
97   Section C, 'Individual Rights', *Towards a New Ireland*, Sept 1972.
98   Haughey, interview.
99   McGrady, interview.
100   Fitt, interview.
101   BBC Radio Ulster, *Behind the Headlines*, 14 Nov 1985.
102   McGrady, interview.
103   'SDLP offers Agreed Ireland', Press Release, 18 June 1974, (PRONI, D. 3072/4/74/23).
104   SDLP Press Release, 3 Sept 1974, (PRONI, D. 3072/4/74/34).
105   McIntyre, 'Modern Irish Republicanism', *IPS 10*, (1995), p. 106.
106   Gerry Adams, *The Politics of Irish Freedom*, p.110.
107   McIntyre, p. 108.
108   Bew and Patterson, p. 59.
109   SDLP Guidelines, 17 June 1974, (PRONI, D. 3072/4/74/23).
110   SDLP Discussion Paper, Aug 1974, paras 2.2,3 (PRONI, D. 3072/4/74/32).
111   Ibid., Paras 5.1, 2.
112   Ibid., Paras 5.4; 7.2.
113   Ibid., Para 7.1.
114   Ibid., Para 7.2.
115   Cmnd. 5675.
116   SDLP Press Release, 3 Sept 1974, (PRONI, D. 3072/4/74/34).
117   Ibid.
118   (PRONI, D. 3072/1D/2).
119   Farren, interview.

NOTES TO CHAPTER TWO

1   *Guardian*, 19 July, 1983.
2   FitzGerald, interview.
3   Ibid.
4   Merlyn Rees, *Northern Ireland: A Personal Perspective*, p. 156.
5   Brendan O'Brien, *The Long War*, p. 170.
6   Rees, p. 166
7   Mark Ryan, *War and Peace in Ireland*, p. 60.
8   Rees, p.109.
9   Desmond Hamill, *Pig In The Middle: The Army in Northern Ireland 1969–84*, pp. 176–7.
10   Austin Morgan, *Harold Wilson*, p. 489.
11   Ryan, pp. 61–2.

12 Ibid., p. 62.
13 Feeney, interview.
14 NICC *Report*, 20 Nov 1975, para 17.
15 SDLP Internal Review, 18 Nov 1974, (PRONI, D. 3072/1B/63).
16 Ibid.
17 SDLP Manifesto, *Speak With Strength.*
18 Ibid.
19 NICC Report, App. 3, 20 Nov 1975.
20 Ibid., para 144.
21 Ibid.
22 Rees, p.135.
23 Morgan, p. 486.
24 Maurice Hayes, *Minority Verdict: Experiences of a Catholic Public Servant*, p. 212.
25 Mallon, interview.
26 Ibid.
27 McGrady, interview.
28 Haughey, interview.
29 Smyth, interview.
30 Ibid.
31 *News Letter*, 4 Feb 1976.
32 Paddy Devlin, *Straight Left*, p. 261.
33 Ibid., p. 262.
34 Hayes, p. 227.
35 Hume, interview.
36 Farren, interview.
37 *Irish Times*, 9 Sept 1976.
38 Hume and Devlin, 8 Sept 1976, (PRONI, D. 3072/1D/3).
39 SDLP Press Release, 20 Sept 1976, (PRONI, D. 3072/1D/3).
40 Para 14, Cmnd. 6387.
41 *Parliamentary Debates* (Commons), 903, (1976), Col. 56.
42 Ibid., 906, (1976), Cols. 1716–7.
43 SDLP Press Release, 15 Sept 1976, (PRONI, D. 3072/1D/3).
44 Ibid.
45 McNamara, interview, 6 Dec 1994.
46 *Belfast Telegraph*, 27 Sept 1976.
47 *Parliamentary Debates* (Commons), 918, (1976), C. 690.
48 Brendan O'Leary and John McGarry, *The Politics of Antagonism*, p. 202.
49 Ivan Fallon and James Strodes, *De Lorean: The Rise and Fall of a Dream Maker*, p.228.
50 *Times*, 4 Oct 1976.
51 SDLP Press Release, 11 Oct 1976, (PRONI, D. 3072/1D/3).
52 Haughey, 13 Oct 1976, (PRONI, D. 3072/1D/3).
53 Haughey, 14 Oct 1976, (PRONI, D. 3072/1D/3).
54 *Irish Times*, 19 Oct 1976.
55 Caraher, 'The British Connection', 9 June 1976, (PRONI, D. 3072/4/76/10).
56 SDLP Press Release, 11 June 1976, (PRONI, D. 3072/1D/3).
57 *Irish Times*, 3 Dec 1976.
58 Ibid.
59 Ibid.

60   Ibid., 6 Dec 1976.
61   Ibid.
62   SDLP Annual Conference, 3–5 Dec 1976.
63   *Irish Times*, 6 Dec 1976.
64   Ibid.
65   Farren, interview.
66   Haughey, interview.
67   Caraher, 5 Oct 1976, (PRONI, D. 3072/1A/35A).
68   *Belfast Telegraph*, 4 Dec 1976.
69   Duffy, interview.

NOTES TO CHAPTER THREE

1   Mallon, 12 Sept 1976, (PRONI, D. 3072, B/1087 (1991)).
2   Farren, interview.
3   Merlyn Rees, *Northern Ireland: a Personal Perspective*, p. 196.
4   Garret FitzGerald, *All in a Life*, p.287.
5   *Parliamentary Debates* (Commons), **918**, (1976), Col. 690.
6   Composite Motion 2, SDLP Conference, 3–5 Dec 1976.
7   *Parliamentary Debates*, (Commons), **925**, (1976), Col. 1645.
8   Ibid., Col. 1646.
9   Christopher Cook, *A Short History of the Liberal Party 1900–1988*, p. 163.
10   David Butler, *Coalitions in British Politics*, p. 107.
11   SDLP Submission, (PRONI, D. 3072/4/77/41).
12   *Irish News*, 2 Feb 1977.
13   *Irish Times*, 3 Jan 1977.
14   McGrady, 5 Apr 1977, (PRONI, D. 3072/4/77/12).
15   *The Northern Ireland Constitution*, Cmnd 5675.
16   Haughey, 8 June 1977, (PRONI, D. 3072/1A/42A).
17   Former SDLP Assembly and Convention member.
18   Mason, 26 May 1977, (PRONI, D. 3072/1A/42A).
19   *Irish News*, 5 Apr 1977.
20   Members of the Subcommittee were John Hume, Austin Currie, Paddy Duffy, Denis Haughey, Seamus Mallon and Hugh Logue.
21   Hume, 13 Aug 1977, (PRONI, D. 3072/4/77/23).
22   Logue, 22 Aug 1977, (PRONI, D. 3072/1D/4).
23   SDLP Statement, 13 Aug 1977, (PRONI, D. 3072/1A/42A).
24   Duffy, 31 Aug 1977, (PRONI, D. 3072/4/77/27).
25   Policy Paper, 17 Sept 1977, (PRONI, D. 3072/1A/42A).
26   Notes, 22 Sept 1977, (PRONI, D. 3072/1B/11).
27   Devlin, interview, 2 Nov 1994.
28   Fionnuala O'Connor, *In Search of a State: Catholics in Northern Ireland*. p. 65.
29   Fitt, interview.
30   Devlin, interview.
31   Duffy, interview.
32   Devlin, interview.
33   Paddy Devlin, *Straight Left*, pp. 154–5.
34   Devlin, interview.
35   Devlin, pp. 280–81.

36   Devlin, interview.
37   Devlin, *Straight Left*, p. 278.
38   *Irish News*, 17 Aug 1995.
39   *Irish Times*, 16 Nov 1995.
40   *News Letter*, 12 Mar 1985.
41   Devlin, p. 277.
42   Devlin, 25 Aug 1977, (PRONI, D. 3072/1D/4.)
43   Devlin, interview.
44   Devlin, p. 281.
45   *Sunday Tribune*, 8 Oct 1995.
46   Duffy, interview.
47   Haughey, interview.
48   Michael Murphy, 'Gerry Fitt: Ulster Politician', (Ph.D. dissertation), p. 245.
49   Devlin, interview.
50   Murphy, p. 245.
51   George Drower, *John Hume Peacemaker*, p. 89.
52   ITV, Paddy Devlin, 20 Jan 1994, NIPC, LHL, PV31.
53   Maskey, interview.
54   Mallon, interview.
55   Cooper, interview.
56   NIPC, LHL, P1716.
57   Hollywood, interview.
58   Currie, interview.
59   Feeney, interview.
60   Paul Arthur and Keith Jeffery, *Northern Ireland Since 1968*, p. 40.
61   Mallon, interview.
62   *Irish Times*, 14 Nov 1977.
63   Ibid.
64   Ibid.
65   *Parliamentary Debates* (Commons), **939** (1977), Col 1727.
66   *Irish Times*, 12 Dec 1977.
67   SDLP Press Release, 19 Oct 1977,(PRONI, D. 3072/1D/4).
68   *Irish Times*, 7 Nov 1977.
69   SDLP Policy, 17 Jan 1978, (PRONI, D. 3072/1A/42B).
70   McGrady, SDLP Press Release, 2 Feb 1978, (PRONI, D. 3072/4/78/6).
71   *Irish Times*, 11 Jan 1978.
72   Notes, 25 Feb 1978, (PRONI, D. 3072/4/78/9).
73   Notes, 4 Feb 1978, (PRONI, D. 3072/B/1084).
74   *News Letter*, 4 Nov 1978.
75   Haughey, Seminar, 27 June 1978, (PRONI, D. 3072/1A/42B).
76   Duffy, Speech, 6 Feb 1978, (PRONI, D. 3072/4/78/6).
77   *Irish Independent*, 24 May 1978.
78   SDLP Agenda, 3–11 Nov 1978.
79   *Times*, 3 Nov 1978.
80   SDLP Motion 70, 3–5 Nov 1978.
81   Mallon and Haughey, Report, (PRONI, D. 3072/1A/ 42C).
82   *Irish Times*, 16 Feb 1978.
83   'Towards a New Ireland', Draft, 15 Sept 1979, (PRONI, D. 3072/1A/8B).

NOTES TO CHAPTER FOUR

1   *Face Reality—The Wasted Years*, 5 Apr 1979, (PRONI, D. 3072/1A/8B).

2   'Towards a New Ireland', 1st Draft, 8–9 Sept 1979, (PRONI, D. 3072/1A/8B).

3   Farren, 29 Oct 1979, (PRONI, D. 3072/1D/6).

4   'Towards a New Ireland', 1st Draft.

5   Mallon and Haughey, *Report*, (PRONI, D. 3072/1A/42C).

6   'Towards a New Ireland', 1st Draft.

7   Ibid., 2nd Draft, 15 Sept 1979.

8   Ibid., 1st Draft.

9   Report, 9 Jan 1979, (PRONI, D. 3072/1A/42C).

10   Motion 65 at the 1979 SDLP Annual Conference endorsing *Towards a New Ireland*.

11   *Towards a New Ireland*, final draft passed at the 1979 Annual Conference.

12   *Irish News*, 1 June 1980.

13   Cmnd. 7763.

14   *Irish News*, 22 Nov 1979.

15   *Irish News*, 29 Nov 1979.

16   Hume, Statement, 8 Jan 1980, (PRONI, D. 3072/1D/7).

17   BBC Radio Ulster, *Inside Politics*, 20 May 1980.

18   Currie, to UCD Law Soc., 21 Feb 1980, (PRONI D. 3072/1D/7).

19   *Irish Times*, 27 Feb 1980.

20   *Parliamentary Debates*, (Commons), **978** (1980), Col. 720.

21   *Parliamentary Debates*, (Commons), **984** (1980), Cols. 503–4.

22   SDLP Proposals, (PRONI, D. 3072/1A/42E).

23   Michael J. Cunningham, *British Government Policy in Northern Ireland 1969–89: its Nature and Execution*, p.144.

24   Cmnd. 7950.

25   Cunningham, pp. 144–5.

26   Para. 15, Cmnd. 7950.

27   Para. 22, Cmnd. 7950.

28   *Parliamentary Debates* (Commons), **994** (1980), Col. 558.

29   *Times*, 5 Feb 1980.

30   McGrady, 4 Feb 1980, (PRONI, D. 3072/11D/7).

31   Currie, interview.

32   Feeney, interview.

33   Fitt, interview.

34   Ibid.

35   Cooper, interview.

36   Barry White, *John Hume, Statesman of The Troubles*, p. 204.

37   Ibid.

38   Murphy, *Gerry Fitt*, p. 263,

39   *Irish Times*, 23 Nov 1979.

40   Fitt, interview.

41   *Irish Times*, 6 Nov 1978.

42   White, p. 210.

43   Richard Davis, *Mirror Hate: The Convergent Ideology of Northern Ireland Paramilitaries, 1966–1992*, p. 16.

44   *Guardian*, 23 Nov 1979.

45   *Times*, 29 Nov 1979.
46   Garret FitzGerald, *All in a Life*, p. 334.
47   James Prior, *A Balance of Power*, p. 185.
48   Brendan O'Leary and John McGarry, *The Politics of Antagonism*, p. 210.
49   Bill Rolston, 'Alienation or Political Awareness? The Battle for the Hearts and Minds of Northern Nationalists,' in *Beyond The Rhetoric: Politics, the Economy and Social Policy in Northern Ireland*, Paul Teague, (ed), p. 61.
50   Fionnuala O'Connor, *In Search of a State*, p. 49.
51   Donald Harman Akenson, *Conor: A Biography of Conor Cruise O'Brien*, 1, p. 377.
52   O'Leary and McGarry, p. 211.
53   Paul Bew and Henry Patterson, *The British State and the Ulster Crisis: From Wilson to Thatcher*, p. 99.
54   John Hume, 'The Irish Question: a British Problem', *Foreign Affairs*, pp. 306–9.
55   Hume, interview.
56   Hume, *Foreign Affairs*, pp. 309–10.
57   Ibid., p. 310.
58   Ibid.
59   Duffy, interview.
60   BBC Radio Ulster, *Inside Politics*, 20 May 1980.
61   Cooper, interview.
62   McGimpsey, interview.

NOTES TO CHAPTER FIVE

1   Currie, Speech to UCD Law Soc., 21 Feb 1980, (PRONI, D. 3072/1D/7).
2   Martin Mansergh, (ed), *The Spirit of the Nation: The Speeches and Statements of Charles J. Haughey (1957–1986)*, p. 335.
3   Ibid, p. 363.
4   Mallon, interview.
5   *News Letter*, 30 July 1980.
6   *Communiqué*, 8 Dec 1980.
7   *Irish Times*, 9 Dec 1980.
8   Motion 65, 1979 SDLP Annual Conference.
9   Hume, interview.
10   *Irish News*, 23 Jan 1981.
11   Farren, Aug 1980, (PRONI, D. 3072/4/80/30).
12   SDLP Policy Document, 1980 SDLP Annual Conference.
13   Ibid.
14   Dáil Éireann (Debates), 326, (1981), Col. 1511.
15   SDLP Review Paper, (PRONI, D. 3072/10/93).
16   New prisoners had to wear prison uniforms and conform to prison discipline. Prisoners refused to wear a uniform and started a campaign of wearing only a blanket. The protest deteriorated into prisoners smearing their cell walls with their own faeces.
17   Prisoners' five demands were: (i) to wear their own clothes; (ii) to refrain from prison work; (iii) to associate freely with one another; (iv) to organise recreational facilities and to have one letter, visit and parcel a week; (v) to have lost remission fully restored.

18   BBC 2 Television, *Timewatch*, 'Hunger–Strike: A Hidden History', 1993.
19   Farren, interview.
20   Haughey, interview.
21   Maskey, interview.
22   Currie, interview.
23   BBC 2 Television, *Timewatch*, 'Hunger–Strike:A Hidden History', 1993.
24   Barry White, John Hume, *Statesman of The Troubles*, pp. 221–3.
25   John T. Greene, 'The Comparative Development of the SDLP and Sinn Féin 1972–1985 (M.Sc. Thesis), p. 156.
26   *Irish Times*, 19 June 1979.
27   Greene, p. 154–7.
28   McGrady, interview.
29   Mallon, interview.
30   Margaret Thatcher, *The Downing Street Years*, p. 391.
31   Hugo Young, *A Biography of Margaret Thatcher*, pp. 464–5.
32   White, p. 223.
33   FitzGerald, interview.
34   *News Letter*, 14 Aug 1981.
35   *Belfast Telegraph*, 6 Apr 1981.
36   *Irish Times*, 29 Aug 1981.
37   *Irish News*, 25 Aug 1981.
38   *News Letter*, 25 Aug 1981.
39   *News Letter*, 2 Oct 1981.
40   Maskey, interview.
41   Abstract of the European Commission of Human Rights Partial Decision on the Admissibility of the Maze Case, Strasbourg 1980. NIPC, LHL (P. 4774).
42   *Times*, 22 Sept 1981.
43   *Republican News*, 26 Sept 1981.
44   *NEC Statement to 1981 Conference*, (PRONI B/051)
45   *Parliamentary Debates* (Commons), 7 (1981), Cols. 1029 and 1030.
46   Michael J. Cunningham, *British Government Policy in Northern Ireland 1969–1989: its Nature and Execution*, p.146.
47   James Prior, *A Balance of Power*, pp. 189–90.
48   *Belfast Telegraph*, 18 Jan 1982.
49   *Irish Times*, 1 Feb 1982.
50   Prior, pp. 195–6.
51   Ibid., p.197.
52   Thatcher, p. 385.
53   Farren, Speech, 22 Mar 1982, (PRONI, D. 3072/ B/1097).
54   *A Framework For Devolution*, April 1982, Cmnd. 8541.
55   *Parliamentary Debates* (Commons), 21 (1982), Col. 699.
56   *Irish Times*, 14 July 1982.
57   John Hume, *Personal Views: Politics Peace and Reconciliation in Ireland*, p. 40.
58   *Parliamentary Debates* (Commons), 22 (1982), Col. 964.
59   Mallon, Speech to INC, 3 May 1984, (PRONI, D. 3072/46 (1993)).
60   *Irish News*, 2 Feb 1982.
61   Cornelius O'Leary, Sydney Elliott and R.A. Wilford, *The Northern Ireland Assembly 1982–1986*, p. 81.
62   *Irish Times*, 28 Aug 1982.

63   O'Leary, Elliott and Wilford, p.81.
64   Currie, interview.
65   Hendron, interview.
66   Haughey, interview.
67   White, p.240.
68   *Irish Times*, 28 Aug 1982.
69   Greene, p. 208.
70   *News Letter*, 10 Apr 1982.
71   Maskey, interview.
72   McGrady, interview, 26 July 1995.
73   SDLP Press Release, 12 Oct 1982, (PRONI, D. 3072/1A/42A).
74   *Itish Independent*, 10 Sept 1982.
75   *Irish Times*, 4 Oct 1982.
76   *Joint Communiqué*, NIIS, 6 Nov 1981, pp. 2–3.
77   Dáil Éireann (Debates), **330** (1981), Col. 1574.
78   White, pp. 227–8.
79   Garret FitzGerald, *All in a Life*, p. 408.
80   Mansergh, interview.
81   *Irish News*, 31 Mar 1982.
82   Mansergh, p. 613.
83   Prior, p. 237.
84   *Irish Times*, 30 July 1982.

NOTES TO CHAPTER SIX

1   Mansergh, interview.
2   Ibid.
3   Hume, interview.
4   SDLP Assembly Election Manifesto.
5   Motion 99, SDLP Annual Conference, 28–30 Jan 1983.
6   Motion 102, SDLP Annual Conference, 28–30 Jan 1983.
7   Hume, SDLP Annual Conference, 28–30 Jan 1983.
8   Farren, 'Northern Ireland Defies an Internal Solution', 13 Jan 1983, (PRONI, D. 3072, No. B. 1097).
9   Haughey, 'The Anglo–Irish Dimension of the Forum', (PRONI, D. 3072/30).
10   Farren, 'Forum For A New Ireland Constitutional Issues', (PRONI, D.3072/30).
11   Farren, 'The New Ireland Forum—a Hope for the Future', (PRONI, D. 3072/30).
12   Logue,'The New Ireland as a Unitary State', 27 Aug 1983, (PRONI, D. 3072/30).
13   SDLP Discussion Document,' Joint Sovereignty', 1 Sept 1983, (PRONI, D. 3072/30).
14   SDLP Discussion Paper, 'Strategical Considerations', 1 Sept 1983, 1, (PRONI, D. 3072/10).
15   Farren, 'The New Ireland Forum—a Hope for the Future', July 1983, (PRONI, D. 3072/30).
16   Barry White, *John Hume,Statesman of The Troubles*, p. 255.
17   *The Fundamental Problems*, 10 Aug 1983, (PRONI, D. 3072/10).

18   SDLP Forum Discussion Paper, 'Constitutional Proposals...', 1 Sept 1983, (PRONI, D. 3072/10).

19   Donlon, interview.

20   Garret FitzGerald, *All in a Life*, p. 462.

21   *Irish Times*, 12 Mar 1983.

22   Margaret Thatcher, *The Downing Street Years*, p. 395.

23   *Irish Times*, 14 Mar 1983.

24   *Irish Times*, 15 Nov 1983.

25   *News Letter*, 31 Jan 1983.

26   *News Letter*, 26 May 1983.

27   *Build a New Ireland*, SDLP Manifesto, 9 June 1983.

28   *Belfast Telegraph*, 17 June 1983.

29   *Irish Times*, 20 May 1983.

30   WD Flackes and Sydney Elliott, *Northern Ireland: A Political Dictionary 1968–1993*.

31   Padraig O'Malley, *Biting at the Grave*, p. 216.

32   Farren, interview.

33   Para. 4.13.

34   Para. 4.14.

35   Para. 4.1.

36   Kevin Boyle and Tom Hadden, *Ireland : a Positive Proposal*, p. 63.

37   Brendan McGarry and John O'Leary, *The Future of Northern Ireland*, p. 67.

38   *Sunday Tribune*, 6 May 1984.

38   Para. 5.2.

39   Martin Mansergh, *The Spirit of the Nation: The Speeches of Charles J. Haughey (1957–1986)*, p. 838.

40   O'Malley, 'The Hollow Assumptions of the Unitary Staters', *Fortnight Magazine*, 206.

41   Brian Barton and Patrick J. Roche, (eds) *The Northern Ireland Question: Perspectives and Policies*, pp. 27–8.

42   Arthur Aughey, *Under Siege*, p. 51.

43   Paul Arthur, *Government and Politics of Northern Ireland*, p. 145.

44   Boyle and Hadden, pp. 21–2.

45   McGimpsey, interview.

46   Maskey, interview.

47   Haughey, interview.

48   *Parliamentary Debates* (Commons), 63 (1984), Col. 57.

49   Hume, interview.

50   *Irish Times*, 4 Oct 1984.

51   *Irish Times*, 7 Nov 1984.

52   *Belfast Telegraph*, 22 Nov 1984.

53   *Guardian*, 26 Nov 1984.

54   *Belfast Telegraph*, 20 Nov 1984.

55   *Belfast Telegraph*, 21 Nov 1984.

56   *Irish Times*, 24 Nov 1984.

57   *Irish Times*, 4 Dec 1984.

58   Arthur, p. 146.

59   Paul Arthur and Keith Jeffery, *Northern Ireland Since 1968*, p. 43.

60   O'Hanlon, interview.

61   Mallon, interview.
62   FitzGerald, p. 489.
63   Mallon, interview.
64   Para 5.10.
65   Hume, interview.

NOTES TO CHAPTER SEVEN

1   *Irish Times*, 20 Nov 1984.
2   Farren, interview.
3   Garret FitzGerald, 'Still making history', *Fortnight*, **205**, Oct 1994.
4   Gerry Adams, *A Pathway to Peace*, p. 58.
5   Padraig O'Malley, 'The Precarious Balance-Sheet of the New Ireland Forum', *Fortnight*, **205**, June 1984.
6   *Irish News*, 4 Jan 1985.
7   BBC, Radio Ulster, *Behind the Headlines*, 31 Jan 1985.
8   Reference to statement from Sean Farren, *Irish Times*, 26 Jan 1985.
8   Motion 121.
9   Para 4.15, 3 May 1984.
10   Para 4.16.
11   BBC, Radio Ulster, *Up Front*, 8 Sept 1985.
12   Hume, interview.
13   Hume, *Personal Views*, p. 42.
14   BBC, Radio Ulster, *Behind the Headlines*, 31 Oct 1985.
15   FitzGerald, interview.
16   Para 3.18.
17   Para 4.4.
18   Para 5.2 (7).
19   Para 5.2 (3).
20   Arwell Ellis Owen, *The Anglo-Irish Agreement: The First Three Years*, p. 14.
21   BBC, Radio Ulster, *Up Front*, 8 Sept 1985.
22   Garret FitzGerald, *All in a Life*, p. 532.
23   Margaret Thatcher, *Downing Street Years*, p. 403.
24   FitzGerald, p. 518.
25   *Belfast Telegraph*, 25 July 1985.
26   Motions 16 and 22.
27   *Guardian*, 19 Aug 1985.
28   *Irish News*, 11 Apr 1985.
29   *Belfast Telegraph*, 11 Nov 1985.
30   FitzGerald, p. 542.
31   *Irish Times*, 15 Oct 1985.
32   *Guardian*, 20 Jan 1986.
33   Article 4 (c), *Anglo-Irish Agreement*.
34   Article 5 (a)
35   Article 5
36   Article 8
37   Article 7
38   Articles 9 and 10.

39   O'Leary, 'The Anglo-Irish Agreement: Meanings, Explanations, Results and a Defence', in *Beyond The Rhetoric: Politics, the Economy and Social Policy in Northern Ireland*, ed. P Teague, pp. 14–15.

40   Brendan O'Leary and John McGarry, *The Politics of Antagonism*, p. 226.

41   FitzGerald, interview.

42   FitzGerald, 'Origins and Rationale of the *Anglo-Irish Agreement* of 1985', in *Northern Ireland and The Politics of Reconciliation*, eds. Dermot Keogh and Michael H. Haltzel, pp. 198, 201.

43   FitzGerald, p. 543.

44   FitzGerald, 'Origins and Rationale of the *Anglo-Irish Agreement* of 1985', p. 196

45   BBC, Radio Ulster, *Behind the Headlines*, 28 Nov 1985.

46   O'Leary, 'The Anglo-Irish Agreement: Meanings, Explanations, Results and a Defence', p. 15.

47   BBC, Radio Ulster, *Behind the Headlines*, 28 Nov 1985.

48   RTE Radio, *Northview*, 3 Dec 1985.

49   BBC, Radio Ulster, *Behind the Headlines*, 28 Nov 1985.

50   BBC, Radio Ulster, *Inside Politics*, 25 Apr 1986.

51   BBC, Radio Ulster, *Talkback*, 10 Nov 1986.

52   BBC, Radio Ulster, *Inside Politics*, 14 Nov 1986.

53   Haughey, Speech on 'The Deterioration in the Northern Situation', Annual Wolfe Tone Commemoration Ceremony, 12 Oct 1986.

54   BBC, Radio Ulster, *Talkback*, 13 Oct 1986.

55   FitzGerald, p. 573.

56   Hume, Address to Bogside Branch of the SDLP, 13 Nov 1986, (PRONI, D. 3072/16).

57   *Belfast Telegraph*, 27 May 1987.

58   W.D. Flackes and Sydney Elliott, *Northern Ireland: a Political Directory 1968–1993*.

59   McGimpsey, interview.

60   Smyth, interview.

61   Flackes and Elliott.

62   Hume, Address to SDLP Annual Conference, Nov 1986.

63   BBC, Radio Ulster, *Inside Politics*, 23 May 1986.

64   Ibid., 21 Nov 1986.

65   Ibid., 23 May 1986.

66   BBC, Radio Ulster, *Behind the Headlines*, 28 Nov 1985.

67   McGlone, Speech, 28 Oct 1987, [PRONI, D.3072/4].

NOTES TO CHAPTER EIGHT

1   Motion 205, SDLP Annual Conference, 25–7 Jan 1985.

2   BBC, Radio Ulster, *Behind the Headlines*, 31 Jan 1985.

3   Gerry Adams, *Free Ireland: Towards a Lasting Peace*, pp. 192–8.

4   BBC, Radio Ulster, *Up Front*, 8 Sept 1985.

5   *Irish Times*, 2 Feb 1985.

6   BBC, Radio Ulster, *Up Front*, 8 Sept 1985.

7   *Guardian*, 5 Feb 1985.

8   FitzGerald, interview.

9   Garret FitzGerald, *All in a Life*, p. 532.
10   Haughey, interview.
11   Adams, p. 197
12   BBC 1 Television, *Panorama*, 30 Jan 1995.
13   *Sunday Tribune*, 25 Sept 1994.
14   *Irish Times*, 22 Aug 1987.
15   *Belfast Telegraph*, 22 Aug 1987.
16   FitzGerald, p. 571.
17   George Drower, *John Hume Peacemaker*, p. 123.
18   BBC, Radio Ulster, *Inside Politics*, 30 Jan 1987.
19   McGimpsey, interview.
20   Ibid.
21   *Common Sense*, Ulster Political Research Group, 29 Jan 1987.
22   BBC, Radio Ulster, *Talkback*, 29 Jan 1987.
23   BBC, Radio Ulster, *Inside Politics*, 30 Jan 1987.
24   Adams, pp. 194–5.
25   BBC 1 Television, *Panorama*, 30 Jan 1995.
26   Adams, p. 194.
27   Mansergh, interview.
28   Brendan O'Brien, *The Long War*, p. 134.
29   Patrick Walsh, *Irish Republicanism and Socialism*, p. 239.
30   Adams, p. 193–4.
31   Drower, p. 133.
32   BBC 1 Television, *Panorama*, 30 Jan 1995.
33   Maskey, interview.
34   Mansergh, interview.
35   Martin Mansergh (ed), *The Spirit of the Nation*, p.1158.
36   *Irish Times*, 7 March 1987.
37   Haughey, in Mansergh (ed), *The Spirit of the Nation*, p.1159.
38   Mansergh, interview.
39   BBC, Radio Ulster, *Inside Politics*, 13 Mar 1987.
40   *Irish Times*, 30 Mar 1987.
41   BBC 1 Television, *Panorama*, 30 Jan 1995.
42   Adams, p.197.
43   *A Scenario for Peace*, May 1987.
44   *Irish Times*, 30 Mar 1987.
45   *A Scenario for Peace*, May 1987.
46   Ibid.
47   McGrady, interview.
48   *Belfast Telegraph*, 22 Aug 1987.
49   *Irish Times*, 20 Jan 1988.
50   *Independent*, 5 Aug 1988.
51   *Times*, 29 Mar 1988.
52   *Belfast Telegraph*, 12 Jan 1988.
53   Eamonn Mallie and David McKittrick, *The Fight for Peace*, pp. 123–4.
54   *Irish Times*, 4 Apr 1988.
55   BBC 1 Television, *Panorama*, 30 Jan 1995.
56   Hume to Adams, Letter, 17 March 1988. NIPC, LHL, (P.3395).
57   *The Sinn Féin/SDLP Talks*, Jan–Sept 1988. NIPC, LHL, (P. 3396).

58   SDLP Document 3 on Sinn Féin document, 2 May 1988, NIPC, LHL, (P.3395).
59   *The Sinn Féin/SDLP Talks*, Jan–Sept 1988, NIPC, LHL, (P. 3396).
60   SDLP Document 3, NIPC, LHL, (P.3385).
61   *The Sinn Féin/SDLP Talks*, Jan–Sept 1988.
62   *Irish Times*, 4 Apr 1988.
63   Adams, 'Why I talked to John by Gerry', *Fortnight*, **259**, Feb. 1988.
64   *Irish Times*, 4 Apr 1988.
65   *Irish News*, 3 Sept 1988.
66   *Times*, 23 May 1988.
67   *Irish Times*, 5 Sept 1988.
68   *Times*, 12 July 1988.
69   SDLP comments on Sinn Féin proposals, LHL P.3396.
70   Hume, interview.
71   *Belfast Telegraph*, 5 Sept 1988.
72   Ibid.
73   *Irish News*, 15 Sept 1988
74   *Belfast Telegraph*, 5 Sept 1988.
75   *Irish Times*, 6 Sept 1988.
76   *Irish News*, 15 Sept 1988.
77   Sinn Féin outlined its position on self-determination as set out in international law 'through the United Nations Charter, Article 2 (1) of the two United Nations Covenants of 1966 on the Right of peoples to self-determination.'
78   *Belfast Telegraph*, 19 Sept 1988.
79   Mark Ryan, *War and Peace in Ireland*, p. 71.
80   Drower, p.139.
81   *Belfast Telegraph*, 12 Jan 1988.
82   *Dáil Éireann* (Debates), **377** (1988), Cols. 601–2.
83   Ibid., Col. 620.
84   *Irish News*, 26 Mar 1988.
85   Northern Ireland Information Service, 27 June 1985.
86   *Irish News*, 8 Apr 1988.
87   Gerard Murray, 'A Review of Government Economic and Social Policy towards West Belfast', Thesis.
88   BBC, Radio Ulster, *Sunday Newsbreak*, 18 June 1989.
89   *Belfast Telegraph*, 27 July 1988.
90   *Independent*, 5 Aug 1988.
91   Motion 79.
92   *Belfast Telegraph*, 9 Nov 1987.
93   Currie, 'A Dialogue for Devolution', *Fortnight*, **252**.
94   *Irish Times*, 12 Sept 1987.
95   Hume, Speech. Glenties Summer School, Aug 1987, (PRONI, D. 3072/17).
96   Hume, BBC, Radio Ulster, *Talk Back*, 1 Dec 1987, (PRONI, D. 3072/17).
97   Tim P. Coogan, *The Troubles, Ireland's Ordeal 1966–1995 and the Search for Peace*, p. 335.
98   *News Letter*, 3 Feb 1989.
99   *Irish Times*, 6 Feb 1989.
100   *Irish Times*, 8 Feb 1989.
101   *Belfast Telegraph*, 4 Feb 1989.
102   *Sunday Times*, 12 Feb 1989.

103 *News Letter,* 6 Feb 1989.
104 *Irish Times,* 6 Feb 1989.
105 *Belfast Telegraph,* 22 Jan 1988.
106 *Irish Times,* 6 Feb 1989.
107 Currie, interview.

NOTES TO CHAPTER NINE

1   Brian Rowan, *Behind The Lines,* p.12.
2   Maskey, interview.
3   Sean Farren, AGM, Cookstown SDLP, 23 May 1988 (PRONI, D. 3072, Box 48).
4   John Hume, SDLP Annual Conference, 25–7 Nov 1988.
5   Concluding SDLP Statement, Hume/Adams Dialogue, 5 Sept 1988, NIPC, LHL, Belfast, P. 3395.
6   *Irish Times,* 4 Nov 1989.
7   RTE 1, *John Hume, A Profile,* 17 Dec 1997.
8   *Irish News,* 18 Jan 1990.
9   *Irish News,* 15 June 1990.
10 SDLP Submission to Inter-Party Talks, 11 May 1992, Cadogan Group web site.
11 *Irish News,* 4 Nov 1992.
12 Kelly, interview 2.
13 *Irish Times,* 17 Dec 1992.
14 BBC, Radio Ulster, *Seven Days,* 23 May 1993.
15 *The Sunday Tribune,* 12 April 1992.
16 Kelly, interview 2.
17 *Irish Times,* 26 Apr 1993.
18 *Irish News,* 27 Sept 1993.
19 *Observer,* 26 Sept 1993.
20 BBC, Radio Ulster, *Sunday Sequence,* 24 Oct 1993.
21 McGrady, interview 2.
22 *The Sunday Tribune,* 28 Nov 1993
23 *News Letter,* 29 Nov 1993.
24 *Belfast Telegraph,* 15 Apr 1994
25 RTE 1 (TV), *John Hume A Profile,* 17 Dec 1997.
26 *The Sunday Tribune,* 26 Sept 1993.
27 Kelly, interview 2.
28 Durkan, interview 2.
29 BBC, Radio Ulster, *Seven Days,* 23 May 1993.
30 Ibid.
31 *Irish Times,* 21 Apr 1989.
32 BBC, Radio Ulster, *PM Ulster,* 26 Apr 1993.
33 *Irish Times,* May 1993.
34 BBC, Radio Ulster, *PM Ulster,* 26 Apr 1993.
35 Stephenson, interview.
36 *Sunday Tribune,* 30 Jan 1994
37 *Irish Times,* 5 Jan 1994.
38 *Sunday Tribune,* 30 Jan 1994.
39 *Belfast Telegraph,* 15 Apr 1994.

40   Joseph Ruane and Jennifer Todd, *The Dynamics of Conflict In Northern Ireland*, p. 299.
41   BBC, Radio Ulster, *PM Ulster*, 1 Apr 1994.
42   BBC, Radio Ulster, *Sunday Newsbreak*, 24 Nov 1991.
43   BBC, Radio Ulster, *PM Ulster*, 1 Apr 1994.
44   *Belfast Telegraph*, 29 Aug 1994.
45   *Irish News*, 1 Sept 1994.
46   *Irish News*, 19 Aug 1994.
47   *Irish News*, 29 Aug 1994.
48   *Irish News*, 1 Sept 1994.
49   BBC, Radio Ulster, *PM Ulster*, 26 Sept 1994.
50   Adams, *Gerry Adams Selected Writings*, p337.
51   Ibid., p.312.
52   *Belfast Telegraph*, 17 Nov 1995.
53   *Belfast Telegraph*, 27 Jan 1996.
54   *Belfast Telegraph*, 31 Aug 1995.
55   *Independent*, 15 Nov 1995.
56   *Irish News*, 2 Nov 1995.
57   *Irish News*, 28 Nov 1995.
58   *Irish News*, 21 Nov 1994.
59   *Belfast Telegraph*, 7 Dec 1995.
60   *Sunday Tribune*, 19 Nov 1995.
61   *Irish Times*, 20 Nov 1995.
62   *Irish News*, 20 Feb 1997.
63   BBC Ceefax, *Election 97*, 29 Apr 1997.
64   Stephenson, interview.
65   *Irish Times*, 29 Nov 1993.
66   BBC, Radio Ulster, *Sunday Newsbreak*, 24 Nov 1991.
67   *Belfast Telegraph*, 20 May 1995.

NOTES TO CHAPTER TEN

1   Richard Jay, 'Nationalism, Federalism and Ireland', in *Federalism and Nationalism*, Murray Forsyth (ed), pp. 227, 232.
2   Cornelius O'Leary, 'Anglo-Irish Relations: The Northern Ireland Problem and the Possible Mediatory Role of the European Community', in *A Constitution For Europe*, Preston King and Andrea Bosco (eds), p. 164.
3   Caraher, interview.
4   Daniel J. Elazar, *Exploring Federalism*, p. 80.
5   *Irish Times*, 22 May 1984.
6   *Socialist International Information Sheet* issued by Socialist International, Maritime House, London.
7   George Drower, *John Hume Peacemaker*, p. 84.
8   Barry White, *John Hume, Statesman of The Troubles*, pp. 202, 205.
9   Drower, p. 87.
10   Committee on Regional Policy and Regional Planning, Doc. 1–517/79.
11   European Parliament Debates, *272*, 18 June 1981, p. 233.
12   Points 24, 25, 26, Committee on Regional Policy and Regional Planning, Doc. 1–517/79.

13 White, p. 230.
14 *Haagerup Report*, 29 Mar 1984, p. 73.
15 Paul Arthur and Keith Jeffrey, *Northern Ireland Since 1968*, p. 89.
16 Adrian Guelke, *Northern Ireland: The International Perspective*, p. 160.
17 Denis Kennedy, 'The European Union and the Northern Ireland Question', in *The Northern Ireland Question: Perspectives and Policies*, Brian Barton and Patrick J. Roche (eds), 1994, pp. 179–80.
18 EP B3–0016/90.
19 EP A3–0042/94.
20 *Irish Times*, 27 Nov 1997.
21 John Hume, 'A New Ireland in a New Europe', in *Northern Ireland and the Politics of Reconciliation*, Dermot Keogh and Michael H. Haltzel (eds), 1993, pp. 227–9.
22 Brendan O'Leary and John McGarry, *The Politics of Antagonism*, p. 210.
23 Paddy Devlin, *Straight Left*, p. 278.
24 Kennedy, in Barton and Roche (eds), p. 167.
25 Hume, 'A New Ireland in a new Europe', p. 226.
26 Paul Arthur, 'Cross-sectarian Support for a European Role in Northern Ireland', in Harald Olav Skar and Bjørn Lydersen (eds), *Norwegian Foreign Policy Studies*, 80, 1993, p.58.
27 Kennedy, in Barton and Roche (eds), p. 177.
28 Kevin Boyle and Tom Hadden, *Northern Ireland: The Choice*, 1994, p. 144.
29 Document 3696 debated before the Council of Europe on 29 January 1976.
30 Arthur and Jeffery, pp. 88–9.
31 Ibid., Document 3696.
32 Arthur, *Government and Politics of Northern Ireland*, p. 143.
33 Kennedy, p. 183.
34 Paul Hainsworth, 'Direct Rule in Northern Ireland: The European Community Dimension 1972–1979', *Administration*, 31, 1983, p. 65.
35 *Irish News*, 27 Nov 1997.
36 BBC, Radio Ulster, *Good Morning Ulster*, 28 Sept 1992.
37 Durkan, interview.
38 Kennedy, in Barton and Roche (eds) p. 177.
39 The Cadogan Group, *Northern Limits: the Boundaries of the Attainable in Northern Ireland Politics*, p. 16.
40 In Paul Hainsworth et al., *Northern Ireland in the European Community: an Economic and Political Analysis*, 1989, p. 186.
41 Richard Kearney, *Across the Frontiers : Ireland in the 1990s*, pp. 50–1.
42 John Hume, 'Report on the Regional Problems of Ireland', EP Document A2–109/87, 1987.
43 Kennedy, p. 181.
44 Gerard Delanty, 'Negotiating Peace in Northern Ireland', pp. 257–64.
45 Hainsworth et al, p. 138.
46 Joseph Ruane and Jennifer Todd, *The Dynamics of the Conflict in Northern Ireland*, p.283.
47 Delanty, pp 257–64.
48 John Hume, *John Hume Personal Views*, p. 96.
49 Mallon, interview.
50 *Irish News*, 5 Dec 1997.

51   White, p. 183.
52   Andrew J. Wilson, 'Irish America and the Ulster Conflict 1968–1985', Ph.D. dissertation, p. 219.
53   Donlon, interview.
54   Michael McKinley, *The Ulster Question in International Politics 1968–1978*, D.Phil. dissertation, p. 429.
55   Wilson, p. 144.
56   Donlon, interview.
57   Ibid.
58   Garret FitzGerald, *All in a Life*, p. 330.
59   Jack Holland, *The American Connection*, pp. 34–5.
60   See Wilson, pp. 99–100 on the origins of the INC.
61   Holland, *The American Connection*, p. 116.
62   Wilson, p. 240.
63   White, p. 191.
64   Wilson, p. 243.
65   Ibid., p. 245.
66   Ibid., p. 130–131.
67   Ibid., p. 247.
68   Hume, interview, 3 Jan 1989; Wilson, p.253.
69   Wilson, p. 132.
70   McKinley, p. 463.
71   Mary Holland, 'Edward Kennedy', *Magill*, Oct 1977.
72   Guelke, p. 136.
73   Donlon, interview.
74   Wilson, pp. 252–3.
75   Ibid., pp. 253 and 254.
76   Mary Holland, 'Carter, Kennedy, and Ireland: The Inside Story', *Magill*, Oct 1977.
77   White, p. 192.
78   Donlon, interview.
79   *Irish Times*, 26 May 1978.
80   McKinley, p. 488.
81   Wilson, p. 304.
82   *Irish Times*, 20 Apr 1979.
83   *Belfast Telegraph*, 9 May 1979.
84   Wilson, p. 312.
85   Adrian Guelke, 'The American Connection to the Northern Ireland Conflict', *Irish Studies in International Affairs*, 1/4, (1984), p. 38.
86   Shane J. Leonard, 'How "Green" is The White House? American Foreign Policy towards Northern Ireland from 1976 to the Present', MA dissertation, p. 22.
87   Garret FitzGerald, p. 349.
88   Seán Cronin, *Washington's Irish Policy 1916–1986*, p. 319.
89   Donlon, interview.
90   *Irish Times*, 7 Nov 1980.
91   Ibid.
92   Leonard, p. 28.
93   Guelke, 'The American Connection to the Northern Ireland Conflict', p. 27.
94   *Belfast Telegraph*, 18 March 1982.

95   Ibid.
96   Martin Mansergh (ed), *The Spirit of the Nation*, p. 663.
97   Presidential Address, 52nd Fianna Fail Ard–Fheis, 31 Mar 1984.
98   Haughey proposed a motion inviting President Reagan to a address a joint sitting of the Houses of the Oireachtas, 15 May 1984.
99   Haughey, speaking at the First Annual Dinner of the Friends of Fianna Fáil in America, New York, 1 Mar 1985.
100 Haughey, The Second Annual Dinner of the Friends of Fianna Fáil, Athletic Club, New York, 6 Mar 1986.
101 Guelke, 'The American Connection to the Northern Ireland Conflict', p. 38.
102 Donlon, interview.
103 FitzGerald, p. 527.
104 Donlon, interview.
105 *Irish Times*, 3 Dec 1984.
106 Leonard, p. 38.
107 Drower, p. 79.
108 *Guardian*, 4 July 1978.
109 *Irish Times*, 1 Sept 1994.
110 O'Clery, *The Greening of the White House*, p. 55.
111 Pers. comm., SDLP.
112 *Irish News*, 10 Jan 1998.
113 *Irish Times*, 1 Sept 1994.
114 Ibid.
115 *Sunday Tribune*, 9 Mar 1997.
116 O'Clery, p.81.

NOTES TO CHAPTER ELEVEN

1   Social Democratic Group, Jan-Dec 1989, (PRONI, D/3072/15).
2   *Irish Times*, 30 July 1986.
3   Seminar on Democratic Development in Northern Ireland. *A Report on the National Democratic Institute's Workshop with the SDLP*, 13–23 July 1986, (PRONI, D/3072/15).
4   National Democratic Institute Project Proposal, 'Northern Ireland—Social Democratic and Labour Party—Party Building, Executive Summary', (PRONI, D/3072/32).
5   Ibid.
6   Membership figures outlined by Anthony Gerard Murray in 'The SDLP 1976–1988: Political Strategy and Identity', DPhil Thesis, 1996, University of Ulster.
7   Kelly, interview.
8   SDLP USA Delegates' Report to Executive Committee, (PRONI, D/3072/17).
9   Kelly, interview.
10   Ibid.
11   Consideration of NDI as an SDLP Institute, (PRONI, D/3072/15).
12   Ibid.
13   Ibid.
14   Kelly, interview 1.

15   Ibid.
16   Social Democratic Group Limited, (PRONI, D/3072/15).
17   Ibid.
18   Objectives of Social Democratic Group, (PRONI, D/3072/15).
19   Seminar on Democratic Development in Northern Ireland. *A Report on the NDI Workshop with the SDLP*, 13–23 July 1986, (PRONI D/3072/15).
20   Ibid.
21   Ibid.
22   George Drower, *John Hume*, pp. 126–7.
23   'Harold McCusker, Jim Allister and Ken Maginnis, 'The SDLP Exposed', documented an investigation in Washington into funding of the SDLP, July 1986, (PRONI, D/3072/15).
24   Co-operative agreement between the NDI and the SDG for July 1987 until 30 June 1988, (PRONI, D/3072/15).
25   Memorandum to Brian Atwood from Patricia Keefer and Karen Clarke—briefing points for NDI- SDG meeting in London, 22 Sept 1987, (PRONI, D/3072/15).
26   Ibid.
27   Ibid.
28   Ibid.
29   Ibid.
30   NDI Northern Ireland Survey Team Report, June 1987, [PRONI, D. 3072, Box 15).
31   Ibid.
32   Ibid.
33   Kelly, interview 1.
34   Kelly interview 1.
35   Ibid.
36   Ibid.
37   'Northern Ireland Survey Team Report', NDI Report, June 1987, (PRONI, D/3072/15).
38   Ibid.
39   Ibid.
40   Kelly, interview 1.
41   'Northern Ireland: Pluralistic Politics In A Divided Society', NDI Report, Oct 1996.
42   SDLP Organisational Committee Minutes, 6 Jan 1982, (PRONI, D/3072/7).
43   Ibid.
44   Ibid.
45   Ibid.
46   Hanna, interview.
47   Hanna, interview.
48   Durkan, interview 2.
49   *Irish News*, 21 Nov 1991.
50   Ibid.
51   *Irish News*, 21 Nov 1991.
52   See Appendix 2, *SDLP Party Constitution*.
53   SDLP Organisational Committee Minutes, 6 Jan 1982, (PRONI, D/3072/7).
54   Hanna, interview.
55   Ibid.

56 McGrady, interview 2.
57 Year ending 30 Sept 1987, SDLP total income was only £103,977 (PRONI, D. 3072, Box 7).
58 Hanna, interview.

NOTES TO CONCLUSION

1 Eddie McGrady, interview 2.
2 Tom Kelly, interview 2.
3 SDLP Definition of Irish Nationalism, (PRONI, D/3072/1A/42E).
4 Ibid.
5 Ibid.
6 Became official SDLP policy in 1985.
7 *Is The SDLP Socialist?* Oct 1988, (PRONI, D. 3072/29).
8 Gerry Adams, BBC, Radio Ulster, News Bulletin, 22 May 1997.
9 *Irish News*, 15 Dec 1997.

Bibliography

(A) Primary Sources

(i) SDLP Records Public Record Office of Northern Ireland (PRONI)

The Public Records Office of Northern Ireland holds extensive files relating to the SDLP, its interests, activities and correspondence dating from 1971 onwards. References have been taken from files relating to branch office minutes, to annual general meetings, to meetings convened on particular issues such as Health and Social Welfare, and to copy letters to and from individual members of the SDLP. These records document the concerns of the Party Officials and membership in the day-to-day running of the Party. They also give vivid analysis of wider issues bearing on the political agenda of Northern Ireland in intimate detail.

Main classified sources used in this book date between 1971 and 1982; thereafter materials remain unclassified. Detailed references occur to appropriate files in footnotes to the text. The list compiled overall for this book was too long and too detailed to include in this bibliography. Should a reader wish for further information, a full list is lodged with the publisher, who may, in turn refer them to the author if necessary. Later source materials including press releases, draft statements, correspondence and administration still need to be classified by library staff.

(ii) Interviews conducted by the author

Dr Garret FitzGerald, 23 Jan 1995

Dr Chris McGimpsey, 5 June 1995

Dr Martin Mansergh, 12 May 1995

Alex Maskey, 23 May 1995

Paddy O'Hanlon, 8 June 1995

Dr Joe Hendron, 19 July 1995

Eddie McGrady, (1) 26 July 1995; (2) 13 August 1997

Austin Currie, 2 Aug 1995

Rev Martin Smyth, 10 Aug1995

John Hume 16 Aug 1995

Gerry Cosgrove, 29 Nov 1995

Seamus Mallon, 4 Dec 1995

Mark Durkan, (1) 18 Dec 1995; (2) 14 August 1997

Seán Donlon, 5 Jan 1995

Denis Haughey, 8 May 1995

Paddy Duffy, 3 Mar 1995

Ivan Cooper, 27 Jan 1995

John Duffy, 23 Jan 1995

Gerry Fitt, 6 Dec 1994

Sean Farren, 30 Sept 1994

Kevin McNamara, 6 Dec 1994

Paddy Devlin, 2 Nov 1994

Ben Caraher, 28 Sept 1994

Sean Hollywood, 2 Jan 1995

Brian Feeney, 20 Feb 1996

Michael McKeown, 13 July 1995

Eamon Hanna, 3 July 1996

Tom Kelly, (1) 9 July 1996; (2) 24 June 1997

Adrian Colton, 17 July 1996

Jonathan Stephenson, 4 June 1997

(iii) SDLP Annual Conference Reports
Annual Conference, 30 Nov - 2 Dec 1973

Fourth Annual Conference, 17 - 19 Jan 1975

Fifth Annual Conference, 28 - 30 Nov 1975

Sixth Annual Conference, 3 - 5 Dec 1976

Seventh Annual Conference, 4 - 6 Nov 1977

Eighth Annual Conference, 3 - 5 Nov 1978

Ninth Annual Conference, 2 Nov - 4 1979

Tenth Annual Conference, 7 - 9 Nov 1980

Eleventh Annual Conference, 13 - 15 Nov 1981

Twelfth Annual Conference, 28 - 30 Jan 1983

Thirteenth Annual Conference, 27 - 29 Jan 1984

Fourteenth Annual Conference, 25 - 27 Jan 1985

Fifteenth Annual Conference, 8 - 10 Nov 1985

Sixteenth Annual Conference, 21 - 23 Nov 1986

Seventeenth Annual Conference, 6 - 8 Nov 1987

Eighteenth Annual Conference, 25 - 27 Nov 1988

Nineteenth Annual Conference, 3 - 5 Nov 1989

Twentieth Annual Conference, 16 - 18 Nov 1990

Twenty - First Annual Conference, 22 - 24 Nov 1991

Twenty - Second Annual Conference, 6 - 8 Nov 1992

Twenty - Third Annual Conference, 26 - 28 Nov 1993

Twenty - Fourth Annual Conference, 18 - 20 Nov 1994

Twenty - Fifth Annual Conference, 17 - 19 Nov 1995

Twenty - Sixth Annual Conference, 8 - 10 Nov 1996

Twenty - Seventh Annual Conference, 14 - 16 Nov 1997

(B) Secondary Sources

(i) Books

Adams, Gerry, *The Politics of Irish Freedom* (Dingle: Brandon, 1986).

Adams, Gerry, *A Pathway to Peace*(Cork: Mercier, 1988).

Adams, Gerry, *Gerry Adams Selected Writings*(Dingle: Brandon, 1997).

Adams, Gerry, *Free Ireland: Towards a Lasting Peace* (Dingle: Brandon, 1995).

Akenson, Donald Harmon, *Conor: A Biography of Conor Cruise O'Brien*, Volume I, Narrative and Volume II, Anthology (Canada: McGill-Queen's University Press, 1994).

Arthur, Paul, *Government and Politics of Northern Ireland* (London: Longman, 1984).

Arthur, Paul, *The People's Democracy 1968 -1973* (Belfast: Blackstaff, 1974).

Arthur, Paul and Jeffery, Keith, *Northern Ireland Since 1968* (Oxford: Basil Blackwell, 1988).

Aughey, Arthur, *Under Siege: Ulster Unionism and the Anglo-Irish Agreement* (Belfast: Blackstaff, 1989).

Aughey, Arthur, Hainsworth, Paul and Trimble, Martin, J., *Northern Ireland in the European Community: an Economic and Political Analysis* (Belfast: Policy Research Institute, Queen's University and University of Ulster, 1989).

Barrington, Ruth and Cooney, John, *Inside The EEC: An Irish Guide* (Dublin: O'Brien, 1984).

Barton, Brian and Roche, Patrick J. (eds) *The Northern Ireland Question: Perspectives and Policies* (Aldershot: Avebury, 1994).

Bew, Paul and Patterson, Henry, *The British State and The Ulster Crisis: From Wilson to Thatcher* (London: Verso, 1985).

Bew, Paul, Gibbon, Peter, and Patterson, Henry, *Northern Ireland 1921-1994 Political Forces and Social Classes* (London: Serif, 1995).

Bew, Paul and Gillespie, Gordon, *Northern Ireland: A Chronology of The Troubles 1968 - 1993* (Dublin, Gill and Macmillan, 1993).

Birrell, Derek and Murie, Alan, *Policy and Government in Northern Ireland: Lessons of Devolution* (Dublin: Gill and Macmillan, 1980).

Bloomfield, Ken, *Stormont in Crisis: A Memoir* (Belfast: Blackstaff, 1994).

Bowyer Bell, J., *The Irish Troubles: A Generation of Violence 1967-1992* (Dublin: Gill and Macmillan, 1993).

Boyle, Kevin and Hadden, Tom, *Ireland: A Positive Proposal* (Harmondsworth: Penguin, 1985).

Boyle, Kevin, and Hadden, Tom, *Northern Ireland: The Choice* (London: Penguin, 1994).

Burgess, Michael (ed), *Federalism and Federation in Western Europe* (Beckenham: Croom Helm, 1986).

Butler, David (ed), *Coalitions in British Politics* (London: Macmillan, 1978).

Cadogan Group, The, *Northern Limits: Boundaries of the Attainable in Northern Ireland Politics,*(Belfast: Cadogan Group, 1992).

Callaghan, James, *Time and Chance* (London: Collins, 1987).

Catterall, Peter and McDougall, Sean (eds), *The Northern Ireland Question in British Politics* (Basingstoke: Macmillan, 1996).

Caul, Brian, *Towards a Federal Ireland* (Belfast: December, 1995).

Coogan, Tim P., *The Troubles: Ireland's Ordeal 1966-1995 and the Search for Peace* (London: Hutchinson, 1995).

Cook, Chris, *A Short History of the Liberal Party 1900-1988* (Basingstoke: Macmillan, 1989).

Cronin, Seán, *Irish Nationalism: A History of its Roots and Ideology* (Dublin: Academy, 1980).

Cronin, Seán, *Washington's Irish Policy 1916-1986: Independence, Partition, Neutrality* (Dublin: Anvil Books, 1987).

Cunningham, Michael J., *British Government Policy in Northern Ireland 1969-89: Its Nature and Execution* (Manchester: Manchester University Press, 1991).

Daly, Cathal B., *The Price of Peace* (Belfast: Blackstaff, 1991).

Darby, John (ed), *Northern Ireland: The Background to The Conflict* (Belfast: Appletree, 1983).

Davis, Richard, *Mirror Hate: The Convergent Ideology of Northern Ireland Paramilitaries, 1966-1992* (Aldershot: Dartmouth, 1994).

De Paor, Liam, *Unfinished Business* (London: Hutchinson Radius, 1988).

Devlin, Paddy, *The Fall of The Northern Ireland Executive* (Belfast: P. Devlin, 1975).

Devlin, Paddy, *Straight Left* (Belfast: Blackstaff, 1993).

Drower, George, *John Hume Peacemaker* (London: Gollancz, 1995).

Duchacek, Ivo D., *Comparative Federalism The Territorial Dimension of Politics*

(Lanham: University Press of America, 1987).

Elazar, Daniel J., *Exploring Federalism* (London: University of Alabama Press, 1987).

Faligot, Rodger, *Britain's Military Strategy in Ireland: The Kitson Experiment* (Dingle: Brandon, 1983).

Fallon, Ivan and Strodes, James, *De Lorean: The Rise and Fall of a Dream Maker* (London: Hamilton, 1983).

Faulkner, Brian, *Memoirs of a Statesman* (London: Weidenfeld and Nicolson, 1978).

FitzGerald, Garret, *All in a Life* (Dublin: Gill and Macmillan, 1991).

Flackes, W.D. and Elliott, Sydney, *Northern Ireland: A Political Directory 1968-1993* (Belfast: Blackstaff, 1994).

Forsyth, Murray (ed), *Federalism and Nationalism* (Leicester: Leicester University Press, 1989).

Gaffikin, Frank and Morrissey, Michael, *Northern Ireland: The Thatcher Years* (London: Zen Books, 1990).

Gallagher, Michael, *The Irish Labour Party in Transition 1957-82* (Manchester: Manchester University Press, 1982).

Guelke, Adrian, *Northern Ireland: The International Perspective* (Dublin: Gill and MacMillan, 1988).

Guelke, Adrian (ed), *New Perspectives on the Northern Ireland Conflict* (Aldershot: Ashgate, 1994).

Hadden, Tom and Boyle, Kevin, *The Anglo-Irish Agreement: Commentary, Text and Official Review* (London: Sweet and Maxwell, 1989).

Hadfield, Brigid, *The Constitution of Northern Ireland* (Belfast: SLS, 1989).

Hainsworth, Paul et al., *Northern Ireland in the European Community: An Economic and Political Analysis* (Newtownabbey: University of Ulster 1989)

Hainsworth, Paul (ed), *Breaking and Preserving the Mould: The Third Direct Elections to the European Parliament (1989) - the Irish Republic and Northern Ireland* (Belfast: Policy Research Institute, Queen's University and the University of Ulster, 1992).

Hainsworth, Paul, *Towards 1992: Europe at the Crossroads* (Newtownabbey: University of Ulster, 1989).

Hamill, Desmond, *Pig in the Middle: The Army in Northern Ireland 1969-84* (London: Methuen, 1985).

Hayes, Maurice, *Minority Verdict: Experiences of a Catholic Public Servant* (Belfast: Blackstaff, 1995).

Holland, Jack, *The American Connection: US Guns, Money and Influence in Northern Ireland* (New York: Viking 1987).

Holland, Jack and Phoenix Susan, *Phoenix, Policing the Shadows* (London: Hodder and Stoughton, 1996).

Hume, John, *John Hume Personal Views: Politics, Peace and Reconciliation in Ireland* (Dublin: Townhouse, 1996).

Kearney, Richard (ed), *Across the Frontiers Ireland in the 1990s* (Dublin: Wolfhound 1988).

Kearney, Richard, *Postnãtionalist Ireland, Politics, Culture, Philosophy*(London: Routledge, 1997).

Kenny, Anthony, *The Road to Hillsborough: The Shaping of the Anglo-Irish Agreement* (Oxford: Pergamon 1986).

Keogh, Dermot and Haltzel, Michael H. (eds), *Northern Ireland and the Politics of Reconciliation* (Cambridge: Cambridge University Press, 1993).

King, Preston and Bosco, Andrea (eds), *A Constitution For Europe* (London: Lothian Foundation, 1991).

Knight, James, *Northern Ireland: The Election of the Constitutional Convention May 1975* (London: Arthur McDougall Fund, 1975).

Lennon, Brian, *After the Ceasefires: Catholics and the Future of Northern Ireland* (Blackrock: Columba, 1995).

McAllister, Ian, *The Northern Ireland Social Democratic and Labour Party* (London: Macmillan, 1977).

McElroy, Gerald, *The Catholic Church and the Northern Ireland Crisis 1968-86* (Dublin:

Gill and MacMillan, 1991).

McGarry, John and O'Leary Brendan, *The Future of Northern Ireland* (Oxford: Clarendon, 1990).

McGarry, John and O'Leary Brendan, *Explaining Northern Ireland: Broken Images* (Oxford: Blackwell, 1995).

McKeown, Michael, *The Greening of a Nationalist* (Lucan: Murlough, 1986).

Mallie, Eamonn and McKittrick, David, *The Fight For Peace: The Secret Story Behind The Irish Peace Process* (London: Heinemann, 1996).

Mansergh, Martin (ed), *The Spirit of the Nation: The Speeches of Charles J. Haughey* (Dublin: Mercier, 1986).

Michie, Alaister and Hoggart, Simon, *The Pact* (London: Quartet Books, 1978).

Morgan, Austin, *Harold Wilson* (London: Pluto, 1992).

Moxon-Browne, Edward, *Nation, Class and Creed in Northern Ireland* (Aldershot: Gower, 1983).

O'Brien, Brendan, *The Long War: The IRA and Sinn Fein 1985 to Today* (Dublin: O'Brien, 1993).

O'Clery, Conor, *The Greening of the White House* (Dublin: Macmillan, 1996)

O'Connor, Fionnuala, *In Search of a State: Catholics in Northern Ireland* (Belfast: Blackstaff, 1993).

O'Halloran, Clare, *Partition and the Limits of Irish Nationalism* (Dublin: Gill and Macmillan, 1987).

O'Leary, Brendan, and McGarry, John, *The Politics of Antagonism: Understanding Northern Ireland* (London: Athlone, 1993).

O'Leary, Cornelius, Elliott, Sydney and Wilford, R.A., *The Northern Ireland Assembly 1982-1986* (London: C. Hurst, 1988).

O'Malley, Padraig, *The Uncivil Wars: Ireland Today* (Belfast: Blackstaff, 1983).

O'Malley, Padraig, *Northern Ireland: Questions of Nuance* (Belfast: Blackstaff, 1990).

O'Malley, Padraig, *Biting at the Grave* (Belfast: Blackstaff, 1990).

Owen, Arwel Ellis, *The Anglo-Irish Agreement: The First Three Years* (Cardiff: University of Wales Press, 1994).

Pimlott, Ben, *Harold Wilson* (London: HarperCollins, 1992).

Quinn, Dermot, *Understanding Northern Ireland* (Manchester: Baseline Books, 1993).

Prior, James, *A Balance of Power* (London: Hamish Hamilton, 1986).

Rea, Desmond (ed), *Political Co-operation in Divided Societies* (Dublin: Gill and Macmillan, 1982).

Rees, Merlyn, *Northern Ireland: A Personal Perspective* (London: Methuen, 1985).

Roche, Patrick J. and Barton, Brian (eds), *The Northern Ireland Question: Myth and Reality* (Aldershot: Academic Publishing Group, 1994).

Rose, Richard, *Northern Ireland: A Time of Choice* (London: Macmillan, 1976).

Routledge, Paul, *John Hume A Biography* (London: Harper Collins, 1997).

Rowan, Brian, *Behind The Lines* (Belfast: Blackstaff, 1995).

Ruane, Joseph and Todd, Jennifer *The Dynamics of the Conflict in Northern Ireland* (Cambridge: Cambridge University Press, 1996)

Ryan, Mark, *War and Peace in Ireland* (London: Pluto Press, 1994).

Sacks, Paul M., *The Donegal Mafia: An Irish Political Machine* (New Haven: Yale University Press, 1976).

Skar, Olav Harald and Lydersen, Bjørn, *Northern Ireland: A Crucial Test for A Europe Of Peaceful Regions* (Norway: Norwegian Institute of International Affairs, 1993).

Smith, Anthony D., *Nations and Nationalism in a Global Era* (Cambridge: Polity, 1995).

Teague, Paul (ed), *Beyond the Rhetoric: Politics, the Economy and Social Policy in Northern Ireland* (London: Lawrence and Wishart, 1987).

Thatcher, Margaret, *The Downing Street Years* (London: Harper Collins, 1993).

Townshend, Charles (ed), *Consensus in Ireland: Approaches and Recessions* (Oxford: Clarendon Press, 1988).

Urwin, Derek W., *The Community of Europe: A History of European Integration since 1945* (London: Longman, 1991).

Walsh, Patrick, *Irish Republicanism and Socialism* (Belfast: Athol, 1994).

White, Barry, *John Hume, Statesman of The Troubles* (Belfast: Blackstaff, 1984).

Whitelaw, William, *The Whitelaw Memoirs* (London: Aurum, 1989).

Whyte, John, *Interpreting Northern Ireland* (Oxford: Clarendon, 1990).

Wichert, Sabine, *Northern Ireland Since 1945* (London: Longman, 1991).

Wilson, Andrew J., *Irish America and the Ulster Conflict 1968-1995* (Belfast: Blackstaff, 1995).

Young, Hugo, *A Biography of Margaret Thatcher* (London: Macmillan,

Ziegler, Philip, *Wilson: The Authorised Life of Lord Wilson of Rievaulx* (London: Weidenfeld and Nicolson, 1993).

(ii) Articles

Delanty, Gerard 'Negotiating Peace in Northern Ireland', Journal of Peace Research, 32/3, 1995, pp. 257-64.

Guelke, Adrian, 'The American Connection to the Northern Ireland Conflict', *Irish Studies in International Affairs*, 1/4, 1984, p.38.

Hainsworth, Paul 'Direct Rule in Northern Ireland: the European Community Dimension, 1972-1979', *Administration*, 31, 1983, p. 65.

Holland, Mary 'Carter, Kennedy and Ireland: the Inside Story', *Magill*, 1/10/77.

Holland, Mary ' Edward Kennedy: an Interview', *Magill*, 7/10/77.

McIntyre, Anthony 'Modern Irish Republicanism', Irish Political Studies, 10, 1995, p. 106.

(iii) Theses

Bradley, Ciaran, 'The Sinn Féin/SDLP Talks and Related Issues', (MSc Thesis, Queen's University Belfast, January 1989).

Fallon, Michael, 'Irish Government Policy Towards Northern Ireland 1922-1992'. A

thesis submitted as part fulfilment of the requirements for the Degree of Master of Philosophy in Peace Studies, (Irish School of Ecumenics, Dublin, 1992).

Greene, John T, 'The Comparative Development of the SDLP and Sinn Féin 1972-1985', (MSc. Thesis, Queens University, Belfast, 1986).

Leonard, Shane J., 'How Green Is The White House?: American Foreign Policy Towards Northern Ireland From 1976 to the Present'. A degree submitted as part fulfilment of the requirements for the degree of Master of Arts in Politics, (University College Dublin, 1994).

McKinley, Michael, 'The Ulster Question in International Politics: 1968-1978'. (D. Phil. dissertation, The Australian National University, Canberra, 1981).

Meehan, Margaret, 'The Anglo-Irish Agreement: Impact On The SDLP Policy And Development' (MSc. Thesis, Queens University, Belfast, 1987).

Murphy, Michael, 'Gerry Fitt: Ulster Politician' (Ph.D. dissertation, Loyola University of Chicago, 1992).

Murray, Anthony Gerard, 'The SDLP 1976 - 1988: Political Strategy and Identity'(D. Phil. dissertation, University of Ulster at Jordanstown, 1996).

Murray, Gerard, 'A Review Of Government Economic and Social Policy Towards West Belfast.' (Thesis, University of Ulster at Jordanstown, 1992).

(iv) Parliamentary Records

Dáil Debates Official Reports, Stationery Office, Dublin, 1976-1988.

House of Commons Reports, Hansard, HMSO, London, 1976-1988.

European Parliamentary Debates, Office for Official Publications, Luxembourg, 1979-1988.

(v) Reports and Official Documents

Northern Ireland Constitutional Proposals. Cmnd 5259 HMSO, 1972.

Northern Ireland Office. Northern Ireland Discussion Paper 2. *Constitutional Convention: Procedure.* HMSO, Belfast, 1974.

The Northern Ireland Constitution. Cmnd 5675. HMSO, 1974.

Northern Ireland Office. Northern Ireland Discussion Paper 3. *The Government of Northern Ireland: A Society Divided.* HMSO, Belfast 1975.

'The Northern Ireland Constitutional Convention. Text of a letter from the Secretary of State for Northern Ireland to the Chairman of the Convention'. Cmnd 6387. HMSO, 1976.

Report of the Committee of Inquiry into Police Interrogation Procedures in Northern Ireland. The Bennett Report. Cmnd 7497. HMSO 1979.

'The Government of Northern Ireland: A Working Paper for a Conference.' Cmnd

7763. HMSO, 1979.

'The Government of Northern Ireland: Proposals for Further Discussion'. Cmnd 7950. HMSO, 1980.

Anglo-Irish Joint Studies. *Joint Report and Studies.* Cmnd 8414. HMSO, 1981.

'Northern Ireland: A Framework for Devolution'. Cmnd 8541. HMSO, 1982.

'Anglo-Irish InterGovernmental Council: Communiqué of the Anglo-Irish Summit on 7/4/83 and related documents'. Cmnd 9094. HMSO, 1983.

Agreement between the Government of the United Kingdom of Great Britain and Northern Ireland and the Government of the Republic of Ireland. Cmnd 9657.

Haagerup, Neils *Report of the European Parliament Political Affairs Committee on the Situation in Northern Ireland.* Doc 1-1526/83 (19 March 1984).

Hume, John *Report of the European Parliament Committee on Regional Policy and Regional Planning on the Regional Problems of Ireland.* EP A2-109/87 (9 July 1987).

New Ireland Forum, May 1984, Stationery Office, Dublin.

(vi) Journals, Newspapers and Magazines

Belfast Telegraph

Fortnight

Guardian

Irish Independent

Irish News

Irish Political Studies

Irish Studies In International Affairs

Irish Times

News Letter

Magill (Linen Hall Library)

Northern Ireland Office Information Service

Parliamentary Affairs

Sunday Tribune

Times

The Independent

The Irish Review

Index